POTABLE WATER FROM WASTEWATER

POTABLE WATER
FROM WASTEWATER

Edited by M.T. Gillies

NOYES DATA CORPORATION

Park Ridge, New Jersey, U.S.A.

1981

Published in the United States of America by
Noyes Data Corporation
Noyes Building, Park Ridge, New Jersey 07656

Library of Congress Cataloging in Publication Data
Main entry under title:

Potable water from wastewater.

    (Pollution technology review ; no. 76)
    Bibliography: p.
    Includes index.
    1. Water reuse. I. Gillies, M. T. II. Series
TD429.P67   627'.56   81-1886
ISBN 0-8155-0845-X   AACR2

Foreword

The idea of obtaining potable water from wastewater is a psychologically difficult one for many people to accept. The tendency is to think that wastewater is "dirty" and cannot be converted to "clean" water. This book describes significant advances in wastewater treatment technology which make possible the control and/or removal of conventional pollutants, thus making potable water from wastewater technically feasible today.

Water is one of our few renewable resources. It can be and is reused continuously due to natural hydrologic cycling powered by solar energy. However, as populations grow, as water demands increase, and as temporary water shortages develop, due either to natural or manmade disasters, the need for supplementary, reclaimed sources of water will become more widespread.

The book covers direct and indirect water reuse. Direct reuse implies the piping of wastewater directly to a user after appropriate intervening treatment; indirect reuse occurs when water from a particular source, such as a river, serves more than one community and/or industry, one after another, as it moves from its origin to its outlet.

Methods of wastewater treatment and purification in varying stages of development are presented. Ongoing experimental and pilot studies around the world have been described. Analytical testing methods for water purity are detailed, and a discussion of contaminants associated with municipal wastewater reuse as well as a chapter on health effects of reuse have been included. Possible approaches to educating the public about water reuse are also considered.

This book will be of interest to anyone involved with problems relating to water reuse for potable purposes—water treatment personnel and environmental engineers, municipal and public health officials.

The information contained here is based on studies and conferences sponsored by various government agencies. Because the material was obtained from multiple sources, it is possible that certain portions may disagree or conflict with other parts of the book. These differing points of view have been included, however, to make the book more valuable to the reader.

Advanced composition and production methods developed by Noyes Data are employed to bring these durably bound books to you in a minimum of time. Special techniques are used to close the gap between "manuscript" and "completed book." Industrial technology is progressing so rapidly that time-honored, conventional typesetting, binding and shipping methods are no longer suitable. We have bypassed the delays in the conventional book publishing cycle and provide the user with an effective and convenient means of reviewing up-to-date information in depth.

The expanded table of contents is organized in such a way as to serve as a subject index and to provide easy access to the information contained herein. The primary sources are listed at the end of the volume under the heading Sources Utilized. The titles of additional publications pertaining to topics covered in this book are listed at the end of several chapters and sections.

A List of Abbreviations has been included to aid in the use of this book.

CONTENTS AND SUBJECT INDEX

INTRODUCTION 1
  Necessity for Reuse 2
    How Much Water Do We Use? 2
    Future Demand. 4
    Planned and Unplanned Reuse 4
    Obstacles to Reuse. 5
  Government Involvement 7
    Federal Legislation 7
    Interim Primary Drinking Water Regulations. 7
    The EPA Role. 8
    Office of Water Research and Technology 10
  A Special Situation—California. 11
    Need for Water Reclamation 11
    Status of Water Reclamation 12
    Public Health 12

INDIRECT POTABLE USES OF WASTEWATER 13
  Introduction. 13
  Feeding Reclaimed Water into a Supplying Reservoir 13
    Necessity for Increased Water Supply 14
    Occoquan Policy. 14
    Design of Plant 15
    Plant Performance. 18
    Operation and Maintenance Cost 19
    Future. 19
  Discharge of Treated Wastewater into Underground System. 20
    Introduction. 20
    Treatment Requirements and Processes 21
    Plant Performance. 22

Costs. 24
Conclusions 26
Groundwater Recharge at Water Factory 21 27
Introduction. 27
Seawater Intrusion Problem. 28
Facilities Description 29
Water Factory 21 Performance. 29
Barrier Performance. 32
Operational Costs 33
Aquifer Recharge 35
Introduction. 35
Existing Water Sources 35
Future Water Sources. 36
Development of Project 37
Treatment Process Development Objectives 38
Process Selection. 39
Pilot Testing. 41
Recharge System. 44
Costs. 45
Conclusions 45
Shallow Well and Basin Recharge 45
History of the Project. 46
Reuse and Recharge Studies 46
Reclamation Plant. 49
Recharge System. 51
Construction Costs 52
Operation 52
Operation and Maintenance Costs. 53
Schedule for First Year of Operation. 53
Highlights of Other Developments in Indirect Water Reuse 55
Woodlands, Texas 55
Aurora, Colorado 55
Three Indirect Use Projects Examined for Washington, D.C. 56
U.S. Army Engineer Corps Report 56
Berlin Project 58
South African Recharge 58
Aquifer Recharge Plans in Victoria, Australia 59

SMALL-SCALE PURIFICATION SYSTEMS AND A PRELIMINARY
STUDY 60
PureCycle's Domestic Wastewater Recycling System 60
Introduction. 60
The PureCycle System 60
U.S. Army Field Hospital Wastewater Treatment for Water Reuse. 62
Introduction. 63
Experimental Set-Up 63
Results and Discussion 65
Summary. 67

Treatment of Municipal Wastewater Effluent for Potable Water Reuse. . . . 67
  Introduction. 67
  Materials and Methods 67
  Results 69
  Conclusions 70

INTERNATIONAL DEVELOPMENTS IN WATER REUSE 71
  The CCMS Drinking Water Study 71
    Introduction. 71
    Regulatory and Legislative Control of Discharges of Pollutants into
      Surface Waters 72
    Measurement of Water Reuse. 73
    Extent of Current Reuse. 74
    Treatment Options 74
    Potential Health Problems. 75
    Water Resources Management 75
    Case Studies. 76
  Water Reuse in the Netherlands 78
    Introduction. 78
    Dordrecht Pilot Plant. 80
    Reverse Osmosis System. 85
    Future Investigations 89
  Reuse of Wastewater in South Africa. 89
    Introduction. 90
    Promotion of Reuse Through Government Policy 90
    Reclamation of Purified Effluents in South Africa 92
    Reclamation for Potable Use 92
    Further Studies. 96
    Integrated Physical-Chemical-Biological Treatment at Pretoria Plant . . . 97
    Operational Results (Pretoria) 99
    Athlone Pilot Plant 103
    Running Costs 103
    Discussion 103
    Conclusions 105
  Singapore Demonstration for Possible Potable Reuse of Wastewater 105

THREE CASE STUDIES 107
  The Dallas Study. 107
    Introduction. 107
    Background of the Dallas Program 109
    Description of Facilities 109
    Unit Processes. 111
    Sampling Procedures 113
    Analytical Procedures. 114
    Plant Operation and Performance. 114
    Process Reliability. 116
    Compliance with the National Interim Primary Drinking Water
      Regulations 119

Conclusions 121
Recommendations. 122
The Denver Project 123
Introduction. 124
Program History 124
Demonstration Plant 125
Treatment Train 129
Costs. 129
The Experimental Estuary Water Treatment Plant 131
Introduction. 131
Description of the EEWT Plant 131
Side Stream Processes. 134
Testing and Evaluation Program. 134

TREATMENT TECHNIQUES FOR WASTEWATER SCHEDULED FOR
REUSE 137
Treatment Technology for Water Reuse. 137
Evaluation Methods. 137
Organic Compounds and Wastewater Treatments. 142
Introduction. 142
Experimental 143
Quality Assurance 145
Discussion of Results 145
Conclusions 148
Composite Membrane for RO Use. 149
History of RO in Water Treatment 149
Asymmetric Membranes 149
Composite Membranes 150
PA-100 and PA-300 Membranes 151
Other Experimental Membranes 152
References 154
Use of Ozone in Wastewater Treatment 154
Introduction. 155
Applications for Ozone. 155
Summary and Discussion 160
Treatment of Acid Mine Drainage. 161
Introduction. 161
Process Description 162
Process Engineering and Operation 163
Conclusions 166
Recommendations. 167
Reductive Degradation Treatment for Chlorinated Hydrocarbons 168
Introduction. 168
Process 169
Process Operation 170
Degradation of Trihalomethanes. 171
Treatment Cost. 171
Conclusions 172

TESTING METHODS 173
  Bioassays Plus Chemical Analyses. 173
    Biological Screening Assays. 173
    The Bioassay Method. 174
    The Response of Tissue Cultures to Toxic Chemicals and Mixtures . . . 174
    Comparison of Treated Wastewater with Cincinnati Tap Water. 176
    Reduction of Toxicity of RO-Treated Wastewater by Ozonation 177
  Trace Element Analyses of AWT Effluents. 178
    PIXE Technology 179
    Results and Discussions 180
  Testing for Trace Organics and Mutagens 182
    Introduction. 182
    Concentration and Extraction 183
    Mutagenic Activity 183
    Organics 186
    Results and Discussion 187
  Testing Volatiles in Wastewater Treatment Plant Effluents 189
    Objectives 189
    The "Purge-and-Trap" Method for Volatiles: Outline of Procedure. . . 190
    Nonvolatile Compounds 192
    Summary. 192
  Testing for Nonvolatile Organic Compounds in Wastewater 193
    Overview of Testing Method 193
    Experimental Procedure 194
    Secondary Liquid Chromatography: Chemical Analysis of the
      Fractions from the Bondapak-C_{18} Column 196
    Conclusions 199
  Toxicity and Mutagenicity Testing Suitable for Reused Water 199
    Introduction. 199
    Choice of a Metabolic Pathway 200
    Methodology 201
    Results 202
    Discussion 203
    Summary and Conclusions 203

CONTAMINANTS ASSOCIATED WITH REUSE OF MUNICIPAL WASTE-
  WATER. 205
  Introduction. 205
    Definitions of Direct and Indirect Use. 206
    Selection of Contaminants for Consideration 206
  Wastewater Inputs. 207
    Elemental Contaminants. 209
    Biological Contaminants. 210
  Primary Treatment 210
  Secondary Treatments 210
    Activated Sludge. 210
    Trickling Filter. 212
    Aerated Lagoons. 213

Ponding. 214
Tertiary Treatments. 215
   Filtration. 215
   Adsorption. 216
   Chemical Treatment. 218
   Ion Exchange 220
   Nitrogen Removal Processes 221
Disinfection 222
   Chlorination. 222
   Ozonation 225
Wastewater Disposal. 226
   By Land to Groundwater 226
   To Fresh Surface Water 230
Conventional Water Treatments 238
   Chemical Coagulation and Flocculation plus Solids Separation. 238
   Disinfection 242
Advanced Water Treatment. 245
   Adsorption onto Activated Carbon and Other Materials 245
   Ion Exchange 248
   Reverse Osmosis 248
References. 252

HEALTH EFFECTS OF WASTEWATER REUSE 280
Epidemiological and Pathological Evaluation of Wastewater
  Contaminants. 280
   Introduction. 280
   Water Quality Parameters 281
   Elemental Contaminants. 282
   Biocidal Contaminants 284
   Synthetic/Organic Contaminants 285
   Biological Contaminants. 287
Evaluation of Toxic Effects of Organic Contaminants in Recycled
  Water 293
   Introduction. 293
   Evaluation Method 294
   Results 296
   Summary. 297
Removal of Mutagens and Carcinogens During AWT. 297
   Introduction. 297
   Experimental 298
   Results and Discussion 300

SOURCES UTILIZED 303

LIST OF ABBREVIATIONS 305

Introduction

The material in this chapter has primarily been excerpted from the following papers delivered at the Water Reuse Symposium held in Washington, DC in March 1979. The collected symposium papers, *Water Reuse—From Research to Application. Proceedings of Water Reuse Symposium Held at Washington, DC on March 25-30, 1979* [Volume 1 (NSF/RA-790224) is hereinafter referred to as "Conference I," Volume 2 (NSF/RA-790225) as "Conference II," and Volume 3 (NSF/RA-790226) as "Conference III"], were prepared by the American Water Works Association Research Foundation for the National Science Foundation, March 1979.

Each paper used in this chapter has been assigned a letter which appears in parentheses before the paper title. At the end of each paragraph taken from one of these papers or at the end of a title, the letter reference will be found, also in parentheses. When only one or two sentences have been quoted, the reference has been omitted.

(A) "Water Reuse: It is Time for Implementation," by T.C. Jorling, of the U.S. Environmental Protection Agency.

(B) "The Environmental Protection Agency's Research Program for Water Reuse," by S.J. Gage, of the U.S. EPA.

(C) "Treatment Technology for Water Reuse," by R.B. Williams, G.C. Culp and J.A. Faisst, all of Culp/Wesner/Culp.

(D) "Toward the Goal of Direct Water Reuse—What Should We Do Next?" by J.-C. Huang, the University of Missouri—Rolla.

(E) "Applied Science and Its Role in Addressing Problems Relating to Renovation and Reuse of Water," by J.T. Sanderson, of the National Science Foundation.

(F) "OWRT's Water Reuse R&D Program," by R.S. Madancy of OWRT, Dept. of Interior.

(G) "Wastewater in Drinking Water Supplies," by M.D. Swayne et al.

(H) "Water Reclamation Efforts in California," by K. Wassermann and J. Radimsky of the Office of Water Recycling, State Water Resources Control Board, CA.

Water used to be one of our cheapest natural resources. In recent years, we have discovered that water is no longer an abundant commodity in many places in the U.S. and in other countries of the world. Reasons for this include population growth, increases in the average water consumption for domestic and industrial purposes, pollution, and climactic changes. Although there are annual changes in our water reservoirs, the long-term trends show that shortage of water is going to be a problem in many places that have not experienced this phenomenon before.

NECESSITY FOR REUSE

Water can no longer be considered a stepchild among the resources—taken for granted and used without thought. It is a reclaimable resource of inestimable value and increasing scarcity. Like clean air it is basic. Inadequate water supplies limit the quality of life and limit municipal and industrial growth.

There is increasing recognition at every level of society that water reuse is a fundamental component of the wise and efficient management of an increasingly scarce, but essential, natural resource. A number of things have led to this recognition. Foremost has been the experience of a series of droughts in the mid-seventies which taught us that our best laid plans for water storage are no match for nature's uncertainties. We are reminded almost daily that water is not an exhaustible resource. Reports of steadily declining aquifers and completely appropriated stream flows mount on the one hand even while the memories of recent droughts have not faded. Studies at every level demonstrate this to be a major national problem and point toward the inadequacy of conventional, technological solutions. We are running out of acceptable reservoir sites and areas with surplus water for inter-basin transfers. The costs for developed water have increased enormously in recent years. If not addressed quickly the situation may erupt into an economic and legal competition . . . . Reclaimed water will increasingly become too valuable a commodity to simply use once and dump. Moreover, reclaimed water supplies are much more reliable than stream flows which vary seasonally (A).

How Much Water Do We Use?

The Water Resources Council indicates that total freshwater withdrawals in 1975 in the U.S. were 362 bgd (see Figure 1.1). Of these, about three-quarters are from surface supplies and the remainder from groundwater sources. The demand for potable water represented 7.5% of the total or about 27 bgd. On a per capita basis, domestic use is estimated to be about 75 gallons per capita per day; this includes bathing, lawn watering and sanitary waste disposal. Commercial, industrial and public uses of water range from 30 to 130 gpcpd, depending on local conditions. A typical figure for overall municipal potable water consumption is 160 gpcpd (C).

According to a recent House Science and Technology Subcommittee report, the nation's withdrawals of groundwater have more than doubled over the past 25 years and are increasing at the rate of 4% annually. In many areas, these withdrawals cause severe problems, including increased drilling and pumping costs due to declining water levels, conflicts between urban and agricultural use, and contamination of the aquifers both by salt and by disposal of pollutants on the surface. Some areas may eventually run out of groundwater (E).

Figure 1.1: National Freshwater Withdrawals—1975

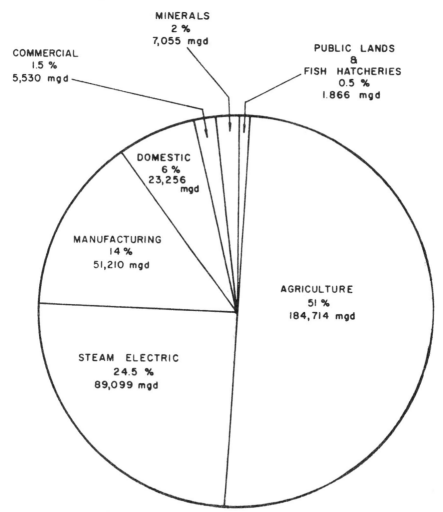

MINERALS
2 %
7,055 mgd

PUBLIC LANDS
&
FISH HATCHERIES
0.5 %
1.866 mgd

COMMERCIAL
1.5 %
5,530 mgd

DOMESTIC
6 %
23,256 mgd

MANUFACTURING
14 %
51,210 mgd

AGRICULTURE
51 %
184,714 mgd

STEAM ELECTRIC
24.5 %
89,099 mgd

Source: (C) NSF/RA-790224

Future Demand

Estimates of future water withdrawals vary widely. According to Dr. Huang, natural runoff averages about 1,200 bgd and our total water demand is about 500 bgd now and is expected to increase to 1,370 bgd by 2020, thus exceeding the natural runoff (D).

On the other hand, the Second National Water Assessment by the Water Resources Council and an evaluation of reuse needs and potential done by OWRT indicate that total freshwater withdrawals of more than 362 bgd in 1975 are expected to decrease to about 330 bgd in the year 2000. This hopeful projection is based upon the continuation of present trends in industrial recycling and improved irrigation efficiency. Increasingly stringent wastewater discharge limitations, coupled with recurring drought periods in water-short areas of the country can provide major impetus for going considerably beyond these current trends. It is now estimated that the total industrial water recycling rate could increase from about 1.9 bgd in 1975 to 8.8 bgd in the year 2000. The reuse of municipal wastewaters could increase from the present relatively insignificant quantity to almost 5 bgd in the same period (E).

Technical Feasibility for Reuse: Is direct water reuse technically feasible today? The answer to this question is generally "yes." In the last two decades, significant advances have been made in water and wastewater treatment technologies. The conventional types of pollutants such as BOD, SS, coliforms, pathogens, nitrogen and phosphorus, etc. can all be removed effectively from wastewater. In fact, some treated effluents may have lower concentrations of these pollutants than those considered satisfactory in raw water sources of domestic water supply (D).

Planned and Unplanned Reuse

Planned, direct reuse of wastewater has been practiced in the United States on a small scale to date, primarily for agricultural and industrial use. The widespread and continued unplanned, indirect reuse of treated wastewaters through the discharge of these waters to streams, lakes and reservoirs for reuse to other communities has been a long accepted practice in the U.S. (C).

One of the major constraints to effective implementation of water reuse has been the aversion to any kind of identifiable association with human waste within our immediate environment. Ironically, this concern has not extended to the transmission of the wastewater to other people's environments. Thus, an upstream community has rarely exhibited concern over transferring its waste products, treated or otherwise, to residents downstream (A).

Even groundwater, which is thought of as being pure, is often "reused" in the sense that wastewater from septic tanks or ground spread by treatment plants leaches into aquifers which feed the wells supplying water for the same or other communities.

Table 1.1 presents a list of twenty-five population centers estimated to have the greatest loading or exposure to municipal wastewater in drinking water supplies. The cities are ranked according to product of population and conservative estimate of percent of wastewater (G).

Table 1.1: Source Water Impact According to Population and Percent Wastewater

State	City	Line	Source Water	Population (x 1,000)	Conservative Estimate of Percent of Wastewater*
PA	Philadelphia	155	Schuylkill River	1,950	3.5
SC	Columbia	259	Saluda River	228	16
PA	Bryn Mawr	149	Neshaminy Creek	820	3.8
IN	Indianapolis	464	White River	680	4.3
PA	Middletown	140	Neshaminy Creek	759	3.8
TX	Dallas	539	Lake Ray Hubbard	878	2.8
AL	Birmingham	207	Cabaha River	650	3.6
NJ	Elizabeth	166	Delaware-Raritan Canal	500	4.3
MD	Baltimore	124	Susquehanna River	1,755	1.2
NJ	Little Falls	055	Passaic River	333	4.9
MO	St. Louis	381	Mississippi River	600	2.2
LA	New Orleans	525	Mississippi River	550	1.8
NJ	Millburn	054	Passaic River	234	4.8
OH	Cincinnati	447	Ohio River	850	1.3
LA	Marrero	524	Mississippi River	600	1.8
MD	Hyattsville/ Wash., DC	178	Potomac River	1,300	0.8
KY	Louisville	454	Ohio River	700	1.4
MO	Kansas City	359	Missouri River	750	1.2
TX	Fort Worth	538	Ben Brook Lake	490	1.6
MO	St. Louis	362	Missouri River	600	1.3
CO	Pueblo	495	Arkansas River	95	7.6
SC	Rock Hill	266	Catawba River	426	1.4
NJ	Elizabeth	167	Raritan and Millstone	500	1.1
IL	East St. Louis	382	Mississippi River	215	2.2
GA	Columbus	237	Lake Oliver	134	3.2

*Cumulative percent wastewater estimates under average source water flow conditions.

Source: (G) NSF/RA-790224

Obstacles to Reuse

For a long time, the word "wastewater" has been linked with a psychological implication of "filth" and "dirtiness" no matter how well it has been treated. Although there is concrete evidence that impurities and harmful substances can be removed from wastewater by today's treatment technologies, the public has not been convinced, and the sanitary engineering profession has not actively tried to convince them, that properly treated effluent can be reused for domestic purposes (D).

Steps to Overcome the Psychological Barrier (G): In order to overcome the public's deeply-rooted psychological rejection, or at least reluctance, toward direct water reuse, intensive public education plus enthusiastic professional campaign are necessary so that the public can be convinced that wastewater, like a piece of equipment or other merchandise, can be "repaired" or "renovated" to make it clean and wholesome again. In carrying out the public education and professional campaign, the following actions should be seriously considered.

(1) Consideration should be given to change some of the common terminologies used today which either explicitly or implicitly link wastewater with a sense of feeling of filth and dirtiness, such as:

Existing Terms	Suggested New Terms
Wastewater or sewage	used water (making it synonymous to used car or other merchandise that can be fixed and reused)
Waste treatment plant	water renovation plant or water reclamation center
Treated sewage effluent	renovated water or reclaimed water
Sewage sludge	municipal humus
Sewage treatment plant operator	water renovator

The main objective of using the above new terminologies is to impress the public that "wastewater" is just like a "used car" or a "used typewriter," that can be fixed and reused. It is hoped that with these terminologies the public will gradually be convinced that wastewater is really not that bad at all. It is only temporarily "used" and can be reused again after it is cleaned up.

(2) The public must be informed clearly that "water reuse" is not new at all. We have been reusing our wastewaters for decades! Of course, the reuse is neither deliberate nor direct; it merely occurs from one community to another as water flows downstream through surface or underground drainage systems. However, in any dry season, much of the water in a natural stream may be from municipal sewage effluents. Under such extreme situations, a practice of direct reuse has already been in effect.

(3) The sanitary engineering professional group should take the lead in publicizing the fact that today's advanced water and wastewater treatment technologies are absolutely able to convert wastewater to potable water. They should also take the lead in demonstrating their willingness to drink the treated sewage effluent first.

(4) More intensive research must be taken immediately to assess the real toxicological implications of the various impurities present in wastewater effluent. At the present time our knowledge in this field is still in the stage of infancy. Because of this, many new standards established today may be unduly conservative. This definitely makes direct water reuse more difficult. It must be pointed out here that in many underdeveloped countries people are still drinking water from fairly polluted sources without having adequate treatment. Yet there is

still no concrete evidence that these people have the kinds of chronic toxicity (except bacterial and viral infections) that can be linked directly with the chemical impurities present in their polluted drinking waters.

GOVERNMENT INVOLVEMENT

Federal Legislation

Recent Federal legislations are expected to have significant impact on the quality of wastewater discharges and on water reuse. The Safe Drinking Water Act of 1974 (PL 93-423) and the Clean Water Act of 1977 (PL 95-217) will both result in significant improvements in the quality of wastewater discharges in many instances that will allow the incremental quality improvement which is needed for reuse to become economically feasible. This is legislation that must be supported by sound administration.

In addition, the Water Research and Development Act of 1978 (PL 95-467) authorizes the Office of Water Research and Technology of the Department of the Interior to continue its comprehensive research and development program in water reuse.

Interim Primary Drinking Water Regulations

The Interim Primary Drinking Water Regulations (IPDWR) listed in Table 1.2 were established by the EPA and became effective on June 24, 1977. They are subject to revision before becoming final and may be superceded by more stringent state or local standards. The secondary standards pertain to aesthetics rather than health. The adoption of the trihalomethane limitation of 0.10 mg/ℓ is still in question since meeting this MCL requires processing not ordinarily used in water treatment (with granular activated carbon) and carries with it significant costs (C).

Table 1.2: Drinking Water Quality Meeting IPDWR Requirements

Parameters	Drinking Water Minimum Contaminant Levels
Primary Regulations	
Arsenic, mg/ℓ	0.05
Barium, mg/ℓ	1
Cadmium, mg/ℓ	0.010
Chromium, mg/ℓ	0.05
Fluoride, mg/ℓ	1.4-2.4*
Lead, mg/ℓ	0.05
Mercury, mg/ℓ	0.002
Nitrate (as N), mg/ℓ	10
Selenium, mg/ℓ	0.01
Silver, mg/ℓ	0.05
Radium, pCi/ℓ	5
Endrin, mg/ℓ	0.002

(continued)

Table 1.2: (continued)

Parameters	Drinking Water Minimum Contaminant Levels
Lindane, mg/ℓ	0.004
Methoxychlor, mg/ℓ	0.01
Toxaphene, mg/ℓ	0.005
2,4-D, mg/ℓ	0.01
2,4,5-TP Silvex, mg/ℓ	0.01
Turbidity, TU	1**
Coliform bacteria, colonies/100 ml	1***
Secondary Regulations	
Copper, mg/ℓ	1
Iron, mg/ℓ	0.03
Manganese, mg/ℓ	0.05
Sulfate, mg/ℓ	250
Zinc, mg/ℓ	5
Color, units	15
Foaming agents (as MBAS)	0.05
Odor, TON	3
Other	
Trihalomethane, mg/ℓ	0.10†

*Varies with average annual maximum daily air temperature.
**Monthly average.
***Monthly average, membrane filter technique.
†Proposed minimum contaminant level.

Source: (C) NSF/RA-790224

The IPDWR represent standards to be met regardless of the source of supply. As the prospect of potable reuse comes closer to being a reality, there is some concern that raw water criteria should be regulated. There is particular concern with groundwater supplies subject to recharge by direct injection or land spreading. Historically, the quality of raw groundwater has been much higher than that of surface water; therefore, treatment prior to use has been minimal (disinfection only, in most cases). The extent and reliability of treatment by percolation through the soil mantle over an aquifer may necessitate strict raw water quality criteria in addition to finished product requirements (C).

The EPA Role

The President and the Congress, in passing the 1977 Amendments to the Clean Water Act, clearly set forth a policy that water reuse is to be more aggressively implemented. Section 210 (g)(5) of the Clean Water Act states that a construction grant shall not be made "unless the grant application has satisfactorily demonstrated to the Administrator [of EPA] that innovative and alternative wastewater treatment processes and techniques, which provide for the reclaiming and reuse of water . . . have been fully studied and evaluated by the applicant" (A).

In the last eight years EPA has sponsored a substantial number of research, demonstration and full-scale nonpotable reuse projects. These projects have provided a significant body of data on the feasibility, economics, health effects, and reliability of nonpotable reuse projects. These projects have demonstrated the natural cleansing capabilities of the soil mantle. EPA has additionally instituted a national pretreatment program to control toxic pollutants at the source, thus reducing the concentrations of contaminants that might otherwise preclude certain reuse options (A).

Water Reuse in Municipalities: In the municipal research area, the major goal is to prove the feasibility and practicability of reusing municipal wastewaters through research and experimental demonstrations. This includes source substitution to conserve high quality supplies, direct potable reuse, indirect reuse for domestic purposes through recharging of surface and groundwaters that serve as drinking water supplies, and water conservation techniques. The components of the Environmental Protection Agency involved in this program are the wastewater and water supply divisions of the Municipal Environmental Research Laboratory (MERL) in Cincinnati and the Health Effects Research Laboratory (HERL), also in Cincinnati, both of which are in the Office of Research and Development (B).

Congress reemphasized its interest in potable reuse in Public Law 95-477, the Environmental Research, Development, and Demonstration Authorization Act of 1979, by appropriating $8 million to expand this program in FY 79. The EPA is concentrating on a new potable reuse demonstration initiative, which includes $7 million for a direct municipal reuse project at Denver, Colorado (B) (see Chapter 5).

Research on Health Effects of Water Reuse: In the health effects area, the research program will evaluate the potential health effects associated with reuse of highly treated wastewater for potable purposes, with the ultimate objective being to develop the data base necessary to recommend criteria for such use. In addition, health effects data will be provided to assist in determining safe practices, proper management and criteria which are protective of public health when wastewaters are applied to land. The program is conducted by the Health Effects Research Laboratory in Cincinnati, Ohio (B).

The research program for direct reuse of wastewater for potable purposes, which was initiated five years ago, has emphasized the testing of effluents from advanced wastewater treatment plants. The organics found in such effluents have been chemically analyzed and, upon concentration, have been tested for mutagenicity and chronic toxicity. Most organic compounds found to date have been in the parts-per-trillion range. About 20 percent of the concentrates have caused mutagenic responses in in vitro screening tests. In short-term animal studies significant adverse effects have not been found, however (B).

The HERL researchers have studied the contaminants associated with both direct and indirect reuse of municipal wastewaters and have shown that the potential problems of the two approaches are similar. They have evaluated the safety of wastewater recycle in two food processing projects and have indicated that recycle could be accomplished without compromising the quality of the food product. Finally, they have extensively investigated the microbiological aspects of wastewater reuse, determining that viruses will penetrate soils under certain conditions and that aerosols from spray application can contain pathogens which may travel considerable distances from the spray site. However, with proper management of the site and the application technique, they have found that the health risks from such techniques may be kept to an acceptable level (B).

The current health effects research effort, totalling about $2 million in this area, is increasingly focusing on human exposure and effects. An epidemiological study is being initiated at a California location where an aquifer used for a community water supply has been recharged with treated wastewater for the past seventeen years. Long-term studies using laboratory animals fed concentrated effluent from an advanced wastewater treatment plant effluent are being undertaken. The animals will then be sacrificed and checked for chronic health effects. Organic chemicals will also continue to be identified in wastewater, and rapid toxicity screening techniques for those effluents will be developed. Criteria for short-term use of renovated wastewater for potable purposes will be developed for the EPA by the National Academy of Sciences (B).

Future Health Effects Research: The future program on health effects of wastewater reuse must necessarily address potable reuse, land application, aquaculture, and industrial recycle at food processing plants. The Office of Research and Development is committed to a continuing program of about $1 million per year on the health effects of potable reuse, about the same for health effects of land application, and somewhat less on the effects of aquaculture and industrial recycle. Progress is now being achieved at a pace such that by 1984 it is expected that the Office will be able to recommend criteria in each of the reuse categories, although future refinements will undoubtedly be required (B).

Office of Water Research and Technology

The Office of Water Research and Technology (OWRT) of the U.S. Department of Interior is authorized to conduct a broad research and development program for water reuse under the provisions of the Water Research and Development Act of 1978 (PL 95-467) enacted in October 1978. The Office of Water Resources Research, one of OWRT's predecessor agencies, was established by PL 88-379 in 1964. This Act was passed to establish a partnership between the Federal Government and the State Land Grant universities through a network of university-based State Water Resources Research Institutes, which were intended to accelerate research in water resources problems and to provide training for scientists and engineers (F).

The new Water Resources Research and Development Act of 1978 authorizes the OWRT, among other things, to conduct a research and development program for water reuse. The development of technology to reclaim wastewater economically for beneficial reuse to supplement and extend existing water supplies is becoming a key element in utilizing our limited water resources fully. We are now starting to realize that water is a reclaimable resource and its efficient reclamation and reuse is a vital short-term consideration in many water-short areas of the United States (F).

A SPECIAL SITUATION—CALIFORNIA (H)

The importance of an adequate water supply for California's 22 million people and its agriculture and industry cannot be overemphasized. Due to its steady economic and population growth, California's water demand is continuously increasing. This fact, combined with the uneven distribution of population and surface waters (population in the South and Coastal areas, water in the North) as well as the fluctuation in annual precipitation, necessitates very careful water resources management to secure adequate water supplies for all needs of Californians. Massive water shortage and transport projects have helped to offset geographically imbalanced supplies and allowed the state to grow and prosper. During years with normal rainfall, water delivery from state and federal projects is almost taken for granted. The critical nature of California's water supply and its growing shortages can only be appreciated fully during drought periods. More than anything in recent history, the 1976-1977 drought in California focused attention on the need to develop several water resource management alternatives to assure that California's water needs are met at all times. These alternatives include measures to reduce water consumption, water exchanges and transfers, conjunctive use of ground- and surface waters, and water reclamation. While the drought underscored the need for water reclamation, reclamation is by no means a water management alternative for drought years only, but should be considered an integral and permanent part of California's water supply.

Need for Water Reclamation

In 1972, the annual water demand was 31 million acre-feet (m acre-ft) and shortage was 2.5 m acre-ft. In 1977, the demand was 35.4 m acre-ft and the shortage, because of the drought, was a staggering 10.8 m acre-ft. It is estimated that by the year 2000 the demand will be 39.1 m acre-ft with an annual shortage of about 4.3 m acre-ft assuming normal rainfall and that several currently proposed water development projects such as Auburn Dam, Peripheral Canal, and others will be completed.

In the past, the continuous and increasing shortages have been met by import from unreliable sources and from groundwater overdraft. Groundwater overdraft has caused land subsidence, depletion of water supplies, increased pumping costs, and saltwater intrusion in many areas of the state. Prior to the 1976-1977 drought, groundwater was being overdrafted at the rate of about 2 m acre-ft annually. During the drought, an estimated 10,000 new wells were constructed and overdraft increased to over 8 m acre-ft per year (m acre-ft/yr). The groundwater basins are vital for California's water resource management; they supply up to 50 percent of the water consumptively used by agriculture and municipalities and it is therefore essential that this trend be halted and overdrafted basins be restored to their natural balance.

Without any action to improve water resources management and development of new supplies, statewide net demands in the year 2000 could exceed dependable supplies by as much as 6.6 m acre-ft/yr. In order to prevent such unacceptable conditions, the Department of Water Resources developed a comprehensive water management program to meet projected water supply demands through the year 2000. New reclamation is expected to contribute at least 600,000 acre-ft/yr. In addition to providing a new and more dependable water supply and saving energy, water reclamation can also result in significant water quality benefits. Pollutants will no longer be discharged to surface waters, saltwater intrusion and groundwater overdraft can be reduced or eliminated.

At a time when Southern California is importing large quantities of water from the Colorado River and Northern California, about 93% of the area's wastewater is being wasted by discharge to the ocean and therefore lost as a valuable resource. By the year 2000, an estimated 3.2 m acre-ft of treated wastewater will be discharged from California's coastal areas, about 2.6 m acre-ft of which is reclaimable. Reuse of this water could significantly reduce the anticipated annual shortages.

Status of Water Reclamation

Although the majority of water reuse projects in California involves irrigation, other types of reuse are also represented and their number is steadily increasing. Significant groundwater recharge operations in California include Montebello Forebay recharge by the Los Angeles County Sanitary District, where about 30 million gallons per day (mgd) have been recharged since 1962 and the Orange County Water District's Water Factory 21 where 15 mgd are injected into aquifers to form a saltwater intrusion barrier (see Chapter 2).

Public Health

Although technology is available today to treat sewage to meet traditional drinking water standards, concerns over effects of reclaimed water on public health persist. This is because of limited knowledge in several areas related to reclaimed water reuse, particularly stable organics and virus removal, long-term effects of ingesting trace organics as well as the bioaccumulation of heavy metals. The difficulties in assuring the continuous reliability of treatment processes wherever public contact is involved present a challenging problem. Present methods of reliability assurance are very costly. Further research is needed to evaluate capabilities of various treatment processes and improve the reliability of available technology to produce reclaimed water of suitable quality at reasonable costs. Because of the major potential for using reclaimed water for recharge of groundwater used as a domestic water supply, health related water quality criteria must be developed.

Indirect Potable Uses of Wastewater

INTRODUCTION

Polls have shown that most people in the United States are very unenthusiastic about the prospect of reusing wastewater for drinking and cooking purposes—the so-called direct reuse of wastewater. However, as was pointed out in the last chapter, it seems inevitable that for many communities, particularly in the western United States, wastewater will have to be used in the near future to a far greater extent than it is being used at present.

Many people feel that these uses should be limited to the needs of industry and agriculture or, at least, to nonpotable purposes in the home such as sanitary waste disposal, failing to recognize the enormous extra expense which would be entailed in the provision of separate water lines, pumping equipment, etc., for separate potable and nonpotable uses.

Because of the distaste of most of our citizens for the direct reuse of wastewater, officials in sections of the country where water shortages are becoming critical are looking into indirect reuses of reclaimed water to augment the supply. These uses may be either direct or indirect recharge of treated wastewater to aquifers or reservoirs from which their water is drawn. This course of action provides more or less dilution of the treated wastewater and, in some cases, extra filtration by the soil. A few of the plans devised for this kind of water reuse will be described briefly in this chapter.

FEEDING RECLAIMED WATER INTO A SUPPLYING RESERVOIR

The information in this section is based on a paper from Conference II entitled, "Water Reclamation for

Reuse in Northern Virginia," by M.H. Robbins, Jr., Upper Occoquan Sewage Authority and G.A. Gunn, CH2M Hill of Virginia, Inc.

Necessity for Increased Water Supply

The Occoquan Watershed is located southwest of Washington, DC, a short distance beyond the highly developed urban area surrounding the city. The watershed encompasses 600 square miles, 570 of which drain into the Occoquan Reservoir. This 1,700-acre reservoir is the principal raw water source for the Fairfax County Water Authority, which serves over 660,000 people in Alexandria, Fairfax County and portions of Prince William County. The reservoir has a capacity of 9.8 billion gallons of water with a safe yield of 65 million gallons per day.

Despite the rapid population increase in the Washington Metropolitan area, the Occoquan Watershed until the 1960s remained largely rural. However, with the construction of the interstate highway system, the watershed came within easy commuting distance of Washington and pressure to expand and develop new housing in the watershed increased tremendously.

Because of the water quality implications of a large population increase, the Virginia State Water Control Board attempted to control development by limiting the number and size of sewage treatment plants in the watershed. This policy not only had severe adverse impact on the commercial well-being of the area, but also resulted in many small, inefficient publicly and privately owned secondary sewage treatment plants with highly variable performance. These increased discharges of inadequately treated sewage resulted in the progressive deterioration of the reservoir. By 1969, the reservoir had heavy algal blooms, mainly blue-green algae, and the water below 10 feet in depth was anaerobic.

Recognizing that a solution to the problem required a coordinated, basin-wide comprehensive plan, the State Water Control Board employed the consulting firm of Metcalf & Eddy to develop such a plan. Following extensive studies, the State Water Control Board in the Occoquan Policy chose a plan which called for providing the most advanced waste treatment and limiting of population as the most cost effective method to protect the watershed.

Occoquan Policy

The Occoquan Policy mandated the following actions:

(1) A regional water reclamation plant utilizing the best treatment technology available would replace the existing sewage treatment plants in the watershed. The effluent requirements for the regional plant were among the most stringent in the United States (Table 2.1).

(2) The regional system would incorporate extensive fail-safe features including the following facilities at the plant and all pump stations:

    (a) standby units for all electrical and mechanical com-
ponents;

    (b) three separate sources of electric power; and

    (c) emergency holding basins.

(3) Until the regional plant was available, all existing sewage treatment plants would use chemical additions to increase treatment
efficiencies.

(4) A watershed monitoring laboratory was required to monitor
conditions of the reservoir and its tributaries.

Table 2.1: Upper Occoquan Sewage Authority Wastewater Characteristics

Constituent	Expected Raw Sewage Characteristics	Required Effluent Quality
BOD_5, mg/ℓ	250	1.0
COD, mg/ℓ	—	10.0
Suspended solids, mg/ℓ	225	<1.0
Phosphorus (total), mg/ℓ	18	0.1
Nitrogen (total unoxid-ized), mg/ℓ	25	1.0
Methylene blue active substances, mg/ℓ	—	0.1
Coliform bacteria, MPN/100 ml	—	<2

Source: NSF/RA-790225

The Upper Occoquan Sewage Authority: The Upper Occoquan Sewage Authority (UOSA), was established in 1971 to meet the Occoquan Policy mandate
to construct and operate a regional water reclamation system. The authority
selected CH2M Hill, Inc. as consulting engineers for the project.

Construction of Plant: The construction of the project was substantially impaired by regulatory actions subsequent to the passage of the Water Pollution
Control Act amendments of 1972 (PL 92-500). These regulatory actions resulted
in a very large increase in project costs and a delay in project completion of
three years.

Design of Plant

A schematic of the UOSA treatment plant is presented in Figure 2.1.

Primary and Secondary Treatments: The first treatment processes are fairly
conventional primary and secondary treatments, with the exception of the fail-
safe or redundant units provided in accordance with the Occoquan Policy. For
example, each primary clarifier is rated at 7.5 mgd.

Figure 2.1: Plant Schematic Flow Diagram

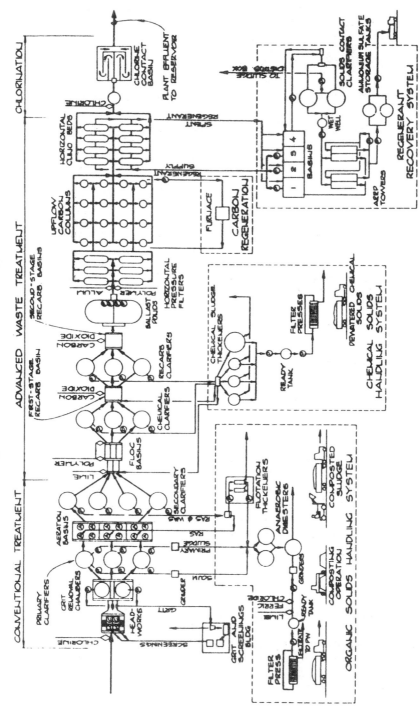

Source: NSF/RA-790225

Therefore, in accordance with the policy, three primary clarifiers are provided, two clarifiers to handle the design flow of 15 mgd and a third as a redundant unit. The same redundancy is provided for all mainstream unit processes in the plant. Another fail-safe feature in this plant section is the capability to divert a portion or all of the plant influent or primary effluent to an emergency retention pond with a capacity of 45 million gallons. The contents of this pond are returned to the plant headworks after the emergency.

Monitoring: A computer-based instrumentation and control system is used to monitor all critical functions in the UOSA system, and the secondary portion of the plant involves the first use of the computers for process control. The dissolved oxygen in the completely mixed activated sludge process is controlled by varying the depth of submergence of the aerator impellers. The impeller submergency is varied by computer adjustment of the aeration basin discharge weirs based on the dissolved oxygen levels.

The advanced waste treatment unit processes in the plant are normally operated in an automatic mode by the computer-based central control system. However, to protect against computer failure, each system is provided with a back-up analog automatic control unit. The first AWT process is chemical clarification using lime to precipitate phosphorus. Lime additions are computer controlled to raise the pH to 11.3. The precipitate is then flocculated and settled. An anionic polymer is added to enhance settling. The pH is reduced to 7.0 by two-stage recarbonation with intermediate settling.

Ballast Ponds: Ballast ponds, or equalization basins, are used to provide constant flows to the remaining processes. The ballast pond water is pumped through trimedia pressure filters, activated carbon adsorption columns, and ion exchange columns for ammonia removal. The water is then chlorinated and discharged to a final effluent reservoir with 20 days' detention. An automatic analyzer continuously monitors the final effluent for the NPDES discharge parameters. If a parameter exceeds its limit, the computer closes the discharge valve, and the unacceptable water is recycled for additional treatment. The final effluent is the water source for all plant processes.

Anaerobic Digestion: Organic solids are processed by two-stage anaerobic digestion, dewatering on filter presses, and composting. The compost will be used by local park authorities as a soil amendment in their nurseries. The methane from digestion is used as fuel in the boilers to produce heat for the plant, and the stack gases are used in the recarbonation process.

Chemical Clarification: Chemical solids are gravity thickened and dewatered on filter presses. These solids are presently landfilled, but UOSA in cooperation with the Virginia Department of Agriculture plans to explore agricultural uses for the chemical solids.

The ion exchange beds are regenerated by purging the ammonia with a concentrated sodium chloride regenerate solution, and the ammonia is removed from the regenerant solution by an air stripping and absorption system developed for the UOSA plant. In this system, the regenerant solution pH is raised to volatilize the ammonia, ammonia gas is stripped into an air stream in a stripping tower, and the ammonia-laden air stream then flows through an absorption tower. The absorbent liquid is sulfuric acid resulting in the ammonia ions being absorbed as ammonium sulfate. The ammonium sulfate will be marketed as a fertilizer.

Plant Performance

The UOSA plant began operations on June 26, 1978. All unit processes are operative except the ion exchange facilities for ammonia removal. It has been found during the first 8 months of operation that most of the fail-safe features incorporated in the UOSA system are essential to meet the NPDES permit limits consistently. The fail-safe features were particularly valuable during one period of three months. The sewage collection systems operated by the juris-dictions served by UOSA were known to have infiltration/inflow problems, but the enormity of the problem was not fully recognized until UOSA was able to intercept and treat these flows. The influence of infiltration/inflow on UOSA flows is illustrated in Figure 2.2. It will be observed that the fairly steady flows during the fall became highly variable during the wet months of December, January and February. During the last week in February, the flows to the UOSA plant increased from 7.8 mgd to 40.8 mg in a four-day period. The actual peak flow rate was much higher, but by utilizing the emergency storage facilities at the pumping stations the peak flow was reduced 40.8 mg on February 25. Despite these highly fluctuating flows, plant performance has been very good.

Figure 2.2: Plant Flow Data Summary

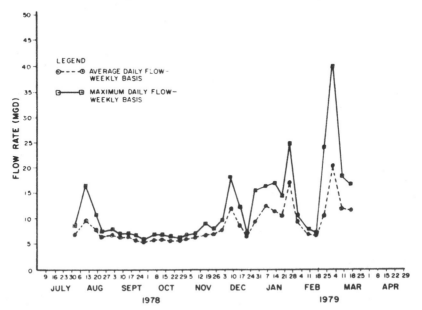

Source: NSF/RA-790225

Operation and Maintenance Cost

The operation and maintenance cost to date (1979) has averaged 70¢ per 1,000 gallons. When the ion exchange facilities for ammonia removal become operational, it is expected that the O&M cost will be about 90¢ per 1,000 gallons.

In Table 2.2, the UOSA operation and maintenance cost is compared to the costs incurred by some of the jurisdictions to operate their small secondary treatment plants replaced by UOSA. This comparison shows that due to economy of scale and certain efficiencies incorporated in the UOSA design, the UOSA plant is able to produce a very high-quality water for a cost comparable to the cost to the jurisdictions to operate their own small secondary treatment plants.

Table 2.2: Comparison of Operation and Maintenance Costs

Jurisdiction	Number Plants	O&M Cost per 1,000 Gallons, $
Fairfax County	5	1.47
Prince William County	1	0.43
City of Manassas	2	0.71
UOSA	—	0.90*

*1978 costs.

Source: NSF/RA-790225

Future

The UOSA plant has already had a substantial impact on the reservoir according to data collected by the Occoquan Watershed Monitoring Laboratory. This laboratory, also required by the Occoquan Policy, is operated by Virginia Polytechnic Institute and State University. The laboratory reports that the water quality in the Bull Run arm of the reservoir last fall was the best ever observed in the six years of the monitoring program.

The quality of the UOSA water will be especially important during low flow periods of the year. In recent dry years, the water authority withdrawals exceeded inflow to the reservoir from April to October, and thus all inflow was retained in the water pool.

During an extended dry period, the wastewater discharges constitute the majority of the flow into the reservoir and as the pool level drops, the percentage of treated wastewater in the raw water supply increases. During the 1977 drought, for example, 80% of the flow to the reservoir during September was from wastewater discharges.

The impact of UOSA on the water resources of Northern Virginia is expected to increase in the future. Much of the growth in Northern Virginia during the next few years is planned for the Occoquan Watershed provided such growth can be accomplished without degrading the reservoir. Thus, UOSA is faced with the challenge of not only protecting the reservoir from wastewater pollution but serving as the source of an ever-increasing supply of reclaimed wastewater for potable reuse.

DISCHARGE OF TREATED WASTEWATER INTO UNDERGROUND SYSTEM

> The material in this section is abstracted from a paper in Conference II titled, "Tahoe-Truckee Water Reclamation Plant," by S.A. Smith and R.L. Chapman, CH2M Hill and O.R. Butterfield, Tahoe-Truckee Sanitation Agency.

Introduction

The Tahoe-Truckee Sanitation Agency was formed in May 1972 to carry out the mandate of the Porter Cologne Water Quality Act, a California law requiring exportation of all sewage from the Lake Tahoe Basin. Upon its formation, the agency immediately embarked on a program to plan, program, design, and construct a regional system which would transport all sewage from an area encompassing the California north shore of Lake Tahoe and Truckee to a regional plant. Construction of this facility would result in the replacement of the existing interim treatment facilities operated by the agency's five-member entities. The Tahoe-Truckee Sanitation Agency (T-TSA) is governed by a Board of Directors comprised of five appointed directors, one from each member district.

Retention of the effluent in the Truckee River Basin was decided to be of prime importance in order that the quantity of water available to downstream users not be diminished by this project. It was also determined that treatment of the wastewater to a high degree at a location near Truckee was the most economical solution and that this plan had the least adverse impact on the environment. Third, the existing high water quality standards required on the Truckee River could not be adhered to by upgrading of the existing treatment plants. The State of California's rigid waste discharge requirements necessitated the implementation of the most sophisticated treatment available.

The project finally selected as the most advisable required the construction of an interceptor line from Tahoe City to Truckee, California, the construction of a 4.83-mgd (212 ℓ/sec) regional sewage treatment plant in Martis Valley, and the installation of an underground disposal system that would allow the effluent to percolate into the permeable glacial outwash soil near the plant. Full tertiary treatment, including maximum removals of nitrogen and phosphorus, was deemed necessary to protect the quality of the Truckee River into which the effluent would ultimately find its way and to ensure the safety and integrity of this primary water source for Reno, Nevada, a major city downstream.

Design of the water reclamation plant was initiated in January 1975. The contract for construction was awarded in November 1975 to Del E. Webb Corporation and University Mechanical Contractors, a joint venture. Because of the urgent need for the facility, the contractor was allowed only 24 months to have the complex plant operational and was permitted additional time for final completion. The plant began treating sewage on February 1, 1978, 27 months after award of contract.

Treatment Requirements and Processes

The discharge requirements for the plant are very stringent and were established to protect the beneficial uses of the Truckee River and groundwater sources. The discharge requirements limit constituent concentrations in the plant effluent as well as limit constituent increases in the Truckee River. The plant effluent limitations are listed in Table 2.3.

Table 2.3: Effluent Limitations

Constituent	Mean Concentration	Maximum Concentration
COD, mg/ℓ	15	40
Suspended solids, mg/ℓ	2	4
Turbidity, NTU	2	8
Total nitrogen, mg/ℓ	2	4
Total phosphorus, mg/ℓ	0.15	0.4
MBAS, mg/ℓ	0.15	0.4
TDS, mg/ℓ	440	—
Chloride, mg/ℓ	110	—
Total coliform organisms, MPN/100 ml	—	23

Source: NSF/RA-790225

Processes installed to meet the discharge requirements include the following:

- Primary treatment.
- Pure oxygen activated sludge.
- Lime treatment with two-stage recarbonation.
- Dual-media filtration.
- Activated carbon adsorption with on-site regeneration.
- Selective ion exchange using clinoptilolite for ammonia removal.

Biological sludges are anaerobically digested. Both biological and chemical sludges are dewatered in a plate and frame filter press and landfilled.

Nitrogen Removal: The nitrogen removal process is a unique feature of the plant. The clinoptilolite ion exchange beds are regenerated using a 3% salt solution in conjunction with an ammonia removal and recovery process (ARRP). The salt regenerant solution is circulated through an exhausted-ion exchange bed to purge the bed of ammonia. The portion of the salt solution with the highest ammonia concentration, approximately 300 mg/ℓ, is elevated to pH 11.1 using sodium hydroxide. This high pH solution is then clarified and pumped to an ARRP module. An ARRP module is a closed air system consisting of a stripping tower, absorber tower, interconnecting duct work and fan.

Ammonia is stripped from the spent regenerant solution in the stripping tower and absorbed in the absorber tower where the pH is maintained at 2 by addition of sulfuric acid. The end result is that ammonia is removed from the regenerant solution and recovered as concentrated ammonium sulfate. The salt regenerant solution is used repeatedly for regeneration of ion exchange beds and all recovered ammonium sulfate is used as a commercial fertilizer in the Sacramento Valley of California.

Ion exchange used in conjunction with the ARRP is believed to be the best process available to provide the ammonia removal required at this location. The low winter temperatures prohibit effective use of biological nitrogen removal or conventional air stripping.

Discharge Arrangement: Another rather unusual and interesting feature of the T-TSA water reclamation plant is that even though the plant effluent is of very high quality, with virtually all contaminants removed, current regulations still prohibit it from being directly discharged into the receiving waters of the Truckee River Basin. This requirement came about because of the pristine quality of the Truckee River in this vicinity and because it is the primary source of the Reno, Nevada water supply. Consequently, as a further precautionary measure, the effluent is discharged into an underground disposal system near the plant.

The combinaion of advanced waste treatment processes and the underground disposal system is believed to provide the best assurance possible of the protection and preservation of this environmentally sensitive and pristine receiving water.

Plant Performance

Raw Sewage Characteristics: The treatment plant receives wastewaters strictly from domestic and commercial sources; there is no industrial contribution. The wastewater characteristics are fairly typical of a moderate-strength domestic sewage except during spring snowmelt conditions when infiltration and inflow dilute the wastewater about 50%. The majority of the year, BOD concentrations are typically in the range of 175 to 250 mg/ℓ and total suspended solids concentrations vary from 175 to 225 mg/ℓ. Total phosphorus and total nitrogen concentrations average about 10 and 40 mg/ℓ, respectively.

Sewage flows and hence total pollutant loadings are highly variable because of the recreational nature of the area. Maximum loadings historically occur during August which is the peak summer vacation period at Lake Tahoe. Other peak loadings occur during the winter ski season, particularly during the Christmas holidays, Washington's birthday weekend, and Easter week. Peak flows to the plant occur during spring snowmelt conditions concurrent with a holiday period.

Maximum hydrualic loads occurred on the plant during Easter week when daily sewage flows averaged about 4.8 mgd (210 ℓ/sec). However, the wastewater was fairly dilute at that time due to the effects of infiltration and inflow. Maximum pollutant loading conditions occurred during the month of August when the plant was operating at about 80% of its design loading.

Removals Obtained: The plant began operation on February 1, 1978, when about 0.5 mgd (20 ℓ/sec) of sewage was diverted from the Truckee Sanitary District system. During the month of February, construction was still continuing and a good deal of performance testing had not yet been accomplished. By March 1, the plant was accepting flow from all scheduled sources.

Initial performance of the plant was extremely successful, particularly considering that construction of the plant was not truly complete and the startup occurred during severe winter conditions. As a result of infiltration and inflow during the spring snowmelt conditions, the concentrations of COD, suspended solids, phosphorus and nitrogen were relatively low during the spring. The concentrations jumped dramatically in June and remained high throughout the remainder of the year. Maximum strengths occurred during July and August as was expected.

During the initial months of operation, there was naturally a period of troubleshooting and initial process optimization efforts. While effluent quality was relatively good from the start, the quality in general gradually improved during the initial months of operation. Fairly stable operation was achieved during the last 7 months of 1978, and an exceptional effluent quality was consistently achieved.

Table 2.4 summarizes the plant effluent quality during the last 7 months of 1978 with respect to the various constituents included in the discharge requirements. During that time, the plant performance essentially met all of the very stringent discharge requirements with exception of the effluent limitations on total dissolved solids (TDS) and chloride concentration. The effluent limitations on TDS and chlorides were established after initiation of the plant design. Consequently, there are no processes included in the plant design to remove these dissolved inorganic constituents.

The TDS and chloride concentrations in the raw sewage, coupled with increases through the plant inherent with the chemical treatment and sludge handling processes, essentially preclude the plant's ability to control the concentrations of these constituents in the effluent. In recognition of these factors, T-TSA staff has requested and hopes to receive a relaxation in the discharge requirements for TDS and chloride. Further optimization of chemical treatment and the ammonia removal system may result in eventual lower levels of TDS and chlorides in the effluent.

Table 2.4: Plant Performance June Through December 1978

Constituent	Average Effluent Concentration	Effluent Limitations
COD, mg/ℓ	10	15
Suspended solids, mg/ℓ	0.8	2
Turbidity, NTU	0.6	2.0
Total nitrogen, mg/ℓ	2.3	2.0
Total phosphorus, mg/ℓ	0.15	0.15
MBAS, mg/ℓ	0.04	0.15
Total dissolved solids, mg/ℓ	633	440
Chloride, mg/ℓ	206	110
Total coliform organisms, MPN/100 ml	<2	23

Source: NSF/RA-790225

Sampling of the Truckee River both upstream and downstream of the plant has indicated the project is meeting its primary objective: returning reclaimed water to the basin with no detrimental effect on water quality. Table 2.5 illustrates the high quality of the Truckee River and indicates the only parameters that show significant increase downstream of the plant are TDS and chlorides. It is not known how much of this increase is due to the plant discharge and how much is due to other sources of runoff.

Table 2.5: Truckee River Water Quality June Through December 1978

Parameter	Upstream of T-TSA	Downstream of T-TSA
Nitrates, mg/ℓ	0.09	0.09
Kjeldahl nitrogen, mg/ℓ	0.26	0.28
Total phosphorus, mg/ℓ	0.04	0.06
Dissolved organic carbon, mg/ℓ	1.1	1.1
MBAS, mg/ℓ	0.01	0.01
pH	7.7	7.6
TDS, mg/ℓ	56	64
Chlorides, mg/ℓ	2.7	6.3

Source: NSF/RA-790225

Costs

Capital Cost: The total capital cost of the plant was approximately $19,976,000. Table 2.6 shows this cost distributed according to major process units. The costs of the sludge handling facilities are included in the costs listed for primary and secondary treatment and chemical treatment.

Table 2.6: Capital Costs

Process Unit	Capital Costs, $	Percent of Total
Primary and secondary treatment	7,666,000	38
Chemical treatment and filtration	4,881,000	24
Carbon adsorption	3,928,000	20
Ammonia removal	3,501,000	18
Total	19,976,000	100

Source: NSF/RA-790225

A major factor that significantly influenced the capital cost is the plant's location. The Lake Tahoe area is historically one of the most expensive areas in California for construction projects. Also, because of the high Sierra location, the facility was designed for snow loads to 150 psf and temperatures to –45°F (–43°C). The severe climate required that nearly all facilities be covered or enclosed for proper operation and maintenance.

Operating and Maintenance Costs: Labor, chemicals, and power are the major costs associated with operation of the treatment processes. Other costs include administration, miscellaneous expenses, and final sludge disposal. These costs are presented in Table 2.7 for the period June-September 1978.

Table 2.7: Operating and Maintenance Costs by Expense Category

Expense Type	$/Million Gallons	Percent of Total
Labor	580	34
Chemicals	475	28
Power	160	10
Administration	140	8
Final sludge disposal	51	3
All other expenses	294	17
Total	1,700	100

Source: NSF/RA-790225

In Table 2.8 the operation and maintenance costs are summarized according to major process unit. Approximately 81% of the current operation and maintenance costs are associated with the AWT processes.

It is anticipated that the cost per million gallons will decrease as plant flows increase and optimization of the chemical dosages continue. [During the period June-September, the raw sewage flow averaged approximately 3 mgd (130 ℓ/sec).]

Table 2.8: Operating and Maintenance Costs by Major Process Unit

Process	Cost $/Million Gallons	Percent of Total
Primary and secondary treatment	331	19
Chemical treatment and filtration	760	45
Carbon adsorption	125	7
Ammonia removal and recovery	484	29
Total	1,700	100

Source: NSF/RA-790225

The cost information presented here was the first effort in analyzing actual plant operations and maintenance costs. It is anticipated that there will be some future shift in the distribution of costs shown in Table 2.8. The labor costs associated with operating the chemical treatment and ammonia removal systems should decrease as operating procedures become more efficient and remaining equipment problems are resolved. Chemical usage should also decrease with these two processes as optimum dosages are determined. The cost of carbon adsorption should increase due to more frequent regeneration of the carbon. During this first year of operation, the need for regeneration has been held to a minimum because of the high-quality virgin carbon.

The cost of operation and maintenance is directly related to the stringent discharge requirements. As an example, the effluent limitation of 0.15 mg/ℓ phosphorus requires a high lime dosage and nearly constant operator attention. Malfunctions must be quickly identified and corrected or the effluent limitation will be exceeded for that day. The same operator vigilance is required for all processes because of the extremely low levels of COD, nitrogen, and solids permitted in the effluent.

Conclusions

The $20 million T-TSA Water Reclamation Plant was successfully put on line beginning February 1, 1978, 3 years after authorization to proceed with design. Performance data collected during 1978 clearly demonstrate the plant's ability to produce an effluent of superior quality basically in conformance with all of the very stringent effluent limitations, exclusive of chlorides and total dissolved solids. Monitoring of the Truckee River has also demonstrated the project is achieving its primary goal of returning reclaimed water to the basin while maintaining exceptional water quality.

Operation and maintenance costs during the first year of operation are estimated at $1,700 per million gallons. The current sewer service charge is approximately $10 per single family residential unit. While these costs are substantial, they are judged reasonable by most people considering the unique environmental setting and the demanding goals.

GROUNDWATER RECHARGE AT WATER FACTORY 21

> The information in this section is based on a paper from
> Conference I entitled, "Groundwater Recharge at Water
> Factory 21," by N.M. Cline, Orange County Water Dis-
> trict.

Introduction

In 1956 the population of the Orange County Water District within Orange
County, California was 500,000 persons. The annual water requirement was
232,000 acre-feet of which 123,000 acre-feet, 53%, were used for irrigation
and 109,000 acre-feet, 47%, for municipal and industrial purposes. The County
was in the midst of a growth boom that had proceeded unabated following
World War II. To support the postwar expansion the community was relying
to a large extent upon groundwater, which resulted in a serious overdraft of
groundwater supply. The Orange County Water District, organized in 1933 to
protect local interests in the Santa Ana River and manage the area's groundwater, reported seawater had intruded as much as 3½ miles inland.

In 1979 the population of OCWD was nearly 1.5 million people. The annual
water requirement was 400,000 acre-feet, of which 50,000 acre-feet, 12%,
was applied for irrigation and 350,000 acre-feet, 88%, for municipal and industrial consumption. Groundwater remains the principal source of water supply
for the burgeoning community, however. Even though the demand for water
far exceeds the safe yield of the local watershed there is every reason to believe
that groundwater resources will continue as the backbone of local water supply.

The District, with the support of local water users and in cooperation with the
Metropolitan Water District of Southern California (MDW), has developed
management procedures that will perpetuate groundwater reliability.

For the last 60 years Southern Californians have been pursuing programs to supplement local water supply by importing additional water. The first major import system to be developed was the Owens Valley Aqueduct, contracted by
the City of Los Angeles in 1913. In the 1920s MWD was organized to transport Colorado River water to the South Coastal plain, and in 1960 MWD contracted with the State of California for additional water to be transferred from
Northern California via the California aqueduct. Orange County was among the
original MWD members, and presently is utilizing groundwater accumulated as
a consequence of flow from the Santa Ana River and local drainage, Colorado
River water and Northern California water. Since 1949 Orange County Water
District has been importing large amounts of Colorado River water for groundwater recharge to supplement Santa Ana River flows. To date more than 2.2
million acre-feet of imported water have been percolated into the area's groundwater reserve for use to meet increasing demand and to repel saline intrusion.

It has been apparent for some time that to sustain an adequate water supply for

Orange County's expanding economy additional supplementary sources must be established.

The interbasin transfer of water is becoming less and less possible. By 1985 California will lose 50% of the volume of water it now draws from the Colorado River, and the prospect of drawing millions of gallons of water from Northern to Southern California seems to be less attractive every year. The energy shortage adds to the difficulties of importing large quantities of water. It is not surprising therefore that in Southern California it is anticipated that, in part, the area's future water requirements will be satisfied through increased water conservation and wastewater reclamation programs. The region's water supplies will ultimately be composed of fully developed local resources, conjunctively used with a combination of imported Northern California and Colorado River water, reclaimed wastewater and limited desalted brackish supply.

In the expectation of what is now occurring, the Orange County Water District has developed a wastewater reclamation system to provide a source of supply to hydraulically prevent seawater intrusion into the area's invaluable groundwater reserve.

Seawater Intrusion Problem

The Orange County groundwater basin is the depositional plain of the Santa Ana River. The principal features of the region are surrounding hills and a broad poorly drained alluvial plain with alternating gaps and minor hill systems along the coast. A major fault system somewhat parallels the coastline, which, as far as has been determined, seals the basin from the sea at deeper levels. However, in several gaps along the ocean front there is hydraulic continuity between seawater and groundwater in the upper 150 to 200 feet of recent alluvial fill.

In general, the aquifers of the area are composed of fine- to coarse-grained sand, separated by silt and clay aquicludes. The Talbert aquifer, the principal zone of production in the area, is Recent age and uncomfortably overlies the Pleistocene deposits within the gap created by the Santa Ana River. The Talbert is the only aquifer in direct contact with the ocean. The lower three zones of local production are subject to intrusion by virtue of their contact with the Talbert.

Early settlers of the Orange County area had found an ideal area for agriculture due to the moderate climate and availability of artesian wells. Agricultural pumping exceeded the safe yield of the system; consequently in the early 1920s artesian pressure levels were lowered below sea level and by 1931 the Talbert aquifer was intruded by seawater as far inland as 1.4 miles. Seawater intrusion continued, moving steadily inland and forcing the City of Laguna Beach to abandon their wells in 1947. Newport Beach lost their wells in 1953 and by 1963 seawater had moved as far as 3½ miles inland from the ocean. Although the Orange County Water Department (OCWD) managed to prevent further and more widespread damage through massive percolation of imported water into the forebay, the need for a coastal barrier system was obvious.

Preliminary studies indicated that to develop an efficient hydraulic barrier to maintain intrusion control would require 30,000 acre-feet of water per year. In water-scarce Southern California this is a substantial quantity; and after weighing all the factors, including consideration of availability of supply, reliability, environmental problems, quality, and program costs, it was determined the best source for barrier injection would be reclaimed water. Since 1962 OCWD has been in the process of developing its coastal barrier project to utilize salvaged wastewater.

Facilities Description

The Coastal Barrier Project currently consists of Water Factory 21, an advanced waste treatment facility; a series of 23 injection wells; 31 monitoring wells; 5 supplementary deep wells and a battery of 7 extraction wells.

The water factory is designed to treat 15 million gallons per day of activated sludge secondary effluent provided through the facilities of the Orange County Sanitation District. The advanced waste treatment process includes lime clarification, ammonia stripping, recarbonation, mixed-media filtration, activated carbon adsorption, demineralization and chlorination.

The 23 injection wells are multiple casing units that inject into the four aquifers subject to the effects of seawater intrusion. The wells are located at 600-foot intervals in precast 6' x 10' concrete vaults located in a city street 3½ miles inland from the coast. The wells vary in depth from 90 to 430 feet. Each well has the capacity to inject 450 gallons per minute. Figure 2.3 is a typical injection well.

The 31 monitoring wells are distributed landward and seaward of the injection line. The majority of the monitoring wells are multiple casing facilities mirroring the injection well installations.

To provide necessary supplementary waters to assure barrier supply, 5 conventional wells have been drilled to produce from a deeper aquifer not subject to seawater contamination. These wells, ranging from 850 to 1,150 feet deep and capable of furnishing 3,500 gpm each, are located adjacent to Water Factory 21.

To assure a seaward gradient from the injection mound, and to regulate the amount of water that will move towards the ocean, 7 extraction wells have been constructed about 2 miles inland. These wells, optimized, produce 300 gpm each.

Water Factory 21 Performance

Because the reclaimed water produced by the plant will ultimately commingle with native groundwater and eventually be used for domestic, agricultural and industrial purposes, very stringent quality standards have been imposed by the California Regional Water Quality Control Board and the State Department of Health. The requirements are tabulated in Table 2.9.

Figure 2.3: Typical Injection or Observation Well

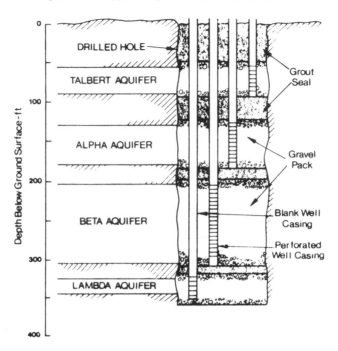

Source: NSF/RA-790224

Because the average wastewater in Orange County typically contains approximately 1,000 mg/ℓ total dissolved solids, it is necessary to provide demineralization for a part of the reclaimed effluent in order to satisfy injection quality standards for TDS. Since July 1977 the District has been operating a 5-mgd reverse osmosis demineralization plant designed to provide 99% rejection of all salts while achieving an overall product water recovery of 85%. The system is composed of pretreatment of the activated carbon effluent by adding chlorination and filtration, followed by RO membrane processing and posttreatment.

By regulation the wastewater must be blended at least 50% with demineralized or deep well water prior to injection into the subsurface. Table 2.10 is a compilation of the quality of blended injection water compared to regulatory requirements for all quality parameters.

In addition to these quality considerations as indicated in Table 2.9, the District conducts a virus monitoring program to ascertain the efficiency of virus removal through the AWT process. To date, no viruses have been determined to have survived the treatment procedure.

The District maintains its own State-approved laboratory to monitor the chemical and biological performance of the plant. Virus work is performed by contract with a local consulting firm.

Table 2.9: Regulatory Agency Requirements for Injection Water OCWD Wastewater Reclamation and Injection Project

Constituent, mg/ℓ	
Ammonium	1.0
Sodium	110.0
Total hardness (CaCO$_3$)	220.0
Sulfate	125.0
Chloride	120.0
Total nitrogen	10.0
Fluoride	0.8
Boron	0.5
MBAS	0.5
Hexavalent chromium	0.05
Cadmium	0.01
Selenium	0.01
Phenol	0.001
Copper	1.0
Lead	0.05
Mercury	0.005
Arsenic	0.05
Iron	0.3
Manganese	0.05
Barium	1.0
Silver	0.05
Cyanide	0.02
Characteristics	
Electrical conductivity, μmho/cm	900
pH	6.5–8.0
Taste	None
Odor	None
Foam	None
Color	None
Filter effluent turbidity, JTU	1.0
Carbon adsorption effluent COD, mg/ℓ	30
Cl contact basin effluent	Free Cl residual

Note: Reclaimed wastewater must be blended at least 50% with demineralized (RO effluent) or deep well water. Reclaimed wastewater must be tested for virus.

Source: NSF/RA-790224

Table 2.10: Blended Water Quality (Typical)

Constituent	Regulatory Limit	Quality Achieved
EC, μmho/cm	900	784
Turbidity, JTU	1.0	0.42

(continued)

Table 2.10: (continued)

Constituent	Regulatory Limit	Quality Achieved
Na, mg/ℓ	110	108
Ca, mg/ℓ	—	37
Mg, mg/ℓ	—	0.5
Cl, mg/ℓ	120	103
SO₄, mg/ℓ	125	83
Alk (CaCO₃), mg/ℓ	—	121
NH₃-N, mg/ℓ	1.0	0.86
Org-N, mg/ℓ	—	0.70
PO₄-P, mg/ℓ	—	—
B, mg/ℓ	1.0	0.86
F, mg/ℓ	0.8	0.50
COD, mg/ℓ	30	10
TOC, mg/ℓ	—	—
MBAS, mg/ℓ	0.5	0.08
Phenol, µg/ℓ	1.0	1.0
CHCl₃, µg/ℓ	—	—
PCBs, µg/ℓ	—	—
Pesticides, µg/ℓ	0.01*	—
As, µg/ℓ	50	2.6
Ba, µg/ℓ	1,000	14.0
Cd, µg/ℓ	10	0.6
Cr, µg/ℓ	50	8.8
Cu, µg/ℓ	1,000	12.3
Fe, µg/ℓ	300	71.0
Pb, µg/ℓ	50	2.8
Mn, µg/ℓ	50	4.6
Hg, µg/ℓ	5	2.4
Se, µg/ℓ	10	1.8
Ag, µg/ℓ	50	0.8
Zn, µg/ℓ	—	156
CN, µg/ℓ	200	<10.0

*Concentration above which pesticides not found in any sample.

Source: NSF/RA-790224

Barrier Performance

Quality Procedures: The product water from the treatment process is pumped to the 23 injection wells for placement in the subsurface. The maximum injection pressure is 20 psi, to prevent damage to gravel pack and well seals of the injection units. The injected water and receiving groundwater is measured quantitatively and qualitatively on a daily basis, following a fixed schedule that provides for daily, weekly and monthly measurements. The injection water quality is continuously monitored and analyzed. Twice daily, grab samples are measured for chlorine residual, and every two hours the pH, conductivity and turbidity are analyzed. Each 24 hours a composite sample is tested for ammonia nitrogen, organic nitrogen, total Kjeldahl nitrogen, calcium, alkalinity, fecal coliform, and total coliform. Once a week composite samples are tested for TDS, hardness, magnesium, sodium, chloride, fluoride, boron, sulfates, foaming agents, color, cyanide, and phenol.

The groundwater quality monitoring program is conducted on samples collected from the four aquifers exposed to seawater intrusion. At weekly intervals four preselected wells are tested for COD, conductivity, ammonia nitrogen, and chloride, color and odor. Monthly and semiannually all the observation wells are checked for conductivity and the presence of chloride.

Due to the special nature of the injection water, particular interest centers on the measured conductivity of the water, the determination of the presence of coliforms, and the potential presence of virus. The conductivity of the receiving waters varies from 1,175 μmho/cm to as low as 375 μmho/cm, with an average of near 600 μmho/cm which is somehwat similar to the injection source, resulting in the potential of obscuring the determination of displacement of native water by injection supply.

Tests for total coliform bacteria and fecal coliform are conducted at least each 48 hours on the final blended supply. No fecal coliform has ever been detected in the injection water. During calendar year 1978 tests for total coliform indicated positive results in 16 occasions. An analysis of coliform occurrence indicates that bacteria were present only when the plant was operating at low flows or coming back on line following a shutdown, which implies some limited bacteria growth during shutdown periods.

Water Levels: Since the inception of the hydraulic barrier program in October 1976, OCWD has injected 33,338 acre-feet of water into the subsurface. The principal objective of the program is to maintain sufficient water levels to prevent seawater from further penetration into the groundwater reserves of the county. It is essential that adequate pressures be established to protect the fresh water, particularly during times when the basin, for any circumstance, might be drawn down substantially below sea level.

Not surprisingly it has been concluded that steady flow averaging between 12 and 20 mgd, depending upon inland water elevation, is the optimum operational level. Studies are continuing in order to optimize injection rate for any given overdraft condition or limitation on the barrier supply.

Because of the excellent permeability of the receiving sediments and the high quality of the injection water, the injection wells, after initial development, have been in continuous operation. It is anticipated that redevelopment will be required as injection rates diminish through clogging or other phenomena. This work is scheduled to occur when the line pressure on the distribution system equals the aquifer system pressure, and the District is not able to sustain an adequate hydraulic mound.

Operational Costs

A summary of the AWT, RO and barrier costs is shown in Tables 2.11 and 2.12. Table 2.11 is a compilation of the annual operations and maintenance costs of the entire system, and Table 2.12 is a summation of total costs including capital and annual expenses. The costs are a tabulation of actual expenditures during one-year operation of the District's Water Factory.

Detailed cost records are maintained to account for treatment processes including personnel expenses, utility costs, chemicals, and all maintenance expenses. All capital costs are amortized over service life of 20 years at 7% interest rate with a plant factor of 90%.

Table 2.11: Water Factory 21 and Barrier Facilities Annual Cost of Operations and Maintenance

		Total, $
. . . . .15 mgd AWT Plant—5 mgd RO Plant		
Salaries		613,000
Operations	315,000	
Maintenance	238,000*	
Admin/Eng.	60,000	
Utilities		1,000,000
Electricity	828,000	
Gas	166,000	
Water	6,000	
Chemicals		222,800
Lime	61,000	
Alum	2,400	
Polymer	15,000	
Sulfuric acid	24,000	
Chlorine	112,000	
SHMP	8,400	
Maintenance		513,600
Parts and materials	260,000	
Equipment rentals	18,000	
Uniforms	10,000	
Special dept. expense	12,000	
RO maintenance contract	213,600**	
Total annual O&M cost		2,349,400
. . . . .Injection System		
Personnel		69,000
Utilities (gas)		43,000
Maintenance		64,000
Total injection system cost		176,000
Total annual costs		2,525,400

*Maintenance labor costs include some plant modifications completed during the year which were not capitalized, e.g., modification of upflow carbon columns to downflow.
**RO maintenance contract includes all membrane replacement costs, cartridge filter replacement, membrane cleaning, routine preventative and emergency maintenance.

Source: NSF/RA-790224

Table 2.12: Operating and Capital Cost Summary, $/mg

	Capital	O&M	Total
AWT plant	209	285	494
RO plant	171	449	620
Injection system	17	35	52
Blended water cost (plant product only)	340	496	836
Injected water cost (includes deep well water)	—	—	700

Source: NSF/RA-790224

AQUIFER RECHARGE

The information in this section is based on an article in Conference I entitled "Aquifer Recharge," by D.B. Knorr, Parkhill, Smith & Cooper, Inc., which discusses the development, planning, and testing work done to date on a water reuse project in El Paso, Texas involving aquifer recharge by direct injection of reclaimed sewage.

Introduction

Area Description and Water Demand: El Paso is located in westernmost Texas along the international border with Mexico which is formed by the Rio Grande. The city has had rapid growth in recent years (3% per annum since 1970), and as of 1978 the city population was about 400,000. The metropolitan region, including Ciudad Juarez, contains about 1,000,000 residents.

In 1977 the El Paso water utility produced and distributed 92,800 acre-feet of water (1.145 x 10^8 m^3) with a per capita consumption of about 210 gallons (795 ℓ) per day. About 36% of the demand occurs in winter months while 64% occurs in April-September. During dry summer periods (especially June) daily demands can reach 400 gpcpd (1,515 ℓ/person/day). Water demands are forecasted to be 14.5 million acre-feet (17.9 x 10^9 m^3) from 1980 to 2050, with only 2.5 million acre-feet (3.08 x 10^9 m^3) available from steady state supplies, i.e., surface water and natural groundwater recharge.

Existing Water Sources

Currently the City of El Paso obtains approximately 10% of the supply from the Rio Grande, 25% from the groundwater sources in the Cantuillo area, and 65% from the Hueco Bolson groundwater source. The bolson supply is the dominant source for the city at present due to its low cost, good quality and the ease with which it can be obtained and distributed, even during the peak summer season. Studies made by the U.S. Geological Survey indicate that the bolson has approximately 10 million acre-feet (12.33 x 10^9 m^3) of freshwater in storage in the Texas portion of the aquifer. A significant supply of saline water adjoins and underlies the fresh reserves. Annual bolson recharge is about 5% of current withdrawals, including the inflow from New Mexico.

It is estimated that 9 million acre-feet (11.1×10^9 m^3) of bolson water are available to the city, plus the entire annual recharge amount. If pumping over the next 60 years averages 150,000 acre-feet (1.85×10^8 m^3) per annum, then the aquifer will be 97% exhausted in the year 2040. This calculation is crude and based on several simplifications; however, it illustrates the basic point that the low-cost water supply available to the city from the Hueco Bolson is finite, and that within the foreseeable future there will be a significant need to obtain new water supplies to supplement the Hueco Bolson.

Future Water Sources

Several alternatives are available to augment the water supplies in the future although all are costly and not all are steady state supplies but a continuation of the current practice of mining. Some of the water resources adjacent to El Paso are not available as water sources to the city.

Substantial reserves of groundwater occur in bolson deposits in New Mexico, adjacent to the El Paso Area. This source would provide a low-cost supply for the city, but is not available due to restrictions in New Mexico state law. The large flow of the Rio Grande is a relatively low cost, but erratic, source of supply for the city. However, the water is controlled by the local irrigation district and, historically, attempts to increase municipal use of this supply have not been successful in the courts.

Alternatives which are available and their forecasted contribution to future supplies are shown on Figure 2.4. These include conservation, small amounts of surface water rights, desalinization, wastewater recycling, importation from other bolsons and continued mining of the Hueco Bolson.

Conservation, that is the avoidance of increased demand by education programs, ordinances, rate increases and rate designs, will provide substantial savings in water use without radical changes in the local economy or life style. For planning purposes, a decline in water use of 5 to 10% is anticipated.

One of the options, slight expansion of river use under existing contracts provides a small increment in available water. Desalinization provides a modest additional supply at high costs and is estimated at 2 million acre-feet (2.47×10^9 m^3). Recharge of the Hueco Bolson with highly treated wastewater consumes large quantities of chemicals and energy but does provide a steady state supply. Recharge is forecasted to supply about 30% of the future demand.

Importation from another West Texas bolson some 150 miles to the east of El Paso is expensive. Implementation of this alternative will require difficult land acquisition problems and large front-end capital investments. The commitment to energy-intensive pumping will exceed that required to reclaim wastewater.

Figure 2.4: Cumulative Demand for and Supply of Water Resources in the City of El Paso, 1980–2050

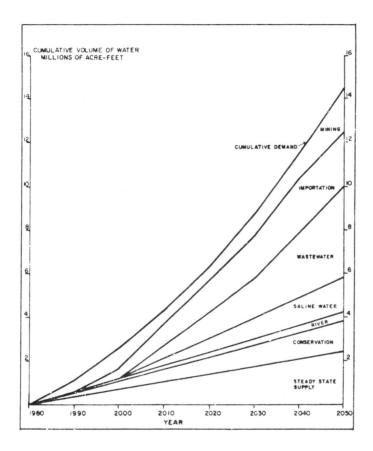

Source: NSF/RA-790224

The option of exchanging a treated wastewater for river water or potable water used by industry is limited due to court decision regarding river water and the lack of large water-using industries.

Development of Project

Sewage Treatment Requirements: The requirement for additional sewage treatment facilities in the Northeast area of El Paso prompted a PL 92-500 Section 201 study of the Northeast service area. Existing treatment facilities consist of three oxidation pond cells and an evaporation pond constructed in the early 1960s. The total pond surface area is about 322 acres (130 ha) and was designed for no discharge. Since the current flow rate grossly exceeds the evaporation capabilities of the system, an overflow evaporation/percolation pond has resulted on property not owned by the city. The resulting percolation of oxidation pond effluent is also contaminating the Hueco Bolson.

Alternatives Considered: The Facilities Plan and concurrent "piggyback" E.I.S. prepared for the service area studied several alternatives. These alternatives included discharge to the Rio Grande, agricultural reuse, industrial reuse, and groundwater recharge. Most alternatives involved multiple reuses since only a few of the reuse opportunities could use all of the wastewater. All alternatives used a 10 mgd (38,000 m^3/day) design flow. The cost effective alternative, selected on the basis of economics and public input, was the alternative involving industrial reuse and direct recharge of the Hueco Bolson.

Treatment Process Development Objectives

Objectives: The recharge alternatives considered that the reclaimed wastewater would meet all drinking water standards as well as other non-drinking water requirements prior to recharge on a continuous basis. Several sources were investigated to determine what parameters should govern the quality of the recharged water.

The primary regulatory requirements are the National Interim Primary Drinking Water Regulations, including the proposed organic chemical requirements, and the Texas Department of Health Drinking Water Standards. Additionally the regulatory requirements for the Orange County Project were also considered. The proposed treatment plant would be designed to meet the criteria decided on. Considering that the raw water supply is relatively protected and would not have the pollutant load of wastewater stream, it was felt that the treatment process must have a high factor of safety for removal of those pollutants which are difficult to identify, particularly toxic materials, trace organics, and viruses.

Effluent parameters affecting recharge wells are anticipated to be turbidity and entrained air. Chemical incompatabilities are not expected to be a problem based upon a U.S.G.S. analysis of Hueco Bolson chemistry and the proposed effluent. Turbidities of less than 0.5 NTU are set as a requirement.

The treatment process selection for the recharge alternative must be one which gives the highest degree of reliability and removal of all potential contaminants through multiple units. Ideally each unit should be chosen so that it adds to the reliability of the overall process by providing redundancy for another process unit. Effluent quality reliability is not only the most important criterion from a health standpoint but from a physical and monetary standpoint as well since only effluent meeting quality criteria may be discharged. Thus water not meeting the criteria after treatment will require the expense of retreatment.

Influent Characteristics: The influent is moderately weak sewage, primarily domestic in origin. Current contributions are about 85 gpcd (322 ℓ/person-day) and flows are around 5.5 mgd (20,900 m^3/day).

Process Selection

Several treatment trains were studied to obtain the optimum treatment technique. Process units involving ponds were not evaluated due to the high evaporation rates in El Paso and the resulting TDS increases.

Primary Treatment: All treatment flow schemes investigated utilized primary treatment and equalization of the primary effluent. The use of primary clarifiers lowers the amount of inert materials in the following process units and removes settleable solids which simplifies the design and operation of the equalization basins. In all cases the primary clarifiers followed screening and degritting.

Primary clarifiers with integral thickeners were chosen to produce a higher density sludge without the odor and other operating problems associated with primary sludge thickeners. Sludge densities of 6% should be obtainable with the integral thickener. Anaerobic digestion was recommended as the sludge stabilization process since it is a net energy producing process and the sludge process used extensively in El Paso. The anaerobic digesters selected were single-stage high-rate complete-mix with dewatering on sand beds. Dried sludge will be composted as is done at other El Paso treatment plants and sold as a soil conditioner.

Equalization: The process proposed, where numerous chemical feed rates are involved and high product quality control is of utmost importance, would benefit greatly from flow equalization. Equalization was located after primary treatment since the primary treatment process is relatively unaffected by flow equalization, given properly designed clarifiers, and storage of primary effluent is relatively simple. The existing oxidation ponds on the treatment plant site hold approximately 300 mg (1.14×10^6 m^3) and are currently the only method of treatment. This volume provides a volume sufficient not only for equalization but for a 30-day plant shutdown as well.

Carbonaceous Material Removal: A great portion of the BOD and the related COD of the incoming sewage should be removed in a biological system. This is suggested since very high removals are required and there are certain BOD- or COD-causing constituents which are easily biodegradable and can be removed through physical or chemical means only with great difficulty.

Since the El Paso wastewater temperatures vary between $16°$ and $31°C$, removals of 96% of the soluble BOD_5 are possible with sludge retention times (SRT) of 3 to 4.5 days. The SRTs required for this removal will also be sufficient for nitrification.

Several methods of biological treatment for carbonaceous material removal were examined, including biodiscs, conventional suspended growth, combined carbonaceous and nitrogen removal (BARDENPHO), and a suspended growth biological system with powdered activated carbon (PACT).

Nitrogen Removal: The nitrogen removal method selected must remove nitrogen which is in the nitrite or nitrate form since the sludge retention time (SRT) necessary for high carbonaceous material removals and the temperature of the wastewater will encourage the growth of nitrifying bacteria. When this occurs, such processes as ammonia stripping, ion exchange, and breakpoint chlorination would not be effective and were therefore not considered.

The expected effluent quality on a soluble basis from a PACT system is:

	mg/ℓ
COD	<10
Total Kjeldahl nitrogen	<1
Ammonia nitrogen (NH_3-N)	<1
Phosphorus	<5
Total nitrogen	<1
TOC	<5

The PACT system was selected for it offers the benefit of a total of 20 days SRT, a two-stage operation, reliability, and potential savings when the cost of downstream carbon processes are considered.

Lime Treatment: The use of a high lime process was considered mandatory due to the wide band heavy metal removals, high viral kills, and phosphorus removal performance of the process. A pH level of 11.1 was selected based upon viral removal and metal removal performance.

Lime treatment was located after denitrification even though it is not the lowest cost location. This eliminates the disadvantage of possible insufficient biology for stable denitrification, since biology and methanol considerations would not be of concern and filtration after the lime process would contain lime carryover in the lime/filtration system. It is best from a virus kill standpoint to lime-treat the water at the lowest practicable turbidity level. Application after denitrification would be slightly better since TSS levels are lower. Lower turbidities would also be expected to give lower interferences with the lime-heavy metal reactions.

Recarbonation: A two-stage recarbonation system is utilized in the process to provide calcium carbonate equilibrium.

Turbidity Removal: Sand filtration was located after recarbonation and before disinfection. The recarbonated effluent is readily filterable and a low turbidity at the point of disinfection is necessary.

Disinfection: Although bactericidal considerations are important, viral and cyst removal requires special consideration in this type of a project. The influent concentrations of viruses and cysts are expected to be quite high compared with normal water sources and measurement techniques are relatively inexact, the organisms are small, and some viral organisms live for several months. Current technology uses various chlorine compounds, ozone, and ultraviolet radiation for disinfection.

All options considered high lime for gross reductions. Ozone was selected as the final disinfecting process due to its advantages over chlorine in disinfection performance and in halogen formation properties. Ozone also provides the potential of improving the performance of the following GAC process by breaking down organics and assisting bio-activity on the carbon.

Removal of Residual Organic Compounds: Reduction of taste and odor compounds, pesticides, herbicides, synthetic organics, trihalomethane precursors, and trihalomethanes is required through existing or proposed drinking water criteria.

The literature reports four general treatment unit processes currently available for removal of the organic compounds. They are: precipitation/filtration, oxidation, aeration, and adsorption. Of these methods granular activated carbon has been chosen as the best "broad spectrum" unit process for controlling organic contaminate concentration. Another combined process, Biologically Activated Carbon (BAC), that of oxidation and adsorption using ozone and activated carbon, has recently been developed.

Since the residual organics seem to be the major health question where recycling is concerned, several of the unit processes selected for El Paso are to provide organics removal. In order of application, the two-stage PACT system is proposed to do the bulk of the organic removal. Following this a high lime coagulation process will provide some treatment of the undissolved organics. Filtration after lime treatment will further reduce the suspended organics. Ozonation is planned after filtration and prior to a final GAC filter thus providing a BAC system for final polishing.

Mineral Removal: The total dissolved solids (TDS) in the plant influent are approximately 300 mg/ℓ higher than the water delivered into the potable water system. The TDS buildup must be considered in the process design since the water produced from the recharged areas of Hueco Bolson could potentially exceed the allowable TDS value (1,000 mg/ℓ). Additionally, the TDS values of the nonrecharged Hueco Bolson water increases as the reservoir is depleted; thus the two increasing TDS trends aggravate the problem. Currently, the mineral buildup is not of concern although future injection projects on the Hueco Bolson of a greater magnitude may require a demineralization process.

Pilot Testing

The PACT portion of the process was piloted for about four months. The PACT effluent was lime treated, filtered, ozonated, and GAC filtered on a batch basis to obtain unit process information and to determine final effluent qualities.

PACT System: The PACT pilot plant was a small (200 ml/min) rack-mounted unit. As a result of the size, some upsets occurred due to plugged tubing and poor performance of the small clarifiers. The pilot schematic is shown in Figure 2.5.

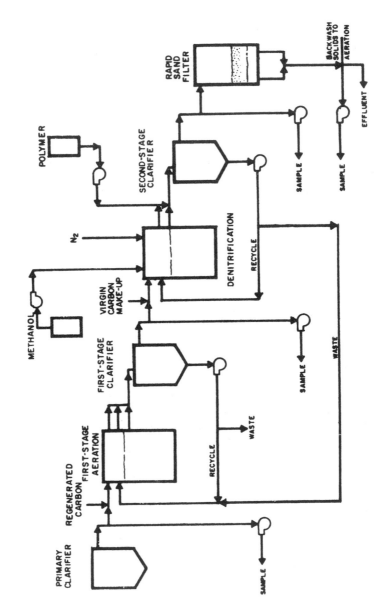

Figure 2.5: Pilot Plant Schematic

Source: NSF/RA-790224

Table 2.13 shows the preliminary data obtained during the last month of piloting. COD values are within the process requirements. TOC and ammonia removals are about as expected. Nitrogen removals are only 76% leaving an effluent concentration of 7.59 mg/ℓ nitrate as N. This level was high because methanol dosage was limited to about 8 mg/ℓ to avoid the possibility of overdosing and the resulting effluent TOC, COD and BOD increase. These nitrogen levels were accomplished at a methanol to nitrate N feed ratio of 0.5 which is much better than 3.0 used in conventional biological denitrification systems. The overall methanol feed rate is held to about 8 mg/ℓ due to denitrification in the first-stage clarifier The effluent values were lowered to zero by increasing the methanol feed rate to a 1.4 ratio; however, methanol overdosing problems resulted due to the small pilot plant and the lack of adequate real time influent nitrate measurement capability.

Table 2.13: PACT Pilot Plant Performance*—January 1979

Parameter	Influent	Effluent	% Removal
BOD	153.4	4.75	96.6
COD	273.6	10.9	96.0
TOC (soluble)	31.4	2.86	90.9
TKN-N	30.5	0.59	98.0
NH_3-N	23.3	0.153	99.3
NO_3-N	0.12	7.59	—
TN	30.5	8.22	73.0
TSS	42.3	3.11	92.6
PO_4-P	14.9	13.1	12.1
Alkalinity as $CaCO_3$	228.0	117.6	48.4
THM, $\mu g/\ell$	2–4	0.03–0.13	96.0
THMFP, $\mu g/\ell$ (24 hours)	100–1,000	20–300	70–80

*Values in mg/ℓ except as noted.

Source: NSF/RA-290224

The performance of the PACT system as a THM removal system is high, averaging 96%. THM precursor removal is not known, although the few samples chlorinated to 0.5 mg/ℓ free chlorine residual indicate influent values from 100 to 1,000 $\mu g/\ell$ and PACT effluent values from 20 to 300 $\mu g/\ell$ after 24 hours.

Trace organics testing of the PACT influent and effluent was done during the pilot period. Samples were analyzed by GC-MS techniques for the 125 organic chemicals included on the list of "Priority Pollutants" and on the list of "Chemical Indicators of Industrial Contamination." Results of this testing indicate methylene chloride concentrations of 72 ppb in the drinking water and 38 ppb in the PACT effluent. Laboratory contamination is suspected here as it is very unlikely the Hueco Bolson is contaminated with methylene chloride. In a different set of tests, 95 ppb of bis(2-ethylhexyl) phthalate were found. This chemical is used in the production of Tygon tubing which is used extensively for pilot plant sampling lines.

One sample of the PACT effluent used in the GC-MS analysis had a TOC of 250 mg/ℓ due to a methanol overdose, but none of the 125 organics were found. Trace organics originating from methanol do not therefore seem to be a problem.

Overall Process Performance: The pilot work indicated the proposed process could meet drinking water standards operating as designed. It was not determined, however, how often the final GAC filter would need to be regenerated but data indicated trihalomethane precursors running as high as 300 μg/ℓ would govern the bed life. It is planned that the bed life will be determined in the full-scale operation since piloting the entire plant long enough to determine the effect of ozone on the carbon is not practicable.

The process provided the unexpected benefit of lowering sodium and TDS levels across the PACT system. This is probably due to the biological nitrogen removal system and the alkalinity change.

An effort was made to evaluate the carcinogenicity of the product water since the removal of carcinogenic materials is a major consideration in a treatment process such as the one proposed. Accordingly, various water samples were tested with a modified Ames procedure. The tests involved using the histidine-dependent strains of *Salmonella,* TA 98, TA 100, TA 1535, TA 1537 and TA 1538 with and without rat liver microsomes to detect mutagenic and/or carcinogenic compounds in unconcentrated water samples.

Initial tests indicated PACT effluent was mutagenic and that El Paso drinking water (Nevins Reservoir) was not mutagenic with or without 2% PACT effluent added to it. Further testing was done to determine if the treatment processes downstream of the PACT units would remove the mutagenic properties. Here, the product water was ozonated effluent, without GAC treatment, chlorinated to 0.5 mg/ℓ free residual. The testing indicated exceedingly small mutagenic properties with 1:1 and 9:1 mixtures of Nevins reservoir water and product water. Undiluted product water did not display mutagenic properties.

The limited data suggests that the product water used in the tests was at least as good as Nevins reservoir water and that the combination of lime, filtration and ozonation does remove the mutagenic property.

Recharge System

Recharging of the Hueco Bolson may be accomplished through percolation basins or through the use of injection wells. Injection wells were selected due to low surface area requirements, higher recoveries and the potential for energy recovery. Artificial recharge of the northernmost well fields appear to offer the greatest potential benefit to the City of El Paso when compared to the other well fields in the aquifer. The City of El Paso owns most of the water in this locality and would receive the most benefit from an artificial recharge program. The recharge wells are located so that it is likely all of the recharged water will be recovered by the city since gradients are generally toward the city's production wells.

Injection rates are expected to be one-half to two-thirds of the capacity of production wells in the area. Existing wells range in capacity from 1,000 to 1,500 gpm (5,472 to 8,208 m^3/day); thus injection rates from 600 to 850 gpm (3,283 to 4,636 m^3/day) are expected. At these rates, 10 injection wells are necessary to handle the 10 mgd (38,000 m^3/day) plant capacity. The wells will be constructed in a manner similar to the existing production wells. A pump will be installed in each for periodic backflushing and redevelopment.

Liquid levels in the injection wells during operating will most probably be around 300 feet (91.5 m) below the ground surface if no provisions are made to increase the injection well head losses. Injection tests in the Hueco Bolson have shown that provisions must be made to control the head loss, preventing air entrainment and the resulting loss of injectivity.

A potential for energy recovery exists due to the 300 foot (91.5 m) head loss incurred by 10 mgd (38,000 m^3/day). Assuming an 80% recovery about 320 kW could be recovered by down-hole turbines which would effectively solve the air entrainment problem. The turbine could be reversible for use as a backflushing device. Injection tests will more accurately determine the injection well performance so that a detailed evaluation of the turbine technique can be made.

Costs

The capital costs for the project are $29,000,000 using 1981 construction costs (STP CCI 316) and operating costs are estimated to be $2,200,000 per year in 1983 dollars.

Conclusions

Recharge was chosen for El Paso because (a) it solves existing wastewater problems; (b) it adds to the steady state drinking water supply; (c) it is a prototype for larger-scale recycling which would provide more than one-fourth of El Paso's water needs over the next 70 years; (d) the water supply benefits of recycling are judged by the public to warrant increased dollar costs, resource use and environmental impacts; (e) alternative wastewater recycling projects do not address municipal water supply concerns; and (f) alternative water supply projects, such as importation, are even more expensive and will result in significant resource use and environmental impact.

The treatment process selected adequately met the process requirements with some benefits, i.e., sodium removal and TDS removal, which were unexpected.

SHALLOW WELL AND BASIN RECHARGE

The material in this chapter was obtained from a paper in Conference I entitled "Observations on the Start-Up of the Water Reclamation-Recharge Project in Nassau County, N.Y.," by J.A. Oliva, F.J. Flood, Jr., and J.S. Gillen, all of the Nassau County Department of Public Works.

History of the Project

Nassau County is one of four counties located on Long Island, New York. Although a groundwater aquifer underlies all of Long Island, only Nassau and Suffolk Counties utilize this aquifer as their only source of potable water. For this reason, the Environmental Protection Agency recently declared this aquifer as a "Sole Source Aquifer."

The increased urbanization of Nassau County, (1979 population 1,480,000) after World War II has been accompanied by increased groundwater pumpage and the contamination of the upper glacial aquifer. In order to retard the contamination of the glacial aquifer and to protect the remaining aquifers (the Magothy and the Lloyd), Nassau County embarked upon a sewering program in the early 1950s, which when completed in 1985 will result in the sewering of greater than 85% of Nassau County. The sewage effluent from the treatment facilities constructed as part of the sewering program is discharged to marine surface waters after undergoing secondary treatment.

The effect of the sewering program, together with the increased groundwater pumpage, has been a net decline in the water table which has resulted in a decrease in freshwater stream flow, increased bay salinity, and the local landward movement of salty groundwater. The effects of the declining water table have provided Nassau County with the need to study methods of replenishing the groundwater aquifer in an effort to offset these effects.

Reuse and Recharge Studies

1963: A Greeley and Hansen Report recommended that Nassau County initiate research into water reclamation and groundwater recharge with emphasis on the construction of a hydraulic dam to retard saltwater intrusion.

1968: After a series of bench-scale studies were completed to provide the basis for the design of a pilot facility, the 400-gpm Water Renovation Plant and 500 foot deep injection well were placed into operation at Bay Park. The Nassau County Department of Public Works was responsible for the operation of the reclamation facilities while the United States Geological Survey (USGS) was responsible for the operation of the 500-foot recharge well. The result of the operation of this facility, which was terminated in April 1973, was that while water reclamation was feasible, deep well injection was not. This result was due to the fact that recharge took place into the relatively fine Magothy aquifer and was accompanied by a long-term well clogging rate of 3 feet of excessive head build-up per 1,000,000 gallons of injected water. This excessive head build-up indicated that frequent redevelopment of the well was necessary to maintain a practical injection specific capacity.

1971: A second Greeley and Hansen Report recommended that Nassau County adopt means of supplementing its groundwater supply. The alternatives suggested include:

(1) Import water from Suffolk County.

(2) Import water from upstate New York water resources.

(3) Water renovation and groundwater recharge.

This report summarized investigations of the USGS and the Nassau County Health Department, which indicated that saltwater intrusion was not a major concern and that nitrate contamination in the central part of Nassau County was a more serious problem. The report recommended the upland recharge of 92 million gallons per day for the year 1990.

Feasibility Study: Based on the results of the above projects and studies, the Environmental Protection Agency (EPA), Region II, prepared an Environmental Impact Statement (EIS) in 1972. This EIS recommended that Nassau County study the feasibility of constructing a 5-mgd water reclamation-recharge, demonstration facility at its Cedar Creek Water Pollution Control Plant site. The EPA then authorized a $95,000 Federal Grant (R801478) for Nassau County to complete this recommended feasibility study. The County of Nassau entered into an agreement with the firm of Consoer, Townsend and Associates to conduct the feasibility study.

The result of this study, which lasted 12 months and was completed in August 1973, was a report which listed the modifications and additions which must be made to convert part of the Cedar Creek Water Pollution Control Plant into a 5-mgd water reclamation facility. This report was submitted to the EPA for approval, and in August 1974, the EPA approved this report and authorized the commencement of work on plans and specifications under the Construction Grants Program. This was a departure from the original plan of conducting the recommended demonstration project under the R&D program. By switching to the Construction Grants Program, many side stream units and processes had to be deleted from the project as they were not fundable under this EPA program. The county, in October 1974, executed an agreement with Consoer, Townsend and Associates to develop plans and specifications for the Cedar Creek Water Reclamation-Recharge Facilities.

Design and Construction: The plans and specifications were completed in early 1976. In June 1976, Nassau County was notified that it was awarded Federal Grant Number C-36-982.01 in the amount of $24,588,497. This grant award was for a combined Design and Construction Grant. Costs under this grant were to be shared as follows: EPA—75% or $24,588,497, New York State Department of Environmental Conservation (NYSDEC)—12½% or $4,098,083 and Nassau County—12½% or $4,098,083 for a total project cost of $32,784,663. In November, 1976, the EPA and NYSDEC approved the plans and specifications for this project.

The design of the reclamation plant was based on producing an effluent which would meet the parameters shown in Table 2.14. In order to meet these proposed standards, the flow diagram shown in Figure 2.6 was developed. This design utilized the existing unused portions of the Cedar Creek Water Pollution Control Plant where possible. A description of the units shown in Figure 2.6 follows.

Figure 2.6: Schematic Diagram of Water Reclamation-Recharge Facilities

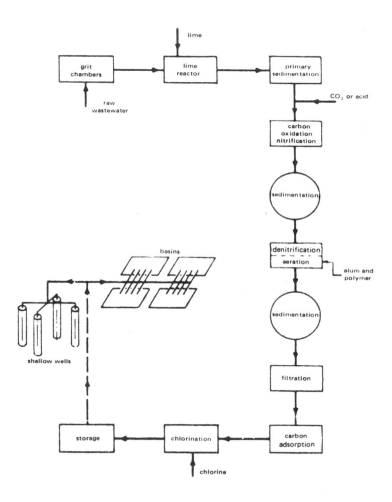

Source: NSF/RA-790224

Table 2.14: Water Quality Standards for Cedar Creek Reclamation-Recharge Project

Constituent, mg/l	Desired Limit	Microbiological characteristic	Desired Limit
ABS	0.5	Coliform org.	4/100 ml
Aluminum	0.1		max.
Arsenic	0.05		1/100 ml
Barium	1.0		avg.
BOD$_5$	2.0	Pesticide, mg/l	
Boron	1.0	Aldrin	0.017
Cadmium	0.01	Chlordane	0.003
Calcium	<Sat. Con.	DDT	0.042
CCE	0.2	Dieldrin	0.017
Chloride	250	Endrin	0.001
Chlorine res. (free)	1.0	Heptachlor	0.018
Chromium (hexavalent)	0.05	Heptachlorepoxide	0.018
Copper	0.2	Herbicides	0.1
Cyanide	0.1	Methoxychlor	0.035
Fluoride	1.5	Org. PO$_4$ + carbamates	0.1
Iron and manganese		Toxaphene	0.005
combined	<0.3	Physical characteristics	
Lead	0.05	Color	15 units
Mercury	0.005	TON	3 units
Nitrogen, total	3.0	TDS	500
O$_2$ consumed	2.0	Turbidity	0.5 JTU
Phenols	0.001	Entrained air	None
Phosphorus	0.1	SS	1.0
Selenium	0.01	pH	6.5–8.5
Silver	0.05		units
Sodium	20*		
Sulfate	250		
TOC	3.0		
Uranyl ion	5.0		
Zinc	0.3		

*Or 50% of cations.

Source: NSF/RA-790224

Reclamation Plant

Chemically Aided Primary Treatment: The influent flow to the water reclamation plant is screened and degritted wastewater withdrawn under controlled conditions from the existing plant primary influent flow. The wastewater is conveyed to chemical treatment facilities. Contained in the chemical treatment facilities are a rapid mix tank for disposal of the lime, automatic lime slaking and feeding equipment, a slurry sludge tank and the required control and monitoring devices. The lime mixed effluent from the rapid mix tank is discharged by gravity to two flocculation chambers. In each of the chambers a horizontal shaft slow-speed turbine mixer is installed for flocculation. The flocculated effluent then flows to existing primary tanks No. 5 and 6 which are used in the reclamation process.

The primary treatment system employs addition of lime followed by primary sedimentation to facilitate removal of phosphorus. Other benefits of lime addition include improved removal of BOD_5, suspended solids and heavy metals, thereby optimizing and protecting the biological nitrification system.

Two-Stage Biological Treatment System: Utilizing all four passes of existing aerator No. 3 and final clarifiers No. 5, 7 and 8, the secondary treatment system has been designed to promote biological nitrogen removal in conjunction with oxidation of the remaining carbonaceous material. The design allows for the operation of the secondary system as a two-stage growth system, with combined carbon oxidation-nitrification, intermediate clarification, denitrification, post-aeration-stabilization and final clarification. The settled wastewater from the primary tank flows by gravity to existing aeration tank No. 3. Passes 1 and 2 of the existing four-pass aeration tank No. 3, which provide a detention time of 5.9 hours based on 5.5 mgd, will be utilized to introduce oxygen to the wastewater. An oxygen transfer rate of 11,200 scfm will be adequate to meet the increased oxygen demand of the combined carbon oxidation-nitrification system. From this combined carbon oxidation-nitrification portion of aerator No. 3, the mixed liquor enters existing 100-foot-diameter final clarifier No. 5 which provides an overflow rate of 700 gpd/ft^2. Activated sludge removed from this clarifier is returned to the carbon oxidation-nitrification tank, utilizing the existing return sludge well, pumps, meters and lines. The nitrified effluent from clarifier No. 5 passes to the denitrification tank (pass No. 3) which provides a detention time of two hours. Methanol is added to the tank influent flow at a rate of 3.54 lb/lb of nitrate nitrogen and is applied as a supplemental organic carbon source in the denitrification process.

The denitrified liquor flows to a postaeration-stabilization tank (pass No. 4) to remove any supersaturated nitrogen gas, to avoid rising sludge problems in the final clarifier, to provide a mixing zone for the addition of alum and polymer for secondary phosphorus removal, and to provide an additional aeration period for the removal of excess methanol. The aerated liquor is conveyed to existing clarifier No. 7 for final clarification.

Operational flexibility is provided to allow conversion from a two-stage to a three-stage biological treatment system as a fail-safe mechanism to assure the production of a high-quality effluent. Clarifier No. 5 is utilized between a high rate activated sludge unit and nitrification unit, clarifier No. 7 is utilized between the nitrification unit and the combined denitrification-postaeration unit, and clarifier No. 8 is utilized for final clarification.

Filtration and Carbon Adsorption: The design of the filtration and carbon adsorption system is based on the use of multiple individual units, the size of which can be incorporated directly into a future full-scale Nassau County recharge system.

The clarified effluent from the secondary system flows by gravity to the filter feed wet well where it is pumped under controlled conditions to automatically backwashed, mixed-media filters. Two gravity-type filters are provided with two additional filters on standby. Each filter is 13' 4" wide and 38' 8" long, providing a surface area of 515 ft^2 and a filter rate of 3.75 gpm/ft^2 based on a flow of 2.75 mgd. Backwash will be at a rate of from 15 to 20 gpm/ft^2. Surface washing equipment and air scour are provided. After passing through the filter media, the backwash water is pumped back to the Cedar Creek Water Pollution Control Plant influent well.

The carbon adsorption facilities consist of two contactor units in parallel, with two standby units provided. Each unit is 13' 4" wide and 38' 8" long, providing 515 ft^2 of surface area. Each unit will be filled with carbon to a depth of 8 feet. This will provide approximately 500,000 lb of carbon and an empty bed detention time of 16 minutes per unit. The adsorption units are operated as downflow packed bed units. Backwash of the adsorbers will be similar to the backwash of the filters. When exhausted, the carbon will be regenerated in an on-site multi-hearth regeneration furnace.

Chlorination and Storage: A 30-minute chlorine contact chamber followed by a clearwell with a storage volume of 1.6 million gallons provides sufficient detention time for disinfection of the plant effluent. The clearwell serves as a pump suction chamber for service pumps to deliver treated water to the recharge site. The clearwell also provides the necessary equalization to permit continuous delivery of 5.0 mgd to the injection wells, despite fluctuations in plant output due to backwashing of filters and carbon adsorbers.

Recharge System

Transmission Main System: The proposed demonstration project involves the use of a 24" diameter concrete pipe transmission main to convey reclaimed water to the recharge site. A number of routes were investigated to determine the most cost-effective transmission system. The selected routing parallels the Wantagh State Parkway from the Cedar Creek treatment plant to the East Meadow recharge site. The length of transmission main required, using this route, is approximately 6.25 miles, or 33,000 linear feet.

Recharge Facilities: The proposed East Meadow recharge site is a triangular-shaped piece of county-owned land located in approximately the geographic center of the county. It includes approximately 60 acres of land which is occupied in part by the Nassau County Correctional Center and the structures and leaching basins of the Meadowbrook Sewage Treatment Plant.

Both shallow well and basin recharge studies will be conducted at the East Meadow site. The proposed program will recharge 4 mgd, with approximately 2.0 mgd recharged through wells. Five wells and ten basins will be used for the recharge studies.

The basins will be used to determine the management practices that are most effective for optimizing recharge; the evaluation of the clogging phenomena associated with the application of reclaimed wastewater; and the evaluation of the potential for the unsaturated zone to improve water quality. Of the five recharge wells to be installed at the East Meadow site, four will be in operation at any specified time, with one on standby. Each well recharges 0.5 mgd.

The East Meadow recharge site is surrounded by a monitoring network of 46 observation wells at 22 sites and manholes in basins No. 2 and 3. In addition, a sampling pump coupled with a composite sampler will be provided on the recharge site storage reservoir. The composite sampler will analyze reservoir water for dissolved oxygen, turbidity, temperature, pH, chlorine residual and specific conductance. Water from recharge basins No. 2 and 3 will be analyzed for pH, dissolved oxygen and sulfide.

Construction Costs

Final bids for construction of the reclamation plant and the recharge facilities amounted to a total of $22,154,997.

Operation

Since a NYSDEC State Pollutant Discharge Elimination System (SPDES) permit would be required in order to recharge the effluent from the reclamation plant, it was decided to make application for this permit in early 1978. Initial contact with EPA, NYSDEC and local and state health departments indicated that obtaining a SPDES permit would not be an easy task. The chemical and physical parameters to be listed in the permit were not the cause of concern, as New York State Drinking Water Standards, Part 72 or better were selected for the proposed reclamation plant effluent quality standards, and these standards were utilized in the selection and design of the various unit processes for the plant. The problem in finalizing the permit was caused by the fact that between 1972 and 1973, the period during which the preliminary design of the reclamation plant was developed, organic analysis had not progressed to the point where long lists of specific organic compounds were listed within drinking water standards or operating permits. During the time NCDPW was trying to finalize its SPDES permits, several Nassau and Suffolk County potable water wells were being closed due to organic contamination, and many organic compounds were classified as being carcinogens, teratogens, or mutagens. Finally, it was decided to perform an organic analysis (GC-MS) on the Cedar Creek Water Pollution Control Plant influent and effluent and to list those organics identified in the SPDES permit with the condition that all unidentified peaks which are exhibited in subsequent analysis shall be identified and reported. The list of organics which are presently specified in the SPDES permit are shown in Table 2.15 on the following page.

Once the permit was formalized, it was time to develop a preliminary operating budget. Unfortunately, at this time, Proposition No. 13 was passing in California. The County of Nassau found itself in the position of adding a $2,000,000 annual operation and maintenance expenditure at a time when most department budgets were being cut and layoff lists were being prepared.

The result of this crisis was that the number of personnel to operate these facilities was reduced and certain line items for the first year of operation had to be deleted.

Table 2.15: Organics Specified in SPDES Permit

Effluent Parameter—Organic	Discharge Limitations Daily Max. (μg/ℓ)	Monitoring Requirements Measurement Frequency	Sample Type
Chloroform	100	Weekly	Grab
Trichloroethylene	10	Weekly	Grab
Tetrachloroethylene	50*	Weekly	Grab
Ethylbenzene	50*	Weekly	Grab
1,1-Dichloroethane	50*	Weekly	Grab
1,1,1-Trichloroethane	50*	Weekly	Grab
Carbon tetrachloride	5*	Weekly	Grab
Methylene chloride	50*	Weekly	Grab
Dichlorodifluoromethane	50*	Weekly	Grab
Toluene	50**	Weekly	Grab
Benzene	ND	Weekly	Grab
para-dichlorobenzene	4.7	Weekly	Grab
ortho-dichlorobenzene	4.7	Weekly	Grab

*Total aggregate concentration of these constituents shall not exceed 100 μg/ℓ.
**Not detectable by tests or analytical determinations referenced in Section 703.4 NYCRR.

Note: All unidentified peaks which are exhibited in analyzing for the above constituents shall be identified and reported. Analysis shall be performed by utilizing the purgeable, headspace or solvent extraction methods appropriate for the constituents in question and performed in a State Health Department-approved laboratory.

Source: NSF/RA-790224

Operation and Maintenance Costs

The operation and maintenance, including staff, associated with the project are anticipated to be $8,159,600 to $14,340,750 for a three- to five-year operating period.

Due to the highly technical nature of the reclamation-recharge project, Nassau County will enter into contracts with outside consultants for expertise in the area of tertiary plant operations, virological/microbiological work, organic analysis and systems analysis. An agreement has been executed with the USGS giving them full responsibility for operation of the recharge facilities. NCDPW personnel will provide maintenance services at the recharge site.

Schedule for First Year of Operation

Since the recharge facilities are completed and it will be at least 9 months before the reclamation plant effluent will be available for recharge, the USGS personnel will have time to perform the following operations:

(1) Install and calibrate the instrumentation in each of the observation wells and the manholes in basins No. 2 and 3.

(2) Sample all of the observation wells in order to obtain background analysis for physical, chemical and organic contaminants present in the groundwater table around the recharge site.

(3) Prepare the surface of each of the recharge basins.

When construction of the reclamation plant is complete, there will be a three- to six-month period set aside for debugging equipment and training personnel in the operation of the reclamation plant.

Operation of all facilities will be for a minimum period of three years and a maximum period of five years. As the operation of the reclamation plant proceeds during the three- to five-year test period, various side stream unit processes may be investigated as follows:

(1) Ozone or chlorine dioxide disinfection.

(2) Use of fluidized bed reactors for carbonaceous removal, nitrification and denitrification.

During recharge, the USGS will be conducting the following investigations:

(1) Comparing shallow well recharge to basin recharge.

(2) Comparison of basins with and without surface vegetation.

(3) Comparison of various vegetation covers.

(4) Comparison of various basin surface soils.

(5) Comparison of various basin surface maintenance practices.

(6) Comparison of various basin application rates and cycles.

The USGS will also monitor the observation wells to determine the path the recharge water is taking and to examine any changes which take place during its travel.

After the above operating period has been completed, the biological portion of the Cedar Creek Plant will be reconverted back to a secondary treatment, step aeration, facility. Assuming the operation proves successful, additions can be made to the permanent filter and adsorption building, while the conventional biological portion of the plant will have to be converted to provide chemical addition and nitrogen removal in a new, permanent facility. The transmission main has been designed to carry 20 mgd and therefore can be utilized along with the recharge facilities.

[Note: It is now expected, as learned from a telephone communication with Mr. Oliva, that recharge will begin early in 1981. The construction of the reclamation plant and recharge facilities has been completed without any serious cost overrun and reclaimed water is being produced at the rate of approximately 5.5 mgd.]

HIGHLIGHTS OF OTHER DEVELOPMENTS IN INDIRECT WATER REUSE

The material in this section is based on a report entitled *Water Reuse Highlights, A Summary of Wastewater Reclamation and Reuse Information* (NTIS PB-289 386), prepared by the American Water Works Association (AWWA) Research Foundation for the Office of Water Research and Technology of the U.S. Department of the Interior, January 1978.

Woodlands, Texas

In the December 1976 issue of *Water and Wastes Engineering* was a description of a reuse project in Woodlands, Texas, a new, fully planned community being developed in a heavily forested area 30 miles north of Houston. When completed in 1977, the new town was to provide work, recreation and living facilities for 150,000 people.

To preserve the forested environment, the owners have incorporated ecological planning into the development process which is reflected in the selected wastewater treatment plant. Treated wastewaters will be recycled into Lake Harrison, a 60-mg recreational facility in the village which also serves as a reservoir for irrigation demands. Overflows from the lake are discharged into Lake Houston watershed which is the source of domestic water for Houston. Quality requirements are BOD, 5 mg/ℓ; SS, 5 mg/ℓ and a P of 2.0 mg/ℓ on a monthly average.

The plant, to be developed in four incremental stages, has a present capacity of 0.5 mgd with an ultimate 6 mgd rating. Should nitrogen removal become a future requirement, ammonia stripping will be employed. Dual-media filters are employed with the ozone contact tower being a vessel 5 feet in diameter and 12 feet high filled with 3-inch polypropylene packing with a liquid detention time of 30 to 60 seconds.

Initial tests have resulted in the following effluent characteristics:

Parameter	Influent	Effluent
BOD	200	1
COD	330	6
SS	40	4
P	20	1.9
Fecal coli	—	0

Aurora, Colorado

The City of Aurora, Colorado on Denver's eastern border, is investigating the possibility of municipal wastewater reuse. For many years, filtered secondary effluent has been used for golf course irrigation, but the new plans call for eventual potable reuse. In a preliminary report prepared by CH2M Hill engineers for the city, a 20-mgd AWT plant would be constructed and be operating by the early 1980s. Conventional primary and secondary treatment for 20 mgd is to be followed by disinfection and filtration steps for 12.5 mgd only. This water would then be used via a secondary distribution system for agricultural purposes (parks, greenbelts, golf courses, etc.) and industry. The remaining 7.5 mgd of flow would undergo further treatment and eventually be discharged into a terminal water supply reservoir to be followed by conventional water treatment and public use. The direct pipe-to-pipe link is missing but the potable reuse acronym is still evident. The preconceptual treatment sequence for the higher grade water consists of lime clarification, two-stage recarbonation, filtration, ammonia removal with ion exchange, breakpoint chlorination, carbon adsorption, reverse osmosis and chemical oxidation. Estimated costs for the industrial/irrigation portion of the project approach $12.1 million, with an additional $43 million for the potable quality plant. Additional information about this ambitious program can be obtained by contacting Mr. C.A. Wemlinger, Director of Utilities, Municipal Building, Aurora, Colorado, 80010.

Three Indirect Use Projects Examined for Washington, D.C.

In the U.S. Army Corps of Engineers' evaluation of water supply alternatives for the Washington, D.C. area, three indirect reuse projects were examined, their purposes being to supplement the base flow of the Potomac River by making highly treated wastewater available for use during drought conditions. Two of the projects considered, the Fairfax County Plant and the 60 mgd Montgomery County Plant, would also serve to reduce the wastewater management plant in the Washington Metropolitan area. The third project would employ AWT at Blue Plains, pumping the effluent upstream of the water intakes.

The advantage of piping highly treated effluents upstream was to reduce the potential health hazard with dilution and utilize the so-called "instream purification processes." As indicated in previous Planning Reports, the Montgomery Plant effluent would have been considerably better than the river quality itself. The Corps, in an effort to find the answers needed, has decided to test estuary waters and Blue Plains effluent in what has been nicknamed the "Six-Million Dollar Plant."

U.S. Army Engineer Corps Report

A U.S. Army Corps of Engineers' November 1975 interim report entitled "Critical Choices for Critical Years" contains information on the water supply needs for the northeastern United States, including several references on wastewater reuse.

Initial findings clearly showed that three metropolitan areas—New York, Eastern Massachusetts-Rhode Island, and Washington, D.C.—have the most critical and immediate need to develop water supply sources to meet growing water demands. Studies of the 200,000-square-mile region indicates a population of 50 million persons, but with an increase by the year 2020 to 80 million. A severe drought in the Northeast in the 1960s caused Congress to pass PL 89-298 directing the Corps to work with appropriate federal, state and local officials to insure against future drought-related water shortages.

Since the drought, no major water supply projects have been built in the three most critical areas and the general purpose of the interim report is to briefly present a wide range of available alternatives based on a separate and ongoing major water supply survey.

As a planning premise it was generally assumed that direct wastewater reuse would not be generally acceptable during the time frame of the study. However, deliberate indirect reuse was acknowledged as impacting available supply. Planned indirect reuse in the East (AWT effluents into water supply reservoirs) is considered direct reuse in several western states.

The statement was made that indirect reuse could be made safe by employing carefully controlled AWT methods or land treatment. AWT plants, whether using biological or PCT processes, can produce effluent that is eminently suitable for indirect water supply use. The effluent can be safely discharged into a stream or surface water body that is used as a water supply source. While the emphasis and interest in AWT has in the past centered on their role as a pollution control tool, their usefulness as a viable source of water supply cannot be overlooked.

Basic plans for the three areas are summarized as follows.

The Washington, D.C. Metropolitan Area: One of the Corps' alternatives concerns construction of a pilot estuarine water treatment plant to determine the technical feasibility of full-scale use of the Potomac estuary for water supply and to answer the health-related questions. Formal plans include the treatment of sewage effluents from the Blue Plains facility as well. In many cases, the secondary effluent is of a higher quality than the Potomac itself. Addition references were given to the planned Montgomery and Occoquan AWT plants.

The New York Metropolitan Area: Emphasis was given to surface water sources in that complex region but groundwater recharge programs in two Long Island counties, Nassau and Suffolk, merited considerable attention. Surface water augmentation with treated wastewaters also received consideration. The Connecticut plan of conservation and development contained a rather limiting policy of not even considering streams within the watershed which might contain sewage discharges.

Eastern Massachusetts and Rhode Island: While surface water development and conservation were stressed, some interest in land treatment and recovery of effluent was shown.

Since public works projects normally take many years to plan, authorize, design and build, it is critical that all parties involved in the water supply decision-making process be made aware of the choices available to avert shortages. With rapidly increasing technology, reuse may come to the forefront as a viable solution.

Berlin Project

Dr. H. Sontheimer of the University of Karlsruhe in West Germany is involved in a Berlin Project to recharge aquifers with treated wastewater. Within the next 12 months, a pilot plant will be constructed to remove nutrients and biological soil clogging organisms. Early research has indicated that ozonation prior to recharge changes the nonbiodegradable organics in such a way that there is a complete biological oxidation within the ground. Other tests have shown that when ammonia and nitrates are in a stoichiometric correlation, biological oxidation in the ground leads to nitrogen formation and removal of all inorganic nitrogen compounds.

Extraction for potable purposes is not expected until much more is known about the combination treatment and ground processes.

South African Recharge

In the 1976 Annual Report from the South African Water Research Commission (WRC) two on-going reuse research projects in the Cape Town region are described. The first involves treatment research at the Athlone Sewage Works on a 300 m^3/day pilot plant which is operated by the municipality while the National Institute for Water Research (NIWR) provides specialist services (see Chapter 4).

During the year 1976-77, extensive studies were undertaken on the hydraulic suitability of the sand beds for storage, infiltration and withdrawal of natural waters or treated effluents. Geohydrological studies showed a daily subterranean flow to an ocean bay of 75 x 10^6 ℓ or approximately 3 m^3/day per meter of coastline. This freshwater could be intercepted and used but at the expense of seawater intrusion. To create a hydraulic barrier against the saltier source, artificial recharge by covered infiltration channels or ponds appeared feasible with 200 x 10^6 ℓ per day of treated domestic sewage as the source. After one year of storage in the coastal aquifer it too would be abstracted for all uses.

A preliminary mathematical model has been developed for simulating the behavior of the groundwater resource under a wide range of conditions.

Three sewage purification works, with an eventual combined capacity of 400 x 10^6 ℓ per day are currently under construction along the bay coast. In two of the three installations, provision is being made for nutrient removals, which simplifies the subsequent reclamation plant. The Cape Flats plant, which will replace the oxidation pond system, will be commissioned by the end of 1978, offering an improved effluent to the proposed 4.5 x 10^6 ℓ per day demonstration AWT plant. A new agreement between the WRC and municipality will postpone the full reclamation plant until the Cape Flats facility becomes operational. In the meantime, only a portion of the demo plant will be built to enable infiltration studies.

Aquifer Recharge Plans in Victoria, Australia

Aquifer recharge is being considered as a water supply alternative in the Victoria State of Australia. The Koo Wee Rup Plain, an extremely productive farmland area, lies southeast of the City of Melbourne. The primary source of water has been the subartesian basin which is connected to the bay at the City of Western Port. Drawdown due to pumping has caused a reversal of flow and contamination of the aquifer with saltwater.

Two proposals were suggested to remedy the situation:

(1) Piping reconditioned wastewater from the Board of Works Southeastern Purification Plant at Carrum, 25 miles to the plains and then reticulating it to farms in order to reduce or eliminate the dependence on groundwater. Nutrients would be effectively absorbed, but the peak water demand which occurs in summer does not coincide with peak supply which occurs in winter.

(2) Piping the reconditioned water to Koo Wee Rup and charging it directly into the aquifer which would obviate the complex farm distribution system and overcome problems created by varying supply and demand. It would, however, introduce the problems of the complex physical, chemical and biological reactions between the natural groundwater, the aquifer medium and the charging water.

An initial testing program has been undertaken by the Department of Mines on charging and discharging a similar sedimentary aquifer at Carrum. In other research performed at the University of Melbourne, a computer model was developed that purports to predict aquifer response to given input conditions.

An entirely separate proposal for the employment of all or part of the 5 million cubic feet per day flow from the Southeastern Plant has been made by Australian Groundwater Consultants Pty. Ltd. In that proposal, it is envisioned that a substantial part of the water requirements of Mornington and Western Port could be met by a scheme entailing the spreading of effluent over the dune limestone deposits of the Nepean Peninsular south of Rosebud.

Modeled on schemes overseas at Santee and Tel Aviv, effluent would be injected into the ground and pumped out some distance away, having been relieved of its BOD, bacterial and phosphate loads. The water would mix with the natural groundwater and, when removed, be blended with waters from the Tarago and Bunyip Rivers north of the Mornington Peninsula to produce a potable supply.

Small-Scale Purification Systems and a Preliminary Study

PURECYCLE'S DOMESTIC WASTEWATER RECYCLING SYSTEM

The material in this section is based on a report in Conference I by R.O. Mankes of PureCycle Corporation of Boulder, Colorado.

Introduction

The conservation of water resources has become increasingly important in the past decade and will increase in importance in future years due to population growth, increased consumption and pollution of existing supplies.

The combining of conservation of water, control and monitoring of the treatment of water, at an affordable capital and operating expense, was the objective of PureCycle Corporation of Boulder, Colorado. By confining and integrating five subassemblies, wastewater is treated and purified for reuse as potable water. The system is controlled and monitored by a microprocessor which is tied into a common telephone line for communication with a service center (see Figure 3.1).

The PureCycle System

The spent water from a domestic residence is delivered to the system usually using a four-inch line with a slope of ¼ inch per foot. The spent water is first treated via anaerobic digestion and solids settling. Following this, aerobic digestion is employed using a rotating biological contractor (RBC). The primary function of the aerobic digestion is conversion of organic matter to stable forms such as carbon dioxide and water. The anaerobic process is designed to stabilize compounds with nitrates and sulfates. The complete digestion of these organic and inorganic compounds is not necessary because following the process are organic adsorption and demineralization. Because there are these subsystems following the digestion, temporary failure of the digestor does not imply that water quality will be impaired during these times.

Figure 3.1: The PureCycle System

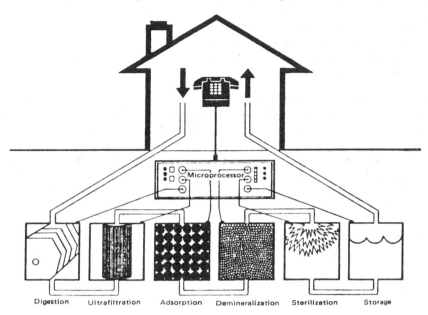

Source: NSF/RA-790224

Separation of solids from the effluent of the digestor is accomplished by an ultrafilter. The ultrafiltration membranes have a pore size of 50 angstroms. This pore size prohibits the passage of bacteria, viruses, other biological contaminants down to a molecular weight of 50,000. A backflush system is employed to periodically clean the filter. Should the ultrafilter rupture and allow passage of solids, a nephelometer would detect them at a level of 0.02 nephelometric turbidity unit (NTU). The microprocessor has been preprogrammed to shut the system down at a turbidity of a 0.33 NTU and autodial a service center to notify a failure.

Organic compounds not destroyed in the anaerobic/aerobic digestor, or not retained by the ultrafilter, are adsorbed by the activated carbon in the adsorption system. Although the ability of activated carbon to perform over a broad range of organic carbons is difficult to predict, activated carbon adsorption has been used successfully in this application many times over. The United States Environmental Protection Agency has proposed that some municipal water utilities use activated carbon to reduce the level of trihalomethanes in water supplies. The monitoring of the adsorption system is done by an on-line ultraviolet light absorbance monitor capable of detecting organic carbons at less than 100 ppb.

Inorganic material and polar organic matter are extracted using ion exchange resins. The hydrogen form and hydroxide form of the ion exchange resins are similar to resins used in commercial applications to provide deionized water. To determine when the resin capacity has been reached and regeneration is necessary, a conductivity cell monitors the effluent of this subsystem. A separate subsystem, the chemical plant, is designed to provide, by electrolysis of aqueous sodium chloride, sufficient amounts of acid and base. The acid and base are used to wash the appropriate resins for regeneration. Again the microprocessor controls this function as needed.

Ultraviolet (UV) sterilization is the final treatment of the water in the purification system. Disinfection of waters via UV radiation is dependent upon energy and exposure, transmission of the liquid, and the liquid flow rate.

UV radiation must hit the microorganism to destroy it and each organism must absorb a specific amount of energy to be destroyed. Varying amounts of UV energy are necessary to kill various microorganisms. The germicidal spectrum of the ultraviolet wavelength is from 2,000 to 3,000 angstroms, with the peak at 2,537 angstroms. The intensity of the ultraviolet radiation is expressed in microwatts per square centimeter at a given distance. The total UV energy emitted from all sides of the UV lamp is expressed in watts. The total exposure of the liquid is expressed as microwatt seconds per square centimeter, or "Ultrads," which is a product of energy, time and area. The same number of Ultrads can be accomplished with a short exposure at a high intensity of UV or a long exposure at a low intensity of UV.

The amount of energy available to an organism from a given ultraviolet source is dependent upon the UV transmission of the liquid. The transmission of the liquid is dependent upon the quantity and types of dissolved and suspended matter in the liquid. The highly polished water with average turbidity of 0.15 NTU produced by the system has an absorption coefficient of less than 0.008. The system's UV sterilizer produces an excess of 300,000 Ultrads for sterilization. After sterilization, the processed water is stored in a 1,500-gallon tank and on demand pumped to the house for all normal uses, such as drinking, cooking, bathing, laundry, etc.

The water quality of the process water is equal to or better than most municipal supplies.

The system has been designed to resolve the problem of building homes where water, either quality or quantity, is a problem and/or on-site treatment of wastewater is a problem.

U.S. ARMY FIELD HOSPITAL WASTEWATER TREATMENT FOR WATER REUSE

The information in this section is based on a report in

Conference II entitled "Ozone–Ultrasound Treatment of a Hospital Wastewater for Reuse" by R.A. Sierka of the University of Arizona and R.L. Skaggs of the University of Nevada at Las Vegas.

Introduction

The U.S. Army provides field hospital medical facilities derived from a modular building block concept termed MUST: Medical Unit, Self-Contained, Transportable. An integral part of this system is the Water Processing Element (WPE) which will treat nonsanitary wastewaters emanating from the following MUST activity centers: showers, operating rooms, kitchen, x-ray laboratory and clinical laboratory. The current WPE process configuration includes equalization tankage, 40 mesh screening, ultrafiltration (UF), reverse osmosis (RO), ultraviolet (UV)/ozonation and hypochlorination.

The ultimate objective is to produce recycleable water, meeting U.S. Drinking Water Standards, for use within the MUST complex. Additionally, 5 mg/ℓ total organic carbon (TOC) and 10 mg/ℓ chemical oxygen demand (COD) limits are imposed. A near-term objective is to produce a treated composite wastewater acceptable for discharge to the environment. To meet these requirements, UF permeates after equalization and screening were to be ozonated in the presence of UV light, then passed through the hypochlorination operation prior to discharge.

The UV/ozonation process was relied upon to meet the organic quality standards outlined above regardless of the final disposition of the treated water. Since this portion of the system was not optimized, research was initiated to acquire design information on the effect that mechanically generated sonic and ultrasonic waves had: (1) in an ozone reactor during the oxidation of synthetic MUST Hospital Composite UF and RO permeates using low volumetric gas flow rates [i.e., volume of gas per minute per volume of liquid (vvm) of 0.1, 0.2, and 0.4 vvm] ; (2) on the mass transfer of oxygen into solution at the above vvm; and (3) on the air-stripping of UF permeates at 45°C.

Experimental Set-Up

The wastewaters employed throughout the course of this research were synthetic UF and RO permeates manufactured from the ingredients listed in Table 3.1. These formulations were derived by the U.S. Army Medical Bioengineering Research and Development Laboratory (USAMBRDL) from gas chromatograph mass spectrometer (GCMS) data on pilot-plant UF- and RO-processed MUST wastewaters. For each day's operation, analytical reagent-grade chemicals were mixed in 64.0-ℓ batches with City of Tucson, Arizona tap water serving as the solvent. The batch pH was adjusted to 9.0±0.1 with sodium hydroxide.

The experimental apparatus employed included a reactor, a 6.0-in i.d. by 7.5-ft high section of glass pipe with bottom and top closure plates constructed of 304-type stainless steel. The bottom plate served as acceptor for the sound wave generator (Biosonic IV). Two lines (0.25-in i.d.) served as drain and sample ports for the reactor which was run in the semibatch (i.e., continuous gas addition and fixed liquid volume) mode. Ozone and its carrier gas were admitted through one port of the top plate through Tygon tubing to the gas sparger while the unreacted gases, after sparging through the reaction liquid, escaped through the second port.

Table 3.1: Organic Chemical Composition of Hospital Composite Ultrafiltration Permeates and Reverse Osmosis Permeates

	UF Permeate	RO Permeate
Methanol	29.8 μℓ/ℓ	16 μℓ/ℓ
Acetone	6.3 μℓ/ℓ	5 μℓ/ℓ
Acetic acid	3.4 μℓ/ℓ	2.8 μℓ/ℓ
Diethyl ether	0.6 μℓ/ℓ	0.1 μℓ/ℓ
N,N-diethyl-m-toluamide	0.8 mg/ℓ	0.2 μℓ/ℓ
Ethanol	0.5 μℓ/ℓ	0.5 μℓ/ℓ
Oleic acid	0.5 μℓ/ℓ	0.1 μℓ/ℓ
Phenol	1.3 mg/ℓ	0.4 mg/ℓ
Urea	18.0 mg/ℓ	12.0 mg/ℓ
Kodak X-Omat developer	942 μℓ/ℓ	283 μℓ/ℓ*
Kodak X-Omat fixer	942 μℓ/ℓ	283 μℓ/ℓ*

*Assumed RO membrane 70% rejection based on Du Pont B-10 separation characteristics and an estimated 2:1 ratio for hydroquinone: acetic acid content which forms the major organic portion of the fixer/developer.

Source: NSF/RA-790225

The 316-type sintered stainless steel sparger was of doughnut design with an o.d. of 5 inches while the i.d. hole was 1.5 inches. The ultrasonic probe tip was inserted through the hole in the gas sparger and therefore sound waves flowed concurrently with the gas bubbles (average initial bubble diameter -5 μ).

Included in the ultrasonic system was a power monitoring device which indicated peak envelope power (PEP), delivered from the sound generator to the head in the probe tip. The amount of acoustical power delivered was variable (0 to 300 watts) and controllable.

Ozone was generated from commercial air delivered from cylinders at 15 psig and from pure oxygen tanks at 10 psig to the OREC ozonator Model 0381-0. Ozone concentrations in air ranged from 0.86 to 1.9% while from pure oxygen it was 2.20 to 2.40%.

COD, TOC, temperature (°C) and pH were measured on all liquid samples taken at 30-minute intervals over the 2-hour ozonation period. Ozone gas samples from the ozonator and reactor effluent lines were measured at irregular intervals. COD and ozone gas concentrations data were obtained by employing standard methodologies. TOC data were measured by directly injecting liquid samples (in triplicate) and standards into a Beckman Model 915 Total Organic Carbon Analyzer.

A series of oxygen uptake runs was performed in the reactor. Laboratory distilled water was placed in the column to a depth of 6.0 ft. Sodium bisulfite and cobalt chloride were added according to the 13th Edition of *Standard Methods*. The water was discarded after companion runs were conducted (i.e., with and without sound) to prevent spurious results due to the buildup of salts or catalyst. Dissolved oxygen measurements were made with a Yellow Spring Dissolved Oxygen Meter Model 57 placed at depths of 6 inches, 12 inches and 55 inches above the gas sparger. The time to reach each 0.5 mg/ℓ change in dissolved oxygen of the reactor contents was recorded and used to calculate the overall oxygen gas transfer coefficient ($K_L a$).

Results and Discussion

The Effects of Sound Waves on the Ozone Oxidation of MUST UF and RO Permeates: To provide data to derive kinetic equations for the design of ozone reactors employing sound waves as a catalyst and to improve gas mass transfer, a series of semibatch experiments was carried out. Three experiments each were performed at constant vvm and variable ozone inlet gas concentrations and three experiments with variable vvm and constant ozone inlet gas concentrations with UF and RO permeates serving as substrates. The following operating conditions were maintained in these experiments:

(1) a starting pH of 9.0 and uncontrolled during the reaction,
(2) ambient temperature operation (approximately 26±1°C),
(3) a 6.0-ft water depth in the reactor, and
(4) a batch reaction time of 2.0 hours.

During the first three runs, conducted with UF permeate, an approximately constant ozone concentration of 1.0 wt % (0.96 to 1.03%) in air was employed. The reaction gas was applied at three different vvm: 0.1, 0.2 and 0.4.

As vvm was increased, the rate and extent of the organic destruction was enhanced. After 2 hours of ozonation, the TOC remaining for the 0.1, 0.2 and 0.4 vvm runs was 88, 70 and 48%, respectively, while on a COD basis the corresponding percentage remaining at the end of these runs was 72, 48 and 22%. These results basically reflect the difference in the nature of the TOC and COD tests. Where the TOC test quantifies the loss of organic carbon by total oxidation to carbon dioxide, the COD test indicates the change in molecular chemistry of the dissolved substrate and measures the oxygen demand of the substance remaining. The COD test, in other words, gives indication of the partial oxidation of the dissolved organics in solution.

The ozone concentrations of the gas leaving the reactor was monitored at irregular times throughout the run. All of the ozone applied to the reactor was utilized when the UF permeate was being oxidized by ozone at the 0.1 vvm condition. Thus, the run was totally mass transfer controlled and represents the major reason that only 12% of the TOC and 28% of the COD was oxidized. The average ultrasound PEP level for the experiment was at the 1.0 wt % ozone-in-air concentration; no residual ozone was found in the gas coming from the top of the reactor until 60 minutes of the run had been completed. From that time on, to the end of the run at 120 minutes, the effluent ozone gas concentration ranged between 34 and 46%. Finally, when the vvm was increased to 0.4, ozone first appeared in the effluent gas stream from the column at 10 minutes into the run. The increase in ozone concentration from 10 to 120 minutes was linear with batch reaction time, until at the termination of the run, 96% of the ozone gas admitted was found to be exiting the reactor.

Ultrasound Scale-Up Experiments with UF Permeates: The benefits of sound inclusion into any ozone reactor are expected to come from improvement in gas transfer and decomposition of ozone to various free radicals.

For larger systems the question of scale-up procedure must be addressed. Today, there does not exist a sufficient body of technical expertise for reactor design employing ultrasonics to permit scale-up based on well-defined scientific principles and, therefore, an empirical approach must be used. Since the experiments performed during this research were limited to the use of a sound generator, operating basically at one frequency (20 kHz), liquid height in the reactor was varied and maximum achievable sound power was employed in an attempt to characterize this effect.

The results of these experiments indicate a direct proportional increase in the mass of TOC removed with liquid height. Also it was evident that ozone utilization increased with liquid height.

The Effect of Ultrasound on Oxygen Mass Transfer: To evaluate the effect that ultrasound had on mass transfer, a series of oxygen uptake runs was performed in the reactor at 0.1, 0.2 and 0.4 vvm. Overall oxygen transfer coefficients ($K_L a$) were measured at the 6.0, 12.0 and 55.0-inch levels from the gas sparger surface.

It was found that the $K_L a$ at any given position in the column increased with increased vvm regardless of the presence or absence of sound waves. However, the presence of sound waves in the reactor always yielded an improvement in oxygen mass transfer over the companion no-sound condition. The range of improvement was between 1 and 48%.

The Effect of Ultrasound on the Air-Stripping of UF Permeates: The effectiveness of air-stripping to remove dissolved organics contained in RO permeates from MUST laboratories was investigated. It was concluded that air-stripping of UF permeates was of little value. Experiments were then carried out by the authors to determine if air-stripping aided by ultrasound could reverse this conclusion. The air-stripping was not particularly successful. However, it can be stated that the rates of COD and TOC removal in the presence of ultrasound did exceed those obtained by USAMBRDL. This increase can be attributed to the enhanced mass transport properties of the air-sound system.

The results indicated that, particularly speaking, air-stripping even in the presence of sound would preclude the use of this concept in the field due to the unreasonably high hydraulic detention times required.

Summary

Organic oxidation rates for synthetic UF and RO permeates, as measured by COD and TOC destruction, were increased by either increasing vvm at fixed ozone gas concentration or increasing inlet ozone concentration at a fixed vvm in a reactor employing sound waves. The benefits due to increasing ozone partial pressure were somewhat negated by the increased amounts of unreacted ozone exiting the reactor. It was also shown that ozone utilization could be increased by increasing the liquid height in the reactor through which the ozone was being bubbled. A mathematical model was developed to relate organic oxidation rates to reactor inlet ozone concentration, vvm and organic concentration.

The positive effect of ultrasound on the transfer of oxygen to distilled water was demonstrated. K_La increased directly with increases in vvm and position above the gas sparger. The improvement ranged from 1 to 48% over the no-sound condition.

This result partially explains the improvement in the air-stripping rates of organics from UF permeates when sound waves were employed.

TREATMENT OF MUNICIPAL WASTEWATER EFFLUENT FOR POTABLE WATER REUSE

> The information in this section was based on the paper of the same title, published in Conference I by D. Roy and E.S.K. Chian of the Georgia Institute of Technology.

Introduction

The subject of water reuse has become an extremely important topic in recent years, and it will become even more important as arid regions of the world become more industrialized. An area of water reuse which has had limited use but is becoming more and more important is that of water reuse for potable purposes. This study was aimed at developing a treatment scheme which has the potential for purifying secondary effluent sufficiently to insure potability and to test the performance of such a treatment scheme. The treatment scheme consists of chemical coagulation, sedimentation, sand filtration, reverse osmosis and ozonation.

Materials and Methods

Approximately 50 gallons of secondary effluent was collected from the East Side Sewage Treatment Plant, Urbana, IL, at the outlet end of chlorination unit. The secondary effluent was dechlorinated after collection to remove any residual chlorine. The East Side Plant uses primary settling, activated sludge and trickling filters in parallel at a ratio of 3:2 activated sludge to trickling filter, final clarification and chlorination. The typical flow through this plant is 12 mgd and other characteristics of the secondary effluent are summarized in Table 3.2.

Table 3.2: Secondary Effluent Characteristics

Parameter	
Effluent BOD, mg/ℓ	23
Chlorine dose, mg/ℓ	7.3
pH	7.3
Turbidity, FTU	6.2
TDS, mg/ℓ	500
Color, units	0.06
TOC, mg/ℓ	32

Source: NSF/RA-790224

The primary purpose for coagulation in the area of water treatment is the removal of suspended solids. Aluminum sulfate was used as the coagulant, and it was attempted to reduce the turbidity from an initial value of 6.2 FTU to approximately 1 or 2 FTU. To evaluate the optimum coagulation dose and pH, conventional jar tests were performed using Phipps and Bird flocculator (Phipps and Bird, Inc., Richmond, VA) with one-minute rapid-mix at 100 rpm followed by 20 minutes' flocculation and 30 minutes' settling. The temperature of water was approximately 20°C. Using the optimum conditions and coagulant dose, as obtained by the jar tests, the secondary effluent was then treated in a simulated laboratory-scale coagulation-flocculation unit and allowed to settle for 30 minutes.

One of the important parameters in the study on water reuse is the removal of organic materials, but very little is known about the ability of chemical coagulation to accomplish this. It is thought that if the organic material is associated with particulate matter, it will be removed well by coagulation-flocculation followed by sedimentation, but if it is in solution, some other process must be employed for organics removal.

The effluent from the settling unit following flocculation-coagulation was filtered through a rapid sand filter bed to remove the solids remaining after the secondary treatment and subsequent coagulation and sedimentation. This was necessary to prevent fouling of advanced treatment processes such as reverse osmosis.

The filtration effluent was then treated by the reverse osmosis (RO) unit. Reverse osmosis is in principle a relatively simple unit process which separates solutes from a solvent on the basis of differences in molecular size, shape and chemical structure through the use of a semipermeable membrane. The RO unit used is a DuPont B-10 module. From the head tank, the feed solution was circulated through the test section and bypass lines with a 5-gpm positive displacement pump. The RO unit was operated at 700 psi and the permeate flux was held constant at 2 gpm.

The RO permeate, having a TDS of 6 mg/ℓ and a TOC of approximately 6 mg/ℓ, mainly consisted of low molecular weight (MW <150) organics. The RO permeate was finally treated with ozone for further removal of organics and disinfection purposes. Ozonation was used as the final unit process of the treatment scheme because of its reported ability as a strong disinfecting agent for resistant pathogenic organisms and good polishing agent for the removal of residual organics. Also, recent findings indicate the formation of undesirable toxic end products when chlorine is used as the disinfectant, whereas nontoxic end products are formed if ozone is the disinfectant.

The laboratory-scale ozonation experiments were performed in an agitated vessel reactor, with ozone/air gas mixture flow rate of 1 ℓ/min. The ozone gas was generated by a Welsbach T-408 laboratory ozonator (Welsbach, Philadelphia, PA) under operating conditions of 60 volts and 8 psig.

Results

The results of laboratory-scale coagulation experiments, using the optimum dose of 40 mg/ℓ in the simulated laboratory-scale coagulation process, followed by 30 minutes of settling, are presented in Table 3.3.

Table 3.3: Results of Coagulation Experiments

Parameter	Influent	Effluent	% Reduction
Turbidity, FTU	6.2	1.4	78
pH	7.3	6.5	—
TDS, mg/ℓ	500	550	—
TOC, mg/ℓ	32	18	44
Color, units	0.06	0.003	95

Source: NSF/RA-790224

Turbidity removal was the main purpose of the filtration unit and approximately 71.4% of turbidity and 33.3% of effluent color removal were achieved by this unit process. Total dissolved solids were not removed at all by filtration, since filtration is a physical process to remove suspended solids. There was a slight increase in TOC level through the filter bed, which is probably because of the organics present due to improper backwashing in the previous runs. The pH, as expected, remained unchanged after filtration.

The filtration effluent was then treated by the RO unit process. Permeate and retentate volumes through the RO unit were measured so that an accurate estimate of the TOC could be achieved by a mass balance on the total and inorganic carbon. The results of the experiments are presented in Table 3.4.

A preliminary set of ozonation experiments were initially performed on the RO permeate by varying the operating parameters. Based on the preliminary experiments, the following conditions were selected as optimum for the final ozonation process.

(1) mixing rpm – 500
(2) initial pH – 6.0 or the unadjusted pH of the RO permeate if it is of that order.
(3) without ultraviolet irradiation.

The results of the final ozonation experiments using the optimum conditions are summarized in Table 3.5.

Table 3.4: Results of RO Experiment

Parameter	RO Influent	RO Effluent	% Reduction
Turbidity, FTU	0.40	0.12	70
pH	6.65	5.7	–
TDS, mg/ℓ	550	17	97
TOC, mg/ℓ	24	6.7	72
Color, units	0.002	–	–

Source: NSF/RA-790224

Table 3.5

Contact Time (min)	Dissolved Ozone Concentration (mg/ℓ)	pH	Inorganic Carbon (mg/ℓ)	TOC (mg/ℓ)
0	0.0	5.7	7.0	6.0
5	0.2	6.0	2.0	2.0
10	0.25	6.1	2.0	1.0
15	0.25	6.2	3.0	2.0
20	0.32	6.35	2.0	2.0

Note: Sample: RO permeate; pH: 5.7; Mixing: 500 rpm.

Source: NSF/RA-790224

Conclusions

A tertiary water treatment scheme consisting of coagulation and flocculation, settling, rapid sand filtration, reverse osmosis and ozonation was evaluated to produce potable water from the municipal secondary effluent. The treatment scheme was able to produce a final effluent with total dissolved solids and TOC contents of 17 and 2 mg/ℓ, respectively, which is comparable to that of distilled water. Turbidity and color were reduced to levels below that of distilled water. Thus, it may be concluded that a tertiary treatment scheme such as the one described above has the potentiality of producing potable water from secondary effluents.

International Developments in Water Reuse

THE CCMS DRINKING WATER STUDY

The information in this section is based on the paper "Waste Water Reuse—The CCMS Drinking Water Study," by R. Richards, B.G. Tunnah, A.M. Shaikh and K.M. Stern, all of Gordian Associates, Inc., and published in Conference I.

Introduction

The provision of potable water that is bacteriologically and chemically safe as well as esthetically acceptable is becoming considerably more complex, particularly in industrialized nations. As the quantity of available water becomes more critical due to population growth and industrialization, the availability of clean uncontaminated water for human consumption poses an increasingly serious problem.

Providing safe drinking water in the highly industrialized nations leads to considerably different problems than are usually encountered in less developed countries, where basic supply and microbiological quality are generally major concerns. For the most part, the industrialized nations have been able to control waterborne disease transmission. However, new and potentially serious questions are raised by the proliferation of industrial chemical discharges into drinking water sources, urban runoff, water polluted by human waste (both treated and untreated), and finally by the formation of new chemicals in drinking water from the interaction of disinfectant chemicals with the natural and synthetic chemicals which are commonly present in drinking water.

The NATO Committee on the Challenges of Modern Society (CCMS) was created in 1969 in order to bring the combined resources of the NATO mem-

bership to bear on environmental and other common problems that have a significant impact on the quality of life in modern industrialized societies. The
aim of CCMS is to "examine how to improve, in every practical way, the exchange of views and experience among allied countries in the task of creating a
better environment for their societies. . .and to consider specific problems of the
human environment with the deliberate objective of stimulating action by member governments."

The working methods of CCMS are based on three concepts, namely, a pilot
country, orientation towards action, and open publicity. The CCMS entrusts
the pilot country that has proposed a project with the responsibility for carrying
it out. This includes planning the study, preparing necessary reports, and the
subsequent action necessary for its realization.

In view of the existing and potential problems in the supply of drinking water
which are faced by the NATO members, the U.S. submitted a proposal for a
CCMS study at the end of 1976. The first meeting of experts from a total of
eleven nations and two international organizations took place in Brussels in
April 1977, and a series of meetings have been held subsequently. The primary
objectives of the NATO-CCMS Study are to achieve a better understanding of

> (1) The drinking water problems shared by industrial-
>   ized countries.
>
> (2) Solutions to these problems now available.
>
> (3) Potential problems for which solutions are currently
>   not available, except perhaps at prohibitive cost.

Six international working groups have been studying various topics related to
drinking water supplies. These topics are analytical methods, advanced treatment technologies, microbiological factors, human health effects, groundwater
protection, and wastewater reuse. In the water reuse group, seven nations
participated: the U.S., France, the United Kingdom, the Netherlands, Sweden,
Spain and Germany.

Regulatory and Legislative Control of Discharges of Pollutants into Surface Waters

In the United States, the enactment of the Federal Water Pollution Control
Act Amendments of 1972 began a comprehensive effort to "restore and maintain the chemical, physical, and biological integrity of the Nation's Waters."
Similarly, other countries participating in the NATO-CCMS effort have introduced, within the past ten years, legislation to maintain or upgrade the quality
of surface waters. The NATO-CCMS report is based on responses from five
member nations: Germany, France, The Netherlands, Sweden and the United
States.

Administrative Responsibility: In all five countries, any special use of water
must first be authorized by a special license. The terms, duration and degree of

detailed control in these licenses vary from one country to another. However, in all cases they are the most important means through which effective control is maintained over the discharge of pollutants. The strongest national role in the administration of water pollution control occurs in the United States. The Environmental Protection Agency is authorized to issue permits to industrial and agricultural users, and may veto any permits issued by state authorities. Furthermore, it is also the principle enforcement agent, with responsibilities in the areas of inspection, review and imposition of penalties.

The Swedish system provides a strong role for the National Franchise Board, but the Board's functions are limited to the review of applications and the issuance of permits. Inspection and enforcement are shared by lower level boards, by local authorities, and by representatives of specialized agencies, none of which operate at the national level. In the Netherlands, national and provincial functions are delineated only on the basis of the waterways for which each level of government has jurisdiction. Finally, in Germany and France, both the granting of licenses and enforcement of compliance with them, are the responsibilities of state government agencies.

Financing: The issue of how water pollution abatement programs should be financed is intimately linked to the nature of the incentives the programs offer. The principal question at stake is the use of tax incentives. Such incentives serve to discourage pollution in excess of the permitted standards and to generate revenue with which to support both monitoring and regulatory activities, as well as direct water purification efforts.

Tax incentives have the advantage of "making the polluter pay." In addition, they allow a measure of flexibility in establishing the maximum amount of permissible pollution. However, they run two important risks: first, if such taxes become an important source of revenue for abatement programs, the incentive to end the revenue-generating sources of pollution is diminished; second, they permit polluters to opt for the tax if he finds it too costly to institute pollution abatement programs—even if the social costs of pollution are extremely high. France, Germany, and the Netherlands have all chosen to include a pollution tax as part of their regulatory systems. It is particularly important as a revenue source in the Dutch system. Neither the United States nor Sweden uses such a tax.

Measurement of Water Reuse

It is difficult, if not impossible, to measure the levels of organic compounds and pathogenic organisms found in rivers which are sources of drinking water. These pollutants are generally found in proportion to the wastewater content of the river. Therefore, in order to protect consumers of water abstracted downstream of industrial and/or municipal discharges, it is desirable to determine the degree of reuse that occurs at the point of abstraction. This is expressed by the reuse factor which is the percentage (or decimal fraction) of the river's flow which is comprised of wastewater.

Reuse can be quantified by a mass balance of the river system by using river flow, discharge and abstraction data. However, this data is not easily obtained and may not be available. In addition, the water in a river can be temporarily exchanged with groundwater resulting in less actual reuse than calculated from flow data. Therefore, several substances are being investigated for use as indicators of municipal/industrial pollution. The criteria for an indicator substance are: that its concentration in municipal/industrial effluents be known; that it have negligible background levels in the stream; and that it be carried freely in the river.

Several indicator substances are being investigated and are discussed by the CCMS study. Of particular interest is boron which can provide a good index of the reuse of municipal effluents since it is found at fairly constant levels in sewage effluent. The source of boron is the perborates in domestic detergents. Total organic chlorine also has been suggested as a reliable indicator of man's activity in the environment. Other indicator substances discussed include: chloride, total organic carbon and phosphates. Although reuse indices cannot determine the toxicity of the water supply, they are valuable as measures of the proportion of harmful materials likely to be present.

Extent of Current Reuse

The direct use of water today occurs almost entirely in industry and agriculture. Industrial and agricultural reuse is an important point in any discussion of the supply of potable water since this reuse reduces the demand for natural water which then can be reserved for potable use.

Treatment Options

The treatment options for two different types of potable reuse were considered: indirect reuse via groundwater recharge; and direct reuse. It should be emphasized that these systems for the reuse of municipal wastewater should only be depended on to supplement, not replace, potable water supplies derived from natural sources.

Groundwater Injection: Groundwater supplies can be augmented through the injection of wastewater that has undergone primary and secondary treatment. Reinfiltration provides additional treatment for the wastewater as does the buffering and dilution capacity of the underground reservoir. Care must be taken, however, that adequate treatment is provided prior to injection to prevent the degradation of the groundwater resource. The design of the treatment process should take into account the quality of untreated water, the hydrogeology of the recharge site, the method of recharge, and the relative proportions of artificial and natural inputs. Generally speaking, this treatment should eliminate suspended solids, organic matter and ammonia and reduce nitrates. In addition, activated carbon and ozonization can be used to remove and enhance the biodegradation of organic matter.

Direct Reuse: Perhaps the greatest problem associated with direct reuse is the buildup of dissolved solids in the recycled water. There are two approaches to solving this problem. The first is the semiclosed system which recycles water until the concentration of dissolved salts reaches the limits fixed by the potability norms. Water is then taken in from another source until the level of salts is reduced to the desired level. The second approach is to demineralize the water using reverse osmosis, electrodialysis, ion exchange or distillation.

The treatment train should also include activated carbon and aeration to remove organic compounds and chlorination should be used to eliminate pathogenic organisms.

Potential Health Problems

The risks to human health from the use of renovated wastewater are due to the possible presence of microbiological and chemical contaminants in the water. The degree of risk rises with the degree of human contact or exposure. The Area V CCMS report examines in detail the risks associated with microbiological and chemical contaminants (inorganic and organic) in recycled drinking water. Chemical and microbiological contaminants are examined at the levels and type of specific contaminant, known health effects, problems of detection and of elimination.

The report finds that present microbiological or chemical standards are inadequate, and that the lack of economically viable methods of detecting low level viruses or organic chemical contaminants is a serious obstacle to the use of reclaimed water. However, the most important objection against the use of renovated water for drinking is that there is, to date, insufficient information on the health risks associated with the various contaminants which may be present in reuse water.

Water Resources Management

All the NATO countries have introduced legislation concerning water pollution control/water resources management within the last 20 years and particularly since 1970. These laws have a common feature in that all countries have organized water management at three levels: national, regional and local. As a general rule, the national level is concerned with the coordination of water policy; the regional level is concerned with systems management (particularly pollution control); and the local level is concerned with the actual management of resources, such as water purification and sewage treatment plants. In countries with a federal form of government (United States, West Germany), the trend is towards greater central government involvement in pollution control. However, in countries where the government is more centralized, the trend is to set up regional management agencies (Finland, France, United Kingdom).

There are two approaches that can be used to obtain compliance with water resources policy: legislative/regulatory constraints; and economic inducements. The former approach requires certain actions, say the reduction of water consumption or pollution discharges by an industrial facility, to be authorized by the government. In the latter approach, penalties (pollution taxes, water charges) can be levied at a level that results in the industrial facility finding it economic to reduce its water consumption/pollution. Spain and France currently employ economic inducements to control pollution discharges.

Water quality targets are desirable so that the reduction of individual pollution discharges to a body of water can be coordinated. There are two different strategies for developing such targets. Long-term targets can be set which require a large reduction in pollution in the hope that the technology to accomplish this reduction will be developed in the future. Alternatively, less severe targets can be set, which are more realistic and are achievable on a short-term basis.

The CCMS member nations have directed most of their energies in the management of water resources towards surface water. However, it is recognized that groundwater resources will require similar attention if the quality and quantity of these sources of potable water are to be maintained. The CCMS report has identical areas that require study before comprehensive groundwater management plans and policies can be developed.

Case Studies

Many communities throughout the world draw their potable water supplies from rivers into which sewage has been discharged upstream. Although indirect reuse may have significant implications for public health, these communities are not always aware of the extent of this reuse. The Case Studies included in the CCMS report review instances where indirect reuse has been documented and measured.

Ruhr Valley (West Germany): Perhaps the best known case involving indirect reuse is the Ruhr River. The Ruhr Valley is a densely populated industrial region in West Germany. The river is used extensively both as a source of drinking water and for the disposal of treated municipal wastewater. By careful management of reservoir discharges, the reuse factor can be kept below an acceptable 22% even at extremely low flows.

Thames River (England): The reuse of the River Thames has been quantified by both boron analysis and by using flow, discharge and abstraction data. Those studies indicate that, at the point where water is withdrawn to supply London, the reuse factor is 13 to 14% during normal flows.

Porsuk River (Turkey): The Porsuk River in Turkey provides an example of innovative planning regarding reuse. Eskisehir, which lies on the Porsuk River, is the seventh largest city in Turkey and had a population of 270,000 in 1975. The present water supply of the city is provided by springs; however, these sources are being used to full capacity and will not be able to meet the future needs of the city. The projected population of Eskisehir in year 2000 is greater than 750,000 and the water demand is expected to increase sevenfold between 1975 and 2000.

Obviously, the City of Eskisehir must find a new source of potable water. The Porsuk River appears to be the best available source for this additional supply. It is estimated that Eskisehir could depend on the Porsuk Reservoir, which is located on the river, for 70 million cubic meters per year. The chief obstacle to this plan is the water quality of the river. There are several discharges upstream of Eskisehir which make the river water unsuitable for drinking without extensive treatment. These discharges are municipal sewage from the City of Kitahya; and effluents from three industrial facilities: a fertilizer factory, a slaughterhouse, and a sugar factory.

The results of water quality survey showed symptoms of typical organic pollution: high levels of BOD, alkalinity, hardness, suspended solids and total dissolved solids. In addition, very high levels of nitrogen were found in the river downstream of the fertilizer factory. While the organic pollution can be treated at source by conventional means, the nitrogen problem is more difficult to solve.

Nitrogen in the Porsuk Reservoir is found in three forms: ammonia, nitrate and nitrite. Nitrite is directly toxic to humans due to its ability to disrupt the normal uptake of oxygen by hemoglobin in the blood. Nitrate is indirectly toxic since it is reduced to nitrite in the stomach. These compounds also stimulate the growth of algae in the Porsuk Reservoir which would impede treatment processes at a water purification plant. With the exception of reverse osmosis (and other membrane processes) no single treatment process can effectively remove all three forms of nitrogen. However, reverse osmosis is very expensive.

The State Hydraulic Works of Turkey examined two alternative plans for utilizing the Porsuk River as a source of drinking water. The first alternative would involve the removal of nitrogen compounds by reverse osmosis after water purification by conventional means at a purification plant in Eskisehir. It is estimated that this alternative would have a capital cost of $65 million and a total annual cost in excess of $16 million. A disadvantage of the reverse osmosis process is that it concentrates the nitrogen compounds (and other dissolved solids) into 25% of the incoming water while 75% is purified. The 25% must be discarded which is a significant water loss.

The second would require the discharges from the Kutahya municipal sewer system, the sugar factory and the slaughterhouse to undergo conventional sewage treatment before discharge to the river. The Eskisehir water purification plant would provide the same treatment as the first alternative, with the exception that reverse osmosis would not be included. The nitrogen problem would be solved by pumping the fertilizer factory effluent to agricultural land for irrigation. In this way, the nitrogen content of the wastewater would be used as fertilizer. This system would require lagoons to store the wastewater during the winter and a distribution network. It would cost just slightly more than $2.5 million to construct this system plus $18.6 million for the wastewater treatment plant at Kutahya. The total annual costs for this alternative would be less than $2.5 million, just 14% of the cost of the reverse osmosis alternative.

WATER REUSE IN THE NETHERLANDS

> The material in this section is based on a paper presented
> at Conference I entitled, "Studies on Water Reuse in the
> Netherlands," by J. Hrubec and B.C.J. Zoeteman, both
> of the National Institute for Water Supply, Voorburg
> and J.C. Shippers of the Netherlands Waterworks Testing
> and Research Institute KIWA NV.

Introduction

The Netherlands is a country rich in water. It is also a highly industrialized area
with one of the world's highest population densities.

There was rapid increase in demand for public water supply from World War II
up to the early seventies. A similar rapid increase of water consumption till
the year 2000 was expected. However, lower population growth, changes in the
water consumption pattern both in households and industry, and a retarded
economic growth in 1978 resulted in a modified prognosis with a much smaller
rate of increase of the water consumption.

The reduction in consumption of water in industry since the early seventies
has mainly been caused by a decrease of water consumption per unit of production, which was encouraged by the Water Pollution Control Act which came into
force in 1970. Under this Act a system of levies for discharge of wastewater was
introduced leading to a limitation of the volume of discharged wastewater in
the industry and consequently to a reduction of the water consumption.

At present about two-thirds of water for domestic and industrial purposes in
The Netherlands is derived from underground sources and one-third from
surface water sources. As the exploitation of the underground sources practically
is approaching the capacity of the aquifers in the country the additional water
demand mostly has to be covered from other sources.

The most important source of surface water in the country is the river Rhine.
The river is strongly polluted. Production of drinking water from the Rhine,
therefore, may be considered as indirect reuse of wastewater for human consumption. The pollution is caused mainly by discharges of untreated or only
partly treated sewage water from a catchment area with a population of about
60 million inhabitants and by discharges of wastes from chemical industries. A
consequence of these discharges is the pollution of the river with refractory
organic compounds. During the early part of the seventies the load with dif-
ficultly degradable organic compounds increased yearly by 6-8% and it is predicted that the load of refractory organic compounds from the catchment area of
the river will increase from around 240,000 ton carbon in 1970 to 500,000 ton in
2000, in spite of biological treatment of all municipal and industrial wastewater.

Furthermore, the chloride and sodium concentrations in the river are steadily increasing as a result of the discharge of salt wastes from the mine industry and other more diffuse sources. The load of chloride in the river Rhine at the Dutch-German border increased from approximately 175 kg/sec in 1950 to more than 350 kg/sec in 1975 and the concentration of chlorides of the river water during the low flow in 1975 was higher than 250 mg/ℓ.

The sodium concentration is coupled with chlorides and hence increasing also. Due to the acceptance of the new drinking water standard of the European Community for sodium (175 mg Na/ℓ) this constituent will become one of the critical parameters for the quality of the river Rhine. To overcome periods during which the quality of the river water does not meet the required quality standards for preparation of drinking water, water storage in open or underground reservoirs is necessary. The realization of these reservoirs which are often located in areas of great ecological value is a subject of growing public criticism. Substantial improvement of the water quality of the river Rhine could be achieved by intensive water pollution control within the whole catchment area.

However, an effective pollution control is a difficult international political problem which recently has been partly regulated in a Treaty on the Chemical Pollution of the Rhine. Up till now no appreciable improvement of the quality of the river water has been achieved.

Taking into consideration climatological, geographical and economical aspects the following supplementary alternatives within the country for the water supply seem to be most suitable:

- limitation of the use of groundwater for industrial and agricultural purposes by means of the use of surface water or by means of direct or indirect reuse of industrial and municipal wastewater;
- use of desalinated brackish groundwater for potable water supply;
- direct or indirect reuse of municipal wastewater for nonpotable domestic use (e.g., reuse in buildings, university complexes etc.).

Reuse of municipal wastewater is a possible alternative for the present indirect reuse via the river Rhine.

At a regional scale the reuse of municipal wastewater for artificial groundwater recharge destined for drinking water supply and for salt intrusion control, provides an alternative for the water supply of the islands located along the Dutch northwest coast. These islands suffer from a serious shortage of drinking water during the recreational summer season, when the population number is multiplied several times. To evaluate the possibilities of the water reuse a program of studies on different aspects of direct and indirect reuse was encouraged in the early seventies. One of the objectives of the studies is to evaluate the efficiency of the available wastewater technologies especially with respect to the removal of potential hazardous materials and to quantify the risks involved in the extreme case of direct reuse of municipal wastewater for potable and non-potable purposes and in the indirect reuse via the river Rhine.

Dordrecht Pilot Plant

The pilot plant is located on the site of the Dordrecht municipal wastewater treatment facility. The feed is secondary effluent of the activated sludge plant that treats wastewater, mostly of domestic origin, from the city of Dordrecht. The industrial wastes of the major industries in the area are treated separately and then discharged directly into the river system.

The Dordrecht waste treatment plant consists of grit removal, primary sedimentation, activated sludge process and secondary sedimentation. About 10% of the effluent from the plant is recycled for scrubbing flue gas from the incineration plant for household refuse and sludge from the wastewater treatment plant. The heated wash water containing ash, HCl, HF and H_2SO_3 is mixed with the raw wastewater influent following neutralization and sedimentation. The secondary effluent was monitored during 1975/76 to obtain information on seasonal fluctuation in quality. Fluctuations in COD and some heavy metal concentrations (Cd, Pb) were found. Fluctuations in quality are especially due to rainfall when mixing of raw water with runoff water occurs. Typical quality characteristics of the secondary effluent are presented in Table 4.1.

Table 4.1: Characteristics of Secondary Effluent (1975/76)

Parameter	
COD, mg/ℓ	35–100
Ca^{2+}, mg/ℓ	75–135
Mg^{2+}, mg/ℓ	12–36
PO_4^{3-}, mg/ℓ	4.5–36
Alkalinity, mg/ℓ	200–400
Suspended solids, mg/ℓ	3–43
Cd, μg/ℓ	0.2–7
Cr, μg/ℓ	1–6.5
Cu, μg/ℓ	3–42
Hg, μg/ℓ	0.1–2.8
Pb, μg/ℓ	4–26
Zn, μg/ℓ	60–580
Ni, μg/ℓ	5–68
Li, μg/ℓ	17–38

Source: NSF/RA-790224

Figure 4.1 shows a chromatogram of Dordrecht secondary effluent in comparison with that of Rhine water and illustrates the fact that the concentrations of many synthetic organic compounds are higher in the river water than in the biological effluent. In 1978 mutagenicity of unconcentrated samples of the secondary effluent was determined six times by means of the Ames test. In no

Figure 4.1: Chromatogram of River Rhine Water
and Dordrecht Secondary Effluent

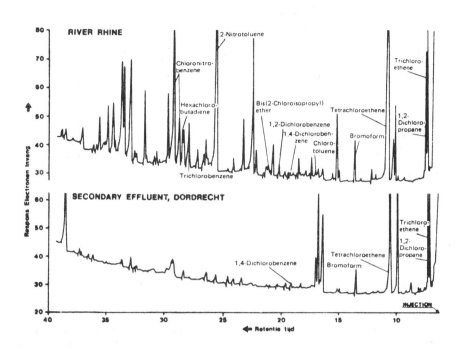

Source: NSF/RA - 790224

sample was mutagenic response detected, while the Rhine water showed significant mutagenicity with a similar determination procedure.

The pilot plant consists of two systems: a combined biological and physical-chemical treatment scheme and a system in which reverse osmosis is incorporated.

Description of the Physical-Chemical System: The physical-chemical system was selected on the basis of experience with advanced wastewater treatment in the USA and South Africa, showing that water of high quality could be produced in an effective and economic way with a combination of the various physical-chemical processes incorporated in the scheme. The system is shown in Figure 4.2.

Lime Treatment at pH 11.2 — This process was preferred over other chemical-coagulation processes for removal of phosphorus and suspended and colloidal

Figure 4.2: Scheme of the Physical-Chemical System

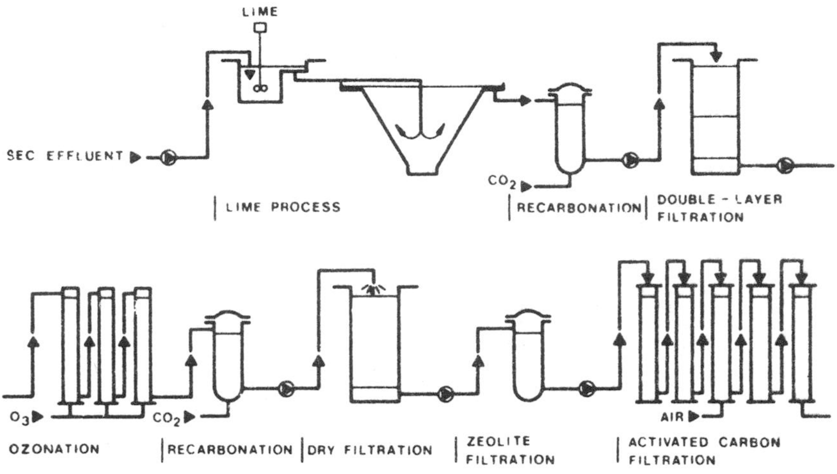

Source: NSF/RA-790224

solids because partial disinfection and more effective removal of potentially toxic trace elements can be achieved at high pH. Furthermore, in contrast to coagulation processes with aluminum and ferric salts, no anions, like chlorides and sulfates, are introduced during lime treatment. Coagulation is accomplished with lime at doses of 250-600 mg $Ca(OH)_2$/ℓ using a rapid-mixing tank and a flocculation tank followed by a sludge-blanket reactor. The retention time for the average design flow of 4 m^3/hr is 1.5 hr. The upflow rate for the sludge-blanket reactor is 1 mm/sec. Polyelectrolyte (0.5 mg/ℓ) is added to the influent of the flocculation tank to enhance flocculation and to improve sedimentation.

Recarbonation — Recarbonation for pH correction can take place after the sedimentation tank or after the ozonation columns. Hence, the possibility for ozonation at high pH exists. First-step recarbonation is carried out in a column, 3.0 m high and 0.5 m in diameter. The hydraulic retention time is 9 minutes with a linear liquid velocity of 20 m/hr. Dosing of CO_2 is controlled automatically. The second recarbonation unit consists of two columns, 2 m high and 0.3 m in diameter, with a retention time of 4.5 min and a water flow rate of 50 m/hr; these can be used individually, in series or parallel.

Double-Layer Filtration — The double-layer filter bed consists of an 80 cm high layer of 1.5-2.5 mm crushed sand and a 20 cm layer of 2-4 mm anthracite. The relatively course filter material was chosen to prevent rapid increase of head loss and thus to obtain longer filtration runs. The filter is operated in the downflow mode with a filtration rate of 5 m/hr. Backwashing and air scouring is controlled manually.

Ozonation — The primary purpose of the ozonation step is disinfection. In addition, improvements in taste, odor, color and turbidity are expected along with partial removal of organic matter and oxidation of some organic micropollutants (phenols and polycyclic aromatic hydrocarbons). The ozonation is carried out in three 4.0 m high columns, with a minimum retention time of 12 minutes. Gas dispersion tubes for O_3-dosing are used to obtain fine gas bubbles. The maximum O_3 dose is restricted to 15 mg/ℓ because of the capacity of the ozone generator.

Selective Ion Exchange and Dry Filtration — A combination of biological dry filtration (trickling filtration) with selective ion exchange of ammonium ion by means of clinoptilolite was chosen for removal of nitrogen compounds. Dry filtration has been used widely in The Netherlands since the early 1950s for removal of ammonia from groundwater. The dry filtration has also been used with success on a pilot plant scale for removal of ammonia from river water.

Dry filtration is based on percolation of air with water through the filter bed. The aeration of the bed must be intensive enough to maintain aerobic conditions in the bed even when rapid oxygen consumption occurs during the nitrification of large ammonia concentrations. Artificial aeration of the filter bed is necessary to obtain full nitrification. In practice complete removal of concentrations of ammonia as high as 30 mg NH_4^+/ℓ was achieved with artificial aeration. A disadvantage of this process is a substantial decrease in removal efficiency at low water temperatures. Ammonia was only partly removed in the treatment of Rhine water at temperatures below 5°C. However, such low temperatures are normally not expected for the effluents of wastewater treatment plants.

There are two dry filters in the scheme, which can be operated either in parallel or in series. The depth of the bed of each filter is 1.55 m; the filter material in the first filter is river sand with a diameter of 4-6 mm and in the second one is crushed sand with a diameter of 2-3 mm. The maximum filtration rate with parallel operation is 4 m/hr and with series connection is 8 m/hr. The aeration is accomplished by blowing in air beneath the filter bottom at a rate of 8 air volumes per volume of water. There is a provision for backwashing of the filter with water (max rate of 120 m/hr) with or without air.

The zeolite filters serve as a polishing step for ammonia removal. Furthermore, it is hoped that a combination of the dry and zeolite filters can be used to prevent high concentrations of nitrate in the product water. A partial by-pass of the dry filters will be used during periods of high nitrate concentrations in the effluent of the dry filters. The two zeolite filters are operated alternatively. When one is actively functioning, the other one is in reserve. Anaconda clinoptilolite with ion exchange capacity of 0.3 meq ammonia per gram at an ammonia concentration of 30 mg/ℓ in the influent and 0.5 mg/ℓ in the effluent has been used. The maximum velocity is 7 bed volumes of water per bed volume of the zeolite per hour. The clinoptilolite is regenerated with 1.2% of NaCl at pH 11.

Activated Carbon Filtration — Four 0.5 m diameter activated columns in series, each with a 1.5 m carbon bed, may be used in either upflow or downflow. The contact time at a maximum flow rate of 2.5 m^3/ hr is 28 minutes. An aeration column filled with Raschig rings is placed between the 2nd and 3rd column. The purpose of the aeration is to prevent anaerobic conditions during the last part of the adsorption process.

Disinfection by Sodium Hypochlorite or Chlorine Dioxide — Final disinfection is provided by addition of sodium hypochlorite to the effluent of the activated carbon columns. Chlorine dioxide can be used as an alternative. The dosage is based on the attainment of residual free chlorine equal to 0.5 mg/ℓ in the effluent of the contact tank after a retention time of 30 minutes.

Preliminary Results of the Lime Process: The first part of the system, the lime process, has been operational since 1977; the other parts of the system are in use only since the beginning of 1979.

Phosphorus and Inorganic Substances — Phosphates were removed quite effectively; especially during summer and autumn the mean concentrations in the effluent were very low (0.05 mg PO_4/ℓ). During the severe winter of 1978/79 the raw water temperature dropped to 10°C and a decrease in removal efficiency was observed: the average phosphate concentration in the effluent increased to 0.15 mg PO_4/ℓ. High degrees of removal of magnesium and of iron were achieved during the tests without iron dosing.

Calcium concentrations in the effluent showed large fluctuations; greater concentrations in the effluent than those in the influent were frequently measured. This is due to frequent overdosing of lime during periods of rapid fluctuation of the influent alkalinity, when it was difficult to maintain a constant pH.

Because of the possibility of higher fluoride concentration in the biological effluent containing wash water from the flue gas of the incineration plant, determination of fluoride was instituted in 1978. The mean fluoride removal was about 30% and the concentration in the effluent of the sludge-blanket reactor became 0.8 mg F/ℓ.

Organic Compounds — Removal of organic matter, as measured by COD, was not as effective as expected. The average removal was only 25% in 1977, for COD values of the effluent of the process equal to 20-30 mg O/ℓ.

Reduction of color-causing substances was also moderate. A positive effect of iron dosing on color improvement was evident: during Fe-dosing color removal increased to about 79%.

Volatile halogenated organic substances and nonpolar organic chlorine were determined occasionally. As expected, no removal of these components by the lime process was detected. The low concentrations of all detected trihalomethanes in the raw secondary effluent are interesting, because these were lower than the mean concentrations in the drinking water of Dordrecht. The concentrations of nonpolar organic chlorine in the biological effluent (1-4 $\mu g/\ell$) are lower than in the Rhine water, which are of the order of 10 $\mu g/\ell$.

Trace Elements — Determinations of concentrations of seven trace elements confirmed the effective removal of heavy metals by the lime process. An exception is an anomaly in the behavior of chromium, its concentration being greater in the effluent than in the influent. The reason was the Cr content of the lime used. In addition, the percentage of As removal was low. Nevertheless, the concentrations of all determined trace elements in the effluent water were well below drinking water standards.

Bacteria and Viruses — The number of bacteria and viruses was determined during three months in 1977 (see Table 4.2). The table shows that bacteria removal was fairly effective. The organism *Pseudomonas aeruginosa* seems to be most resistant to the high lime treatment. Enteroviruses were determined in the influent and effluent water 10 times. Enteroviruses were detected in four samples of the influent and ranged to a maximum of 560 PFU/ℓ. The percentage removal was 35-100%.

Table 4.2: Removal of Microorganisms by High Lime Treatment

| | . . . . . Concentration, 10^3 counts/ml . . . . . | | | | Average |
| | . . . .Influent . . . . | | . . . . Effluent. . . . . | | Efficiency, |
Organism	Minimum	Maximum	Minimum	Maximum	%
Coliphages	1.2	100	0	1.5	97.3
Coliforms	43.000	640.000	25	22.000	98.9
E. coli	380	290.000	3	460	97.0
Ps. aeruginosa	1.100	30.000	8	3.200	94.5
Clostridia	9	630	0.2	19	97.3
Fecal streptococci	1.700	5.100	1.2	160	98.0

Source: NSF/RA-790224

Conclusion: The data on the performance of the lime process confirmed that this process can achieve effective removal of phosphates, microorganisms and heavy metals. The removal of organic compounds was lower than was expected. The reliability of the process was not satisfactory. Particularly a breakthrough of sludge-blanket caused serious problems. Furthermore, due to high lime consumption the costs of the process are relatively high.

Reverse Osmosis System

The principal reasons for the incorporation of reverse osmosis in the Dordrecht pilot plant study were the high efficiency of this system with regard to removal of almost all inorganic, organic and biological constituents and the fact that the reverse osmosis seems to be the best available alternative for elimination of a buildup of refractory pollutants during multiple reuse.

Description of the System: In Figure 4.3 the pilot plant scheme for the reverse-osmosis system is shown.

Figure 4.3: Scheme of Reverse Osmosis System

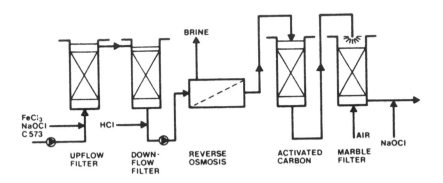

Source: NSF/RA-790224

The pilot plant consists of: dosing pumps for sodium hypochlorite, ferric chloride and polyelectrolyte; an upflow contact filter and a downflow rapid filter; dosing equipment for hydrochloric acid; the reverse-osmosis unit itself; an activated carbon filter; a dry marble filter; and a final dosing pump for sodium hypochlorite.

In the design of the pilot plant installation special attention was given to the following technical aspects:

      (a) keeping membrane fouling to a minimum;
      (b) prevention of biological attack of the membrane;
      (c) assurance of complete removal of ammonia, which
          is only partly rejected by reverse osmosis;
      (d) reduction in content of organic pollutants, including
          low molecular micropollutants, to a minimum;
      (e) prevention of formation of trihalomethane;
      (f) elimination of corrosivity of product water.

Results: *(a) Technological Aspects* — In Table 4.3 the data on flux decline and on salt rejection during 10,000 hours of continuous operation are presented.

Table 4.3: Course of Waterflux and Salt Rejection in Reserve Osmosis

Time	200	6,000	10,000
	. . . . (hours)		
Flux (m³/m² day)	0.56	0.50	0.47
Rejection (%)	97.4	97.9	97.3

Source: NSF/RA-790224

The flux is recalculated to a pressure of 40 bars at 20°C. Rejection is based on conductivity determinations. The salt recovery ratio over the reported period was 60-80%. The flux decline rate is typical for cellulose acetate membranes used to treat secondary effluents and gives good hope that a projected module life of three years may be achieved. The membranes are cleaned every three weeks by depressurization and flushing with foam balls. Once every two months an enzyme product is used. Up till now no sign of membrane abrasion has been observed.

(b) Water Quality Aspects — A summary of data on effluent quality at various stages in the treatment process is presented in Tables 4.4, 4.5 and 4.6. As expected, the percentage rejection of the inorganic constituents is great with exception of those for ammonia and nitrates, for which the removals are 90%. Nearly complete elimination of ammonia is achieved with the marble dry filter.

Also, the data on organic matter and trace elements, presented in Table 4.5, indicate high rejection of all determined constituents. Data on organic micropollutants are summarized in Table 4.6. The table shows that particularly the groups of halogenated aliphatics, benzene, C_{1-2} alkylbenzenes, naphthalene, alkylated naphthalenes, sulfonamides and alkylphenols are removed ineffectively by reverse osmosis. Alkanes, alkylated benzenes with longer side chains, indane and alkylated indanes, organic phosphates, chlorophosphates, phthalates and cyclic hydrocarbons are rejected rather effectively.

By means of activated carbon filtration substantial additional removal of almost all detected micropollutants was achieved with exception of cyclic hydrocarbons.

Table 4.4: Removal of Inorganic Constituents During
the Reverse-Osmosis System

Parameter*	Secondary Effluent	. Reverse Osmosis. .		Effluent Marble Filter
		Feed	Effluent	
Conductivity, μS/cm	1,220	1,220	50	215
Cl⁻	–	161	12	–
SO₄⁼	–	107	2	–
F⁻	0.6	0.5	0.07	0.05
HCO₃⁻	365	357	15	128

(continued)

Table 4.4: (continued)

Parameter*	Secondary Effluent	. Reverse Osmosis .		Effluent Marble Filter
		Feed	Effluent	
pH	7.5	7.5	5.2	7.9
Ca^{++}	102	104	3	43
Mg^{++}	15	14	1	1
Na^+	110	110	3.5	3.5
K^+	17	16	1	1
NH_4^+	–	14.5	1.4	0.18
NO_2^-	1.0	1.0	0.01	0.01
NO_3^-	30	30	3.0	7.3
PO_4^{3-} ortho	15	11	0.07	0.04
SiO_2	25	21	1	5

*units in mg/ℓ unless otherwise stated.

Table 4.5: Removal of Organic Compounds and Trace Elements
During the Reverse Osmosis System

Parameter*	Secondary Effluent	. Reverse Osmosis .		Effluent Marble Filter
		Feed	Effluent	
COD, mg/ℓ	47	32	3	2
DOC, mg/ℓ	14	11	1.7	1.3
As	5	4	0.5	0.5
Cd	1.2	0.4	0.1	0.1
Cr	2.4	1.8	0.5	0.5
Cu	3.0	1.8	0.5	0.5
Hg	0.1	0.1	0.1	0.1
Mo	7	7	2	2
Ni	6.3	6.8	1	1
Pb	9.4	3.3	0.5	0.5
Se	2	2	2	2
Zn	80	40	10	10

*units in μg/ℓ unless otherwise stated.

Source: NSF/RA-790224

Table 4.6: Removal of Organic Micropollutants
During the Reverse Osmosis System

Compounds	Secondary Effluent	Reverse Osmosis		Effluent Marble Filter
		Feed	Effluent	
	. . . . μg/ℓ			
Halogenated aliphatic hydrocarbons	21	8.5	11	1.1
Benzene + C_1 and C_2 alkyl-benzenes	0.3	0.3	0.25	0.1
Sulfonamides	3.3	3.3	3.1	–
Alkylphenols	0.69	0.69	0.31	0.36
Naphthalenes + alkyl-naphthalenes	0.2	0.1	0.05	0.01

(continued)

Table 4.6: (continued)

Compounds	Secondary Effluent	Reverse Osmosis Feed	Reverse Osmosis Effluent	Effluent Marble Filter
	. . . . μg/ℓ			
Hydronaphthalenes	0.12	0.19	0.06	–
Alkanes	0.2	0.9	0.05	0.05
C_{3-8} alkylbenzenes	5.7	3.36	0.76	0.13
Indane + alkylindanes	0.75	0.75	0.05	–
Phosphates + chloro-phosphates	0.5	0.5	0.06	–
Phthalates	10.2	1.7	0.23	0.13
Cyclic hydrocarbons	1.13	1.13	0.11	0.2

Source: NSF/RA-790224

Conclusion: Experience accumulated during the 14 months of operation of the scheme incorporating reverse osmosis shows that this system has a satisfactory reliability and is capable of producing water of high and constant quality with an economically acceptable decline in membrane flux at a constant ratio of salt rejection. Fouling of the membranes can be overcome by an easy and economical cleaning procedure. The analyses of the effluent water indicate that practically all determined chemical parameters meet the current quality standards set for drinking water.

Future Investigations

Future investigations will be focused especially on the comparative study of the water quality produced with both pilot plant systems and drinking water of Dordrecht, which is produced from Rhine water. Special attention will be paid to qualification of health hazard pollutants and to determinations of viruses after concentration by means of a filter adsorption technique.

To evaluate toxicological aspects toxicity tests with amphibian *Xenopus laevis,* which has been started in the beginning of 1979, will be continued and in addition, to test mutagenicity, Ames tests will be carried out with highly concentrated water.

REUSE OF WASTEWATER IN SOUTH AFRICA

The information in this section is from two papers given at Conference I, the first entitled "Reuse of Wastewater in South Africa—Research and Application," by P.E. Odendaal, Water Research Commission, Republic of South Africa and L.R. van Vuuren of the National Institute for Water Research, Republic of South Africa; and the second, "The Reclamation of Industrial/Domestic Wastewater," by L.R. van Vuuren and M.P. Taljard of the City Engineer's Department of Cape Town.

Introduction

In any water stress economy water reuse is one of the obvious first-line approaches in an overall strategy to optimize the utilization of available supplies. The implementation of water reuse over a broad front is no simple matter, however: once reuse has been accepted as a policy objective, the responsible authorities will have to take special steps to create a climate which will be conducive to positive reuse decisions by consumers.

South Africa is a relatively dry country with an average annual rainfall of only 483 mm, compared to 735 mm for the USA and to a world average of 860 mm. In addition, the distribution of rainfall is uneven, varying from 50 mm p.a. on the west coast to 2,500 mm p.a. in the mountains of the south, western and eastern regions. About a third of the country receives an annual rainfall of less than 300 mm.

Within the framework of present knowledge and expertise, it is estimated that South Africa's total water credit, i.e., distributable water supplies, is 33,000 million m^3 per year. Demand is rising rapidly and projections indicate that by the year 2000 the demand will be 30,000 million m^3 per year, only 3,000 million m^3 less than the total quantity of water available.

Measures could be applied, however, to reduce water demand and the following figures are based upon estimates by the Commission of Enquiry into Water Matters:

Savings through improved utilization of irrigation water	1,500 million m^3 p.a.
Savings through water reclamation and reuse	7,200 million m^3 p.a.
Total Reduction in Demand	8,700 million m^3 p.a.

It is important to note that the estimated 7,200 million m^3 p.a. which can be saved by reuse constitutes almost 22% of the country's distributable water supplies. It is evident, therefore, that reuse is destined to play a key role in the South African water economy. This being the case, the question arises as to what policies, incentives and pressures exist in South Africa to promote water reuse.

Promotion of Reuse Through Government Policy

Commission of Enquiry into Water Matters: In 1966 the State President appointed a Commission of Enquiry into Water Matters "to report upon and to submit recommendations on all aspects of water provision and utilization within the Republic of South Africa, as well as the broad planning of policy in this connection."

The Commission tabled its report in Parliament in 1970. With specific reference to reuse, the Commission pointed out that reuse will in future assume an increasingly important role in augmenting the country's limited water resources and considered it essential that at least 50% of the gross water demand by municipalities serving large industrial centers, should be met by the reclamation of effluents. The Commission recommended that:

(1) the Department of Water Affairs, in administering the Water Act (to be discussed further on), place the internal water use by industry and the reclamation of effluents for reuse on a practical footing, first, by issuing the necessary policy directive for the execution of a long-term water plan, and secondly, by defining the administrative procedures and instructions for the planning and erection of water reclamation schemes as integrated parts of the water economy of the areas to be served by them;

(2) in order to promote sewage reclamation as an essential part of water supply on a national basis, consideration be given to subsidizing water reclamation schemes for local authorities where consumption exceeds 1,137 m^3/day (250,000 gpd); and

(3) adequate financial support be given to ensure that research work into water reclamation and the internal reuse of water in industry can be placed on a practical footing and substantially intensified.

The South African Water Act: In implementing its reuse policy, the Government has a powerful tool in the Water Act, which is administered by the Department of Water Affairs. Some of the features of the Act which have impact on water reuse are the following:

(1) For the use of more than 250 m^3 per day on average, or more than 300 m^3 on any one day, a permit is required from the Department of Water Affairs. In granting such permits, the Department has the authority to specify that reuse, recycling and hierarchical use of water should be practiced as far as possible.

(2) Wastewaters must be purified to standards laid down by the South African Bureau of Standards.

(3) Water abstracted from a stream and used for industrial or municipal purposes must be returned to the stream of origin after purification. Before return, the water must be diminished only by essential consumptive use. For instance, evaporation of a tractable wastewater to avoid the expense of purification, or irrigation of inferior land where there is a possibly better form of reuse, would not be ac-

ceptable. This requirement is intended to ensure
the indirect reuse of wastewaters.

(4) Local authorities may use purified sewage effluent
for any approved purpose or discharge it to a public stream. This provision was designed to overcome older legislation which forbade the discharge
of effluent to public streams and also opens the way
for the reuse of sewage effluent.

Reclamation of Purified Effluents in South Africa

Thirty-two percent of the total quantity of sewage effluent produced by 33
major cities, towns and industrial complexes in South Africa is reused for irrigation, power plant cooling and industrial use.

Included in these figures are those for the Pretoria-Witwatersrand-Vereeniging
complex (PWV-complex), the most densely populated and industrialized area in
the country, which produces almost 50% of South Africa's gross national product. This area is under mounting pressure as far as water supply is concerned,
and it is significant to note that the PWV complex reuses 50% of its effluent.

The much higher reuse percentages for the PMV-complex are indicative of the
quantitative control on water supplies, in terms of the Water Act, which are
operative in the area.

Reclamation for Potable Use

The well-known Windhoek reclamation plant is still the only full-scale facility in
the world where sewage effluent is directly reclaimed for potable use. Windhoek
is the capital of South West Africa, a territory which is being administered by
South Africa under a mandate from the old League of Nations. Although the
city, therefore, is not in the Republic of South Africa, the reclamation plant
resulted from research which the NIWR in Pretoria had done in collaboration
with the City Engineer's Department in Windhoek.

In spite of the fact that the original Windhoek plant was commissioned in 1969,
no other reclamation schemes for potable water have subsequently been established in South Africa. The reason is simply one of relative urgency. Windhoek
is situated in a very arid region, and at the time when the reclamation plant was
commissioned, the city could no longer meet its water demands from the available conventional supplies. In South Africa no city has yet reached the same
state of urgency, but in a few areas the economically feasible alternatives are
rapidly being exhausted and South Africa's first operational reclamation plants
for potable water can be expected to appear during the late eighties.

In this realization, South African research into water reclamation for unrestricted
reuse has continued, and in fact intensified, since completion of the Windhoek
project. It should be realized that the situation in Windhoek in two respects
uniquely facilitated the introduction of reclamation: In the first instance, in-

dustrial effluents could be easily segregated, leaving an essentially domestic effluent for reclamation; secondly, the particular siting of the sewage purification facilities allowed the reclamation plant to be integrated with the conventional water purification plant, which meant considerable savings in pumping and piping and enabled the same staff to operate both plants.

For this reason the Windhoek scheme could not serve as a blueprint for potable water reclamation in South Africa, where a high level of industrialization has been achieved and where the planning of reclamation schemes will have to contend with a status quo where sewage purification facilities have not been sited and planned with future reclamation in mind.

South African research relating to water reclamation has mainly been associated with the Windhoek plant and with four pilot plants, two in Pretoria and two in Cape Town, as indicated in Table 4.7. The main problems receiving attention are discussed below.

Table 4.7: Plants Featured South African Research on Water Reclamation

Plant	Capacity, m^3/day
Windhoek	5,400
Stander experimental plant (Daspoort, Pretoria)	4,500
NIWR pilot plant (Daspoort, Pretoria)	80
Athlone pilot plant (Cape Town)	300
Cape Flats experimental plant	4,500

Source: NSF/RA-790224

Health Aspects: If the large-scale reclamation of sewage effluent for potable use is to become a reality in South Africa, the Department of Health with whom the final clearance will rest, must obviously be satisfied that health requirements will be met. A strong research effort is, therefore, being maintained to provide the scientific data which can guide the Department in its decision making. The lines of investigation have been the following:

(1) *Monitoring of Plant Performances* — One of the conditions on which the health authorities approved the direct reclamation of sewage effluent for potable use in Windhoek, was that a strict quality surveillance program should be maintained. Virological surveillance is being done independently by the South African Institute for Medical Research (SAIMR) and the National Institute for Water Research (NIWR); bacteriological surveillance by the SAIMR, NIWR, Windhoek Municipality and the Department of Water Affairs. The results of the different laboratories generally correlated well and thus far the quality of the final water has always conformed to standards for drinking water (USPHS, WHO and the South African Bureau of Standards). Viruses have not been isolated from any final water sample.

The SAIMR, NIWR, National Institute for Virology, Rand Water Board, and the Pretoria Municipality are all collaborating in the bacteriological and virological monitoring of the Stander reclamation plant in Pretoria. In this case too, the final water consistently conformed to international standards for public water supplies.

(2) *Epidemiological Surveys* — Epidemiological studies by the SAIMR have now been proceeding for a number of years in the Windhoek municipal area. Thus far the studies have indicated that disease patterns in the area show no relation to the quality of the water supply. Data will be accumulated for several years and computer stored for analysis.

Projections indicate that water reclamation for potable use, may well have to be introduced in the Cape Town area in the late eighties. For this reason, it is considered a matter of urgency that epidemiological studies commence as soon as possible to establish health patterns for communities that may receive reclaimed water. Comparative data would be required for such communities before and after the introduction of reuse, and comparisons should also be drawn with other communites that are supplied from conventional sources only. Negotiations are now proceeding whereby such studies will be undertaken by the Department of Community Health at the University of Cape Town.

(3) *The Occurrence and Fate of Micropollutants* — A twofold study was carried out by the NIWR on the occurrence of organics in the feed and final water of the Stander plant and on the efficacy of a pilot plant to remove inoculated toxic organic compounds.

In the feed to the Stander plant, a total of ten polynuclear aromatic hydrocarbons were detected in the ng/ℓ range, while the final water contained only two of these compounds (pyrene and fluoranthene), neither of which have toxicological importance. The percentage reduction of organic material through the plant was 84%. The total number of chromatogram peaks in the final water was almost the same as in the feedwater, but a marked change had taken place in the distribution of the peaks. The final water mainly contained peaks (more than 61%) in the concentration range 10-100 ng/ℓ, whereas the peaks in the feedwater were mostly (65%) in the range of 100-1,000 ng/ℓ.

Eighteen known toxic compounds were inoculated in rather large concentrations (up to 4.3 mg/ℓ) into the feedwater of the pilot reclamation plant. The plant reduced the toxicants by more than 99.9% to values ranging from 0 to 6 μg/ℓ in the final water.

(4) *Toxicological Studies* — In an experiment which was run over a period of 25 months, the National Research Institute for Nutritional Diseases of the South African Medical Research Council and the NIWR subjected four different waters (reclaimed water from the Stander plant, humus tank effluent, distilled water, and tap water) to biological assaying, using rats. In addition spent and new active carbons were also included in the diets of the rats. During the experi-

mental period a careful note of the health behavior and sexual patterns of the rats was kept. All were autopsied and the liver, kidneys, lungs, heart, spleen, pancreas, gonads, esophagus, stomach, intestine and any apparently abnormal tissues were fixed, stained and microscopically examined. Results indicate that the feedwater to the reclamation plant (humus tank effluent) was the only water which exerted obvious deleterious effects on the test animals. No indication of the presence of carcinogens in reclaimed water was detected in this study. The lifelong ingestion of spent active carbon appeared to be without ill effects on the health of the rats, which substantiated results achieved in an earlier study.

The Ames *Salmonella* auxotroph test for the detection of mutagenic substances in water is now being applied by the NIWR.

(5) *Development of Biomonitoring Systems* — Research by the NIWR on the development of biomonitoring systems which can be used at water reclamation and conventional purification plants, has thus far concentrated on the respiratory performance of the protozoan *Tetrahymena pyriformis* in the presence of toxicants and the effect of toxicants on fish movement patterns and breathing rates.

(6) *Monitoring the Chemical and Biological Quality of Water Supplies* — On behalf of the South African Department of Health, the NIWR is maintaining a monitoring program on the chemical and microbiological quality of various waters, including conventional drinking-water supplies, reclaimed water, purified effluents, rivers, dams and boreholes in the PWV-complex.

A list of 11 compounds classified by an expert committee of WHO as being very toxic and frequently present in water, was modified from various publications, and adapted to South African conditions by the NIWR. This list includes the trihalomethanes and other organohalogens, chlorophenols and chlorinated and polynuclear hydrocarbons. Based on toxicity data and limits set elsewhere (e.g. by the U.S. EPA), limits of detection were established: 1 μg/ℓ for the chlorophenols and volatile organohalogens, and 0.1 μg/ℓ for the others.

Results indicated that the waters were generally of excellent quality. No polynuclear aromatics occurred above the minimum limits, with only traces of fluoranthene ($<$0.05 μg/ℓ). Maximum values for organohalogens were 40 μg/ℓ, which is below the limit of 100 μg/ℓ suggested by EPA. Chlorophenols were found in the range 1-10 μg/ℓ. Only one water source (Hartebeespoort Dam) receiving heavy inflows of secondary effluent and serving several small communities near Pretoria, contains chlorinated hydrocarbons in the range 0.1 to 1 μg/ℓ (EPA limit is 4 μg/ℓ).

Segregation of Industrial Effluents: In view of the world-wide controversy over the presence and possible deleterious effects of certain organic compounds in water supplies, it seems only logical to have a closer look at the sources of these compounds. It is likely that in most instances refractory organics will originate from a few point sources only. If these could be traced and eliminated at source by separate treatment or containment, it would make a tremendous contribution towards safeguarding the quality of receiving waters which serve as raw water supply for conventional purification plants. In cases where the direct reclamation of sewage effluent for potable use is under consideration, it would also remove much of the misgivings, whether justified or not, which may still exist about health aspects. The application of this philosophy was in fact a key factor which facilitated the introduction of reclamation for potable use in Windhoek, in that industrial effluents were segregated from the 'catchment' for the reclamation plant.

As mentioned previously, it is likely that Cape Town will have to reclaim water for potable use in the late eighties. In its planning for the future, the city has already taken steps to segregate industrial effluents from the sewage flow which could eventually be reclaimed for potable use. Two pilot plants are being operated in the area: one at the Athlone sewage works which receives most of the industrial effluents, and where investigations are carried out on the reclamation of the effluent for industrial use; the other pilot plant is on the Cape Flats where a new sewage works is under construction which will treat predominantly domestic sewage. The Cape Flats pilot is used to investigate reclamation for unrestricted reuse.

The segregation of industrial effluents as achieved in Windhoek and Cape Town may not always be feasible in other situations. Should reclamation for potable use be contemplated in such instances, catchment quality control should be practiced for the sewerage networks involved, as a supplement to analytical monitoring and toxicological testing. Where sources of hazardous compounds are identified, they should be treated or contained on site or transported to sites reserved for the treatment and disposal of hazardous wastes. In a project which is now under consideration, it is proposed that a detailed analytical survey be made of industrial discharges to the sewerage system which serves the Daspoort sewage works in Pretoria, which supplies the feedwater to the Stander reclamation plant.

Further Studies

The National Institute for Water Research (NIWR) has extended its research on reclamation technology to cover integrated physical-chemical and biological processes to provide for the integration of wastewater treatment and reclamation into the engineering discipline.

Pilot plant studies at Pretoria using combined physical-chemical-biological methods for the renovation of wastewater mainly of domestic origin and results obtained from a second pilot-scale study (Athlone plant) with wastewater containing a higher proportion of industrial effluents will be briefly discussed below.

Improvements Made at Windhoek Plant: For unrestricted reuse of wastewater, as in the case of the City of Windhoek, it was regarded as essential that the wastewater should be predominantly domestic in origin as already discussed. Nitrogenous compounds from the local abattoir and meat-packing industries were duly separated before the secondary effluent, which was also passed through a series of algae maturation ponds, was considered amenable to advanced treatment. In the long run, however, the trickling filters and algae maturation ponds proved to be unreliable for securing consistently low ammonia residuals which, in turn, were essential for effective disinfection. High lime treatment with partial ammonia stripping was subsequently implemented to ensure better utilization of the Windhoek reclamation facilities.

Daspoort Plant: A similar water reclamation plant at Daspoort served as a research and demonstration facility for reclamation of effluents derived initially from trickling filters and subsequently from activated sludge. In the case of the trickling filters, a balancing and quality equalization basin was found highly advantageous for improved ammonia removal and fail safe disinfection control. The use of activated sludge effluents as opposed to trickling filter effluents was found to be much superior as an intake source for reclamation purposes in terms of smaller quality fluctuations, reduced ammonia and residual COD.

Integrated Physical-Chemical-Biological Treatment at Pretoria Plant

The NIWR has developed a 60 m^3/day pilot plant for the treatment of screened raw sewage with a relatively low industrial effluent component. This facility was flexibly designed to enable various process configurations and operational modes to be compared. Extensive studies with high lime treatment and dissolved air flotation followed by biological treatment (LFB process) have been made. More recent studies have included the use of ferric chloride as primary coagulant and partial denitrification with a view to cutting down on the chemical and maintenance costs experienced in high lime treatment.

A flow diagram of the modified LFB plant is shown in Figure 4.4 and the individual process units are briefly described below. The process stages may be classified into biological, chemical and polishing stages. The performance of the biological and chemical units is discussed in greater detail because of their overriding importance in the process as a whole.

Denitrification Reactor: Raw screened sewage enters a reactor vessel of 16 m^3 capacity at a rate of 40 ℓ/min. Recycled streams from several succeeding stages are returned to the reactor. These include fully nitrified effluent together with chemical organic sludge and waste activated sludge. The recycled sludges serve as a source of carbon and for seeding of organisms for the purpose of partial biological denitrification. The recycle rate of nitrified effluent affects the extent to which denitrification is achieved. A ratio of 1:1 effectively reduces final nitrate to about 12 mg/ℓ as N. Limited runs with a recycle ratio of 1.5:1 confirmed that the nitrate could be controlled at less than 8 mg/ℓ.

Chemical Clarifier: Ferric chloride is dosed to the blended streams of the reactor outflow and lime added to control pH. Sludge is drawn continuously from the chemical clarifier (24 ℓ/min) and split into three equal streams of which one is returned to the reactor unit, one to the chemical flocculation tank and one wasted to the thickener prior to anaerobic digestion. The waste

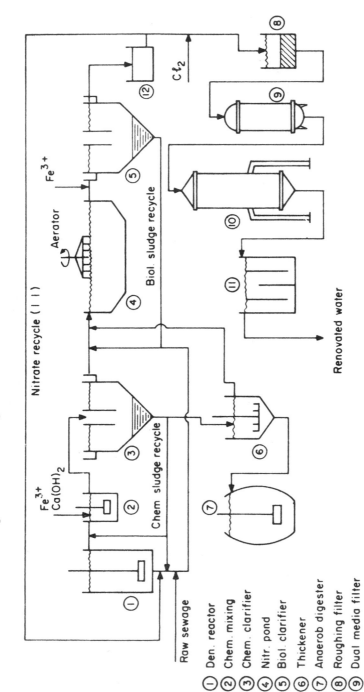

Figure 4.4: Flow Diagram of Modified LFB Pilot Plant (60 kl/d)

① Den. reactor
② Chem. mixing
③ Chem. clarifier
④ Nitr. pond
⑤ Biol. clarifier
⑥ Thickener
⑦ Anaerob digester
⑧ Roughing filter
⑨ Dual media filter
⑩ Act. carbon
⑪ Chlorination
⑫ Flow division

Source: NSF/RA-790224

sludge serves as a reserve carbon source during periods of weak sewage strength. Nighttime flows in particular are low in organic content and are best treated by not wasting the chemical organic sludge.

Ferric chloride dosages (as $FeCl_3$) based on the inflow rate of raw sewage can be cut from an initial 160 mg/ℓ to 75 mg/ℓ as a result of continuous recycling of chemical sludge. Low turbidity (<2.0 JTU) in the effluent from the chemical clarifier is the criterion used which also coincides with efficient phosphate removal.

Nitrification Pond: An aeration pond and secondary clarifier serve as an activated sludge process stage. Addition of a further dosage of ferric chloride (10 mg/ℓ) enhances the settleability of the activated sludge and secures a low effluent turbidity for further polishing.

The results reported here are representative of a sludge age of 15 days with an MLSS and VSS corresponding to about 1,100 and 600 mg/ℓ respectively. These results confirm that nitrification was highly efficient with low residual COD and ammonia levels.

The aeration pond was designed for a nominal retention of 7½ hours, based on a raw intake flow of 130 m^3/d during earlier runs with the high lime treatment. This flow had to be reduced to 60 m^3/d to allow for recycle and hydraulic limitations of the clarifiers whereby the nominal retention in the aeration basin was inadvertently increased to about 16 hours.

Polishing Process Units: The effluent from the activated sludge clarifier with a turbidity of less than 2 JTU, is prechlorinated and passed through a roughing filter, followed by a dual media filter (turbidity <0.6). The filtered effluent is finally polished by means of a single active carbon packed column and free residual chlorination is applied for final disinfection. In view of the low demand and low organic carbon content the formation of halogenated hydrocarbons is expected to be minimized.

Operational Results (Pretoria)

Chemical Quality: The improvement in quality through the chemical-biological stages is illustrated in Figure 4.5. The effluent from the activated sludge stage was allowed through the polishing units only during special runs for the purpose of microbiological monitoring and final quality assessment. A typical quality of the product water achieved during these runs is shown in Table 4.8.

The effluent from the activated sludge clarifier was found to be consistently of a very high average quality in terms of COD (<30 mg/ℓ), NH_3 (0.2 mg/ℓ as N) and soluble phosphate (<0.2 mg/ℓ as P). This quality proved to be excellent for further polishing in that the chlorine demand for complete disinfection was extremely low (<3 mg/ℓ). This finding is considered to be of great significance in that multiple safety barriers can be created by successive chlorination points without extravagant costs. In this particular study the two chlorina-

Figure 4.5: Quality Improvement Through Chemical and
Biological Stages

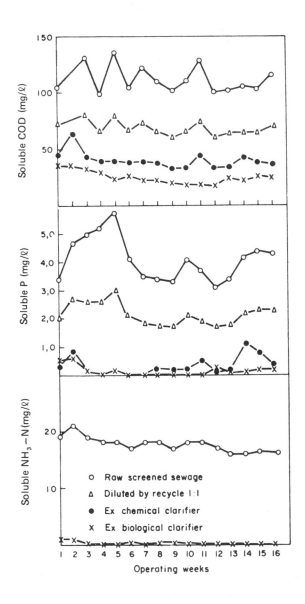

Source: NSF/RA-790224

Table 4.8: Quality of Raw and Final Product Water

Quality Parameter	Raw Screened Sewage	Final
Turbidity (JTU)	8	<0.6
Color (Hazen)	120	8
pH	7.3	7.8
Electrical conductivity, mS/m	69	67
Na, mg/ℓ	45	40
K, mg/ℓ	12	10
Ca, mg/ℓ	38	55
Mg, mg/ℓ	20	22
TKN, mg/ℓ	28	<0.5
NH_3-N, mg/ℓ	18	<0.2
NO_3 + NO_2, mg/ℓ	<1	11.0
Si, mg/ℓ	8	6
SO_4, mg/ℓ	70	35
Total-P, mg/ℓ	6.0	<0.2
Ortho-P, mg/ℓ	4.1	<0.2
Cl, mg/ℓ	50	100
Total alkalinity (as $CaCO_3$), mg/ℓ	220	102
COD, mg/ℓ	350	<10
LAS, μg/ℓ	3,600	620
Al, μg/ℓ	120	<100
B, μg/ℓ	300	100
Phenol, μg/ℓ	<10	<10
F, μg/ℓ	<100	<100
Fe, μg/ℓ	470	<100

Source: NSF/RA-790224

tion points (total of 9 mg/ℓ) proved most satisfactory for disinfection control purposes. The low COD prior to active carbon polishing is also indicative of lower active carbon requirements as compared with effluents from trickling filter plants.

The low phosphate of less than 0.2 mg/ℓ as P which was consistently achieved is also of great significance from a pollution control viewpoint.

Microbiological Quality: The effluent at various stages of processing was monitored weekly for eight consecutive weeks. Owing to the recycling of biomass to the chemical clarifier, this unit process did not achieve any dramatic removal of microorganisms. A marked improvement was, however, effected in the secondary biological clarifier where up to two logs in total plate count, coliforms and coliphage were recorded. By prechlorination coliphage was completely absent during all tests and TPC and coliforms were reduced to extremely low values. After active carbon polishing a two log increase in TPC was recorded, evidently as a result of biological growth on the media, but this was effectively reduced to zero order levels by final chlorination.

Denitrification: A balance of NO_3 plus NO_2 relating to the reactor influent and the chemical clarifier effluent showed virtually complete denitrification ($>$90%) with an average residual nitrate of 0.6 mg/ℓ as N. The reduction of total dissolved nitrogen was 58% of which 47.5% was associated with the denitrification/chemical stages and 10.5% with the activated sludge process state. The polishing stages did not contribute significantly to overall nitrogen reduction.

The rate of denitrification was calculated at 1.1 mg N per gram VSS per hour. The residual nitrate out of the reactor was however found to be critically dependent on the VSS confirming a value in excess of 1,000 mg/ℓ for efficient denitrification. The reactor unit has not as yet been optimized in terms of minimum retention and flow regime. A plug flow arrangement is expected to improve its performance further.

The rate of soluble COD to NO_3-N reduction in the reactor unit was on the order of 4.7. An overall reduction of soluble COD of about 77% was achieved up to the activated sludge stage, more than 60% of which was due to the denitrification/chemical stages. On the basis of a total COD of 350 mg/ℓ entering the plant the overall reduction by chemical and biological treatment exceeded 90%.

Nitrification was readily accomplished in the aeration pond with a biomass corresponding to an MLSS and VSS of about 1,000 and 600 mg/ℓ respectively. The activated sludge showed excellent settling properties on account of a further dosage of ferric chloride (10 mg/ℓ) which evidently also ensured phosphate residuals of less than 0.2 mg/ℓ as P.

Chemical-Biological Sludge: The combined chemical-biological and raw organic sludges drawn from the chemical clarifier served the following important functions:

(1) A source of organic carbon and seeding of microorganisms for denitrification.

(2) Improved settleability and reduced ferric chloride dosage, apparently as a result of sludge recycle.

The settleability of the sludge in the chemical clarifier was also significantly improved by ferric chloride dosage and upflow velocities exceeding 2 m/hr could readily be achieved in both clarifiers.

Complementary laboratory-scale studies were conducted in order to assess the stability of phosphate in the sludge wasted from the chemical clarifier. Samples of thickened sludge were stored under anaerobic conditions in the laboratory and the release of P, NH_3 and COD monitored with time. After 5 days no release of P could be detected whereas an increase of both NH_3 and dissolved COD confirmed anaerobic biodegradation.

In subsequent tests sludge samples representative of varying ferric chloride dosages were stored for periods of up to two months. Phosphate release into the supernatant was minimal (<1 mg/ℓ) and could be roughly correlated with the iron content of the sludges. The stability of the phosphate bonded sludge is most encouraging in relation to phosphate release in the case of pure biological phosphate bearing sludges. These studies are currently being extended to detailed pilot-scale evaluation which will, amongst others, incorporate criteria for thickening and sludge stabilization.

Athlone Pilot Plant

Based on the original development of the LFB process, a second pilot plant (300 m^3/d) was constructed for the reclamation of secondary effluent derived from the Athlone sewage works near Cape Town. This particular sewage works receives a stronger sewage which includes wastewaters of industrial origin. Domestic effluents from this area are partially diverted to a separate sewage works for the purpose of eventual unrestricted reuse.

The Athlone works incorporates the use of trickling filters which produce a final effluent of poor quality as a result of overloading. Nitrification and carbonaceous oxidation are accordingly low as reflected by residual COD values in the final effluent of 220 mg/ℓ, ammonia of 36 mg/ℓ as N and nitrate below 1 mg/ℓ on the average. The AWT pilot plant was designed to investigate the potential reuse of this quality effluent for selected industries such as textiles.

The Athlone pilot plant provides high lime treatment and partial ammonia stripping as pretreatment stages. This is followed by a surface aerated activated sludge process with ferric chloride dosage to improve secondary clarification. The polishing units comprise prechlorination, gravity filtration, active carbon adsorption and free residual chlorination.

Chemical and Microbiological Results: The Athlone AWT plant was commissioned in 1976 and has been in intermittent operation for periods of up to 3 months. A great deal of effort was devoted to the optimization and refinement of individual process units particularly high lime dosage control, ammonia stripping and gravity filtration. As in the case of the Pretoria plant, extremely low ammonia levels could be maintained with efficient disinfection control.

Running Costs

The cost of chemicals based on bulk supply prices (1979) and the electrical power costs for aeration, pumping and ammonia stripping for both pilot plants are compared in Table 4.9 (1 SA cent equals 1.15 U.S. cents).

It should be noted that the total cost for chemicals and electricity for the Athlone plant is about double that for the Pretoria plant. This is essentially due to high lime, carbon dioxide and active carbon requirements and also the need for ammonia stripping in the case of the Athlone plant.

Discussion

Operation of the two separate AWT pilot plants based on integrated physical-

Table 4.9: Running Cost for Integrated Systems
(Electrical and Chemicals only)

Item	Pretoria Plant ..... 60 m³/day ...... Price Delivered ¢/kg	Dosage mg/ℓ	Cost ¢/m³	Athlone Plant ......300 m³/day ...... Price Delivered ¢/kg	Dosage mg/ℓ	Cost ¢/m³
Ferric chloride (as 100% FeCl₃)	12.2	85	1.04	36.8	37	1.37
Lime [as Ca(OH)₂]	4.5	70	0.32	5.0	482	2.41
Polyelectrolyte	265	0.75	0.20	275	1.7	0.45
Chlorine	44	9	0.40	53	11.2	0.59
Carbon dioxide	—	—	—	85	6.4	0.55
Activated carbon	—	—	4.00*	—	—	6.00**
Total Chemicals			5.96			11.37
Power	2.1 ¢/kWh		0.72***	2.76 ¢/kWh		2.40†
Total Chemical and Electrical			6.68			13.77

*Projected from full-scale reclamation plant.
**Projected from full-scale reclamation plant and higher intractable organic load.
***Projected from full-scale activated sludge plant.
†Projected from full-scale activated sludge plant and including ammonia stripping.

Source: NSF/RA-790224

chemical-biological principles have confirmed several distinct advantages both from a pollution control and water reclamation point of view:

Nitrate reduction could be achieved by partial ammonia stripping in the case of the Athlone plant and partial denitrification without addition of an external energy source in the case of the Pretoria plant. In both cases phosphate could be removed to acceptably low residuals.

Chemical pretreatment consistently ensured efficient nitrification and carbonaceous oxidation. This had a beneficial effect on disinfection control and active carbon utilization. Aeration energy and retention time in the aeration basin have not been optimized during these studies but indications are that much lower requirements compared with conventional activated sludge are achievable. Both plants performed satisfactorily with a nominal retention of 7½ hours and sludge age of 15 to 25 days. In the case of the Athlone plant a 25 day sludge age resulted in an MLSS concentration of between 500 and 1,500 mg/ℓ. Values of less than 100 mg/ℓ MLSS were occasionally recorded without loss of nitrification efficiency.

For the reclamation of sewage contaminated with industrial effluents, the integrated approach offers distinct advantages in that the activated sludge process stage is protected by chemical pretreatment. The use of ferric chloride as primary coagulant ensures less operational control problems than high lime treatment and from a cost point of view was found to be more favorable. An increase in total dissolved solids with associated hardness should however be weighed against these advantages.

Conversion of the high lime process to a ferric chloride coagulation system at the Pretoria plant has been highly successful and is also being considered for Athlone.

Conclusions

The two pilot-scale studies reported herein have confirmed the suitability of integrated chemical-biological systems for the reclamation of wastewaters of varying quality. Effluents containing an appreciable proportion of industrial contaminants could be rendered more amenable to biological oxidation by chemical pretreatment. Both lime treatment and ferric chloride have been used successfully but the latter coagulant offers the advantage of partial biological denitrification, better operational control and lower treatment costs.

SINGAPORE DEMONSTRATION FOR POSSIBLE POTABLE REUSE OF WASTEWATER

> The material in this section is from a report entitled *Water Reuse Highlights, A Summary Volume of Waste-Water Reclamation and Reuse Information (NITIS PB-289 386)*, prepared by the American Water Works Association Research Foundation for the Office of Water Research and Technology of the U.S. Department of the Interior, January 1978.

The City of Singapore, with an area of 225 square miles and a population of 2.25 million, is one of the more densely populated areas in the world. Insufficient water supply has led the Public Utilities Board to investigate water recycling and reuse.

In the mid-1960s, the Jurong Industrial Estate was constructed with 5.4 mgd of reclaimed wastewater being used in paper and textile manufacturing as well as for rinsing and cooling purposes with the user costs in the range of $0.076 to $0.24 per 1,000 gallons. Secondary effluent from the nearby Ulu Pandan Plant receives prechlorination, dual media filtration, cascade aeration and post-chlorination before reuse by the industries, or in irrigating public parks and roadway landscaping. No use is made of the water in vegetable gardens or for watering livestock.

In June of 1971, six high rise residential apartments were selected for a dual plumbing system and the use of Jurong reclaimed wastewater for toilet flushing. Visible pipes are colored yellow with the only complaint from users being slight foaming when flushing or odors after long periods of stagnation. Heavier chlorine doses have combated the problem. The acceptance and success of the pilot work has led the government to extend the program to an additional 4,000 apartments.

It became apparent that a higher quality effluent would foster even more reuse. A 100,000 gpd AWT plant was designed by Camp, Dresser & McKee in 1972, constructed in 1973 and placed in operation in Sept. 1974.

Secondary effluent undergoes chemical treatment, ammonia stripping, filtration, carbon adsorption and demineralization by three methods and disinfection with chlorine or ozone. Effluent quality and removal characteristics are shown in Table 4.10.

Table 4.10: Singapore AWT Demonstration Plant Results

Parameter	Secondary Effl Range, mg/ℓ	AWT Effl Range, mg/ℓ	Avg Removal Range %
Alkalinity	190–340	30–116	80
Turbidity	3–750	0.5–4.8	93
SS	16–535	0.4–7.2	95
BOD_5	8–58	0.2–4.6	95
COD	47–645	2–29	89
TOC	9–170	2–24	70
PO_4-P	2–15	0.01–1.65	92
TKN	16–46	0–6.4	93
NH_3-N	15–44	0–5.6	94
NO_2-N	0–0.35	0–0.08	85
LAS	0.14–1.9	0–0.78	85
Fe	0–1.64	0–0.09	95
Zn	0–0.6	0–1.6	50

Source: NTIS PB-289 386

The demo plant is being used to determine the feasibility of treating wastewater to potable water standards within practical economic constraints.

Overall treatment reliability has been demonstrated with the RO process proving superior to the electrodialysis and ion-exchange methods for demineralization.

Virus recovery by the University of Singapore has been negative but this is not to imply their absence because new concentration techniques are needed. Fish bioassays are being performed to determine organic uptake in selected organs.

Based on operational data developed to date, it was the consultants' opinion that reuse could provide a viable means for the Government to augment the water supply.

Three Case Studies

THE DALLAS STUDY

The information in this section is based on *Wastewater Characterization and Process Reliability for Potable Wastewater Reclamation* (EPA Report 600/2-77-210) prepared by A.C. Petrasek, Jr. of Texas A & M University for Dallas Water Utilities under the sponsorship of the EPA Office of Research and Development, Municipal Environmental Research Laboratory, November 1977.

The study described here was undertaken to evaluate the performance and reliability of an advanced wastewater treatment system designed to produce an effluent suitable for potable reuse.

Introduction

The city of Dallas in north central Texas is situated in the upper Trinity River Watershed. This region must be classified as naturally water deficient; in fact, there is only one natural lake in the whole state of Texas. In the upper Trinity River Basin, average annual precipitation ranges from about 40 inches per year in the eastern portions to 20 inches per year in the westerly sections. In general, average annual precipitation and evaporation rates are about equal, and drought periods in excess of 60 days are not uncommon. These factors combine to make water a very valuable resource in north central Texas.

The city of Dallas derives its drinking water supply from an extensive reservoir network and estimates indicate that an adequate supply of freshwater exists to meet demands anticipated to the year 1995. The water supply is derived from six reservoirs on three watersheds, with estimated safe yields for the year 2020 indicated in Table 5.1.

Table 5.1: Summary of Existing Water Supply for the Year 2020

Reservoir and Basin	. . Estimated Safe Yield. .	
	(mgd)	(m³/day)
Trinity River Basin		
Lewisville (Garza-Little Elm)	86.8	328,573
Grapevine	10.0	37,854
Ray Hubbard	55.4	209,711
Lavon	10.0	37,854
Return flows	41.3	156,337
Sabine River Basin		
Tawakoni	162.8	616,263
Neches River Basin		
Palestine	102.0	386,111
Total available supply	468.3	1,772,703

Source: EPA-600/2-77-210

As early as 1955 Dallas seriously evaluated the possibility of an indirect wastewater reuse as an alternate supply of drinking water. With respect to total water resources management in the upper Trinity River Basin, indirect but intentional wastewater reuse is of considerable importance to the city of Dallas. Both the Bachman and the Elm Fork Water Purification Plants withdraw water from the Elm Fork of the Trinity River. Estimated water supply for the year 2020 includes 328,573 m^3/day (86.8 mgd) from Garza-Little Elm Reservoir; 37,854 m^3/day (10.1 mgd) from Grapevine Reservoir; and 156,337 m^3/day (41.3 mgd) in return flows. The return flows are composed exclusively of wastewater effluents discharged approximately 33 km (20 mi) upstream from the water plant intake structures. The return flows constitute 30% of the 522,764 m^3/day (138.1 mgd) that will be used as a source of drinking water, and represent a valuable water resource. However, travel time from the point of discharge to the most distant intake structure is less than one day, allowing little time for significant natural purification to occur. Under these circumstances, Dallas has considerable interest in water and wastewater treatment technology since it is imperative that the public health be safeguarded.

Bearing in mind the occasional shortages of rainfall and the consequences of a prolonged drought, and knowing also that new sources of supply are disappearing rapidly, Dallas has felt for some years that the building of new reservoirs on streams to augment the potable water supply would become virtually impossible. The fact that eastern cities in particular have been able to produce potable, palatable waters from rivers that have been increasingly polluted has led to consideration that some day the actual recycle of wastewater, properly treated, may actually be a means of survival in the semiarid Southwest and West.

Dallas has for several years pursued studies of wastewater and water treatment methods that might lead to the production of potable water completely acceptable for all uses. Because there are technological, legal, and esthetic considerations to be satisfied, Dallas has followed a cautious policy that more must be learned about constituents of any water proposed for reuse, the three large areas still relatively unsatisfied being viruses, heavy metals, and organics. Any or all of these may be found to some degree in recycled waters, and enough work must be done to satisfy all parties that no risk exists to either health or comfort from the prolonged use of such waters. Dallas will want to know that the most stringent standards can be met before proposing recycle.

Background of the Dallas Program

As a result of the drought in 1955 and the consideration then of using the heavily polluted West Fork of the Trinity, the present indirect use of upstream effluents, however minor, and the economics dictating that maximal amounts of wastewaters be salvaged if practical, the Dallas Water Utilities have pursued an active, viable wastewater reuse program since June 1970.

The Demonstration Plant of the Dallas Water Reclamation Research Center was built and brought on-line in late July 1969. Equipment check-out and/or modification consumed at least nine months, and the facility was in service for almost a year before the staff considered it to be truly operational. Additionally, a laboratory and administration building was constructed to provide laboratory capabilities for the research program and office space for several different Water Utilities Department activities. The laboratory facilities were occupied in the spring of 1971.

Grants for the construction of the laboratory, administration building and demonstration plant were made by the EPA and the City of Dallas. The EPA and the city also shared the cost of a Research Center study on the removal of metals and viruses through three different advanced wastewater treatment sequences.

Description of Facilities

City of Dallas Collection System: The sanitary sewer collection system serving Dallas consists of 5,074.005 km (3,136.734 mi) of gravity mains. The best available estimates indicate that the total length of laterals is between one and two times the length of the gravity mains, indicating a total collection system length between 10,000 and 15,000 km (6,215 and 9,323 mi). The city has no combined sewers.

In addition to the normal domestic wastes discharged to the collection system, the city has significant contributions from industrial and commercial establishments. During fiscal year 1974 the industrial discharges represented 12.1% of the total flow received at the Central Plant, or 21.93×10^6 m^3 (5.794×10^9 gal) per year. The 221 significant industries monitored by the Water Utilities Department discharged a total of 1.70×10^7 kg of BOD$_5$ (3.7396×10^7 lb) and 1.375×10^7 kg (3.0263×10^7 lb) of total suspended solids (TSS) to the collection system. When expressed in terms of concentration, the BOD$_5$ and TSS of the industrial discharges are 773 mg/ℓ and 626 mg/ℓ, respectively. The BOD$_5$ discharge represents 37.7% of the total load entering the Central Plant, while the industrial TSS discharges represent 30.7% of the total TSS load.

The activities of commercial establishments, including restaurants, wholesale food preparation facilities, and service facilities (principally car washes), have substantial impact on wastewater characteristics. The predominant effect of commercial activities is to increase the organic and solids loadings; however, certain of the service activities (car washing) can have appreciable impact on metals concentrations.

The concentrations of certain metals in the influents of the Dallas and White Rock plants are given in Table 5.2. The column headed "Combined" is a calculated, flow-weighted concentration for all wastewaters arriving at the Central Plant which comprises both the Dallas and White Rock plants. Most of the industrial waste discharges enter the Dallas sewage treatment plant, and for this reason the wastewaters entering the White Rock plant are more suitable for wastewater reuse studies.

Table 5.2: Influent Metals Concentrations for Fiscal Year 1975

| | . . . . Sewage Treatment Plants . . . . | | |
| Metal | Dallas | White Rock | Combined |
	. . . . .Concentration, mg/ℓ		
Arsenic	0.00474	0.02003	0.0164
Barium	0.660	0.700	0.691
Boron	0.507	0.387	0.416
Cadmium	0.035	0.016	0.0205
Chromium	0.345	0.114	0.169
Copper	0.234	0.142	0.164
Lead	0.443	0.193	0.252
Manganese	0.096	0.080	0.084
Mercury	0.00159	0.00125	0.001331
Nickel	0.210	0.088	0.117
Selenium	—	—	—
Silver	0.0170	0.0155	0.0159
Zinc	0.580	0.227	0.311

Source: EPA-600/2-77-210

Dallas Sewage Treatment Plant: The Dallas STP is the oldest wastewater treatment facility operated by the City of Dallas. This single-stage, standard-rate, trickling-filter facility consists of 4 bar screens and grit channels, 24 Imhoff tanks which are operated as primary clarifiers, 2 rectangular primary clarifiers, 16 standard-rate trickling filters which are 53 meters (174 feet) in diameter, and 3 final clarifiers.

White Rock Sewage Treatment Plant: The White Rock STP is a two-stage, high-rate trickling-filter facility without intermediate clarification. The plant consists of 2 bar screens and grit channels, 6 rectangular primary clarifiers, 4 first-stage, high-rate trickling filters, 8 second-stage, high-rate trickling filters, and 4 rectangular final clarifiers. All trickling filters are 53 meters (174 feet) in diameter, and contain a maximum of 2.286 meters (7.5 feet) of media.

Tertiary Treatment Complex: Under normal flow conditions the effluents from both the Dallas and White Rock facilities will be discharged to the tertiary treatment complex prior to discharge into the Trinity River. The tertiary complex consists of 12 completely-mixed, activated sludge aeration basins and 12 final clarifiers, followed by 14 mixed-media gravity filters. This facility was scheduled to come on-line during the fall of 1976, and pilot plant research indicates that considerable improvement in water quality in the Trinity River can be anticipated.

Demonstration Plant: The Demonstration Plant of the Dallas Water Reclamation Research Center is located with the White Rock Sewage Treatment Plant at the City of Dallas' Central Wastewater Treatment Facility. The Central Plant actually consists of the three treatment facilities described above, two of which are trickling-filter plants. The third facility is completely-mixed activated sludge followed by tertiary mixed-media filtration.

All influents to the Demonstration Plant are pumped from the White Rock STP and all effluents and sludges from the pilot plant are returned to the headworks of the White Rock plant. There are a total of five possible influents which can be supplied at a maximum flow of 47.32 ℓ/sec (750 gpm), with the exception of the raw sewage pump that is rated at 18.93 ℓ/sec (300 gpm). The discharges from all pumps are routed to a valve station at the White Rock plant, from which the flow is directed to the pilot plant through one of three main influent lines. Each influent line services one of the major treatment modules (biological, chemical, or physical) at the Demonstration Plant.

Unit Processes

No. 1 Activated Sludge System: The No. 1 activated sludge system consists of the No. 1 aeration basin and the No. 1 final clarifier, and return sludge and effluent pumps. The return sludge pump has a practical operating range of 6.3 to 47.3 ℓ/sec (100 to 750 gpm), while the effluent pump has an operational range of 3.2 to 20.5 ℓ/sec (50 to 325 gpm).

No. 1 Aeration Basin: The No. 1 aeration basin is a circular mild-steel tank erected above ground. Several different types of mixing and oxygen transfer equipment have been evaluated in this basin. The original equipment, supplied by Dorr-Oliver, consisted of an 18.6 kw (25 hp) surface/submerged turbine variable-speed mixer and an 11.2 kw (15 hp) variable-speed air compressor. This system was removed and replaced with Fiscalin equipment supplied by Aquarius, Inc.

No. 1 Final Clarifier: The No. 1 final clarifier is a circular, mild-steel basin erected above ground. As initially provided by Tex Chainbelt, the unit had peripheral feed and square effluent weirs in the center of the tank. The unit was not originally equipped with a surface skimmer, and the center effluent weir configuration made addition of a skimmer quite complex. Therefore, the basin was modified by removing the center effluent weirs and bolting a new peripheral effluent weir to the inside of the existing influent baffle skirt. A skimmer and scum collector were then fitted to the basin. Sludge is removed by the head differential between the water surface in the clarifier and the return sludge pump well, via a single armed header.

No. 2 Activated Sludge System: The No. 2 activated sludge system consists of the 28.4 m^3 (7,500 gal) completely-mixed aeration basin, and a three-hopper Smith and Lovelace final clarifier. The aeration basin has a diameter of 3.14 m (10.3 ft) and a side-water depth of 3.66 m (12.0 ft). Mixing and oxygen transfer is effected by diffusers, and the maximum air flow is 53.8 ℓ/sec (114 scfm).

Upflow Carrier: An Infilco Densator was used as the chemical treatment unit at the Demonstration Plant. The unit consists of the main tank, 5.5 m in diameter and 5.48 m deep, and an inner cylinder that serves as the rapid-mixing and flocculation zones. Influent enters the top of the inner cylinder and the main tank serves as the upflow clarification compartment. Energy input for mixing and flocculation is supplied via independent turbine-type mixers, each of which is equipped with a U.S. Electric Varidrive that has a 10 to 1 turndown capability. A 2.54 x 10.16 cm (1 x 4 inch) steel fluidizer bar is used to prevent the sludge from overcompacting.

Chemical Storage and Feed Equipment: Facilities are present at the Demonstration Plant to store and feed the following chemicals: hydrated lime, hydrated aluminum sulfate, ferric chloride, dry polyelectrolytes, liquid polyelectrolytes, activated silica, powdered activated carbon, and chlorine.

All coagulants and coagulant aids, with the exception of lime, can be fed to either aeration basin or final clarifier, to the upflow clarifier, or in front of the filters or carbon contactors for use as filtration aids. The lime slurry can be pumped to either of the activated sludge systems or the upflow clarifier.

No. 1 Mixed-Media Filter: The No. 1 filter had filtering media consisting of 0.91 m (3.0 ft) of sand overlayed with 0.30 m (12 inches) of anthracite. The influent flow was split equally between the top and bottom of the filter bed, and the effluent was withdrawn through a mid-bed collector located 15 cm (6 inches) below the sand-anthracite interface. The filter performance can be characterized as having been generally good; however, structural deficiencies with the mid-bed collector resulted in frequent maintenance and the unit was converted to a conventional gravity flow filter.

When the filter was rebuilt media supplied by Neptune Microfloc was utilized and the media consisted of three sizes of gravel, coarse and fine garnet, sand and anthracite. Total depth of the filter media was 99 cm (39 inches). The filter has a nominal diameter of 1.2192 m (4.0 ft) and a surface area of 1.17 m^2 (12.57 ft^2). At a flow of 2.37 ℓ/sec (37.5 gpm) the filtration rate is 174.7 m^3/m^2/day (3 gpm/ft^2). Filter backwashing is conventional and utilizes a surface wash in lieu of an air scrub.

No. 2 Dual-Media Filter: Structurally the No. 2 filter is almost identical to the No. 1 filter, and this unit is also operated in the conventional gravity-flow mode. Media consist of 30.48 cm (12 inches) of sand with 60.96 cm (24 inches) of anthracite cap. The filter sand has an effective size of 0.57 mm and a uniformity coefficient of 1.6. Air scour is normally used prior to backwash at a rate of 20.2 ℓ/sec/m^2 (4 scfm/ft^2).

Activated Carbon Contactors: Both the No. 3 and No. 4 columns at the Demonstration Plant serve as granular activated carbon contactors. Both units are 1.22 m (4.0 ft) in diameter and use a 3.048 m (10.0 ft) charge of carbon, or 1,998 kg (4,396 lb) at a bulk density of 0.56 kg/ℓ (35 lb/ft^3). The carbon contactors use the same air-scrubbing system for backwashing as the No. 2 filter. Calgon Filtrasorb 400, 8 x 30 mesh, was used throughout the study.

Chlorine Contact Basins: The Demonstration Plant has two chlorine contact basins which may be operated in parallel or in series. Each basin is 5.49 m (18.0 ft) long, 2.26 m (7.41 ft) wide, and 0.48 m (1.58 ft) deep. Each basin has a volume of 5.95 m^3 (1,573 gal), which results in a theoretical residence time of 15.7 min at a flow of 6.31 ℓ/sec (100 gpm). Eleven fiber glass baffles were installed in each basin, such that plug flow would be closely approximated. Dye studies have been used to quantify the hydraulic characteristics of the end-around baffling system, and observed residence time distribution functions closely approximate theoretical values. The chlorination equipment is capable of a maximum feed of 22.7 kg (50 lb) of chlorine per day.

Sampling Procedures

The sampling procedures described below were utilized for the duration of the research effort. Samples for routine wet chemistry and metals analyses were collected by the operators on duty at the Demonstration Plant, while samples for microbiological analyses were collected by the staff microbiologist or microbiology laboratory assistants.

Samples for routine wet chemistry analyses were collected by the plant operators seven days a week at 1 AM, 5 AM, 9 AM, 1 PM, 5 PM, and 9 PM. Wide-mouth, half-pint plastic bottles were used for sample collection. These sample bottles were placed in a refrigerator until transported to the laboratory, at which time they were composited by the staff chemists. Since the Demonstration Plant was operated at hydraulic steady-state, equal volumes (400 ml) of each of the six grab samples were used for the 24-hour composite sample.

Samples for metals determinations were collected by the plant operators at the same time samples for routine analyses were collected; 400 ml fractions were composited in 1-gal amber bottles to which redistilled nitric acid (10 ml/ℓ) had been previously added for sample preservation.

Either the staff microbiologist or the microbiology laboratory technicians collected all samples for microbiological evaluation. The samples were collected in 125 ml, wide-mouth glass bottles with glass stoppers that had been previously dry sterilized at 350°F for 1 hr.

The following parameters were measured:

5-day biochemical oxygen demand	total Kjeldahl and organic N
chemical oxygen demand	nitrite N
total organic carbon	nitrate N
total solids	sulfate concentration
total suspended solids	chloride concentration
total dissolved solids	alkalinity
total P	turbidity
ammonia N	color

concentrations of: Al, Ba, Cd, Ca, Co, Cu, Cr, Fe, Pb, Mg, Mn, Ag, Sr, Zn, Na, K, As, B, Be, Hg, Mo, Se, Si, and V.

Sampling Frequency: Most of the more conventional water quality parameters that had process control significance were evaluated daily and on 24-hour composite samples. Those parameters necessary for general background information, such as chlorides and sulfates, were evaluated on weekly composite samples. Due to time and cost limitations, trace element determinations were made on weekly composite samples.

Analytical Procedures

The analytical procedures used in this research effort followed the 13th Edition of *Standard Methods for the Examination of Water and Wastewater* (APHA, Washington, DC, 1971), as far as practicable.

Plant Operation and Performance

The Demonstration Plant of the Dallas Water Reclamation Research Center was configured as shown in Figure 5.1 for the potable reuse research effort discussed in this report. The basic process control philosophy was to produce as high a quality product water as possible by operating the completely-mixed activated sludge system to nitrify, maintaining a pH of at least 11.3 in the upflow clarifier, and employing extended empty-bed contact time by utilizing two granular activated carbon contactors in series operation.

The primary coagulant fed to the upflow clarifier was hydrated lime with a minimal dose of ferric chloride used as a flocculation aid. Single-stage recarbonation of the high pH effluent from the upflow clarifier was accomplished by using liquid carbon dioxide. Two-stage recarbonation with intermediate clarification would have reduced the calcium in the product water and been much more desirable; however, these facilities were not available at the Demonstration Plant.

The recarbonated water was then pumped to the No. 1 mixed-media filter, which is a conventional gravity-flow filter with Neptune Microfloc media and a rate-of-flow controller on the influent line. Both granular activated carbon contactors were operated in series, with the trailing (No. 3) contactor being loaded with virgin carbon. The final effluent was then disinfected with a chlorine solution in the chlorine contact basin.

Figure 5.1: Demonstration Plant Configuration for the Potable Reuse Study

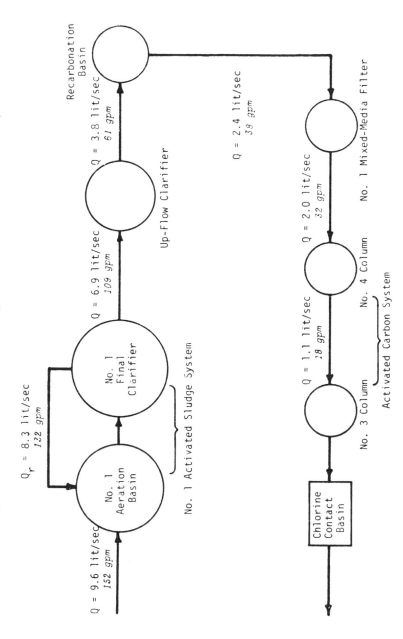

Source: EPA-600/2-77-210

Table 5.3 presents a brief summary of the performance of the Demonstration Plant during this research effort. All values reported are arithmetic means for the study period; the raw wastewater data were obtained from the monthly reports of the Wastewater Treatment Division, Dallas Water Utilities Department.

Table 5.3: Summary of Demonstration Plant Performance

Parameter	Raw Wastewater	AWT Effluent	Reduction
	........(mg/ℓ)........		(%)
TSS	212	2	99.1
BOD_5	198	1.3	99.3
COD	442	3.3	99.3
UOD*	375	14	96.3
NH_3-N	16.9	2.6	84.6
Organic N	14.6	0.6	95.9
NO_2-N	0.0	0.16	—
NO_2- and NO_3-N	0.5	5.9	—
Total N	32.0	9.1	71.6
Total P	12.6	0.4	96.8
pH	7.1	6.9	—

*Ultimate oxygen demand = $1.5 (BOD_5) + 4.6 (NH_3$-N)

Source: EPA-600/2-77-210

The plant performance was excellent during most of the project period, as the effluent quality indicates. Nitrification was not complete, since an average of 2.6 mg/ℓ of ammonia nitrogen was present in the final product water; however, the total nitrogen removal approached 72% with only 9.1 mg/ℓ of nitrogen being found in the product water. The Demonstration Plant has no nitrogen removal process per se, and this significant reduction in total nitrogen was not anticipated.

The observed reductions in gross organic materials as measured by the five-day BOD test and COD test were about as anticipated except that the average product water COD concentration of 3.3 mg/ℓ is somewhat lower than one might predict. Product water total suspended solids averaged 2 mg/ℓ, which is well below the practical working limit of the procedure.

Process Reliability

When considering wastewater reclamation for potable reuse, process reliability must be of paramount concern. During this research effort the three operational problems described below perturbed the routine process control of the Demonstration Plant:

(1) Failure of an operator to close a valve on schedule while wasting activated sludge caused a major loss of sludge and created a major prolonged process upset in December 1974.

(2) Improper backwashing of the mixed-media filter during the first months of the project resulted in two significant turbidity breakthroughs.

(3) Mechanical problems with the hydrated lime feed system made pH control in the upflow clarifier very difficult.

Although these problems were totally undesirable when considered in terms of experimental design, the fact that they occurred makes the research effort more useful, since it permits evaluation of the stability of the overall treatment sequence.

Organic Materials: Although the activated sludge process upset that occurred in early December 1974 had some effect on the quality of the product water, the impact was much less than one might have expected. In fact the three highest COD values measured on the product water (29, 15, and 15 mg/ℓ) were observed during the first week of operation. Previous experience at the Demonstration Plant indicates that about two weeks are required before a new charge of granular activated carbon will consistently produce a high quality effluent. It is interesting to note that the six highest COD values were observed during the first two weeks following the start-up of the No. 3 contactor.

Total Suspended Solids and Turbidity: The effect of the suspended solids and turbidity breakthrough that occurred on the No. 1 filter was obvious. However, since the gravity-flow carbon contactors function as relatively good filters, the quality of the product water remained relatively good.

The turbidity in the effluent from the No. 3 carbon column exceeded 1.0 FTU in 20% of the samples, but only exceeded 3.0 FTU in 3% of the samples. Filtration aids, such as polyelectrolytes or alum, were not used during this project, and their use would have improved product water quality when difficulties with the filter were being experienced.

Total Phosphorus: The median total phosphorus concentration in the activated sludge influent of 8.4 mg/ℓ was reduced to 6.2 mg/ℓ by biological treatment. The effluent from the upflow clarifier had a total phosphorus concentration that exceeded 2.6 mg/ℓ in 10% of the samples. The extreme variability in the observed phosphorus concentrations can be directly related to problems in controlling the lime feed to the upflow clarifier and switching the ferric chloride feed from the upflow clarifier to the activated sludge process.

The effluent from the No. 3 carbon column had very low phosphorus concentrations. Two samples had total phosphorus concentrations exceeding 2.0 mg/ℓ, and only 5 samples exceeded 1.0 mg/ℓ.

Nitrogen Compounds: Nitrification was not achieved consistently during this project as a result of difficulties encountered with the oxygen transfer equipment and operator error. The NH_3-N concentration in the activated sludge effluent exceeded 2.0 mg/ℓ in 40% of the samples, although the median concentration was 0.8 mg/ℓ. No significant changes in ammonia nitrogen concentrations were observed in the processes following the activated sludge system.

The median nitrite-nitrate concentration observed in the product water was 6.4 mg/ℓ, and the nitrite-nitrate concentration exceeded 10 mg/ℓ in only 8% of the samples.

The median organic nitrogen concentration in the activated sludge effluent was 2.8 mg/ℓ, and the AWT processes (principally that of activated carbon) very significantly reduced the median organic nitrogen concentration to 0.45 mg/ℓ.

Metals: Fifteen special weekly composite samples were analyzed for a total of 13 different metals at 4 different points in the treatment sequence.

Silver — Silver was present in such low concentrations that analysis for this metal was terminated after the fifth weekly composite sample. At the low silver concentrations observed in the city of Dallas wastewater, no significant change in the concentration of this metal occurred.

Arsenic — Total removal of arsenic was excellent, averaging almost 86%. High pH lime coagulation and filtration were the most important processes effecting the removal of arsenic.

Boron — No significant removal of boron was observed during this study.

Barium — Barium is a relatively refractory metal, and only a 22.2% total reduction was observed. All of the observed reduction occurred in the activated sludge process.

Cadmium — Total cadmium removal was good, averaging 83.3%. The activated sludge process reduced the mean cadmium concentration from 0.012 to 0.005 mg/ℓ, and was the most significant process with respect to the removal of this metal.

Chromium — The observed chromium concentrations were favorable with the exception of the samples collected during the week of December 27, 1974 through January 2, 1975. The samples of the filter effluent, and most obviously the effluent from the No. 3 carbon column, exhibited peaks that appeared to indicate sample contamination with acid-dichromate. Chromium removal was excellent, averaging 74%. Both the biological and the physical-chemical processes were responsible for significant chromium removal.

Copper — Copper reductions were quite significant during this study. The observed total reduction was 67.4%, and the activated sludge process was responsible for the greatest removal, reducing the mean concentration from 0.141 to 0.029 mg/ℓ.

Iron — Iron reductions were quite significant, averaging 84.6%. The two peaks in the activated sludge effluent occurring during the ninth and tenth weeks were the result of ferric chloride feed to the activated sludge process.

Mercury — Mercury concentrations were very erratic. No significant removal of mercury was observed during this research effort; in fact, an increase of about 0.2 mg/ℓ was observed, although the activated sludge process did reduce the mercury concentration by about 45%.

Manganese — Manganese removal was very good, averaging 84.5% for the project period. The effluents from the No. 1 filter and the No. 3 carbon column average approximately 0.011 mg/ℓ. The activated sludge is quite variable, and a significant peak develops at precisely the same time the major process upset occurred. The manganese concentration in the activated sludge effluent then decreases as the biomass in the activated sludge system becomes reestablished.

Lead — The lead concentrations observed during this study were somewhat erratic. The only significant lead removal observed was the result of biological processes; the physical-chemical processes were rather ineffectual in altering lead concentrations.

Selenium — Selenium is present in the wastewater at very low concentrations. This metal's concentration was reduced by an average of 79.5%, and the physical-chemical processes were particularly effective.

Zinc — The changes in zinc concentrations observed during this research are difficult to quantify because the recarbonation basin was a galvanized steel tank. The data indicated that a relatively constant 44% zinc reduction could be anticipated from the activated sludge process. As a result of zinc pick-up from the recarbonation basin it is impossible to make any definitive statement with respect to the physical-chemical processes.

Compliance with the National Interim Primary Drinking Water Regulations

The objective of this research effort was the production of a product water that was of potable quality, and for the purposes of defining potable water quality, those water quality criteria presented in the National Interim Primary Drinking Water Regulations will be utilized.

Figure 5.2 presents a graphical comparison between the water quality criteria established in the NIPDWR (excepting coliforms) and the arithmetic means for the various water quality parameters monitored in the product water from the No. 3 granular carbon contactor.

Nitrate Nitrogen: During this study the combined nitrite-nitrate nitrogen concentration averaged 5.9 mg/ℓ, and the nitrite nitrogen concentration averaged 0.16 mg/ℓ. Nitrate nitrogen concentrations were equal to, or exceeded, the 10 mg/ℓ standard in approximately 8% of the samples. Due to the instability of the activated sludge process during this study, it is quite likely that higher nitrate nitrogen concentrations would occur if this research was repeated. Additionally, the total Kjeldahl nitrogen concentrations observed in the influent to the activated sludge process (average = 24.1 mg/ℓ) are lower than the 30 to 40 mg/ℓ which might normally be anticipated in a municipal wastewater. For these reasons, nitrate nitrogen concentrations should still be considered a potential problem to the potable reuse of wastewaters.

Turbidity: Although some difficulties were experienced in the operation of the filter, the turbidity values observed for the product water meet the NIPDWR standards in all respects.

Metals: The means of the metals concentrations observed in the product water were considerably lower than the standards promulgated in the NIPDWR. The metals concentrations observed in the activated sludge effluent were also lower than the criteria defined in the NIPDWR. The mean concentrations of only three metals (cadmium, chromium, and lead) in the effluent from the primary clarifiers at the White Rock STP exceeded the EPA standards.

Three individual weekly composite samples exceeded the NIPDWR criteria for one individual metal. Chromium was found at 0.145 mg/ℓ in the tenth week, lead was present at 0.059 mg/ℓ during the twelfth week, and a mercury concentration of 5 mg/ℓ was found during the fifteenth week.

Biocides: Determinations for chlorinated hydrocarbons and chlorophenoxys were made on only one 24-hour composite sample collected from 12 noon October 24, 1974 to 12 noon October 25, 1974. All compounds were present in concentrations much lower than the NIPDWR standards.

Figure 5.2: Comparison Between the NIPDWR Criteria and Product Water Quality

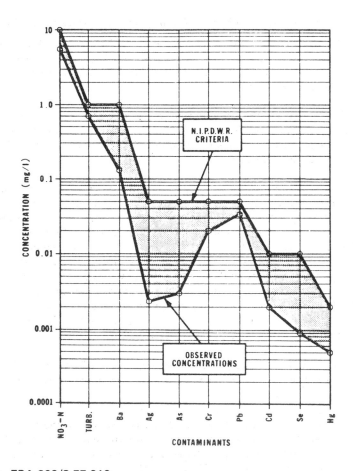

Source: EPA-600/2-77-210

Conclusions

The sequence of unit processes used in this research effort, i.e., screening, de-gritting, primary clarification, biological treatment with completely-mixed activated sludge, high-pH lime coagulation, single-stage recarbonation, gravity filtration, and activated carbon adsorption through two gravity-flow contactors operating in series, produced a consistently high-quality product water. When evaluated in terms of mean observed concentrations, the product water easily complied with the criteria for maximum contaminant levels for potable water promulgated by the U.S. Environmental Protection Agency in the National Interim Primary Drinking Water Regulations.

During this study the activated sludge system experienced one major process upset that resulted in very high COD and TSS concentrations in the effluent from the biological process. However, the 87-minute empty-bed contact time in the activated carbon adsorption system was sufficient to prevent any significant increase in the COD concentrations in the product water, and for this reason extended empty-bed contact time should be considered in the design for potable wastewater reuse.

Although turbidity breakthrough did occur on the mixed-media filter as a possible result of improper backwashing procedure, the downflow carbon contactors provided important supplementary filtering capacity such that the turbidity of the product water was not increased significantly. Difficulties with filter performance should be minimal under normal operating conditions, but the redundancy gained by using downflow carbon columns is a significant factor to be considered when designing a facility for potable reuse.

The metals removals observed during this study were quite variable, ranging from an increase for mercury to an 85.6% reduction for arsenic. Every metal for which there is a standard in the NIPDWR was substantially reduced in concentration by the activated sludge process, and for this reason one may conclude that biological processes are important in limiting the metals concentrations in the product water. Additionally, most of the metals with well-defined adverse health effects were reduced in concentration by at least 50%. Considering the concentrations and removals of the various metals observed during this research, the best technique for controlling metals concentrations in the product water is to limit metals discharges into the collection system, and then employ an effective treatment sequence.

Operation of the activated sludge system to achieve complete nitrification is important for a facility producing an effluent for potable reuse and employing the same treatment sequence used in this study. Lower soluble COD concentrations will result from operation at the elevated sludge ages necessary to develop an adequate population of nitrifying microorganisms. If the activated sludge process is operated to nitrify, and long empty-bed contact times are provided in the carbon adsorption system, the production of a product water with a very low COD concentration (0 to 3 mg/ℓ) is feasible.

Certain water quality parameters that were routinely monitored during this study have great utility as process control parameters for wastewater reclamation facilities that are producing a product water intended for potable reuse. Since operation of the activated sludge process in a nitrifying mode produces water with a lower COD, and since chlorination as a disinfection process is affected by the presence of ammonia, ammonia nitrogen and organic nitrogen are extremely valuable process control parameters. Monitoring and control of pH on the lime coagulation and recarbonation processes are essential if process performance and cost effectiveness are to be maximized. Alkalinity determinations can be used for process control on the chemical treatment systems, and since alkalinity is destroyed during nitrification it is a valuable process control tool for the biological process.

Control of product water turbidity is important for proper disinfection, and the turbidity of various process flows is an important indication of how well the individual unit processes are operating. With the singular exception of biochemical oxygen demand (BOD_5)—because of the five-day period—all of the gross organic parameters have the capability of being important process control parameters.

During this study no nitrogen removal process per se was incorporated in the treatment sequence. Nitrate nitrogen concentrations were consistently below the 10 mg/ℓ standard promulgated in the NIPDWR, but higher nitrate nitrogen concentrations can and should be anticipated. Under these circumstances nitrogen removal will probably be necessary, although the process utilized may only be required to treat 25 to 50% of the total product flow.

The product water produced during this study easily complied with the criteria promulgated in the NIPDWR; however, these water-quality criteria were not developed for potable water derived from wastewater and the comparison must be viewed with this in mind.

[Editor's Note: It must be realized that this research was completed in 1975, and that proposed amendments to the NIPDWR concerning organic chemical contaminants such as the trihalomethanes, organic pesticides, and various individual toxic compounds, were not proposed until 1978. No testing for these compounds was made in this study.]

Recommendations

The following recommendations are made as a result of the potable reuse research program conducted at the Dallas Water Reclamation Research Center, and the experience gained during operation of the Demonstration Plant.

(1) Since the consistent production of a high-quality product water is essential for potable reuse, every effort should be made to optimize the reliability of the entire treatment sequence and each individual unit process.

(a) Demonstrated reliability of the mixing and oxygen transfer equipment used in the activated sludge system should be considered more important than mass transfer efficiency, since mechanical failure will adversely affect all subsequent unit processes and product water quality will be impaired.

(b) Chemical feed equipment should be sized and duplicated so that both reserve capacity and standby capacity assure continuing of operation.

(c) All chemical feed lines, and especially the lime feed lines, must be accessible for routine cleaning and scale removal.

(d) If high pH lime coagulation is employed, the effluent from the chemical clarifier should flow by gravity to the recarbonation basin to avoid scale formation in pumps.

(e) Two-stage recarbonation with intermediate clarification should be used to improve calcium removal and reduce the hardness of the product water.

(f) Downflow carbon contactors should be used so that the facility will have a redundant filtering capability.

(2) Significant removals of toxic metals were observed during this project. However, the employment of adequate processes to remove metals should also be accompanied by a source control program so that metal discharges into the municipal wastewater system can be carefully controlled and limited.

(3) High pH ($>$11.2) lime coagulation is a very effective disinfection process, and for this reason should be considered in the design of any potable reuse treatment sequence.

(4) The activated sludge process should be operated to nitrify such that the COD loading to the activated carbon adsorption system will be reduced, and performance of the carbon improved.

(5) Additional research should be performed to evaluate the capabilities of high-pH lime coagulation as a disinfection process. Particular emphasis should be placed on the destruction of parasitic organisms and enteric viruses.

THE DENVER PROJECT

The information in this section is based on material from the paper in Conference I entitled, "Demonstration of Potable Water Reuse Technology—The Denver Project," by M.R. Rothberg and S.W. Work of the Denver Water Department and K.D. Linstedt and E.R. Bennett of the University of Colorado.

Introduction

The Denver Water Department (DWD) provides water service to over **900,000** people serving approximately 75 billion gallons (0.28×10^9 cubic meters) of treated water annually. The department also supplies raw water, by agreement, to numerous cities and water districts around the Denver metropolitan area. To accomplish this, the utility operates an extensive raw water collection, storage, and transmission system which involves facilities for diversion of both native, indigenous water on the eastern side of the Rocky Mountains and Colorado River water from the western side.

Denver realizes that continued growth in this water-short area will create new demand and necessitate additional raw water supply capabilities. Since the native water supply is essentially fully utilized, within the context of the Colorado water law, it is apparent that future supplies will necessarily derive from additional transmountain diversion and other alternatives to conventional acquisition of raw water. Evaluation of future West Slope diversion shows that this type of raw water acquisition will become increasingly more difficult and will have a major economic impact. Future diversions will require elaborate and lengthy transmission systems, and may involve pumping at a cost estimated to reach $5,000 to $6,000 per acre-foot ($4,065 to $4,878 per 10^3 cubic meters) by the turn of the century. Therefore, while continuing to develop conventional raw water diversion, Denver is pursuing various nonconventional alternatives for increasing water supply, including successive use.

Program History

The Denver Water Department began its successive use program in the late 1960s. Initially the program involved the examination of water reuse alternatives including industrial and agricultural applications. Legal, marketing, planning, and other feasibility studies were performed concurrently with the design and construction of a small-scale pilot facility. This facility (1) was developed jointly with the University of Colorado and provides a flexible laboratory for graduate research in the area of advanced waste treatment.

Evaluation of water use within the Denver area along with marketing studies to determine potential uses of a lower quality water led to the conclusion that the metropolitan area has neither the type nor volume of industry required to make industrial reuse of water feasible from either an economic or net-yield standpoint. In addition, the evaluation of Denver's geography and current downstream uses of Denver's return flow led to the conclusion that intentional agricultural reuse of transmountain waters would not provide sufficient water for the future. Geology has also figured heavily in Denver's early dismissal of groundwater recharge as a viable alternative for water reuse. Denver is located over a geological bowl comprising the downward extension of the Rocky Mountains. The aquifers are extremely deep and very marginal in permeability.

It became apparent then that if the Water Department wished to maximize the benefits of successive use, essentially obtaining a new source of raw water, it must look further and find other forms of successive use.

The only form of successive use which would provide substantial benefit in terms of augmenting present water supplies was—and is—that of potable reuse. In Denver's case, potable reuse is the complete renovation of wastewater to a potable quality water which could, without reservation or restriction, be supplied through the potable system to the residents of the metropolitan area.

Demonstration Plant

Because of the untested nature of potable reuse technology, most national experts agree that any process involved must be demonstrated on a plant scale prior to actual application.

In early 1975, the Denver Water Department charged the consulting firm of CH2M Hill with developing a preliminary design for a potable reuse demonstration plant. The unit processes selected for use in the process train are given below.

Phosphorus Removal: Phosphorus removal can be accomplished by any of four generally accepted treatment schemes: biological, biological-chemical, ion exchange, or physical chemical. Although selective ion exchange utilizing activated alumina was considered, the treatment finally chosen was a physical-chemical one, involving the use of lime, alum or iron salts for chemical coagulation of secondary effluent. Secondary effluent coagulation for phosphorus removal also provides nearly complete suspended solids removal prior to downstream process. Because the coagulation is done in basins separate from other processes, highly reliable and easily controllable operation results.

The influent wastewater quality is the factor which effects the quantity of chemical coagulant required to achieve a given degree of phosphorus removal. Alum, iron and lime requirements are affected by the alkalinity of the wastewater. Numerous plants utilizing lime precipitation clarification have provided valuable data assisting in the choice of the lime process for the Denver Water Department's demonstration plant.

Data obtained through operation of the department's pilot plant have indicated that effective phosphorus removal can be achieved through relatively simple operation of a lime clarification system. The additional benefits of this system also provide positive factors for its consideration. Lime treatment had been chosen in the conceptual design and will be the demonstration plant process.

Suspended Solids Removal: The relatively complete suspended solids removal necessary for potable reuse requires efficient filtration of the chemically coagulated effluent. The extremely efficient phosphorus removal requirements also dictate filtration for polishing. This process is also necessary to protect downstream units and to assure their efficient operation.

Granular media filtration may involve single media operation where graded sand is utilized, or the operation may involve dual media typically utilizing anthracite and sand. An additional alternative is that of mixed media filtration utilizing anthracite, sand, and garnet. All of the various configurations have been used in both pilot and full-scale work involving treatment of secondary or advanced waste treatment effluents.

The demonstration plant will utilize dual media pressure filtration aided by the addition of alum and polymer. This is based on the most satisfactory results obtained through pilot plant operations as well as operating history at numerous plants throughout the country.

Nitrogen Removal: The four most effective treatment processes for nitrogen removal include biological nitrogen removal, breakpoint chlorination, ammonia stripping and selective ion exchange.

Biological nitrification-denitrification processes left concern considering reliability and were affected poorly by the cold climate of the Denver area.

The principal disadvantages of breakpoint chlorination are the large increase in TDS and the high operating costs. Additionally, because of current concerns for chlorinated organics and the potential for breakpoint chlorination to form these compounds, other alternatives are warranted.

The ammonia stripping process for the removal of nitrogen has been used on a plant scale at both South Lake Tahoe and Water Factory 21. At these plant sites the process has shown promise for removal of ammonia from wastewater under favorable temperature conditions. The major restriction of the process for application to the Denver Project is the climate and the temperature dependence of the process. Experience at South Lake Tahoe has indicated unsatisfactory results during the winter time. Because of the problems associated with climate, ammonia stripping was not considered for the Denver Project.

The selective ion exchange process utilizes zeolites which are selective for ammonia relative to calcium, magnesium and sodium. The currently favored zeolite is clinoptilolite, which naturally occurs in several extensive deposits in the United States. Several studies of the process have been conducted as well as the design and construction of two full-scale operating plants at the Tahoe-Truckee Sanitation Agency and Occoquan.

In an effort to effect complete removal of ammonia nitrogen, breakpoint chlorination had been considered as a backup and polishing step for Denver's clinoptilolite system. Since the initial conceptual design, however, major concerns associated with chlorinated organics and other chlorine oxidation products provoked a decision to remove breakpoint chlorination as a process in the demonstration plant. Therefore, the nitrogen removal will rely on clinoptilolite with polishing accomplished by other processes discussed below.

Soluble Organic Removal: The adsorption or chemical oxidation processes that may have application to remove the residual refractory organics from wastewater include granular or powdered activated carbon, polymeric adsorption, ozonation and catalytic oxidation.

The use of granular activated carbon (GAC) for removal of refractory organic material from wastewater has been clearly demonstrated as an efficient, reliable and economical unit process on a plant scale at South Lake Tahoe, Water Factory 21, Pamona, Colorado Springs, and several other plants around the country. The regeneration of the carbon in multiple hearth and other types of furnaces has been perfected with nearly complete recovery of the adsorptive capacity of the carbon while minimizing carbon losses. The technology associated with applying carbon for wastewater treatment processes is well known and has been described in great detail.

Powdered activated carbon provides a very efficient removal of soluble organic materials. The problems in handling the dry powdered activated carbon as well as carbon recovery were a factor in the dismissal of this process for the Denver plant.

Certain synthetic adsorbents consisting of polymeric resins developed for analytical determinations of trace organics and other adsorptive functions have been considered for organic removal. This adsorbent method shows potential as a possible alternative to carbon adsorption particularly for trace organic removals. However, insufficient data with regard to pilot work and the prevailing economic and operational problems indicate that this method is not currently suitable for full-scale operation.

Ozone has been used for the disinfection of water supplies for many years, particularly in Europe. Work at the department's pilot plant has indicated limited effectiveness of ozone for reduction of COD in lime treated filtered secondary effluent. The data does indicate the effectiveness of ozone as a disinfectant, however. The portion of the study utilizing ozone in combination with granular activated carbon shows uncertain performance in initial short-term runs.

The treatment system now proposed will be modified to provide the ability to add ozone between first- and second-stage carbon contact. Recent data concerning biologically activated or ozone enhanced carbon shows promise from the standpoint of both organic and residual ammonia control. The biological growth in the carbon columns assisted by high dissolved oxygen concentrations developed by ozonation can effectively nitrify any residual ammonia leaking past the clinoptilolite exchangers.

The lower concentrations of ozone typically necessary for biologically enhanced carbon should not cause significant problems with oxidation products as opposed to the concerns expressed over the high doses necessary for ozone oxidation or UV catalyzed ozone oxidation.

Demineralization: There are five different methods often proposed for demineralization of water: freezing, distillation, electrodialysis, ion exchange, and reverse osmosis. It is generally felt that those methods requiring a phase change such as freezing, distillation and electrodialysis are most suitable for seawater or other high TDS concentration waters.

While the ion exchange process showed promise, the side benefits of reverse osmosis were a major factor in choosing it over ion exchange. Reverse osmosis is the newest of the salt-removal processes and has been extensively developed during the past few years for treatment of both brackish waters and wastewaters. There have been many pilot plant and demonstration studies on reverse osmosis for municipal wastewater demineralization. Most recently, Water Factory 21 has installed a 5 mgd reverse osmosis demineralization plant.

The Denver Water Department has conducted pilot studies utilizing spiral-wound membranes of both cellulose acetate and polyamide materials from two manufacturers. The removal data was rather impressive for both membranes.

Advantages of reverse osmosis include the fact that the process generally provides a physical barrier to the passage of materials, thus showing consistently high removals of organics, turbidity, bacteria, and virus as well as inorganic material. Removal efficiencies and power consumption remain relatively stable over a wide range of TDS concentrations present in the feedwater. The disadvantages of the reverse osmosis process include the negative effects of scaling and the susceptibility of the system to damage from improper operation. These can be mitigated, however, and the Denver Water Department has chosen the reverse osmosis process as the demineralization step for the demonstration plant.

Disinfection: Complete and total disinfection is necessary for the successful operation of the demonstration plant. The various methods of disinfection available involve use of strong oxidants including chlorine, chlorine dioxide, ozone and ultraviolet light.

The effectiveness of chlorine as a disinfectant is debatable. Numerous studies have indicated varying contact times and dose requirements for disinfection of organisms ranging from indicator bacteria to virus and cysts. The advantages of chlorine as a disinfectant are its ease of application and the detailed information known about its use. The disadvantages are the by-products formed when chlorine oxidizes various organic chemicals.

Chlorine dioxide has shown favor as a disinfectant in the last few years. EPA has conducted several studies utilizing the compound as a disinfectant in water and wastewater. The careful control of chlorine dioxide disinfection reduces the potential for formation of chlorinated organics. Chlorine dioxide must be generated on-site and is usually the product of a reaction of chlorine gas with sodium chlorite. Because of the extremely rapid kinetics of chlorine dioxide reactions, it is necessary to rapidly disperse it into the wastewater and to provide intimate contact for complete disinfection.

As previously discussed, ozone is a very strong oxidant and has been shown from various studies to be an effective bactericide. It has also shown its effectiveness against virus and cysts. Questions concerning the formation of oxidation by-products with ozone are currently under investigation.

Ultraviolet light also has capability for disinfection purposes. The problems associated with ultraviolet disinfection involve the passage of the light through water. Relatively clear solutions are necessary to insure proper disinfection, and design of the UV system must be such that the water passes over the UV source in thin sheets. At large scales, these design constraints cause severe problems.

Chlorine was originally chosen as the disinfectant for the demonstration plant. Because of concern over chlorinated organics and oxidative by-products, however, the disinfection process has been changed from chlorine to chlorine dioxide. Since the feedwater for the demonstration plant will be unchlorinated secondary effluent from the Metro treatment plant, there will be no chlorine added at any point in the system.

Treatment Train

The revised treatment train for the demonstration plant is shown in Figure 5.3. Phosphorus removal will be accomplished by high lime precipitation utilizing single-stage recarbonation. The side benefits of this process are removals of turbidity, disinfection, viral inactivation, suspended solids removal, some softening, and some heavy metals removal. The primary suspended solids removal process will be chemically aided dual media pressure filtration which can provide additional benefits of bacterial and virus removals, and additional reductions in phosphorus. The primary nitrogen removal process will utilize clinoptilolite for the selective ion exchange of ammonia. The process will provide additional filtration.

The soluble organic removal process will utilize granular activated carbon enhanced by ozone between the first and second carbon stage. The process will provide additional removals of virus and bacteria, heavy metals and oxidation of residual ammonia nitrogen to nitrate.

The demineralization process will utilize reverse osmosis. This process will provide additional removals of bacteria and virus, trace metals, soluble organics, and ammonia and nitrate nitrogen.

The disinfection process will involve the on-site generation and addition of chlorine dioxide and should provide final and residual disinfection of the product water.

Costs

The overall costs of this project are currently [1979] estimated at $21.6 million. The Denver Water Department is entering into a cooperative agreement with the U.S. Environmental Protection Agency which will provide $7 million of Federal funds for this project. The demonstration program is developed to provide the necessary information to determine if potable water can, in fact, be produced directly from secondary effluent. If this program proves successful, as the Denver Water Department fully expects it will, Denver will be on its way toward the implementation of a full-scale, 100 mgd reuse program which could provide up to 15% of Denver's municipal water supply by the year 2000.

Figure 5.3:　Revised Process Flow Diagram—Proposed Denver Plant

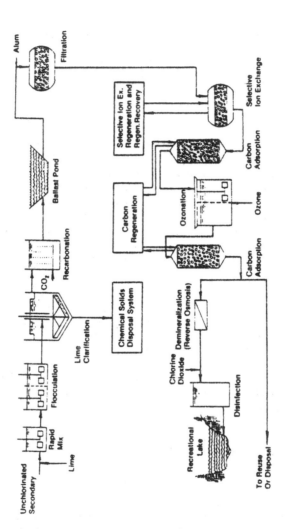

THE EXPERIMENTAL ESTUARY WATER TREATMENT PLANT

The information in this section is from a paper of the same title by C.C. Johnson, Jr. and D.R. Aukamp, both of Malcolm Pirnie, Inc. The paper is published in Conference I.

Introduction

The use of the Potomac River estuary as a possible water supply source for the metropolitan Washington area is one of several alternatives discussed in the Corps of Engineers Northeastern United States Water Supply Study (NEWS). In 1974 the Congress authorized the construction of an experimental estuary water treatment plant (EEWTP) which could be used to investigate the feasibility of this alternative. The design for this experimental plant was completed for the Corps by Malcolm Pirnie, Inc. in 1977. The operation of the experimental treatment plant is scheduled for a two-year period beginning in March of 1980.

Most process units in the plant have been provided in duplicate, some of which can be operated in both series and parallel, and most of which can be by-passed if desired. A side stream which flows up to 10,000 gpd allows the testing and evaluation of special or unique processes for short periods of time. A blending tank allows the mixing of a raw water quality to any specification.

Description of the EEWT Plant

The Experimental Estuary Water Treatment Plant was designed to provide a capability of using in various modes the off-the-shelf unit processes available for treating a raw water supply of questionable and unknown quality to produce a potable water of acceptable quality. It required consideration of all facilities from the intake structure to the final clearwell. It required a capability to blend waters to some future predicted raw water composition. A system capable of handling a flow of 1 mgd was the primary design parameter affecting all unit processes.

Microscreening: Two microscreen units have been provided for the removal of organic detritus, suspended solids and microorganisms associated with the Potomac Estuary water and the secondary effluent. The microscreens are constructed of 35 micron stainless steel mesh and each is designed for a maximum flow of 1.0 mgd. The rotating screen will be backwashed continuously with water from the microscreen effluent chamber. The rotating speed of the screens as well as the quantity of backwash water is controlled automatically based on head loss through the microscreens. The captured solids flow by gravity from the waste collection hopper to the sludge thickener.

Ammonia Removal: A selective ion exchange process is utilized to reduce the concentration of ammonia in the Blue Plains secondary effluent to approximately 1 mg/ℓ. Following passage through the microscreen, the secondary effluent will be pumped through the two ion exchange units. Each unit was designed for a maximum hydraulic flow of 0.5 mgd and contains a natural zeolite (clinoptilolite) medium which has a relatively high affinity for ammonia ions. The ion exchange units are 7 feet in diameter and each contains about 155 cubic feet of media. Backwashing/regeneration will be used as needed and the solution used will be 1.6% NaCl with caustic to raise the pH to 10.

Aeration: The aeration process serves to oxidize iron, manganese and some organic matter, and to increase the palatability of the water by the removal of objectionable gases and other taste and odor producing substances. The square aeration tank will be equipped with a turbine-type aerator and will provide a detention time of approximately 10 minutes.

Rapid Mix and Flocculation: The rapid mix facilities involve a two-stage tank for dispersement of the coagulants into the raw water. The detention time in the tank will be approximately one minute at the maximum flow of 1.0 mgd. The two-stage flocculation basin was sized for a total detention time of 20 minutes at the maximum design flow of 1.0 mgd. Each compartment of the flocculation basin is equipped with two turbine-type mixers with variable speed motors. The speed of the flocculators will be manually controlled.

Settling Basin: The flocculated water will pass through thirty-six 4-inch orifices in the baffle wall into a rectangular settling basin. The basin provides a 2-hour detention with a corresponding surface settling rate of about 1,200 gpd/ft^2 of surface area. A continuously operating sludge scrapper system moves the settled solids to sludge hoppers at the influent end of the basin. From there, the sludge is pumped to the gravity sludge thickener. The sludge pumps are controlled automatically by time clock and sludge density. A skimmer collects any floating materials and discharges them to a dewatering trap. The clarified water will discharge to two effluent troughs through submerged orifices to the predisinfection tanks or directly to the rapid filters. The predisinfection tank was designed for a detention time of approximately 5 minutes and can accommodate either chlorine or ozone. When the lime coagulation mode is being used the clarified water will be passed through a recarbonation tank before predisinfection and filtration.

Filtration: The filtration process involves two dual-media filters consisting of anthracite coal and silica sand. The filters are 30 inches deep and rest on a 10-inch layer of silica gravel. The anthracite coal has a depth of 22 inches, and the remaining silica sand has a depth of 8 inches. The filter bottom is precast Wheeler Bottom Blocks on concrete piers. The filtration loading rate was designed at 6 gpm/ft^2 at the maximum flow of 1 mgd. Filter controls are located adjacent to the filters. The turbidity will be monitored continuously and indicated and recorded in the central operations room. An alarm system has been provided to indicate high effluent turbidity and loss-of-head. Backwashing of the filters is initiated manually with subsequent automatic sequencing of valves and pumps.

Adsorption: Following rapid sand filtration, the water is treated by an adsorption system for the removal of dissolved organic substances. The process consists of three upflow columns and three pressure downflow columns, each containing granular activated carbon. When the adsorptive capacity of the carbon is exhausted, the carbon will be replaced by means of an eductor system. Spent carbon will be regenerated off-site. Both upflow and downflow units were specified to allow comparison of the operating efficiencies of the two unit types. The columns can be operated in two parallel trains or in series, e.g., upflow followed by downflow.

Disinfection: Because of the nature of the raw water source for the pilot plant, the disinfection process will be a critical function. Facilities were provided for both pre- and postdisinfection. Predisinfection can take place prior to filtration or be bypassed if it is not necessary. The product water from the carbon columns will receive postdisinfection. Separate disinfection facilities were also provided for the side stream which has passed through the dissolved solids removal facilities. In order to evaluate the effectiveness of other disinfection processes, facilities were provided for both chlorination and ozonation at the predisinfection location, and facilities were provided for chlorination, ozonation, and ultraviolet irradiation for postdisinfection of both the main stream and the side stream. The postdisinfection facilities are arranged so that any two of the three processes may be operated in parallel with each other. In addition, the ozonation and ultraviolet processes can be followed by chlorination.

The chlorine facilities include a two-bay contact tank which will provide a contact time of approximately 65 minutes at 0.5 mgd and 32 minutes at 1.0 mgd. By using only one bay of the tank these detention times can be cut in half. The gas-type chlorinators have a capacity range of from 5 to 140 lb/day and will be automatically controlled by the chlorine residual analyzer/recorder with control loop. One-hundred-fifty pound chlorine gas cylinders will be used with a 2-cylinder scale.

The ozone contact tank has two compartments and will provide a contact time of approximately 24 minutes at 0.5 mgd and 12 minutes at 1.0 mgd, when both chambers are utilized. Horizontal baffles form an over/under serpentine flow to reduce short circuiting and enhance ozone transfer. The ozone will be produced by a single water cooled generator using ambient room air as its input. The generator has a maximum capacity of approximately 83 lb/day and will supply both post ozonation as well as preozonation, when it is used. A rotometer and manual control valve regulates the quantity of ozone flowing to the predisinfection tank. The feed rate for postozonation can be controlled manually or automatically by the ozone analyzer/controller.

The ultraviolet irradiation equipment consists of a multitube, self-contained unit, with a maximum hydraulic capacity of 0.5 mgd. The unit was designed to maintain a dosage rate of 33,000 MW-sec/cm^2 (Ultrads).

Side Stream Processes

A side stream flow has been provided from the carbon column clearwell, but before postdisinfection, to evaluate the effectiveness of various unit processes in removing dissolved solids. The processes to be evaluated will be reverse osmosis, electrodialysis and ion exchange. Only one process will be operated at a time and each will be designed for a flow rate of 10,000 gpd. The removal of dissolved solids is being investigated in the event the future TDS concentration in the estuary exceeds recommended drinking water limits.

Chemical Recovery System: A recovery system was designed to enable the evaluation of the operating results and coagulation characteristics of recovered and recycled coagulants. The sludge handling system was sized to enable operation of the chemical recovery system for either the alum or magnesium bicarbonate-lime mode. Each mode will be used separately over a predetermined period of operation. In the alum mode, the thickened sludge will be dosed with sulfuric acid to dissolve the aluminum hydroxide floc into a soluble aluminum sulfate, which is recovered by a decant procedure. The remaining sludge will be dewatered in a centrifuge and disposed of in a sanitary landfill.

When operating under the magnesium bicarbonate-lime mode, the thickened sludge is mixed with carbon dioxide gas that has been recovered from the multiple hearth furnace. The addition of carbon dioxide causes the magnesium hydroxide precipitate to be solubilized into magnesium bicarbonate. The sludge is pumped to a classifying centrifuge which dewaters the sludge into a cake containing 40% dry solids. The sludge cake, containing most of the calcium carbonate and suspended solids, is conveyed to the furnace for recalcination. The magnesium bicarbonate centrate is then pumped to a clarifying centrifuge and then to a storage tank for reuse. The residual sludge cake from the clarifying centrifuge will be disposed of in a sanitary landfill.

Testing and Evaluation Program

Objectives and Methods: The objective of the operation of the experimental estuary water treatment plant is to determine the feasibility of producing potable water from the Potomac River estuary. Inherent in such a feasibility study is an evaluation of the performance of the system as a whole, and an evaluation of the reliability, stability and consistency of the unit processes for producing an acceptable finished water quality. To reach this objective, development of the testing and evaluation program was focused on three areas: (1) determination of the quality of the input water to be treated; (2) identification of the processes to treat the water, and determination of the effectiveness of these processes; and (3) evaluation of the quality of the water produced by the experimental plant.

The parameters to be analyzed include parameters from the National Interim Primary Drinking Water Regulations, the EPA proposed Secondary Regulations, and those recommended by the National Academy of Science's "Committee to Review the Potomac Estuary Water Treatment Plant Project."

Sampling: A rigorous sampling program was devised to provide the basis for evaluating the performance of the pilot plant. At the outset some parameters are to be measured on a continuous or semicontinuous basis. These include turbidity, TOC, pH, temperature, and chlorine residual. A few parameters such as dissolved oxygen and coliforms are scheduled to be determined using daily grab samples. Most inorganic parameters, including trace metals, are to be measured using daily composite samples. Most specific organic compounds are scheduled for weekly composite samples.

Nineteen sampling points throughout the system of the demonstration plant were considered critical to evaluation of the effectiveness of unit process operations and/or the quality of water produced by the pilot plant. Additional points would be located on one or more public water supply systems in the Washington, DC area. These latter points enable the collection of information on the quality of water produced by such systems to be compared against the same parameters used to evaluate the water produced by the pilot plant.

Analysis: A large portion of the laboratory analysis work relates to analyses that probably will be performed by specialized laboratories. These include radiological, bacteriological (other than SPC and coliform), and toxicological testing. The testing program calls for the remainder of the work to be conducted in three laboratories that could be established for the project. One laboratory would handle all organic and inorganic analyses. A second would handle the microbiological work. The third laboratory, located in the pilot plant facility, would conduct routine and process control analyses.

The project design calls for the plant to be operated continuously (24 hours per day, 7 days per week) for two years. This period is to be preceded by a predemonstration phase of six months to enable the project team to become thoroughly familiar with the pilot plant, the test protocols, and to conduct the predemonstration sampling that is required.

Evaluation: Final evaluation of the results of the testing and evaluation program essentially involves three facets. These include: (1) quality of water produced by the pilot plant; (2) effectiveness of the unit processes that are tested; and (3) projection of costs associated with staffing and operation of the pilot plant.

The quality of water produced by the pilot plant will be evaluated against existing, proposed, or revised primary and secondary drinking water standards promulgated by EPA prior to the date this demonstration project is completed. In the absence of EPA proposed or promulgated standards, it was assumed that no generally recognized and nationally accepted or proposed standards or regulation existed against which to evaluate the remaining water quality parameters. To provide a basis for comparing water quality produced by the pilot plant with a currently accepted drinking water supply, identical and simultaneous laboratory analyses of all parameters are to be made of the treated water from the pilot plant and the treated water from other water supply systems in the Washington, DC area.

It is important to note that no attempt is intended to be made in this evaluation of water quality, using those parameters for which there are no existing or proposed standards, to determine if the water is or is not an acceptable water from a public health standpoint. The demonstration is intended to determine if, and under what conditions, the Potomac River estuary water can be treated to be at least as good in quality for the parameters measured as the water produced for human consumption by other water supply systems in the Washington metropolitan area.

Treatment Techniques
for Wastewater
Scheduled for Reuse

TREATMENT TECHNOLOGY FOR WATER REUSE

The material in this section is based on a report in Conference II having the above title and written by R.B. Williams, J.A. Faisst, and G.L. Culp, all of Culp/-Wesner/Culp, El Dorado Hills, California. The paper is a summary of the findings of a study, the entire report of which is contained in the following two volumes: Culp-Wesner-Culp, *Water Reuse and Recycling, Volume 1: Evaluation of Needs and Potential,* and Culp-Wesner-Culp, *Water Reuse and Recycling, Volume 2: Evaluation of Treatment Technology,* prepared for the U.S. Department of the Interior, Office of Water Research and Technology, OWRT/RU-79/1; published by Noyes Data Corporation as *Wastewater Reuse and Recycling Technology.*

This study considered specific projects of wastewater reclamation, but went further to present more generalized information. Using the information in the report, treatment trains can be developed to satisfy the quality requirements of virtually any of the beneficial reuses of wastewater.

Evaluation Methods

The contaminant removal capabilities of the treatment processes which can be used for reclamation listed in Table 6.1 were evaluated in detail.

Obtaining Data: The data used to evaluate these processes were obtained from various full-scale and pilot test facilities across the country and are supplemented with information and data reported in the literature. The removal of various contaminants by each unit process was calculated using influent and effluent data to each unit process. This is presented in terms of percents so that it can be applied to waste with any reasonable influent contaminant concentration.

Table 6.1: Treatment Process Used for Reclamation

Process	Principal Contaminants Removed
Primary sedimentation	TSS, BOD, grease and oil
Activated sludge	BOD, COD, TSS, grease and oil, some heavy metals
Nitrification	BOD, COD, TSS, ammonia, some heavy metals
Denitrification	Nitrate
Trickling filter	BOD, COD, TSS
Rotating biological contactor	BOD, COD, TSS, ammonia, some heavy metals
Filtration	TSS, turbidity
Activated carbon adsorption	BOD, TSS, coliforms, TOC
Chemical coagulation-flocculation	BOD, COD, TSS, phosphorus, some heavy metals
Ammonia stripping	Ammonia
Selective ion exchange	Ammonia, TSS
Reverse osmosis	TDS
Chlorination	Coliforms
Ozonation	Coliforms, color, turbidity
Land treatment	BOD, COD, TSS, ammonia, phosphorus, oil and grease, coliforms

Source: NSF/RA-790225

Establishing Reliability of the Process: The statistical analysis was used to establish the reliability of the particular process in question. The values are given in terms of percentiles (10, 50, and 90%) which represent the percent of times a given value was achieved. For example, if the 10 percentile value for suspended solids removal in primary treatment is 75%, then 10% of the time the removal would be greater than or equal to 75% removal of suspended solids.

Evaluating treatment efficiencies in terms of effluent reliabilities is important in light of the current EPA definition for secondary treatment which recognizes the natural variability of treatment capability. Secondary treatment requires a 30-day average BOD and suspended solids of 30 mg/ℓ, while the 7-day average can be as high as 45 mg/ℓ. A recent study shows that the mean values for BOD and suspended solids should be 18 mg/ℓ and 17 mg/ℓ, respectively, in order to attain the 30-day values of 30 mg/ℓ. The data presented in the report can be used to determine similar values for other contaminants and develop treatment systems with greater degrees of reliability.

Analyzing Data: In general, the performance data from wastewater treatment processes do not follow normal statistical distribution. There are many external factors and process control practices which can upset what might otherwise be a natural distribution of data. To compensate for these variations, the data can be analyzed using log-normal distribution.

Effluent Quality for Treatment Levels: Since the basic performance data in the report are for individual unit processes, a method has been presented for combining these data for the various process trains to obtain effluent quality for various levels of treatment. This is easily illustrated for the removal of suspended solids by primary and secondary treatment. The average percent removals for each process, for instance 50% for primary treatment and 80% for secondary treatment, are converted to decimal equivalents (0.5 and 0.8, respectively). They are then added together; the product of the two removals is then subtracted from this sum to give the overall removal in terms of a decimal equivalent, for the two processes [i.e., (0.5 + 0.8) – (0.5 x 0.8) = 0.91]. This procedure can be carried out for any number of unit processes to determine either removal or reliability. However, it must be reiterated that actual operating data should be used if they are available.

Water Quality Criteria: Water quality criteria for beneficial uses were established through extensive review of available publications. The criteria finally selected were intended to be typical of the use, although the requirements could change for different areas. These criteria form the basis upon which treatment systems were developed to attain the values with a 90% reliability.

The level of treatment to meet the possible beneficial uses was derived from commonly used unit wastewater treatment processes as already mentioned. Because secondary treatment is now required for effluent discharge, it was considered to be the minimum degree of treatment or Level 1. The other levels were established by adding processes to meet increasingly more stringent qualities. In some cases, local requirements may prove a higher level to be the minimum acceptable treatment. These systems, summarized in Table 6.2, were based on successfully operating treatment facilities currently in use. Table 6.3 shows the average train performance up through Level 11 treatment.

Table 6.2: Treatment Levels

Treatment Level	Treatment System
1a	activated sludge
1b	trickling filter
1c	rotating biological contactors
2a	2-stage nitrification
2b	rotating biological contactors
2c	extended aeration
3a	nitrification-denitrification
3b	selective ion exchange
4	filtration of secondary effluent
5a	alum added to aeration basin
5b	ferric chloride added to primary

(continued)

Table 6.2: (continued)

Treatment Level	Treatment System
5c	tertiary lime treatment
6a	tertiary lime, nitrified effluent
6b	tertiary lime plus ion exchange
7	carbon adsorption, filtered secondary effluent
8	carbon, tertiary lime effluent
9	carbon, tertiary lime, nitrified effluent
10	carbon, tertiary lime, ion exchange
11	reverse osmosis of AWT effluent
12a	physical-chemical system, lime
12b	physical-chemical system, ferric chloride
13a	irrigation
13b	infiltration-percolation
13c	overland flow

Table 6.3: Level 11 Treatment—
Carbon Adsorption of Lime-Treated Activated Sludge Effluent—
Average Process Train Performance

Constituent	Average Removal (%)	Average Reliability, %			Average Effluent Concentration (mg/ℓ)
		10	50	90	
BOD	100	100	100	89	0
COD	100	100	100	97	0
TSS	100	100	99	87	0
NH_3-N	100	97	81	48	0
Phosphorus	100	100	100	99	0
Oil and grease	97	100	98	73	2
Arsenic	61	93	63	0	0.003
Barium	79	95	79	52	0.092
Cadmium	98	100	98	87	0.0002
Chromium	100	100	98	84	0
Copper	98	100	99	98	0.002
Fluoride	*	*	*	*	*
Iron	99	100	100	94	0.023
Lead	99	100	98	78	0.001
Manganese	98	100	98	86	0.002
Mercury	23	31	18	0	0.028
Selenium	7	26	12	0	0.006
Silver	82	100	99	80	0.004
Zinc	98	100	95	58	0.008
TOC	100	100	98	83	0
Turbidity	100	100	100	95	0**
Color	93	100	94	56	5***
Foaming agents	92	†	84	†	0.17
TDS	95	†	†	†	129

*Data inconclusive.
**TU.
***P-C units.
†Insufficient data.

Source: NSF/RA-790225

Costs: Capital and operation and maintenance costs were developed for three treatment facility plant sizes (1, 10 and 50 mgd). To facilitate the cost-effectiveness analysis a computer program was utilized to derive costs and energy estimates for the various treatment trains. The information stored in the computer includes curves for capital and maintenance materials costs. These are keyed to Bureau of Labor Statistics (BLS) cost indices for construction materials, labor, etc., so they can be updated as prices rise. Certain costs, such as labor, electrical energy, and fuel are updated using fixed unit prices. The program automatically calculates construction, annual O&M, amortized capital, and unit treatment costs (i.e., annual cost/dwelling, cents/thousand gallons) depending on the variables entered in the input (i.e., contingencies, interest rate, amortization period, population per dwelling). A summary of unit treatment costs is given in Table 6.4.

Table 6.4: Summary of Unit Treatment Costs*

Treatment Level	Treatment System	. Unit Cost, ¢/1,000 gal. .		
		1	10	50
		. . . . . . (mgd)		
1a	activated sludge	100.0	47.4	36.3
1b	trickling filter	104.7	52.6	39.5
1c	rotating biological contactors	107.2	65.1	55.8
2a	2-stage nitrification	130.7	58.8	44.7
2b	rotating biological contactors	142.3	98.2	85.0
2c	extended aeration	43.2	28.4	—
3a	nitrification-denitrification	150.2	73.2	56.0
3b	selective ion exchange	189.3	89.9	65.5
4	filtration of secondary effluent	132.8	55.1	42.7
5a	alum added to aeration basin	172.8	70.3	57.4
5b	ferric chloride added to primary	156.4	77.5	57.8
5c	tertiary lime treatment	196.1	81.7	59.3
6a	tertiary lime, nitrified effluent	217.0	83.0	60.6
6b	tertiary lime plus ion exchange	224.4	108.9	77.2
7	carbon adsorption, filtered secondary effluent	176.5	72.7	57.2
8	carbon, tertiary lime effluent	238.7	99.4	74.2
9	carbon, tertiary lime, nitrified effluent	263.8	100.6	75.5
10	carbon, tertiary lime, ion exchange	288.0	126.5	91.9
11	reverse osmosis of AWT effluent	481.3	214.6	171.8
12a	physical-chemical system, lime	250.4	103.3	81.2
12b	physical-chemical system, ferric chloride	255.6	115.0	86.4
13a	irrigation	79.5	61.5	53.5
13b	infiltration-percolation	38.1	19.7	15.8
13c	overland flow	52.4	35.4	30.1

*1979 figures.

Source: NSF/RA-790225

Once the reuse costs were established, they were compared to the costs associated with developing and transporting raw water to the same point of use. Using the values for raw water, a cost-effective treatment plant capacity can be determined. Data on the value of water or the cost of development are limited, so in several cases, general costs obtained from published papers were used. Although sludge processing is an important aspect of wastewater treatment, the specific processes selected for solids handling have little bearing on effluent quality. A basic sludge process train was selected for each wastewater treatment train for the purposes of cost and energy analysis. In some cases this was determined from a comparison of two basic alternatives (biological stabilization or physical/chemical processing), while in some cases only one type of processing was deemed appropriate and no comparison was made.

To assess the economic feasibility of direct potable reuse, the cost of Level 11 treatment is compared with the cost of raw water treatment. The cost of raw water treatment, even at a high level with reverse osmosis, is still less than producing potable water from wastewater. However, as the cost of developing and delivering new supplies increases, the economic feasibility of direct potable reuse will also increase.

ORGANIC COMPOUNDS AND WASTEWATER TREATMENTS

The information in this section is based on the report in Conference III entitled "Behavior of Volatile and Extractable Organics in Combined Biological/Physical-Chemical Treatment of Municipal Wastewater," by T.A. Pressley of the U.S. EPA, Municipal Environmental Research Laboratory of Cincinnati.

Introduction

The increasing pollution of existing freshwater sources, as well as the need for wastewater reuse in many parts of the world, is focusing attention on more efficient methods of wastewater treatment. Effluents from the more common biological treatment processes contain considerable amounts of organic materials which are responsible for taste, odor, and color, some of which may possess the potential for severe toxic effects on the biota of freshwater bodies. In wastewater reuse for human consumption considerable attention has been given to aesthetic as well as physiological effects of the organic residuals thus far identified.

The organic materials in wastewaters affect, and are affected by, many of the physical-chemical and biological processes in use today. A better understanding of the composition and characteristics of the organic materials in raw wastewater, as well as effluents after various stages of treatment, aid in better design and operation of wastewater treatment processes. The purpose of this study was to examine qualitatively and semiquantitatively the behavior of the volatile (purgeable) organic materials and the semivolatile methylene-chloride-extractable organic materials after the major steps of treatment in a combined biological/physical-chemical treatment reuse process.

Conventional Physical-Chemical Treatment: In the physical-chemical treatment of raw wastewater, lime and a mineral salt such as $MgSO_4$, $FeCl_3$ or alum are added to the wastewater in the reactor to attain a pH of 10.5 to 11.6. Under these conditions, bicarbonate ions are converted to carbonate ions and precipitated by the excess calcium ions as calcium carbonate. Phosphorus is precipitated as calcium hydroxyapatite with soluble residuals below 0.1 mg/ℓ (as P). The magnesium or ferric ions, converted to their gelatinous hydroxides, provide very efficient flocculation and sedimentation of the calcium carbonate, calcium hydroxyapatite and particulate organic matter in the clarifier following the reactor.

Following lime clarification and sedimentation, ammonia removal is achieved by biological nitrification-denitrification or breakpoint chlorination. The wastewater is then treated with activated carbon (either granular or powdered) for the removal of dissolved organic materials. In some cases, effluents from carbon adsorption are "polished" by breakpoint chlorination for residual ammonia removal and disinfection.

Treatment Processes Examined: In the combined biological/physical-chemical treatment process examined in these studies, approximately 200 mg/ℓ of CaO and 15 mg/ℓ FeCl$_3$ (as Fe) were added for lime clarification, at pH 10.5 (low pH-lime process). Nitrification (suspended growth) and denitrification (fixed film) were employed for ammonia removal. Methanol dosages corresponding to methanol:NO_3-N ratios of 2:1 to 4:1 were used in denitrification. Dissolved organic material was removed by passing the effluent from the denitrification stage through granular (8 x 30 mesh) activated carbon (Filtrasorb 300) contained in four columns in series at a 4.8 ℓ/m^2/sec loading rate (downflow packed bed operation).

Following carbon adsorption, the wastewater was treated with approximately 5 mg/ℓ of alum as Al and passed at approximately 2 ℓ/m^2/sec hydraulic loading rate, through a dual media filter, containing 0.6 m of coal and 0.3 m of sand. This final flocculation and filtration step was designed to remove particulate matter formed by, or escaping from, the carbon adsorption stage. The wastewater was then chlorinated to achieve a free available chlorine concentration of 1 mg/ℓ for removal of any residual ammonia and for disinfection. The physical-chemical treatment process required a total detention time of 10.6 hr at a flow rate of 35 gpm (2.2×10^{-3} m^3/sec).

Experimental

Sampling: Wastewater samples used in these studies were taken at the U.S. EPA District of Columbia Pilot Plant located in Washington, DC. The pilot plant was designed for research in the development and demonstration of more efficient methods of municipal wastewater treatment. The combined biological/physical-chemical treatment process examined in this study was that described above. Chemical parameters typical of the District of Columbia raw wastewater and effluents after various stages of treatment are shown in Table 6.5.

Wastewater grab samples were taken of the raw wastewater (H-1) and after the following stages within the combined biological/physical-chemical treatment process: denitrification (I-7), carbon adsorption (J-7), alum coagulation and filtration (K-7) and chlorination and filtration (L-7; final effluent).

Table 6.5: Chemical Parameters Typical of the District of Columbia Raw Wastewater and After Various Stages in the Combined Biological/Physical-Chemical Treatment Process*

Chemical Parameters	H-1	I-7	K-7	L-7
Alkalinity, P	—	—	—	—
Alkalinity, MO	126	—	—	96
pH	7.2	—	7.5	7.5
Conductivity (mhos)	—	—	—	710,000
TOC	72	7.0	2.5	2.7
BOD	104	4.5	1.3	2.8
COD	237	18.5	6.6	6.5
Total P (PO_4)	15.0	0.3	0.17	0.16
TKN	19.0	0.76	0.25	0.22
NH_3-N	16.0	0.20	0.95	0.65
$NO_2^- + NO_3^--N$	0.89	4.7	4.8	4.8
Suspended solids	107	3.9	0.97	0.86
VSS	83.0	2.7	—	—
TS	—	—	—	368
Ca^{++}	32	—	—	56
T-Fe	1.3	—	—	0.6
Mg^{++}	6.5	—	—	5.4
Cl^-	—	—	—	68.7
$SO_4^=$	—	—	—	50.7
Na^+	—	—	—	34.1
K^+	—	—	—	8.2
F^-	0.7	—	—	0.7
MBAS	8.9	0.28	—	0.14
Al^{+++}	—	—	0.25	—

*mg/ℓ unless otherwise indicated.

Source: NSF/RA-790226

Samples for volatile organic analysis (VOA) were taken in 15 ml crimp-seal bottles containing a film of $Na_2S_2O_3$ sufficient to reduce the total available chlorine in a 15 ml aliquot of water containing 30 mg/ℓ of total available chlorine. The bottles were completely filled to avoid headspace losses and crimp-sealed with a Teflon seal.

Testing for Volatile Organics: Volatile organic materials were determined by GC/MS on a 5 ml sample employing the purge and trap procedures and apparatus described by Bellar and Lichtenberg (EPA-670/4-75-009).

Testing for Semivolatile Organics: Grab samples taken for the analysis of methylene-chloride-extractable acidic, neutral, and basic organic materials were contained in 1 gal wide-mouth glass jars under an aluminum foil seal. The jars were filled in order to avoid headspace losses. The samples were not dechlorinated. The samples were packed in ice and shipped by air express to the Cincinnati laboratory for extraction. The time interval between sample selection and sample extraction was 24 to 48 hr. The samples, usually 4 ℓ aliquots, were extracted in 6 ℓ separatory funnels with methylene chloride for acidic, neutral, and basic materials. The methylene chloride extracts were dried, concentrated, and the solvent changed to acetone according to the procedure described in the EPA GC/MS Procedure Manual. The final acidic, neutral, and basic methylene chloride extractable organic materials (now in acetone), were concentrated under a gentle flow of dry nitrogen, to 1.0 ml and held at 4°C for GC/MS analysis.

Quality Assurance

Quality assurance measures during the VOA involved achieving ion abundance data from perfluorotributylamine, which matched that taken when the mass spectrometer was properly tuned and verified from ion abundance data from decafluorotriphenylphosphine. Additional sensitivity and chromatographic performance checks were made by running fresh standard solutions.

Quality assurance measurements throughout the analysis of the acidic, neutral, and basic extracts involved strict compliance with the GC/MS tuning and sensitivity recommendations prescribed by Eichelberger and Budd (*Anal. Chem.,* 47:7, June 1975) with decafluorotriphenylphosphine under identical sample analysis conditions. Additional column performance and sensitivity checks were made by running a C_{18}, C_{19}, and C_{20} hydrocarbon mixture. Sensitivity was achieved so that 10 ng of the hydrocarbons produced a 4:1 signal to noise ratio.

Compound identifications were made by computerized spectral matching techniques and by running and matching against known standards when available.

Discussion of Results

Methylene Chloride Extractable Organics: The complexity of the total ion chromatograms of the extracts of methylene chloride extractable materials from wastewater after varying stages of physical-chemical treatment seemed to parallel the TOC and COD values. The methylene chloride extractable materials in the raw wastewaters showed considerable variation in content as well as in complexity of the total ion chromatograms.

No single organic compound was found in the 8/3/76 raw wastewater extracts above 10 ppb. In the 11/4/76 raw wastewater extracts, only stearic and palmitic acids were found at concentrations above 10 ppb. These acids, as well as lauric and oleic, were found in the neutral fraction and were not found at concentrations above 1 ppb in the acidic fraction. Caffein was also found in the neutral fraction and not detected in the basic fraction. The large number of saturated and unsaturated aliphatic hydrocarbons detected in the raw wastewater extracts indicate motor oil and other internal combustion engine by-products. No organic bases were detected in the raw wastewater extracts except caffein and a trace of a compound tentatively identified as N,N-diphenylhydrazine.

Following lime precipitation (clarification), biological nitrification and denitrification, (I-7), the methylene-chloride-extractable organic materials in the wastewater were dramatically reduced from that of the raw wastewater. Only acetic acid was identified in this neutral fraction of I-7 at a concentration greater than 1 ppb. This probably was sample contamination since acetic acid is sufficiently volatile to have been lost during Kuderna-Danish concentration and should not have been extracted into the neutral fraction.

Following carbon adsorption, GC/MS analysis of the K-7 extracts revealed further reduction of complexity in the total ion chromatograms. The TOC and COD analyses revealed a parallel reduction of total organic matter. No compounds were identified in any of the K-7 extracts at concentrations greater than 1 ppb. Likewise, no peaks were observed in the total ion chromatograms of the K-7 extracts that could have represented concentrations greater than 1 ppb.

Following chlorination for residual ammonia removal and disinfection and alum addition and filtration for residual turbidity removal, the total ion chromatograms of the final effluent (L-7) extracts revealed no significant difference from those of the K-7 extracts. All of the compounds identified in the L-7 extracts were at low ppb levels (1-5 ppb) or at the lower limits of detection by GC/MS under the conditions employed in these tests. These low concentrations encountered in the methylene chloride extracts of the final effluents from the wastewater treatment system made spectral identification difficult and were responsible for most of the tentative identifications made.

Considerable quantities of chlorinated and brominated cyclohexanes, cyclohexenes, and cyclohexanols were detected in the neutral and acidic extracts of the final effluent. The presence of these compounds was attributed to the extraction of wastewater containing free chlorine residuals with methylene chloride preserved with cyclohexene.

Volatile (Purgeable) Organics: Halogenated ethanes and methanes were compiled into a separate table for special discussion due to the recent emphasis placed on these materials as possible carcinogens.

In the Washington, DC raw wastewater, chloroform concentrations averaged a rather steady 10 μg/ℓ in the summertime grab samples. Other halogenated methanes and ethanes identified in the raw wastewater were at concentrations below 10 μg/ℓ. The concentration of chloroform in the wastewater was reduced 50 to 100% following biological nitrification and denitrification (I-7). The concentrations of other halogenated methanes and ethanes identified in the wastewater following biological nitrification and denitrification were reduced to levels not detectable by the conditions employed in these tasks.

This reduction in the concentration of volatile halogenated methanes and ethanes was attributed to the purging action of the aeration step incorporated in the nitrification step previously described. No further reductions in the volatile halogenated methanes and ethanes were observed following the carbon adsorption (J-7). Indeed, chloroform concentrations may have increased slightly following carbon adsorption as shown in the 7/1/76 to 7/8/76 tests.

After chlorination to a free chlorine residual of approximately 1 mg/ℓ, the final effluent (L-7) contained concentrations of chloroform ranging from 5 to 10 μg/ℓ. Other halogenated methane and ethane concentrations increased from undetectable levels to levels ranging from 3 to 5 μg/ℓ. More data is necessary to substantiate this apparent formation of halogenated methanes and ethanes by chlorination of treated wastewaters. In these studies no attempt was made to ascertain that the chlorine used in the chlorination step was not contaminated with chloroform and other volatile halogenated materials.

Other volatile (purgeable)/organic materials identified in the wastewaters are tabulated in Table 6.6. Organic compounds other than the halogenated methanes and ethanes were not consistently detected in the final effluent (L-7) above 1 μg/ℓ.

Table 6.6: Other Volatile (Purgeable) Organic Materials Identified in Effluents of the Combined Biological/Physical-Chemical Process

Compound	H-1	I-7	J-7	K-7
	. . . . μg/ℓ			
6/18/76				
Acetaldehyde	—	√	√	—
Methanol	—	—	—	—
Acetone	√	√	√	√
Dichloromethane	10	—	1	1
Acrolein	—	√	—	√
Carbon disulfide	—	—	—	√
Dimethyl disulfide	6	—	—	—
Toluene	2	—	—	—
Xylene	1	—	—	√
Alkylbenzene	1	—	—	—
Benzaldehyde	—	√	—	—
7/1/76				
Acetaldehyde	√	—	—	—
Methanol	—	—	—	—
Acetone	√	√	√	√
Dichloromethane	1	—	1	—
Acrolein	√	—	—	—
Carbon disulfide	√	—	—	—
Dimethyl disulfide	—	—	—	—
Toluene	2	—	√	—
Xylene	—	√	√	√
Alkylbenzene	√	—	—	—
Benzaldehyde	—	√	—	5
7/8/76				
Acetaldehyde	—	—	—	—
Methanol	√	—	—	—
Acetone	√	√	√	√
Dichloromethane	—	√	2	√
Acrolein	—	—	—	—

(continued)

Table 6.6: (continued)

Compound	H-1	I-7	J-7	K-7
			μg/ℓ	
Carbon disulfide	—	—	√	—
Dimethyl disulfide	—	—	—	—
Toluene	2	√	√	√
Xylene	—	√	√	—
Alkylbenzene	—	—	—	—
Benzaldehyde	—	—	—	√

Note: Dash (—) indicates not detected.
Check (√) indicates trace amounts (less than 1 μg/ℓ).

Source: NSF/RA-790226

Conclusions

The dramatic reduction in the total organic material in the wastewater follow-ing lime clarification and biological nitrification and denitrification, as mon-itored by COD and TOC paralleled the reduction in the complexity and number of peaks in the respective gas chromatograms. The efficient removal of the specific organic matter by lime precipitation and biological nitrification and denitrification (ammonia removal step) suggested effective:

Adsorption and absorption by the gelatinous hydroxides formed during the lime clarification step, with subsequent removal by sed-imentation (occlusion);

Purging of the more volatile organic materials from the water during the aeration step of biological nitrification; and

Biological degradation of the organic materials and/or adsorption into the biomass during the nitrification and denitrification proc-esses.

The activated carbon process reduced the wastewater TOC from approximately 6 mg/ℓ to 2 mg/ℓ. The absence of peaks in the gas chromatograms of the acidic, neutral, and basic fractions of the extracts from treated wastewater samples taken after the activated carbon treatment step indicated that the residual or-ganic materials ($\sim$2 mg/ℓ of TOC) may be of amphoteric nature and thus not extractable by organic solvents used in analytical methods, or that any specific extractable organic may be at concentration levels below the level of detection employed in these tests. Further work is needed to characterize the 2 mg/ℓ of residual TOC in the renovated water.

The results of these studies of the behavior of volatile and extractable organics in a combined biological/physical-chemical treatment of a municipal raw waste-water revealed final effluent concentrations of halogenated methanes and eth-ane, other volatile organic materials, and the extractable materials to be similar to those found in finished drinking waters during the EPA National Reconnaissance Survey of 1975. The specific organic compounds identified in the final effluent have also been identified in finished drinking waters (Warner and English, EPA-600/2-78-027, March 1978).

COMPOSITE MEMBRANE FOR RO USE

The information in this section is based on a report published in Conference II entitled "Composite Membrane for Waste Water Reclamation" by R.G. Sudak, and R.L. Fox, of Membrane Systems, Inc.

History of RO in Water Treatment

The generally accepted date for the beginning of commercial application of reverse osmosis membranes is 1970. The first market of any magnitude was the industrial pretreatment of process water in the electronics industry. The use of reverse osmosis for the production of potable water from brackish wells followed, but this has been limited to locations where the lack of a dependable potable water supply retarded development of valuable real estate.

The process is now being introduced on a commercial scale as an alternative to distillation for the demineralization of seawater, and initial results would indicate that reverse osmosis should be regarded as a serious competitor. However, the severity of a seawater environment and the consequent economics will limit the use of either process for the foreseeable future. Another obvious source of potable and industrial waters is the renovation of wastewaters by reverse osmosis. This assumes that the valid issues of health considerations may be successfully resolved. It would appear that some of these problems may have been overcome already in that large-scale plants are in operation or in planning, e.g., Water Factory 21 and the Yuma Desalting Plant.

Asymmetric Membranes

Until recently, the reverse osmosis process has relied solely on the use of asymmetric membranes which were prepared from either cellulose acetate or polyamide. The cellulose acetate membranes were packaged in the spiral wound, tubular and hollow fine fiber configuration, and the polyamide was packaged in the hollow fine fiber configuration. These asymmetric membranes suffered some severe operating limitations.

It is evident that the number of feedwaters that can be desalinated with these membranes is limited and, in many cases, extensive pretreatment is required. Unfortunately, wastewaters emanate from a wide variety of sources, and it would appear that in order to be more effective in the treatment of wastewaters, membranes with more versatility will have to be developed. This could be done with a single membrane having a wider range of operating limits or, as is more likely, with a family of membranes to meet the variable needs.

Asymmetric membranes are fabricated from various homopolymers. The formulation and casting conditions largely determine their reverse osmosis properties. In the last decade it was determined that an asymmetric membrane consists of a relatively thin, dense skin supported by an amorphous underlayer. In general, most sheet membranes are cast on a fabric carrier material which is a mechanical aid to assist in handling. Once the nature of asymmetric membranes was understood, the logical extension was the concept of composite membranes.

Composite Membranes

The first composite membrane was developed at the North Star Research Institute and designated as the NS-1 membrane (1). Polysulfone was used as the porous support and the membrane barrier layer was formed by the interfacial polycondensation of polyethyleneimine (PEI) and toluene-2,4-diisocyanate (TDI). The resultant polyurea had all the advantages and disadvantages of the hollow fine fiber polyamides. Another composite developed at North Star was the NS-200 membrane (1). This membrane barrier layer is formed on a polysulfone porous support by the in situ condensation of furfuryl alcohol into furan.

Additional composite membrane work was done at the Fluid Systems Division of UOP where the PA-100 membrane (2) was formed on polysulfone by the interfacial polycondensation (3) of PEI with isophthaloyl chloride (IPC) to form a polyamide membrane barrier layer (4). The substitution of IPC for TDI gave an improved flux while retaining good rejection characteristics. All of the above membranes have one thing in common in that they are sensitive to residual chlorine in the feedwater.

In the case of membranes formed from PEI, it has been theorized that the residual chlorine sensitivity is the result of secondary amines in the polymer backbone. In an attempt to improve the resistance to residual chlorine, Fluid Systems developed the PA-300 membrane (5). This membrane also utilizes a polysulfone porous support, and the membrane barrier layer is formed from the interfacial polycondensation of epiamine and IPC.

Epiamine is a water-soluble polymer formed by the condensation reaction of polyepichlorohydrin and ethylenediamine. It differs from PEI in that secondary diamines are not in the polymer backbone but are pendant groups. This membrane proved to be more resistant to residual chlorine in that considerably more time is required to achieve the same level of performance degradation that would be achieved by PA-100 membrane at the same concentration of residual chlorine.

Another membrane which has been designated as RC-100 by Fluid Systems is formed on polysulfone by the interfacial polycondensation of epiamine and TDI. A summary of the polymer systems discussed above is shown in Table 6.7. It is understood that the NS-200 membrane has been evaluated for possible commercial production and has been found to be unstable under long-term operating conditions even with dechlorinated feedwaters. Of the membranes mentioned, only the PA-300 and the RC-100 type of membranes are commercially available at this time. In any event, only a small number of polymer systems have been evaluated for composite membrane application, and it is suggested that this represents a small fraction of the possibilities available to polymer chemists.

Table 6.7: Composite Membranes

Membrane	Reactants	Membrane Barrier Layer Polymer
NS-1	Polyethyleneimine-tolylene-2,4-diisocyanate	Polyurea
NS-200	Furfuryl alcohol	Furan
PA-100	Polyethyleneimine-isophthaloyl chloride	Polyamide
NS-100	Polyethyleneimine-isophthaloyl chloride	Polyamide
PA-300	Epiamine-isophthaloyl chloride	Polyether/amide
RC-100	Epiamine-tolylene-2,4-diisocyanate	Polyether/urea

Source: NSF/RA-790225

PA-100 and PA-300 Membranes

The PA-100 system has been investigated at Membrane Systems and has been found to be extremely versatile. By varying the concentration of the reactants it can be used from low-pressure brackish water applications to the desalination of seawater. One formulation will give a membrane that will produce 20 gal/ft^2/day at 97% salt rejection when operated at 250 psig on a feedwater containing 5,000 mg/ℓ of sodium chloride at a temperature of 75°F.

Another variation will give a membrane that will produce 20 gal/ft^2/day at 99.2% rejection when operated at 800 psig on a feedwater containing 35,000 mg/ℓ of sodium chloride at a temperature of 75°F. The PA-300 membrane shows similar versatility with reactant concentration variation. At the low-pressure test conditions specified above, fluxes of 16 gal/ft^2/day and 98% rejection were obtained. Under seawater conditions fluxes of 20 gal/ft^2/day and 99% rejection have been obtained.

Advantages: The PA-100 and PA-300 membranes have the following advantages over cellulose acetate membranes:

They can operate over a broader range, i.e., pH 3 to 12. However, it is noted that flux and rejection vary as a function of pH and the optimum rejection is found between pH 4 to 6;

Flux decline, or compaction, is of less consequence. A log-log compaction slope of −0.01 at 1,000 psig and 25°C have been shown, whereas recently developed cellulose acetate membranes show a compaction rate of −0.04;

There is no evidence of biological degradation in the limited data available;

The membrane has been shown to be stable to alcohols, esters, ketones, and hydrocarbons and demonstrates better rejections of these compounds; and

They can be operated at elevated temperatures, i.e., 140°F compared to 95°F for cellulose acetate.

As previously mentioned, both of these membranes are susceptible to attack by residual chlorine.

Other Experimental Membranes

To eliminate the susceptibility of polyamides to residual chlorine, several membranes have been prepared with the difunctional secondary amine, piperazine. By reacting piperazine with IPC, the secondary amine is converted to a tertiary amine and, theoretically, the resultant polyamide is resistant to residual chlorine. At Membrane Systems this technique was used to form the membrane barrier layer on polysulfone. Short-term testing showed that this composite membrane was indeed resistant to residual chlorine. However, the best flux and rejection obtained at low-pressure brackish water test conditions were 5 gal/ft^2/day and 90% rejection.

As noted above, the prepolymer, epiamine, has been used successfully in the PA-300 membranes. It was theorized that piperazine, instead of ethylenediamine, could be reacted with polyepichlorohydrin to form a poly(epichlorohydrin-secondary diamine) as the prepolymer. This would then be reacted with IPC to form a polyamide membrane barrier layer without a secondary amine in either the backbone or the crosslinking sites. The prepolymer has been synthesized at Membrane Systems and composite membranes have been prepared which, under low-pressure brackish water test conditions, give a flux of 17 gal/ft^2/day and a rejection of 97%. While the membrane does show an improved resistance to residual chlorine, it is still susceptible to attack. Work on this system is in progress at this time and conclusions are not available.

Another approach utilizing piperazine has been attempted at the North Star Division of the Midwest Research Institute. Prepolymers were formed by reacting either trimesoyl chloride, cyanuric chloride or phosphorus oxychloride with piperazine (6). The product was then reacted with IPC to form the membrane barrier layer. Indications are that this membrane is resistant to residual chlorine and reports of preliminary work show interesting properties for seawater desalination. When tested at 1,000 psig on synthetic 3.5% seawater, typical results were 13.9 gal/ft^2/day and 99.2% rejection. It is suspected that these membranes would also be capable of operation at extended pH ranges and higher temperatures while not being susceptible to biological attack.

Polysulfone Support: To date, the majority of composite membranes have been formed on polysulfone porous support. While polysulfone has served its purpose, it has inherent limitations which prevent its use in the development of a broad range of composite membranes. Polysulfone has excellent thermal stability, and it can be used under continuous service at temperatures up to 170°C. It is highly resistant to oxidizing agents, mineral acids, alkali and salt solutions. Resistance to aliphatic hydrocarbons and detergents is good but it is attacked by chlorinated hydrocarbons and aromatic hydrocarbons as well as polar organic solvents such as esters and ketones. It has fair to good resistance to most alcohols and ethers.

Since the techniques for casting polysulfone are well known, it is not surprising that it was the first choice for use as a porous support in composite membranes. The low temperature used in the formation of the NS-1 membrane barrier layer and the intermediate temperature used in the formation of NS-200 membrane barrier layer are compatible with the nature of polysulfone. In addition, the ultimate use for the membrane (desalination of brackish and seawaters) was also compatible with the chemical and mechanical properties of the support.

Development of other membranes has been impeded due to the lack of a wide range of porous supports. For example, the in situ formation of a polyimide membrane barrier layer requires a higher temperature capability than that possessed by polysulfone. Another example is the thin film deposition of a homopolymer from a chlorinated hydrocarbon solvent.

Recent work at Membrane Systems has resulted in the preliminary development of polycarbonate, polyphenylsulfone, polyimide, polyvinylidene fluoride, and polyphenylquinoxaline as porous support materials. Some of the interesting physical and chemical properties of these polymers are shown in Table 6.8 (7). To date, it has been demonstrated that a porous support can be cast from each of these polymers and that the porous support can be successfully incorporated into a PA-100 type composite membrane. As can be seen from the table, the above porous supports do extend the range of possibilities that are now open to membrane scientists with imagination.

Table 6.8: Porous Supports—Physical and Chemical Properties

Material	Continuous Heat (°C)	. . . . Solvents					
		Acids	Bases	Aromatic	Aliphatic	Chlorinated	Ketones and Esters
Polysulfone	170	G-F	G	X	G-F	X	F-X
Polycarbonate	125	G-F	X	X	G	X	X
Polyphenylsulfone	260	E	E	F	E	G-F	F-G
Polyvinylidene fluoride	170	E	E	E	E	E	X
Polyimide	260	G-X	X	E	E	E	E
Polyphenylquinoxaline	450	G	E	E	E	X	E

Note: E is excellent, no discernible attack; G is good, no significant attack; F is fair, limited attack; and X is unacceptable.

Source: NSF/RA-790225

Ultrafiltration Membranes: To this point the discussion has been limited to the role of composite membranes in desalination with reverse osmosis. In order to produce an effective composite membrane, it is necessary to have a porous support with a small mean pore diameter and a large porosity (number of pores). This necessity is dictated by the fact that the support must not only handle permeate flow with relatively little resistance, but it must truly support the thin film membrane barrier layer without rupture.

Both the mean pore diameter and the porosity can be altered by variation of casting solution formulation and/or casting conditions. By tailoring the pore diameter, it is possible to use any of the six porous supports mentioned above as an ultrafiltration membrane. If desalination of a wastewater is not required and the only requirement to reclaim a wastewater is the removal of suspended solids, then this can be done more economically with ultrafiltration membranes.

In conclusion, the following observations about composite membranes should be made. The concept of thin film composite membranes expands the number of possibilities available to custom fabrication of membranes for specific applications in wastewater reclamation. While initial developments in composite membranes are very promising, it is evident that only a very small number of possibilities have been explored. As the needs in the field of wastewater reclamation are clarified, efforts of membrane scientists will focus on the technical and economic feasibility of adapting composite membrane technology to the problem.

References

(1) Cadotte, J.E., et al, *In-situ Formed Condensation Polymers for Reverse Osmosis Membrane,* Final Report, OWRT Contract 14-30-2883, North Star Research (February, 1975).

(2) Riley, R.L., et al, *Research and Development on a Spiral Wound Membrane System for Single Stage Seawater Desalination,* Final Report OWRT Contract No. 14-30-3303, Fluid Systems Division, UOP, Inc. (1974).

(3) Enkelman, V., et al, "Mechanism for Interfacial Polycondensation and the Direct Synthesis of Stable Polyamide Membrane," *Macromol. Chem.,* 177, 3177 (1976).

(4) Wittbecker, E.L. and Morgan, P.W., "Interfacial Polycondensation," I-X, *J. Polym. Sci.,* XL, 289–418 (1959).

(5) Riley, R.L., et al, *Spiral Wound Poly(Ether-Amide) Thin Film Composite Membrane Systems,* First Desalination Congress of the American Continent, Mexico City, Fluid Systems Div., UOP, Inc. (1976).

(6) Cadotte, J.E., et al, *Research on In-situ Formed Condensation Polymer for Reverse Osmosis Membranes,* Final Report OWRT Contract No. 14-34-0001-6521, North Star Research Div., Midwest Research Inst. (1978).

(7) Harper, C.A., *Handbook of Plastics and Elastomers,* McGraw-Hill Book Co., New York (1975).

USE OF OZONE IN WASTEWATER TREATMENT

This section uses information contained in the paper in Conference II entitled, "Ozone Applications: A Water Reuse Review," by H.M. Rosen of Union Carbide Corporation, Ozonation Systems.

Introduction

Water reuse in most cases will be indirect, i.e., treated wastewater will be ground injected, stored in surface water reservoirs, or mixed with other "pure" water supplies. After some variable time, this water will then undergo a second treatment stage, usually called water treatment, as opposed to the wastewater treatment it received prior to its initial discharge. Often a middle stage of treatment, advanced waste treatment (AWT), is added to the end of more traditional wastewater treatment when reuse is in mind.

Until a relatively few years ago the solution to pollution was dilution, and the same water bodies were often used for wastewater discharges and water supplies, with very little thought or planning about the relationships between the two. This, of course, is changing as the scarcity and value of water resources are realized. Also, the definition of potable water purity has changed and continues to evolve as we recognize the potential dangers of micropollutants and are more easily able to identify and quantify them.

Potable reuse is not new. For many years the rivers of Europe were its sewers, and water withdrawn from these sources required a much higher degree of treatment before use as compared with the much more pristine nature of water sources in the U.S. The use of ozone for wastewater reuse is well established in the field, since the commercial history of ozonation to treat potable water dates back to Europe in the early 20th century.

Ozone is currently being used widely outside the U.S. (over 1,100 water treatment plants in operation) and is rapidly gaining acceptance here in treating both water and wastewater. Ozone has been demonstrated to have a place at both ends and the middle (AWT) of a potable reuse scheme.

Applications for Ozone

As reuse schemes develop and become more direct, the differentiation between treated wastewater and raw potable water begins to disappear. This distinction becomes even less meaningful as the use of ozone for polishing or as part of AWT is considered, since some products of AWT are of higher quality in some areas than raw water sources in others. Thus, for the purposes of limiting discussion primarily to reuse for potable purposes, no differentiation will be made between wastewater and water and, unless otherwise stated, the term "water" will be used generically.

Ozone is the strongest oxidant available for water treatment. In its role as an oxidant it is also the strongest practical disinfectant known with respect to all types of microorganisms. Thus the application of ozone to water and the resulting purification will generally fall into two categories, oxidation and disinfection. In addition, the process of ozonation can lead to improvements in water quality not necessarily connected with either.

While the advantages of ozone are many, ozonation like any unit process does not stand alone, but is part of a multiple unit process treatment scheme to achieve a cost-effective treatment objective. Also, each water is different and, although discussions tend to generalize the utility of any unit process to achieve the cost effective objective when combined with the other possible unit processes, that utility will vary. As a result, for a particular water, ozonation will be only one method of treatment among and in combination with many others that may be necessary.

Disinfection: The difference between water and wastewater disinfection by ozone is only a matter of degree. The disinfection of wastewater requires more ozone because of the demands created by the other materials present which compete for the ozone. Thus, the quality of the wastewater which exhibits a decreasing ozone demand with increasing quality is the prime determinant of the required amount of ozone to achieve disinfection. Other determinants are the level of disinfection desired and the organisms to be inactivated.

Table 6.9 demonstrates the relative efficiency of ozone as compared to other disinfectants on particular microorganism types, and the relative efficiencies of the various disinfectants to a particular class of microorganisms on the basis of a dose-time relationship.

Study of various data shows that ozone disinfection efficiency increases as the effluent quality increases, and that reasonable doses of ozone are required for high effluent disinfection levels, both for bacteria and viruses. The data also present some conflicting specifics which only indicate what is already well known, independent of disinfectant—that the water in question must be examined using the treatment considered, for confidence in resulting quality.

Table 6.9: Comparative Disinfection Efficiency: Ozone vs Chlorine

| Agent | . . . . Λ (mg/ℓ)$^{-1}$ (min)$^{-1}$ at 5°C . . . . | | | |
	Enteric Bacteria	Viruses	Amoebic Cysts	Spores
O_3	500	5	0.5	2
Cl_2 as HOCl	20	1.0 up	0.05	0.05
Cl_2 as OCl$^-$	0.2	<0.02	0.0005	<0.0005
Cl_2 as NH_2Cl	0.1	0.005	0.2	0.001

Note: Λ is specific susceptibility coefficient when organisms are compared.
Λ is specific lethality coefficient when germicides are compared.

Source: NSF/RA-790225

Organic Removal by Direct Oxidation: The second primary use of ozone is chemical oxidation. In this area, ozone is such a strong oxidant that there are essentially no organic compounds that, from the point of view of thermodynamics, it cannot oxidize to CO_2 and H_2O. However, ozone oxidation at the low doses usually employed in water treatment is incomplete, having little effect on

TOC, while at higher doses, usually considered too costly, major TOC reductions can be realized.

Smaller removals of TOC than would be expected from thermodynamic arguments result because, under the usual design conditions for ozonation, dissolved ozone concentrations are low and the kinetics of the organic oxidation reactions limit the utility of ozone to reduce the concentration of TOC. However, as the cost of alternatives increases, so does the cost-effective potential of ozone, especially as a polishing agent where removal of small amounts of TOC is what is required of ozone for reuse situations.

The most definitive study in this area was performed several years ago in the EPA Washington, DC Blue Plains pilot plant (Wynn, C.S., et al, EPA-R2-73-146). One of the conclusions of the study which examined a variety of effluents was that a 50% COD removal (40 to 20 mg/ℓ) could be achieved at a 1973 cost of $0.10/1,000 gal for a 50 mgd plant. Another conclusion was that there appear to be no technical limits on the COD removal. The study further concludes that the rate of COD reduction is increased with increasing pH and increased dissolved ozone concentration.

The study goes on to report that high ozone dose tertiary treatment results in practically bacteria-free water, and turbidity reductions are significant. The efficiency of COD removal generally ranged from 3 parts of COD per part of ozone for high COD concentrations, to 1 part of COD per 3 parts of ozone at low concentrations.

Suspended Solids Removal by Flotation/Oxidation: Some effluents, especially those containing specific organics which, when oxidized, cause froth, will produce a rigid foam which floats to the surface of an ozone contactor and can be removed for disposal by conventional (e.g., water spray) means. The froth flotation mechanism appears to be enhanced by small amounts of iron and/or manganese in the wastewater which, when oxidized by ozone, create pin floc nuclei around which the froth can develop. This flotation mechanism can remove significant amounts of many different wastewater constituents, especially when looked at as part of a tertiary polishing scheme. The froth flotation mechanism is not well understood and many effluents, even of relatively low quality, do not foam when ozonated.

The froth referred to above is not the detergent foam often found as a result of wastewater aeration, but has a more rigid, handleable consistency. In fact, ozone has been shown in some cases to reduce the more traditional effluent foaming problems because of its ability to oxidize surfactants.

Microflocculation: The removal of turbidity and soluble organics, or improvements in these removals, can be accomplished by another ozonation mechanism, usually termed microflocculation. In a sense ozone acts as a flocculent aid, often allowing reduction in coagulants by making them more efficient. This phenomenon has been reported often, especially at low ozone doses in water treatment applications. This is another of the underutilized (because it is not well understood) ozone applications which may have potential in reuse schemes.

Specific Micropollutant Removal: While the gross removal of organics through the measurement of parameters such as COD and TOC has been discussed, it should not be forgotten that ozone can be very selective in its reactions toward particular types of organics.

In an excellent piece of research, Gardiner and Montgomery (*Water and Waste Treatment,* 12, Sept/Oct 1968) reported on the treatment of settled trickling filter effluents. Table 6.10 shows the effect of ozone on pesticides added to this wastewater. When a mixture of phenols, including phenol, o-, m-, and p-cresol and catechol, was added to the wastewater, an absorbed ozone dose of 25.6 mg/ℓ reduced the total phenols concentration from 11.8 to 2.3 mg/ℓ or an 81% reduction, at the same time that the wastewater COD was reduced from 76 to 62 mg/ℓ.

Table 6.10: Effect of Ozonation on Chlorinated Pesticide Removal from Settled Trickling Filter Effluent

Pesticide	Absorbed Ozone (mg/ℓ)	Pesticide Concentration Pre-O_3	Post-O_3	Removal (%)
		. . . . (mg/ℓ)		
γ-BHC	8.8	1.32	0.88	33
Dieldrin	18.3	1.30	0.66	49
DDT	11.7	2.00	0.54	73
TDE	11.7	2.00	0.62	69

Source: NSF/RA-790225

Stripping for Volatile Organics Removal: The process of ozonation is one in which relatively large gas volumes are added to the water. At a nominal 1 wt % concentration of ozone in the gas phase, 100 pounds of air are added for every pound of ozone. Thus, at a 5 ppm dose, 38.8 scfm would be applied to each million gallons. As a result, certain volatiles will be stripped and removed from solution. The pesticide results reported above may be largely due to this phenomenon, since highly chlorinated organics are generally refractory to ozonation.

Pretreatment Prior to Biological Treatment or GAC: *Biological Treatment* — There has been a little work on the treatment of wastes prior to biological treatment in order to detoxify or make the waste less refractory so that biological treatment can be more efficient. This treatment has been considered both prior to biological treatment for removal of carbonaceous material as well as prior to nitrification. Since ozone is very often selective on a kinetic basis for biologically refractory material and tends to produce a higher BOD/COD before BOD is ultimately oxidized and TOC removal occurs, pretreatment with ozone can make a waste more amenable to biological treatment for removal of carbonaceous material. Also, since ozone can detoxify many of the materials which tend to inhibit nitrification, a similar pretreatment may help enhance biological ammonia oxidation. In this area both the oxidation and stripping action resulting from ozone treatment can be useful.

Ozone Enhanced Biologically Active Carbon (OEBAC) — Biologically active carbon, commonly referred to as BAC, is one of the areas of high current interest in ozonation. Since essentially all granular activated carbon (GAC) systems support biological growth, the name is somewhat inappropriate; hence, the title of this section, ozone enhanced biologically active carbon or OEBAC. A good review of OEBAC was recently published by Miller and Rice (*Civil Engrg.-ASCE,* February 1978).

Table 6.11 lists the potential advantages of OEBAC. OEBAC has been studied and is operating for water treatment, wastewater treatment as part of a physical-chemical treatment scheme with no biological treatment, and for tertiary polishing of a biologically treated wastewater with reclamation in mind. OEBAC results from a Swiss study show that effluent quality after 50 weeks is still comparable to that reported for new carbon. All these results suggest that OEBAC can be a powerful tool for water treatment and especially for effluent polishing prior to reuse.

Table 6.11: Advantages of OEBAC

- More effective removal of biodegradable and nonbiodegradable organics than by GAC or ozone alone.
- Increases organic loading compared with GAC significantly.
- Extends time between necessary carbon regeneration (periods of 1 month have been extended to more than 3 years).
- Applicable to both water and wastewater treatment.
- Significantly reduces capital, operating and maintenance costs of GAC systems.
- Prevents anaerobic conditions and resulting problems.
- Ammonia removal (biological nitrification) possible.

Source: NSF/RA-790225

Catalytic Ozonation: The last area of ozonation that requires some discussion because of its potential value in reclamation applications and because it has been studied a good deal is catalytic ozonation. Four categories, soluble chemical catalysis, insoluble chemical catalysis, ultrasonic catalysis, and ultraviolet (UV) catalysis, require mention.

Soluble Chemical Catalysis — While little is known about all the potential catalytic effects of water-soluble catalysts, primarily because of their complexities, two cases are worth pointing out. The first is the catalytic effect of cupric ion on the oxidation of cyanides (Bollyky, EPA-600/2-77-104). While it is not implied that this catalyst and pollutant would necessarily be of specific use in reclamation for potable purposes, it is certainly important in industrial reuse and it does point out the type of catalytic effects possible which may affect the treatment of a specific water.

The second and more important catalytic effect comes as a result of production of hydroxyl radicals. When water is ozonated, it is postulated that oxidation occurs both directly through molecular ozone (Hoigne and Bader, *Water Research* 10:377) and by hydroxyl radicals. The formation of these radicals can be enhanced by several techniques including raising the pH and, if this type of catalytic ozonation is understood and used to advantage, the cost-effectiveness of ozone oxidation may be improved.

Insoluble Chemical Catalysis — Chen et al have reported on the effect of such catalysts as Raney nickel on the oxidation of specific compounds in water. While the catalytic effect is present, a very inexpensive catalyst that would not add greatly to sludge production or is easily recoverable will be required before the use of such catalysts can be justified in wastewater treatment.

Ultrasonic Catalysis — Ultrasonic catalysis is listed as a catalytic effect although, in some instances, an observed improvement in ozone oxidation efficiency may be due to the sonic emulsification of the wastes to produce good mixing and turbulence for ozone mass transfer and reduction of particle size of solids, rather than a true catalysis. Sierka, however, has shown that sonification can apparently catalyze the ozone oxidation of specific compounds.

UV Catalysis — This is the area in which the most work on catalysis of aqueous ozonation reactions has been performed. Table 6.12 presents some data showing this catalytic effect with respect to particular compounds refractory to traditional ozonation.

Table 6.12: RFI* Values—Selected Compounds

Compound	Formula	RFI (O_3)	RFI (O_3 + UV)
Ethanol	CH_3CH_2OH	245	47
Acetic acid	CH_3CO_2H	>1,000	41
Ferricyanide	$Fe(CN)_6^{-3}$	270	8.6
Glycerol	$CHOH(CH_2OH)_2$	112	7.4
Palmitic acid	$CH_3(CH_2)_{14}CO_2H$	27.3	7.2
Glycine	$H_2NCH_2CO_2H$	19.7	6.0

*RFI is Refractory Index. A measure of relative resistance to ozone oxidation based on half-life conversion to CO_2 and H_2O.

Source: NSF/RA-790225

Summary and Discussion

Some of the applications discussed above result only in modification of organic molecules, such as in the case of low dose applications that oxidize trihalomethane precursors to reduce the formation of trihalomethanes upon ultimate chlorination. Other applications result in major TOC reductions. Direct ozone oxidation in some cases and OEBAC and UV ozonation have been shown to do this.

In all cases, ozonation results in improved water quality. One general benefit is high dissolved oxygen. Also, when ozone is evaluated it must be evaluated as part of a total unit process scheme to produce the required product quality, and the multiple effects of disinfection, TOC oxidation, possible solids removal, increase of DO, etc., that may result and how they may create savings in other unit processes require study.

The purpose of the foregoing is to suggest the possibilities available in the use of ozone in treating all quality waters from secondary effluents to high-purity potable waters, and because of its proven versatility and advantages to suggest that the production of high-quality water in any stage of the reuse cycle must consider ozone as a possible part of the treatment sequence, and to evaluate its usefulness through testing.

TREATMENT OF ACID MINE DRAINAGE

> The material in this section is abstracted from a paper in Conference II entitled "Soda Ash Treatment of Acid Mine Drainage Impregnated Streams for Potable Water Use," by D.A. Long, Civil Eng. Dept., Pennsylvania State University and J.A. Butler and M.V. Lenkevich of Gwin, Dobson & Forman, Inc., Altoona, PA.

Introduction

Lime neutralization of coal mine drainage is a well-known and widely applied process for upgrading stream water quality. When a significant portion of the watershed available to a municipality for water supply is affected by mine drainage pollutants, the question as to whether or not neutralized mine drainage can be economically treated to a more beneficial use level becomes a logical consideration. The $4.8 million water treatment plant in Altoona, located in south-central Pennsylvania, was constructed with "Operation Scarlift" funds ($500 million Pennsylvania bond issue money) with a view to addressing both of these problems, i.e., stream pollution abatement and municipal water supply.

The watershed involved drains a portion of the mountainous area to the southwest of Altoona in the vicinity of Penn Central Railroad's well-known Horseshoe Curve. The aftereffects of deep mining coal in this region has rendered two streams acid—Glen White Run and Kittanning Run. The latter, with only half the drainage area of the former, is about seven times more acid than Glen White Run. Early in Altoona's history, a series of three raw water reservoirs, together with transmission lines, were constructed to provide a water supply for the city during periods when the high-quality source (Mill Run Reservoir) became depleted. Under normal conditions, the backup reservoir system in the Horseshoe Curve consisted primarily of the better source, Glen White, with Kittanning Run bypassing the impoundments altogether. During severe drought, however, there were times when the highest reservoir (Kittanning Point) was fed by the Kittanning Run source, and this poor quality of water was the only one available to city consumers.

The rationale for the new treatment plant was to provide two levels of treatment: lime neutralization of Kittanning Run to meet stream release standards (pH 6.0 to 9.0 and iron 7.0 mg/ℓ); and lime neutralization and lime/soda ash softening of the reservoir system supply, fed by the Glen White source, to meet EPA potable water standards. The study was prompted by the question as to whether it would be technically and economically feasible to treat the Kittanning Run raw water source to a more beneficial use quality. It was the main objective of this project to develop the basis for considering this question within the limits imposed by the available treatment units.

Process Description

The treatment system employed consisted of three major process objectives—neutralization, softening and sludge handling. The first stage, or neutralization process, consists of the flash mix, slow mix, aeration and sedimentation units. Detention times in this flow-through sequence are 25 sec, 25 min, 1.1 hr, and 6.17 hr, respectively, based on a flow of 13,200 m^3/day (3.5 mgd). Settled solids are pumped from the sedimentation basin at a controlled rate to the flash mix (recycled sludge) and to the thickener clarifier (waste solids). Lime slurry is fed to the flash mix in a controlled amount to maintain the pH called for in the slow mix tank. In addition, as a result of this investigation, provision has been made to feed potassium permanganate into the influent raw water line.

Effluent from the first-stage sedimentation basin meets stream release water quality and, in the case of Kittanning Run, would normally be discharged from the plant. For purposes of this study, however, the effluent was directed to the mix box where lime can be added prior to softening and recarbonation. The softener unit is a circular tank arranged with separate compartments to provide zones for rapid mix, flocculation, and clarification (Walker Process ClariFlow Unit). In theory, the unit is designed to pump settled solids from the bottom-center of the tank back to the reaction zone.

Chemicals (soda ash, alum, coagulant aid, and potassium permanganate) can also be fed at this point to allow for mixing of the applied flow with previously formed floc and chemicals so that the required reactions, coagulation, and flocculation can occur. Theoretical residence times for the reactor and settling zones are 25 min and 83 min, respectively. Flow from the softener is to the recarbonation chamber 12.2 x 2.4 x 3.0 m (40' x 8' x 10') where carbon dioxide is added. Recarbonation detention time for the 13,200 m^3/day (3.5 mgd) flow is 10 min. The effluent from the recarbonation unit is filtered prior to clearwell storage and chlorination.

The major components of the sludge handling process are the thickener clarifier, holding tank and vacuum filters. For purposes of this discussion, the backwash lagoons, which receive backwash water from the filters, filtrate from the vacuum filter, and thickener overflow, also are included in the solids handling operation. The thickener receives underflow solids from the first stage (sedimentation basin) and the second stage (softener). Thickened sludge is pumped to a holding tank and from there to the vacuum filters as required. The vacuum filters are elevated so that the sludge cake can be conveyed to a hopper and periodically loaded on a truck for hauling to final disposal.

Process Engineering and Operation

Project Plan: The total project was divided into several major phases. The first phase was designed to achieve an effluent quality which would meet EPA requirements for potable water. At the time the study was conducted (August 1974-February 1975), the Interim Primary Drinking Water Standards required under the Safe Drinking Water Act had not been established. Therefore, the 1962 Public Health Service Drinking Water Standards, except for sulfate content, were used to define desired effluent quality. Specific objectives were to produce a finished water with approximately 100 mg/ℓ $CaCO_3$ hardness and containing no more than the permissible 0.3 mg/ℓ and 0.05 mg/ℓ of iron and manganese respectively. This product water was designated as "municipal water supply quality" (MWSQ).

Raw Water Quality: Raw water for the study was a blend of Kittanning Run (KR), a moderate acid mine drainage affected source, and Impounding Dam (ID), a better quality water. Design flow through the portion of the plant used for the study was 13,200 m^3/day (3.5 mgd). Because the sustained yield of Kittanning Run is less than 13,200 m^3/day, it was necessary to blend the two sources as indicated in order to achieve the design flow. Table 6.13 shows the blended water characteristic for a blend typical of that treated during the study, i.e., 5,680 m^3/day (1.5 mgd) of KR plus 7,570 m^3/day (2.0 mgd) of ID.

Table 6.13: Typical Blended Raw Water Characteristics*

Parameter	Value
pH	3.0
Acidity, mg/ℓ as $CaCO_3$	170
Calcium, mg/ℓ	28
Magnesium, mg/ℓ	18
Iron, mg/ℓ	17
Manganese, mg/ℓ	4.5
Aluminum, mg/ℓ	13
Sodium, mg/ℓ	1.8
Hardness, mg/ℓ as $CaCO_3$	260
Sulfates, mg/ℓ	270
Specific conductance, μmhos/cm^2	820

*Kittanning Run:Impounding Dam is 1:1.33.

Source: NSF/RA-790225

Analytical Methods: Samples for the various analyses performed during the study were collected daily and composited by treatment plant personnel. Following collection, the samples were transported to the laboratory for analysis.

EPA methods were used for the determination of acidity, alkalinity, suspended and dissolved solids, aluminum, calcium, iron, magnesium, manganese, sodium, and sulfate.

"Standard Methods" procedures were used to determine pH and specific conductance. All hardness values reported herein were calculated in accordance with "Standard Methods" using the values obtained for Ca, Mg, Al, Mn, and Fe.

Municipal Water Supply Quality Results: For the purposes of this project, municipal water supply quality was defined as treated water having a total dissolved solids (TDS) content of less than 500 mg/ℓ. Further, the target hardness for the treated water during this portion of the study was 100 mg $CaCO_3$/ℓ. Also, as indicated earlier, effluent limits for iron and manganese were 0.3 mg/ℓ and 0.05 mg/ℓ, respectively.

Examination of the characteristics of the typical blended raw water in Table 6.13 indicates that about 28% of the total hardness (TH) was due to magnesium (73 of 255 mg/ℓ as $CaCO_3$). The target hardness of 100 mg $CaCO_3$/ℓ, therefore, should have been achievable by leaving most of the magnesium in the water and by removing calcium hardness down to its minimum practical solubility of 30 to 40 mg $CaCO_3$/ℓ. One concern, however, with this approach is the potential problem of magnesium silicate scaling in the high-temperature service, such as boiler feedwater application, when the magnesium hardness exceeds 40 mg $CaCO_3$/ℓ.

Assuming that a magnesium hardness of approximately 70 mg $CaCO_3$/ℓ is acceptable, the desired hardness should have been achieved by maintaining the softener pH at approximately 9.5 and by using conventional lime-soda ash softening operational parameters. Soda ash addition to remove noncarbonate hardness (NCH) could then be used to control the effluent total hardness.

A probability plot of the softener effluent total hardness indicated that the target hardness of 100 mg $CaCO_3$/ℓ was achieved only approximately 30% of the time. Effluent hardnesses of 125 mg $CaCO_3$/ℓ or less were obtained approximately 70% of the time, and 85% of the time the effluent hardness was 150 mg $CaCO_3$/ℓ or less. It is believed the primary reason for the poor performance of the softening operation was the inability to adequately build up and retain solids in the reaction zone of the ClariFlow unit. Successful solids-contact softener operation is highly dependent upon having enough preformed crystals in the reaction zone to increase the rate of chemical reactions in the process.

Accurate control of pH in the range of 7.0 to 9.5 was impossible during the study due to problems with the pH controllers. The problem of maintaining pH control in this range made proper control of the softening process difficult, and this lack of control may be part of the reason for poor overall performance. Because of the inability of the recarbonation unit to reduce the pH to desired levels during some operating conditions it was not possible to fully evaluate the effect of recarbonation on effluent hardness.

Softener effluent total and dissolved manganese probability plots showed that the drinking water standard limit of 0.05 mg/ℓ was achieved 65 or 80% of the time depending on whether total or dissolved values were used. Manganese oxidation, which is normally the rate limiting step in the removal of manganese from potable water, proceeds rather slowly at pH's between 8.5 to 9.5. During those periods of the study when the neutralization stage was being operated at pH's less than 8.5 and because of the poor pH control achieved, effluent manganese values were often too high to meet the standards.

Data were not collected routinely for those substances listed in the NIPDW regulations developed by the EPA, but the results of one set of analyses, reported in Table 6.14, indicate that effluent from the plant could be expected to meet the standards for those substances that were measured. Not all of the substances included in the NIPDW regulations were included in the analyses performed.

Table 6.14: Water Quality Data Comparison*

| | . . . . Raw Water . . . . . | | Recarbonation | |
Parameter	Kittanning Run	Impounding Dam	Neutralization Stage	Basin Effluent	EPA NIPDWR
	. . . .(mg/ℓ)				
Arsenic	0.030	0.030	0.030	0.030	0.05
Barium	0.05	0.05	0.05	0.05	1
Cadmium	0.004	0.004	0.004	0.004	0.010
Chromium	0.010	0.010	0.010	0.010	0.05
Cyanide	0.005	0.005	0.005	0.005	0.2
Lead	0.030	0.030	0.030	0.030	0.05
Mercury	—	—	—	—	0.002
Nitrate	—	—	—	—	10.0
Selenium	0.010	0.010	0.010	0.010	0.01
Silver	—	—	—	—	0.05
Fluoride	0.33	0.19	0.29	0.29	1.4–2.4
Copper	0.3	0.020	0.010	0.010	1.0**
Zinc	1.1	0.15	0.070	0.030	5.0**

*With EPA National Interim Primary Drinking Water Regulations.
**1962 USPHS Drinking Water Standards and proposed "Secondary Drinking Water Standards."

Source: NSF/RA-790225

Probability plots of the total dissolved solids and sulfates for all data collected during the entire study showed that the softener effluent met USPHS drinking water standards and the proposed EPA Secondary Drinking Water Regulations for these constituents most of the time. No appreciable removal of sulfates was anticipated with the processes used. It should be pointed out again, however, that the raw water was not taken solely from Kittanning Run, the acid mine drainage impregnated stream, and hence, the raw water was lower in total dissolved solids and sulfates than had been anticipated.

Conclusions

A basic requirement of the study method utilized was that a relatively constant hydraulic 13,200 m^3/day (3.5 mgd) and mineral loading should be applied to the treatment process. In this regard, certain qualifying factors should be mentioned prior to discussing the major findings of the study. First, since the Kittanning Run (KR) source is an open channel flow, weather (rainfall) caused some variation in raw water quality. This condition could be controlled using KR exclusively or by blending the total flow in KR with constant quality Impounding Dam (ID) water, a fairly successful procedure so long as KR flow did not exceed the maximum 13,200 m^3/day (3.5 mgd). Temperature, however, was a parameter which could not be controlled.

Another equally important factor was the inability to obtain consistent softener operation with reaction zone solids and good clarification. This situation was a two-edged problem inasmuch as it was necessary to evaluate nontypical process performance of the unit as well as delay filter start-up because of this condition. Data collection of this process was thereby limited for fear of prematurely fouling the filter media. The following conclusions were drawn from the study.

> Coal mine drainage (average characteristics of pH 3.0, acidity 160 mg/ℓ, iron 14.5 mg/ℓ, and manganese 4.5 mg/ℓ) was treated by the neutralization and lime-soda ash process to produce a finished water quality that will generally meet the EPA NIPDWR.

> The cost of producing a water suitable for blending with a potable supply from the subject drainage source is, in 1975 dollars, about 10¢/m^3 (37¢/1,000 gal). This cost includes power, chemicals, operating personnel and maintenance.

> Lime addition to the neutralization process did not contribute an equivalent amount of calcium hardness in the sedimentation basin effluent. Some calcium (approximately 15 mg/ℓ) was apparently precipitated as calcium sulfate, as further evidenced by an equivalent sulfate loss, in the neutralization stage.

> The softener unit operation employed was of the solids contact type that requires the return of settled solids to the reaction zone for intimate mixing of previously formed floc with the applied flow and chemical addition. The buildup of reaction zone solids (10 to 15% settleable solids by volume in 15 minutes) was a prerequisite for efficient reaction and effective clarification according to the manufacturer. With the exception of approximately 3 weeks during the study, it was impossible to obtain the recommended type of softener operation. The reason for failure of the unit to build up solids is not understood.

The operating conditions under which reaction zone solids could be generated required a pH of 11.0 or higher. During these test periods the neutralization stage pH was 7.0 to 8.0. Heavy floc carryover from the sedimentation basin was characteristic of this first-stage operation. It was determined, however, that good softener operation at pH 11.3 also could be obtained without the presence of heavy floc carryover from the first stage. The favorable softener operation with a desired level of reaction zone solids was accomplished during periods when the water temperature was above 12°C. At water temperatures below 12°C, the desired softener process operation could not be reproduced.

The general appearance of the softener effluent for the most part could be characterized as a turbid, homogeneous quality of water containing a finely divided precipitate. Samples drawn from various levels and zones within the tank failed to show any distinct differentiation in the liquid contents which would indicate significant solids buildup.

The use of alum and coagulant aids (CA 233 and CA 253) was not effective in improving the coagulation-flocculation process in the softener.

The capacity of the recarbonation unit was not sufficient to lower the pH of the softener effluent below 9.5 when the softener process was operated at a pH in excess of 11.0. The carbon dioxide feed capacity was 682 kg/day (1,500 lb/day) or about 51 g/m^3 (428 pounds/million gallons) of water to be treated.

A severe filter plugging problem was experienced during the period from October 23 to 28. It was suspected that the cause for this condition was due, at least in part, to coagulant aid fouling of the top 10 to 15 cm (4" to 6") of the filter media.

Settled solids in the thickener could not be effectively moved to the center collection well. The fluid characteristics of the sludge resulted in a condition whereby the solids accumulated in a ring approximately one-third to halfway from the periphery of the tank. Air lancing was partially successful in moving the sludge to the tank-center. Ultimately, it was necessary to lower the level in the thickener and hose the solids toward the middle sump.

Recommendations

Conventional design criteria will generally apply to the softening process (lime/soda ash) so long as the water temperature remains above 12°C (54°F). It is assumed that if Kittanning Run or a similar quality of raw water were to be treated, impoundment would be provided, so in all probability, temperature below this threshold level would not be experienced.

Turbulence should be avoided at transfer points in the system after mixing and particularly ahead of the clarifier to minimize floc breakup.

The use of potassium permanganate should be limited to head-end of the plant application. This study indicated that the addition point ahead of neutralization (7 hr before the softening unit) was best. Potassium permanganate feed directly to the softener was very difficult, if not impossible, to control.

Application of the particular solids contact type of softener unit used in this study appears questionable.

Design of the thickener unit operation for handling a mixture of iron hydroxide/calcium carbonate solids should take into consideration the tendency of this type of sludge to "doughnut," or resist movement to the tank center. The bottom slope in the unit available for the study was about 14.5%. Increasing the floor slope would facilitate sludge removal and solids control.

Provision should be made for feeding coagulant aid to the sedimentation basin (ahead of softening) inlet line. This capability is important because of the characteristic light iron hydroxide floc formed in the neutralization stage. In general, flexibility in chemical addition points is most desirable.

The data analysis indicated that, although on occasion a softener effluent hardness of less than 100 mg/ℓ $CaCO_3$ was obtained, an average of 120 mg/ℓ could be expected, regardless of the amount of soda ash fed. This result must be interpreted with some caution because the process condition did not afford control of temperature, softener reaction zone solids, or continuous filter operation. Where a specific application of this treatment process is being considered, it would be advisable to determine this minimum achievable hardness level in the laboratory.

REDUCTIVE DEGRADATION TREATMENT FOR CHLORINATED HYDRO-CARBONS

> The material in this section is based on a paper in Conference II entitled "Reductive Degradation Treatment of Industrial and Municipal Wastewaters," by K.H. Sweeny, of Envirogenics Systems Company of California.

Introduction

An important problem facing those concerned with maintaining clean waters is from the discharge of halogenated hydrocarbons into the waters. These discharges may arise from manufacturing and processing a variety of chemicals, and upon chlorination of some municipal waters. An area of particular concern is the treatment of the chlorinated hydrocarbons soluble in water, since the soluble material cannot be removed by filtration, and is generally resistant to conventional biological treatment.

An economical and effective means for the treatment of the dissolved halogenated toxicants would permit the reuse of these waters in manufacturing or processing plant recycle, allow the waters to be used safely for groundwater recharge, and to permit safe discharge into rivers and other waters. Treatment of the reportedly carcinogenic trihalomethanes (THM) produced by the chlorination of water containing organic matter is another important application leading to better use of our waters.

A new approach to the treatment of these waters is the technique of reductive degradation. This process appears to be highly effective for the treatment of halogenated toxicants, is very simple, and is projected to be an economical treatment process.

Process

The process is basically one of chemical reduction of the contaminant by a catalyzed metal powder. The reaction can be carried out at ambient temperatures, though it is expectedly more rapid at slightly elevated temperatures.

Reductants: The reductants generally employed have been the powders of iron, zinc and aluminum. All of these metals are effective reductants, though iron is generally preferred on the basis of effectiveness at low cost and freedom from deleterious reductant products; zinc ion in the water, for example, would offer toxicity problems to aquatic life unless removed.

Process Chemistry: The reduction reactions are known to give several different products depending on the material to be reduced, the reductant, and reduction conditions.

The most common of the reductive reactions appears to be the replacement of a halogen atom by a hydrogen. Removal of the halogen atom generally leads to products of greatly reduced toxicity. The initial reduction of DDT by zinc, for example, proceeds by this reaction. Further removal of the aromatic chlorines requires more vigorous treatment.

Substitution of a hydroxyl group for the halogen has also been observed. Saturation of an aromatic structure has likewise been shown in tests involving the reduction of halogenated organic compounds. An example of both hydroxylation and saturation is shown in the case of the catalyzed iron reduction of chlorobenzene, where cyclohexanol has been observed as a reaction product. In a related test, reduction of hexachlorocyclopentadiene led to the production of nonchlorinated branched chain alkanes—evidence of dechlorination and ring opening.

A reductive condensation has also been found to occur where certain toxicants are treated with the reducing agents. An example of this reaction is shown in the reduction of DDT by catalyzed aluminum to produce a butane derivative with extremely low water and fat solubility.

Hydrolysis has also been observed in the presence of the reductants. While the hydrolysis reaction is not considered to be reduction, the hydrolytic reaction has been observed in the presence of the catalyzed metal reductant, and was not observed in its absence. For example, in the presence of catalyzed iron, the aliphatic chlorines in DDT are apparently hydrolyzed to give the acid (as well as the tetraphenyltetrachlorobutane).

The amount of iron consumed in the reductive reaction is generally somewhat greater than the calculated amount consumed by one of the preceding reactions. The additional iron is apparently consumed by reaction of the iron with water. Typically, the effluent from the reductive column will contain 1 to 3 mg/ℓ of ferrous iron when an industrial or municipal water is fed to the unit, and less than 1 mg/ℓ when deionized water is employed. This amount of iron can be readily removed, if desired, by standard aeration and flocculation methods.

Materials Reduced: Tests with a number of chlorinated and nonchlorinated species show that the reductive technique has wide applicability. Some of the variety of materials reduced include the cyclodienes such as aldrin, chlordane, dieldrin, endrin, heptachlor and heptachlorepoxide; DDT, DDD, Kelthane, methoxychlor and Perthane; lindane; toxaphene; carbon tetrachloride, chloroform, methylene chloride and chlorobromomethane; the 2,4-D ester and 2,4,5-T ester of chlorinated phenoxyacetic acid; hexachlorocyclopentadiene and the pesticide Kepone derived from it; p-nitrophenol and the reportedly carcinogenic N-nitrosodimethylamine; s-triazine and atrazine.

This shows the wide range of chemicals known to be reductively degraded by the Envirogenics process. In all of these examples, complete or near complete degradation is obtained, and the analysis of the waters shows that the bulk of the chlorine is removed from the organochlorine compounds. The chemical changes that appear to have taken place in these species all lead to substantially reduced toxicity so that the effluent would appear to be innocuous at the levels expected to be encountered.

Process Operation

While many organic compounds can be degraded by mixing the reductant powder in a solution of the organic compound, much better degradation has been achieved by use of a column. Two versions of the column have been employed, the diluted bed and the fluidized bed.

Reduction is best accomplished by using a large excess of the reductant and a contact time up to 100 min at ambient (~25°C) temperature. These conditions can be achieved with a bed of the reductant diluted with an inert ingredient, such as sand, to give requisite flow and retention properties. The sand-diluted bed may contain 5 to 40 wt % of the reductant, and the flow through a 6' deep bed may range from 0.5 to 3 gpm/ft^2. In order to provide suitable retention and flow properties, sand with approximately the same particle size as the reductant powder is used, so that interstitial particle packing is minimized. Substantial differences have been found in sand diluents; some sand sources retard the rate or extent of degradation.

A fluidized bed reactor is even more efficient. In this process, the catalyzed reductant powder in a column is supported on a distributor plate such as a fine mesh sieve or a porous metal plate. Flow of the liquid into the bottom of the vertical bed expands the powder mass, giving turbulent motion to provide good mixing of the reductant and wastewater to be treated. In a typical reactor, the bed may be expanded two-to-four-fold from the depth of the quiet bed. Flow rates as high as 22 gpm/ft^2 have been achieved with good degradation—this flow rate is approximately ten-fold greater than for the sand-diluted bed. The pressure drop across the system is low, with current systems operating at approximately 15 psi. Contact times are generally on the order of 5 min.

While wastewater streams treated with a sand-diluted reductant bed must have adequate filtration before the reactor, filtration does not appear to be required with the fluidized bed unit. Particulate matter entering a sand-diluted reactor gradually clogs the bed, and any attempt at backwashing leads to particle segregation, since the reductant particles are about three times as dense as the diluent particles. In the fluidized bed, however, a moderate amount of particulate matter of about the same size as the reductant is expected to pass through the reactor into the overflow, because of lower density. Thus, the fluidized bed reactor gives promise of direct reaction of chlorinated organics in silt, in which the decontaminated silt would pass through the bed into the discharge.

Degradation of Trihalomethanes

The degradation of the trihalomethanes has been shown to be effectively achieved in a series of laboratory tests. The initial tests were made with sand-diluted beds in which the toxicant-laden water was allowed to trickle through the 6' deep bed by gravity flow. Flows ranging from 30 to 45 ml/min through a 37 mm diameter bed were employed in the initial test. Samples containing 100 μg/ℓ each of chloroform, carbon tetrachloride, methylene chloride, and bromochloromethane were prepared and passed through the column. Samples of the effluent analyzed by gas chromatography (electron-capture detection) showed no trace of the starting material (<1 μg/ℓ). The degradation of aqueous chloroform and aqueous bromoform was also demonstrated by a laboratory fluidized bed column.

Treatment Cost

The simplicity of the reductive degradation process results in low estimated operating and capital costs.

The reduction column operates most satisfactorily at a pH near 7; too low a pH results in excessive reductant consumption, and too high a pH leads to reductant precipitation in the bed, as well as decreased efficiency. If the pH is less than 5.5 or greater than 8.0, pH sensing and neutralization are necessary. However, with the fluidized bed system and a nearly neutral stream, the system may be as simple as a pump, flow controls and the reductant bed.

An estimate for the treatment cost for a fluidized bed system, using the method and the data from a 1977 study on granular activated carbon absorption indicates substantially lower projected treatment costs for the reductive technique as compared to granular activated carbon treatment. These calculations were made for a municipal water source that did not require pH neutralization, filtration, or iron removal.

Conclusions

Reductive degradation treatment has been shown effective for a wide range of halogenated toxicants dissolved in water. The technique has also been shown to be useful for the nonchlorinated species investigated.

Treatment costs are estimated to be significantly lower for reductive degradation than for activated carbon, when compared for trihalomethane treatment at a variety of water plant sizes. Capital costs are also estimated to be much less for reductive treatment.

Products that have been identified, as well as expected products from the known reactions, all lead to apparently safe products. The process is inherently very simple, requiring minimum labor and space.

> **Note:** Attention is called to Chapter 8 of this book which includes a comprehensive review of the literature on treatment methods for wastewater and for recycled water to be used for potable purposes. A complete bibliography is given.

Testing Methods

BIOASSAYS PLUS CHEMICAL ANALYSES

The information in this section is based on a paper in Conference III entitled, "Integrated Use of Bioassays and Chemical Analyses to Evaluate the Quality of Reuse Water," by T.E. Cody, V.J. Elia, C. Scott Clark, and R.T. Christian, all of the Department of Environmental Health of the University of Cincinnati Medical Center.

Biological Screening Assays

Quality control of potable water supplies, whether drawn from polluted natural sources or produced by recycling wastewater, would benefit from the use of biological screening assays in addition to chemical assays. Wastewater and natural water are complex mixtures of dissolved and suspended materials. Exhaustive chemical analysis of water samples can not be performed in a reasonable time and at reasonable cost. Furthermore, interpretation of data gathered by chemical analyses of water samples can not be readily interpreted in terms of the toxic effects that may result from consumption of the water. Biological methods for evaluation of potential toxic effects of potable water could effectively supplement chemical analyses.

The method of Ames, using strains of *Salmonella typhimurium*, has been widely used for detection of mutagenic substances. This method has been applied to testing recycled water samples. General toxicity testing of potable water supplies with rapid biological screening assays has not been as well studied, although such assays have been applied to recycled water. This paper presents some examples of the use of a mammalian cell tissue culture assay for assessment of quality of recycled wastewater.

173

The Bioassay Method

The goal of developing methods of biological monitoring for trace levels of toxic contaminants in treated water is to provide techniques that are rapid and can be used in conjunction with currently used chemical methods for screening or monitoring produced waters for potential health effects. A bioassay approach that has been very useful has been developed.

Sample Treatment: The water sample is collected and chilled immediately, but not frozen, and stored at about $4°C$ until ready for testing. The sample is passed through a 0.22 μ pore size membrane filter for removal of particulate material, including bacteria and viruses. Salts, glucose, amino acids and vitamins are added to the sample to convert it into tissue culture medium. The media to which the cultures are to be exposed must have a nearly neutral pH that does not vary more than a few tenths of a pH unit during the exposure period. The osmotic pressure of the media must be within the range of 290 to 310 mm osmols/kg H_2O. If the osmolality exceeds this range, a condition that may occur when testing water samples with moderately high levels of dissolved solids, the amount of NaCl added to the water sample when making the medium is adjusted to bring the osmolality within the desired range. The medium is resterilized by membrane filtration. Sterile fetal bovine serum, 1% v/v, and antibiotics are added to the medium.

Assessment of Results: Two days prior to exposure, cultures of mouse fibroblasts (L-cells, Clone 929) are prepared by seeding culture flasks with 20,000 cells/cm^2 of surface. The cells attach to the surface of the flask and approximately quadruple in number by the time the growth medium is replaced with medium prepared from test water. Cultures are exposed for 72 hours at $37°C$. During the exposure the microscopic changes in the cell cultures are monitored daily. At the end of the exposure period quantitative assessment of the effects of the test water is determined through measurement of protein or DNA contents or cell numbers in the cultures.

Chemical Analyses: Chemical analysis of the water sample is usually performed on the samples before and after filtration and on the medium itself. In the experiments the chemical analyses performed were chosen on the basis of what was known about the sample and usually included some or all of the following: total organic carbon; chemical oxygen demand; total dissolved solids; atomic absorption analysis for metals; gas chromatographic head space analysis for volatile organics; and high pressure liquid chromatography for nonvolatile organics.

This approach is adaptable to screening for toxicity for all types of water samples that have been encountered: drinking water; wastewater; recycled water; natural surface and groundwaters.

The Response of Tissue Cultures to Toxic Chemicals and Mixtures

By varying the concentration of chemicals or percentage of test water in the medium, the concentration-dependent response of the cultures to the test sub-

stance may be determined. The data obtained from exposure of cultures to varying concentrations of test substances (Figures 7.1 and 7.2) may be used to determine the concentration of chemical or water sample that will cause a 50% reduction in growth. This value, referred to here as the LC_{50} (50% lethal concentration), is used to compare the effects of different test substances on the cultures.

Figure 7.1: Response of L-Cells to Varying Concentrations of Hydroquinone

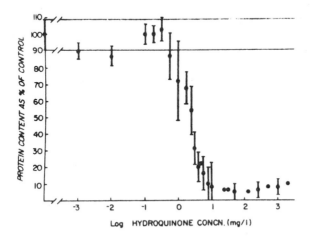

Source: NSF/RA-790226

Figure 7.2: Effects of Reverse Osmosis Permeate on L-Cells

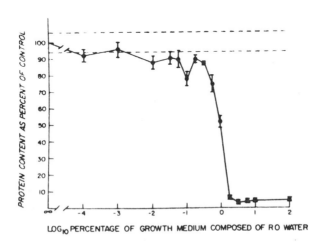

Source: NSF/RA-790226

Comparisons should be made among experiments in which the conditions of exposure are similar. The concentration-dependent responses illustrated in Figures 7.1 and 7.2 were a result of a 72-hour exposure. Figure 7.1 shows an example of a concentration-response curve of L-cells treated with medium containing a single organic toxic chemical (hydroquinone). The vertical bars through the points designate the limits of ± standard deviation. Figure 7.2 shows an example of a concentration-response curve of L-cells treated with medium containing a treated wastewater sample. Vertical bars through the points designate limits of ± standard deviation. Experience has shown that a 72-hour period is long enough to observe a response at the lowest effective concentration and yet not so long as to introduce error due to buildup of excessive metabolites and cell degradation products in the medium.

Both of the curves shown are typical of the type of response usually seen when protein or DNA production is used as the estimation of cell growth. The concentration range and the variability of response will vary depending on compound and mixture tested. However, the sharpness of the response of the cultures to the RO permeate is not atypical for complex mixtures.

Comparison of Treated Wastewater with Cincinnati Tap Water

Synthetic hospital wastewater was treated by ultrafiltration, reverse osmosis, and ozonation. This water sample caused no toxic response in the mammalian cell culture assay. In order to determine how the treated water sample compared with the biological quality of drinking water, samples of the treated wastewater and Cincinnati tap water were concentrated by vacuum fractional distillation. Concentrates of both water samples were obtained that were toxic in the tissue culture assay.

Vacuum Fractional Distillation: Vacuum fractional distillation was used because water could be removed from the samples by reducing the pressure rather than raising the temperature. The low-boiling fractions were distilled and saved to be recombined with the residue in the stillpot after the water-containing fraction had distilled. The volume of the Cincinnati tap sample was reduced to 0.005 of original (200-fold concentrate) and the TOC was increased from <2 to 77 mg/ℓ. The treated wastewater was reduced in volume from 123 liters to 2.2 liters (~0.02 of original volume; 55-fold concentrate). Based on TOC measurements, which increased from 12 to 417 mg/ℓ, 60% of the organic matter was conserved in the concentrate. The remainder was present in the distillate.

Cincinnati tap water was toxic when the volume was reduced to <0.05 of original volume (20-fold concentrate). Protein content of cultures treated with water reduced to 0.005 of original volume (200-fold concentrate) for 72 hours was 25% of control protein. Tissue culture protein was reduced 44 to 55% when treated with water reduced to 0.009 (112-fold) of original volume (Table 7.1).

The most concentrated sample of treated wastewater (~0.02 of original; 55-fold) and a volume reduction to ~0.04 completely killed the cells in tissue cultures. When the Cincinnati tap was tested at these concentrations it reduced the protein content of cultures by <20% and <10%, respectively. The treated wastewater required a concentration of less than one-half before the first toxic effects were observable. Therefore, the treated wastewater was shown by the concentration procedure to be substantially more toxic than Cincinnati tap water. More extensively treated wastewaters prepared for later studies proved to be at least as nontoxic as Cincinnati tap water.

Table 7.1: Cytotoxicity of Treated Waters

	TOC (mg/ℓ)	Inhibition of Protein Synthesis, %
Treated synthetic waste	12	None
55-fold concentrate	417	100
28-fold concentrate	208	100
9-fold concentrate	67	50–60
Distillate	5	None
Cincinnati tap water	<2	None
200-fold concentrate	77	75
112-fold concentrate	43	45–55
64-fold concentrate	25	20–30
20-fold concentrate	8	0–10

Note: Simulated hospital waste was treated with UF, RO, and ozone. Concentration was by vacuum fractional distillation.

Source: NSF/RA-790226

Freeze Concentration: As an alternative to vacuum fractional distillation, freeze concentration has been used with even better retention of organic components. The efficiency of the freeze concentration method declines if the water contains high concentrations of dissolved salts or suspended solids.

Reduction of Toxicity of RO-Treated Wastewater by Ozonation

Cytotoxicity assays may be combined with chromatographic analyses to evaluate the effectiveness of a wastewater treatment step. In the following experiment, samples of a simulated wastewater that was treated with reverse osmosis were ozonated in batches for increasing periods of times. The changes in chemical composition were followed with high pressure liquid chromatography (HPLC) and the changes in toxicity were followed with the tissue culture assay system. The treatment system that was used is described by Elia et al (*Jour. WPCF*, 50:7:1727).

Ozonation Treatment: Ozone was generated from an O_2 stream with a Wellsbach O_3 generator at a concentration of 67.5 (65 to 70) mg O_3/ℓ O_2 at a gas flow rate of 2 standard ℓ/min. The gas stream was introduced through fritted glass spargers into two connected columns containing a total volume of 13 liters of wastewater. The pH of the wastewater was 9.0 to 9.5 and the temperature was 50° to 60°C. O_3 input rate was 131 (130 to 134) mg/min during all exposure periods except during the 120-min period when it was 120 mg/min. O_3 was consumed throughout the exposure periods. The rate of consumption became less as the exposure period was lengthened.

Results: Chromatographic analysis by HPLC showed that treatment with ozone changed the chemical composition of the treated water. The changes were time dependent. An unexpected alteration of the chemical composition occurred when the RO-treated wastewater was treated with O_2 for 15 minutes. The major product formed by the O_2 treatment was not the same as the major product formed by treatment with O_3 in an O_2 carrier stream. Treatment with O_2 for 15 minutes resulted in reduction of the peak with a retention volume of 4.3 ml from >190 to 17 units. At the same time the peak at 2.1 ml increased from 8 to 143 units. In contrast, ozonation eliminated all of the observable peaks in the RO-treated wastewater in <7.5 minutes. New peaks were formed at 2.3 ml, 3.3 ml and 3.7 ml. The peak at 2.3 ml was formed in <7.5 ml and then diminished with increasing O_3 time. The peak at 3.7, after being formed did not change between 7.5 and 15 minutes and, if present, was obscured by the 3.3 ml peak after 30 minutes of ozonation. The major peak in the ozonated samples was the 3.3 ml peak which increased from 50 units after 7.5 minutes of ozonation to 184 units at 30 minutes.

The tissue culture assay response was also influenced by the length of ozonation time. The RO-treated waste was lethal in 72 hours. A 15-minute exposure to ozone did not reduce the toxicity. By 30 minutes the toxicity of the water had been reduced to the extent that it only inhibited protein synthesis by 30 to 35%. There was no further reduction of toxicity even after 120 minutes of ozonation. During the first 30 minutes of ozonation the COD decreased rapidly from 86 to 10 mg/ℓ. It continued to drop slowly to ≤3.5 mg/ℓ by 120 minutes of ozonation.

In 15 minutes of purging with oxygen the toxicity of the water was reduced to the point that it only inhibited protein production by about 50 to 55%. Concomitantly, the COD of the solution was reduced from 86 to 75 and alteration of chemical composition occurred.

Interpretation of Results: The alteration in chemical composition during oxygen purging without a great reduction in COD suggests that reduction in toxicity occurred as a result of alteration rather than substantial degradation of toxic components. In the ozonation experiments, the initial reduction in toxicity may also have resulted from alteration of toxic components but nearly complete removal of COD also occurred in the first 30 minutes of ozone treatment which surely contributed to removal of contaminants that caused the toxic response in tissue cultures.

TRACE ELEMENT ANALYSES OF AWT EFFLUENTS

The information in this section was obtained from a report in Conference III entitled, "Trace Element Analyses

of Several Advanced Wastewater Treatment Plant Effluents," by H.R. Pahren and N.S. Ulmer, both of the U.S.
EPA in Cincinnati, Ohio.

Advanced wastewater treatment (AWT) processes will undoubtedly be used in
any system designed to produce potable water from wastewater. Generally, laboratory analyses to determine the concentration of the elements in AWT processes are limited to a few common metals such as those listed in the National Interim Primary Drinking Water Regulations. The dozens of other elements are assumed not to be present in concentrations at harmful levels. Many of these elements would be very difficult to analyze.

PIXE Technology

A new multielement procedure, involving proton-induced x-ray emission (PIXE)
technology, was utilized for the simultaneous determination of 70 elements
heavier than aluminum in the effluent of four AWT full-scale plants or pilot
plants. Plants cooperating in this short-term screening study were: Orange
County, California, Water Factory 21; South Lake Tahoe, California; Pomona
AWT Pilot Research Facility, Pomona, California; and the U.S. EPA pilot plant
at Blue Plains, Washington, DC. The objective of this screening was to determine
if any element which is not ordinarily checked might be present in the effluent
at a level which would be of a health concern if the water were ever reused for
potable purposes. At the Pomona plant, influent samples were obtained as well
as the effluent so that removals through the system could be determined.

Sampling Methods: One-quart grab samples were taken and preserved with 1.5
ml concentrated HNO_3/ℓ. The polyethylene cubitainers containing the samples
were mailed to the U.S. EPA laboratory in Cincinnati. Three samples were taken
at each location over a five-month period during the last half of 1976. Periodically, a number of samples were shipped to the U.S. EPA contractor, Purdue Research Foundation, in West Lafayette, Indiana where the analyses were performed.

Analysis: The multielemental analysis by PIXE consisted of (1) preparation of
targets from a 1-ml (for calcium and potassium only) and a 30-ml sample aliquot
using a unique vapor filtration technique, (2) bombardment of each target using
a pulsed beam of 4-MeV protons from a FV tandem Van de Graaf accelerator,
(3) detection of emitted x-rays by a Kevex model 3010 silicon-lithium detector,
(4) transmission of the electrical pulses from the detector to a PDP 15/40 computer, (5) conversion of the pulses to a number proportional to the energy of the
x-ray, and (6) calculation and recording of the concentration of the elements by
the computer system which had been programmed to compensate for various interferences, know the precise energy of all x-rays of interest and the shapes of
the peaks, check and adjust the energy calibration, perform a multidimensional
linear least-squares fit to the data, check on the relative intensities of the x-rays
from any given element and record any discrepancies along with the elemental
results. In general, PIXE is useful for detection of elements heavier than aluminum, but results to date indicate that other methods are better for measuring
bromide, chloride, iodide, phosphorus, and sulfur.

Results and Discussions

Elements with at least one positive result among the fourteen effluent samples from the four AWT plants are shown in Table 7.2. Elements not detected are presented in Table 7.3. It should be mentioned that for samples with greater than 50 ppm calcium, as was the case with each of the AWT samples, the cited detection limit is multiplied by the factor (calcium concentration in ppm)/50. This modification does not apply to scandium.

Table 7.2: Elements Detected in Advanced Wastewater Treatment Effluents

Element	Detection Limit (ppb)	Percent Detected	Minimum (ppb)	Median (ppb)	Maximum (ppb)
Potassium	100	100	6,530	8,780	17,600
Calcium	100	100	52,500	64,400	96,000
Vanadium	1	57	<1.0	2.0	7.5
Chromium	0.1	57	<0.1	0.7	12
Manganese	1	71	<1.0	7.7	412
Iron	1	100	18	33.5	17,900
Cobalt	0.1	7	<0.1	<0.1	0.9
Nickel	0.1	100	2.2	9.3	47
Copper	1	93	<1.0	7.1	64
Zinc	1	100	12	26	3,620
Molybdenum	1	79	<1.0	4.1	15
Silver	1	7	<1.0	<1.0	2.4
Cadmium	0.1	36	<0.1	<0.1	5
Lead	0.1	71	<0.1	2.7	63
Titanium	1	36	<1.0	<1.0	33
Gallium	0.1	29	<0.1	<0.1	0.9
Rubidium	0.1	93	<0.1	6.1	11
Strontium	0.1	100	91	432	604
Tin	0.3	21	<0.3	<0.3	7.3
Antimony	0.4	21	<0.4	<0.4	9.8
Barium	2.5	93	<2.5	35.5	77
Thallium	0.3	7	<0.3	<0.3	0.5
Arsenic	0.5	93	<0.5	2.3	9.5
Selenium	1	29	<1.0	<1.0	2.5

Source: NSR/RA-790226

When comparing results to the EPA NIPDWR (Table 7.4), it may be seen that these elements are generally well below the limits. Only one sample exceeded the limits. Lead at the Blue Plains pilot plant had a value of 63 ppb, slightly over the limit of 50 ppb for drinking water, at a time when the plant was being shut down. Earlier values of 2.8 and 4.1 ppb were obtained under normal operating conditions. Although the maximum permissible mercury level is 2 ppb, the PIXE detection limit is 3 ppb. Since mercury was not detected in any of the samples, it is probable that mercury was below the limit for drinking water.

At the Pomona pilot plant, samples were taken of the AWT influent as well as the effluent of two parallel treatment systems. One system consisted of coagulation, sedimentation, filtration, chlorination, and carbon adsorption. The other had two carbon adsorption steps with intermediate chlorination. Table 7.5 lists the removals of those elements found in the wastewater. In certain instances, elements increased during treatment. Both iron and manganese increased significantly in each Pomona treatment system. The unusually high maximum iron value in Table 7.2 was from the Pomona plant.

Table 7.3: Elements Not Detected in Advanced Wastewater Treatment Effluents

Element	Detection Limit (ppb)	Element	Detection Limit (ppb)
Scandium	0.1% Ca	Germanium	0.1
Silicon	5,000	Palladium	0.1
Indium	0.2	Tellurium	0.7
Cesium	2	Lanthanum	2.5
Tungsten	0.3	Platinum	0.3
Niobium	0.1	Bismuth	0.3
Ruthenium	1	Zirconium	1
Rhodium	1	Cerium	20
Praseodymium	18	Neodymium	16
Promethium	13	Samarium	12
Europium	11	Gadolinium	9
Terbium	8	Dysprosium	7
Holmium	6	Erbium	5
Thulium	3	Ytterbium	3
Lutecium	3	Hafnium	3
Tantalum	3	Rhenium	3
Osmium	3	Iridium	3
Gold	3	Mercury	3
Polonium	3	Astatine	3
Francium	3	Radium	3
Actinium	3	Thorium	3
Protactinium	3	Uranium	3
Neptunium	3	Plutonium	3

Source: NSF/RA-790226

Table 7.4: Comparison of Advanced Wastewater Treatment Effluents with Drinking Water Standards

Element	Minimum	Median	ppb Maximum	NIPDWR
Arsenic	<0.5	2.3	9.5	50
Barium	<2.5	35	77	1,000
Cadmium	<0.1	<0.1	5.0	10
Chromium	<0.1	0.7	12	50
Lead	<0.1	2.7	63	50
Mercury	<3	<3	<3	2
Selenium	<1	<1	2.5	10
Silver	<1	<1	2.4	50

Source: NSF/RA-790226

Table 7.5: Percent Removal of Elements at Pomona

Element	Carbon System	Chemical Coagulation System
Potassium	8	3
Calcium	0	0
Vanadium	0	0
Chromium	78	99
Manganese	0	0
Iron	0	0
Nickel	42	44
Copper	90	88
Zinc	42	21
Molybdenum	33	63
Lead	92	99
Titanium	67	67
Rubidium	29	52
Strontium	3	2
Tin	67	100
Barium	20	18
Arsenic	21	0

Source: NSF/RA-790226

In general, results of this screening exercise indicate that trace elements were not a problem at the four advanced wastewater treatment plants. Elements which are not normally checked were either below detectable limits or not of a level to be of serious concern.

TESTING FOR TRACE ORGANICS AND MUTAGENS

The material in this section is based on a report in Conference II titled, "Mutagenic Activity and Trace Organics in Concentrates from Advanced Wastewater Treatment Plant Effluents," by H.R. Pahren and R.G. Melton, both of the U.S. EPA in Cincinnati.

Introduction

There is much interest in certain geographical locations in the potential use of renovated wastewater for potable purpose. These areas may be encountering increased demand for water resources and water planners are looking at various alternatives to supplement existing water supplies.

Since the question of health effects is always raised when consideration is given to potable reuse, the Health Effects Research Laboratory of the U.S. Environmental Protection Agency initiated a project to collect concentrates from advanced wastewater treatment (AWT) plants and to test the concentrates for specific organic compounds and mutagenic activity. AWT plants were chosen since many of the same unit operations will undoubtedly be used if a plant is designed specifically for potable reuse. Data presented in this paper should not be construed as being representative of potable grade water. It is assumed that if research shows the existence of health effects associated with a certain treatment train, the process would be redesigned if potable grade water is to be the objective.

Facilities cooperating in this project are located at South Lake Tahoe, California; Pomona, California; Escondido, California; Orange County, California; Dallas, Texas; and the EPA pilot plant at the District of Columbia. This paper will present the results of mutagenic activity of all samples and organics data from South Lake Tahoe and Pomona.

Concentration and Extraction

Concentrates containing the organic materials from the advanced wastewater treatment systems were obtained by Gulf South Research Institute under a contract with EPA. The basic scheme utilized consisted of two recirculating reverse osmosis subsystems in series. The first system utilized a cellulose acetate membrane. Permeate from the cellulose acetate system was reprocessed in a second reverse osmosis system which had a nylon base membrane. Water permeating the nylon membrane was run to waste. Thus, two concentrates were generated: one retained by the cellulose acetate membrane and another retained by the nylon membrane. Between 1,500 and 1,900 liters of plant effluent were processed through the system.

Nylon (polyamide) membranes have been shown to reject many lower molecular weight organics better than those of cellulose acetate. However, polyamide is sensitive to chlorine. The cellulose acetate removes the chlorine, allowing the polyamide to be used.

The aqueous concentrates isolated by reverse osmosis contained a high salt burden in addition to organics. Solvent extraction was used to avoid the salts as well as concentrate the organics even further. Each concentrate, with volume between 19 and 38 liters, was extracted first with pentane and then with methylene chloride under neutral conditions. Following this, the aqueous phase was adjusted to a pH of 2 and again extracted with methylene chloride. Each of the three extracts was concentrated to one milliliter for testing purposes. Certain modifications of the extraction procedure were incorporated into some of the later samples.

Mutagenic Activity

About 80% of the concentrate of organics was used to check for mutagenic potential. All of the mutagenic testing was carried out by Stanford Research Institute International under contract to EPA.

Methods: Advanced wastewater treatment plant effluent samples and their solvent blanks were tested by the Ames *Salmonella*/microsome assay procedure.

The small amount of sample available necessitated using only *Salmonella typhimurium* strains TA 98 and TA 100 for most samples. Strain TA 98 is sensitive to chemicals that cause frameshift mutations while TA 100 is sensitive to frameshift mutagens and base-pair substitution mutagens. Samples generally were tested with and without metabolic activation.

Result and Discussion: Results for the 63 samples are presented in Table 7.6. Most advanced wastewater treatment plants were sampled more than once. In some cases the repeated samples represented different processes, such as Pomona and Blue Plains. In other cases, such as Dallas, Lake Tahoe, and Orange County the same process existed for the sampling which occurred during two different time periods.

Several observations may be made while examining the results of Table 7.6. Concentrates from the cellulose acetate membrane tended to have more mutagenic potential than concentrates from the nylon membrane. Since the treated wastewaters were passed through the cellulose acetate membrane prior to the nylon membrane, the mutagenic activity possibly may be due to higher molecular weight compounds that did not reach the latter system. The type of solvent extraction would determine the type of organics which would be contained in a given fraction of concentrate and hence whether one fraction may be expected to have greater adverse effects than another. It may be noted that methylene chloride extraction under acidic conditions has a greater number of positive responses for mutagenicity than with pentane or neutral methylene chloride. Although it may or may not be significant, 6 out of 9 systems which had chlorination as the final unit operation showed mutagenic properties in the concentrate. The systems with either activated carbon or reverse osmosis as the final step were all negative. For a substance to be present in the sample, it must be rejected by the reverse osmosis membrane used in the concentration system. Since reverse osmosis was used to treat the wastewater at Escondido, compounds not capable of permeating a membrane most likely were removed.

Table 7.6: Mutagenic Potential of Advanced Wastewater
Treatment Effluents

AWT Plant	Membrane*	Solvent**	Mutagenic
Dallas I	CA	P	No
	CA	MC-neutral	No
	CA	MC-acidic	Yes
	N	P	No
	N	MC-neutral	No
	N	MC-acidic	No
Dallas II	CA	P	No
	CA	MC-neutral	No
	CA	MC-acidic	Yes
	N	P	No
	N	MC-neutral	No
	N	MC-acidic	Slight

(continued)

Table 7.6: (continued)

AWT Plant	Membrane*	Solvent**	Mutagenic
Lake Tahoe I	CA	P	No
	CA	MC-neutral	No
	CA	MC-acidic	Yes
	N	P	Yes
	N	MC-neutral	Yes
	N	MC-acidic	Yes
Lake Tahoe II	CA	P	No
	CA	MC-neutral	Slight
	CA	MC-acidic	Yes
	N	P	No
	N	MC-neutral	No
	N	MC-acidic	Slight
Pomona I	CA	P	Yes
	CA	MC-neutral	Yes
	CA	MC-acidic	Yes
	N	P	No
	N	MC-neutral	No
	N	MC-acidic	No
Pomona II	CA	P	No
	CA	MC-neutral	No
	CA	MC-acidic	No
	N	P	No
	N	MC-neutral	No
	N	MC-acidic	No
Pomona III	CA	P	No
	CA	MC-neutral	No
	CA	MC-acidic	No
	N	P	No
	N	MC-neutral	No
	N	MC-acidic	No
Escondido	CA	P	No
	CA	MC-neutral	No
	CA	MC-acidic	No
	N	P	No
	N	MC-neutral	No
	N	MC-acidic	No
Blue Plains I	CA	P	No
	CA	MC-neutral	Yes
	CA	MC-acidic	Yes
	N	P	No
	N	MC-neutral	No
	N	MC-acidic	No
Blue Plains II	CA	P	No
	CA	MC-neutral	Slight
	CA	MC-acidic	No
	N	P	Slight
	N	MC-neutral	No
	N	MC-acidic	No
Composite			Slight

(continued)

Table 7.6: (continued)

AWT Plant	Membrane*	Solvent**	Mutagenic
Orange County I Composite			No
Orange County II Composite			No

   *CA (cellulose acetate); N (nylon)
  **P (pentane); MC (methylene chloride)

Source: NSF/RA-790225

Organics

About 20% of most concentrates obtained by Gulf South Research Institute is being utilized to determine specific organic compounds in the samples. In addition to attempting to identify the compounds in greatest concentration, the contractor performing the analytical work, Battelle Columbus Laboratories, is searching for and quantifying 54 organic compounds of special interest to the EPA Health Effects Research Laboratory. These special interest compounds are as follows. The organic procedure used will determine compounds generally within the range of molecular weight from 70 to 500.

Chloroprene	Methylchlorophenoxy acetic acid me-ester
Aniline	n-Phenyl-1-naphthylamine
Phenol	Chrysene
Diethylnitrosamine	2,4-Dichlorophenoxy acetic acid me-ester
Styrene	Dibromobenzene
p-Methyl phenol	3,4-Benzpyrene
2-Methyl styrene	Benzfluoranthene (bk)
2,4-Diaminotoluene	Hexachloro-1,3-butadiene
2,4-Dimethyl phenol	Pentachloroaniline
Nitrobenzene	2,4,5-Trichlorophenoxy acetic acid me-ester
2-Chlorotoluene	Hexachlorocyclopentadiene
2-Chloroaniline	Benz-(ghi)-perylene
4-Chlorophenol	Indeno-(1,2,3-cd)-pyrene
3-Nitroaniline	Pentachlorophenol me-ether
4-Chlorophenol me-ether	Hexachlorobenzene
2-Naphthylamine	Lindane
1,4-Dichlorobenzene	Tetrachlorobiphenyl
p-Nitrophenol me-ether	Pentachloronitrobenzene
4-Chlorophenyl methyl ketone	Pentachlorobiphenyl
2-Chloronaphthalene	Triphenyl phosphate
Diphenylamine	DDT
4-Phenylaniline	Hexachlorobiphenyl
2,4-Dichlorophenol me-ether	Aldrin
1,2,4-Trichlorobenzene	Tri-(m)-cresyl phosphate
2,4-Dichloronaphthalene	Heptachlor
Fluoranthene	Dieldrin
2,4,6-Trichlorophenol me-ether	Hexabromobiphenyl

Methods for Chemical Analysis: Basically, the organic concentrates are analyzed by addition of deuterated internal standards to the concentrate, fractionation of the concentrate into acidic, basic, and neutral fractions, partitioning the neutral fraction on a microsilica gel column, and analysis of the unpartitioned concentrate and partitioned fractions by glass capillary gas chromatography using a flame ionization detector (GC-FID) and glass capillary gas chromatography coupled to a mass spectrometer (GC/MS). The GC-FID and GC/MS analyses are conducted on two types of wall-coated open-tubular glass capillary GC columns, one containing a nonpolar liquid phase (SP2100) and the other a polar liquid phase (SP1000). The basic analytical approach was developed at the EPA Health Effects Research Laboratory. This approach requires extensive quality assurance procedures in order to permit meaningful comparison of concentrates over the 3-year period of the project. Details of the chemical analysis procedures are summarized in Figure 7.3.

Figure 7.3: Analytical Scheme for Analysis of Water Concentrate

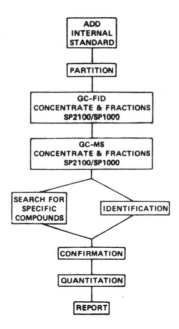

Source: NSF/RA-790225

Results and Discussion

Results of the organics portion of the overall project are available only for the Lake Tahoe II effluent concentrated by the cellulose acetate (CA) membrane, the three CA concentrates from Pomona I, the CA concentrate from Pomona II using acidified methylene chloride extraction, and a composite of the three CA extracts from Pomona III. It is not intended to determine the organic compounds in each sample checked for mutagenic activity, as the cost would be prohibitive. Rather, a representative number of samples have been selected from the various sites so as to include most concentrates showing mutagenic activity as well as several which were free of mutagenic activity. In several cases, as with Pomona III, the concentrates from the several fractions were composited.

A total of 447 compounds were identified in the Lake Tahoe II samples. Using the semiquantitative procedure of relative size to estimate quantities, the compounds in highest concentration were clofibric acid at 2 ppb, followed by di-n-butyl phthalate and tripropylene glycol methyl ether. Most of the compounds were at the parts per trillion level. It is interesting that clofibric acid is the compound in greatest concentration. Clofibrate is a drug used to reduce lipids in the blood stream and a patient is usually given 2 grams per day for this purpose. A person on clofibrates will excrete clofibric acid in the urine. The procedure detected 4 mg in the 400-gallon sample processed.

Ten of the 54 special interest compounds listed were detected. Pentachlorophenol, a wood preservative, was present in highest concentration at 16.58 ppt.

A combined listing of compounds for all three extracts from system 1 at Pomona shows 389 identified compounds. Of these, 194 organic compounds were identified in the acidified methylene chloride extract alone. This compares to 119 compounds in the acidified methylene chloride extract of system 2 and 108 compounds in the composite of all six extracts from system 3. Thus, it appears that ozonation reduces the number of organic compounds and the two systems having activated carbon as the final treatment step results in fewer compounds than with the system 1 where chlorination was the final step.

Compounds in highest concentrations in the Pomona samples, as determined by the semiquantitative relative size procedure, include dioctyl sebacate, 1.5 ppb; di-n-butyl phthalate, 1.5 ppb; and tris-β-chloroethyl phosphate, 1 ppb.

Special interest compounds, with their concentrations, are listed in Table 7.7 for each of the five Pomona samples analyzed. The compound in highest concentration was 2,4-D, a weed killer. Following the trend for the total number of compounds, systems 2 and 3 had fewer numbers of special interest compounds than with system 1, and the concentrations tend to be lower.

As more data become available regarding the analysis of organic concentrates, perhaps patterns will become more pronounced. On the other hand, the possibility is very strong that positive results with the Ames test cannot be related to identified organics or functional groups in a sample. When dealing with complex mixtures of organics at low levels, biological screening tests do not have the same sensitivity as available with chemical testing procedures. Perhaps only when new or improved biological testing systems are available will it be possible to say with assurance whether or not exposure to these materials will result in any adverse health effects.

One cannot rule out the possibility that certain compounds, such as plasticizers, are added to the concentrates during the concentration process. Studies are under way at present to try to identify the degree of such sample contamination.

There are sufficient differences, however, in the mutagenesis and chemical data from site to site for given fractions to conclude that most compounds must have been in the original wastewater and are not an artifact of the concentration process.

Table 7.7: Special Interest Compounds in Pomona Effluent

| | . . . . Concentration in ng/ℓ . . . . | | | | |
Compound	Pomona I Pentane	Pomona I *MC-Neutral	Pomona I MC-Acidic	Pomona II MC-Acidic	Pomona III Composite
Phenol	4.85	19.68	11.26	4.56	3.92
Styrene	0.84	1.41	0.61		0.84
2-Methyl styrene	0.59	0.64	0.28	0.09	0.11
2-Chloroaniline	3.86	24.87			4.52
Diphenylamine	9.77	2.18	0.14		0.05
2,4,6-Trichlorphenol	1.59		2.42	1.31	9.64
1,2,4-Trichlorobenzene	0.70		0.08		
Fluoranthene	3.43	0.22			
Pentachlorphenol	43.92	10.17	6.77	11.06	
Triphenyl phosphate	1.31				
p-Chlorophenol		16.41	54.82		
2,4-D			69.68		
Hexachlorobenzene			3.40	1.55	
p-Chloroacetophenone		7.49			
Tricresylphosphate					2.6
p-Dichlorobenzene			0.56		0.02

*MC = methylene chloride

Source: NSF/RA-780225

TESTING VOLATILES IN WASTEWATER TREATMENT PLANT EFFLUENTS

The information in this section is abstracted from *Health Effects of Consumption of Renovated Water: Chemistry and Cytotoxicity*, (EPA Report 600/1-79-014), by W.R. Chappell, C. Solomons, H.F. Walton, and W.L. Weston, all of the University of Colorado Environmental Trace Substances Research Program, and sponsored by HERL, U.S. EPA, Cincinnati, Ohio.

Objectives

Since 1975 a group of researchers at the University of Colorado has been conducting research into developing better methods for establishing both the chemical identity and the biological effects of contaminants in both untreated and treated effluent from wastewater treatment plants. Most of this effort has been directed at the effluent from the Denver Metro Sewage Plant because the Denver Water Board is engaged in a multiyear effort to evaluate the feasibility of potable reuse of wastewater.

The overall objectives of the research were:

> (1) to develop various analytical methods to concentrate, fractionate, and identify compounds, particularly those that proved to be toxic to the cells used.

> (2) to test the applicability of certain mammalian cells for use as *in vitro* models to evaluate the toxicity of wastewater.

The results of this work have several potential beneficial uses including:

> (1) the eventual development of methods for automatic monitoring;

> (2) methods development for evaluating the human health effects of potable use;

> (3) the setting of guidelines for further toxicological testing and epidemiological studies;

> (4) the identification of the most important pollutants and classes of pollutants; and

> (5) the development of gross tests for groups of contaminants.

The "Purge-and-Trap" Method for Volatiles: Outline of Procedure

Purified nitrogen gas was passed through a 1-liter sample of water to be analyzed, which was contained in a 2-liter 3-neck flask mounted on a heating mantle. One "neck" carried a thermometer. Nitrogen was led into the flask through a tube that terminated in a glass frit; it passed out of the flask into a glass tube or trap, 175 mm long and 4 mm internal diameter, packed with 150 mg of the adsorbent Tenax-GC, a porous polymer of phenylene oxide. This adsorbent strongly retains hydrocarbons and chlorinated hydrocarbons while having little affinity for water. The trap was surrounded by a water jacket and could be cooled.

After loading with volatile organic compounds from the sample, the Tenax trap was removed and mounted at the inlet of a gas chromatograph, which was fitted with a wall-coated capillary column and a flame-ionization detector. The adsorbed organic compounds were transferred from the trap to the capillary column by first cooling the column in dry ice, then quickly heating the trap by mounting a two-piece oven around it. Nitrogen was passed; it swept the organic compounds out of the trap and into the column, where they were "focused" close to the column entrance. The column oven was then turned on, evaporating the dry ice and raising the temperature to 180°C in 3 hours according to a linear program. The FID response was recorded. Peaks were identified by mass spectrometry and by comparison of retention times with those of known compounds.

Environmental Samples: *Wastewater* — Figure 7.4 shows chromatograms obtained from the secondary effluent of the Metropolitan Denver sewage plant, before and after chlorination, along with a system blank obtained with redistilled water. The chlorinated effluent is discharged into the river. Peaks are seen for the following compounds, listed in the order of emergence from the capillary column, with the most prominent peaks indicated by asterisks.

Chloroform*
1,1,1-Trichloroethane
Benzene
Dibromomethane
Trichloroethylene
Dimethyl disulfide*
Toluene*
Tetrachloroethylene*

Xylenes*
Ethylbenzene
Styrene
Methylethylbenzenes
Trimethylbenzenes
Dichlorobenzenes**
Chlorotoluenes

Figure 7.4 shows an effect observed repeatedly, namely, an increase in the toluene and xylene concentrations after chlorination.

Figure 7.4: Chromatogram of Denver Secondary Effluent

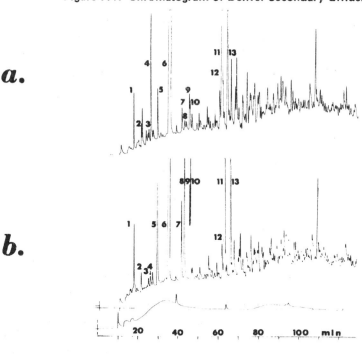

(a) Before chlorination
(b) After chlorination
Key:

(1) Chloroform
(2) 1,1,1-Trichloroethane
(3) Trichloroethylene
(4) Dimethyl disulfide
(5) Toluene
(6) Tetrachloroethylene

(7) p- and m-Xylene
(8) Ethylbenzene
(9) Styrene
(10) o-Xylene
(11)(12)(13) p-, m-, o-Dichlorobenzene

Source: EPA-600/1-79-014

Water from an experimental reverse osmosis unit at the Denver sewage plant showed marked peaks at positions corresponding to chloroform, toluene and tetrachloroethylene, as well as lesser peaks, indicating that reverse osmosis did not remove the more volatile compounds. Activated carbon treatment does not remove these compounds either. Liquid chromatography, however, showed that carbon filtration and reverse osmosis were effective in removing the less volatile and more polar impurities from water.

Tap waters from Denver and Boulder were examined and showed very little volatile content, well below 1 μg/ℓ. The city of Boulder, Colorado, has an unusually clean source of drinking water. Humic material is present, but there is little contamination of human origin. The water is chlorinated and clarified with alum before distribution. No toluene or other aromatic hydrocarbons were found at any stage of the treatment, though trihalomethanes were found in low concentrations. It seems that precursors of toluene may exist in wastewater but not in uncontaminated natural waters.

Pristine mountain water from a spring in the timber at 8,000 feet elevation (2,400 meters) showed five peaks, two of high volatility emerging near the beginning of the temperature program, and three of low volatility emerging near the end. The concentrations were about 0.1 μg/ℓ. Identifications were not attempted, but one may speculate that the compounds came from the decay of humic material. Similar peaks of low volatility appeared in Denver tap water. Water from Grand Lake, Colorado was almost devoid of volatile organic matter.

Nonvolatile Compounds

A discussion, "Testing for Nonvolatile Organic Compounds in Wastewater," by H.F. Walton, the material for which was the same as in this report, will be found in the next section of this chapter.

Summary

Methods are being devised for the chemical analysis of the very complex mixtures of organic compounds found at trace levels in natural waters, treated waters, and wastewaters. One part of the problem has been essentially solved, that is, the identification and measurement of volatile substances that can be swept out of water by warming and bubbling nitrogen. These substances include chloroform, other chlorinated hydrocarbons, benzene and toluene, all of them substances that are toxic to some extent. They are trapped on a special adsorbent (Tenax) and transferred to a gas chromatograph, where they are analyzed and identified by mass spectrometry. Concentrations of one part per billion and less can be measured. Applying this technique to wastewater and drinking water, it is possible to see what substances are present and how they are affected by treatments such as chlorination, ozonation, and filtration through activated carbon. Carbon treatment is being introduced on a very large scale for removing organic compounds from drinking water and wastewater; the findings suggest that it removes toxic substances but is not especially effective in removing traces of volatiles.

The analysis of organic compounds in water that are not volatile is a much more difficult problem. Nobody has found a satisfactory solution, but a start has been made. It has been possible to "strain out" or selectively absorb a part of the organic material, using an absorbent called Bondapak-C_{18}, followed by stripping the absorbed substances off the Bondapak by a series of mixtures of water and methanol. Several fractions were obtained, graded according to "polarity" or compatibility with water, then concentrated by evaporation so that the substances originally present in say 10 liters of wastewater are recovered as a series of six fractions, each of volume 4 ml. To guide the fractionation process the adsorption of ultraviolet light is recorded. The record on the chart paper shows what is going on, and allows a comparison of the results of various wastewater treatments.

The concentrated fractions are submitted for cellular toxicity tests. Lately, samples have also been tested for mutagenic activity. The Bondapak absorbent retains only one-third of the total organic carbon in wastewater, but the nonretained material does not seem to be toxic. The toxicity is concentrated in the less polar fractions. It is here that one would expect to find pesticides and products of industrial contamination. As to mutagenic effects, four sets of samples have been tested and the data are not consistent. In some tests the polar fractions were found to be strongly mutagenic, particularly the green G2 fraction, while the less polar fractions were not. In another test, G1 was mutagenic but G2 had little effect. Clearly, the composition of a municipal sewage effluent varies from day to day, and perhaps consistency should not be expected. Mutagenesis may be due to a minor component appearing on the border between G1 and G2, a component whose concentration varies greatly from day to day. Mutagenesis is a serious matter, however, and more tests will be made. The cellular toxicity of the less polar fractions has been confirmed many times. The cellular toxicity tests have been used to judge the effectiveness of carbon treatment and reverse osmosis.

TESTING FOR NONVOLATILE ORGANIC COMPOUNDS IN WASTEWATER

> The information in this section was obtained from a paper in Conference III, "Chemical Analysis and Toxicity of Nonvolatile Organic Compounds in Wastewater," by H.F. Walton of the Chemistry Department, University of Colorado.

Overview of Testing Method

Organic compounds in filtered wastewater are concentrated by pumping the water through a column packed with the adsorbent Bondapak-C_{18}. This is a superficially porous silica of particle size 37 to 75 microns which carries a chemically bonded layer of octadecyl groups. The material has the adsorbent properties of kerosene. It retains less polar organic compounds while letting pass inorganic salts and ionized compounds like salts of fatty acids, as well as highly polar water-soluble compounds like sugars, amino acids and urea.

To remove the adsorbed compounds the column is first flushed with distilled water, then water mixed with methanol is passed over it according to a linear gradient, starting with pure water and ending with pure methanol 30 minutes later. This is continued until all adsorbed material is removed. Ultraviolet absorbance is used to detect the organic compounds; the absorbance is recorded on a strip chart. The chart record provides some information about the composition of the organic material, and additional information is obtained by collecting and examining fractions of the solution flowing from the column.

Experimental Procedure

Collection and Initial Treatment of Samples: Wastewater is collected on the site in sterile one-gallon bottles. Generally, chlorinated, secondarily treated effluent is taken just above the point of discharge into the river. It is brought to the laboratory and heated to $60°C$, then filtered through glass fiber filter paper, first the relatively coarse Whatman GF/A, then Whatman GF/F, which retains 0.7-micron particles. Filtering is done under suction, thus removing dissolved air and carbon dioxide. The pH rises to above 8, and is brought back to 7.5 by adding nitric acid.

Bondapak Column: Ten to twelve liters of filtered, degassed wastewater are now pumped through a stainless steel column, 1 cm x 50 cm, packed with Bondapak-C_{18}, using the arrangement shown in Figure 7.5. In an alternative procedure, unfiltered wastewater is pumped through a series of sand and glass filters and through a short "collector column" of Bondapak-C_{18}, which is later attached to the inlet of the column shown in Figure 7.5. The flow rate during this loading step is 7 ml per minute.

Flushing: When sufficient wastewater has been passed, the flow is reduced to 5 ml/min, the inlet valve of Pump A is turned and the column is flushed with distilled water for 15 minutes. Then the linear water-to-methanol gradient is started. A schematic graph of absorbance vs time is shown in Figure 7.6, which also indicates where the fractions were taken. Chromatograms of water supplied by the San Jose Creek Water Quality Laboratory near Pomona, California showed the effect of carbon treatment of wastewater, which is to remove the less polar fractions of organic material while having little effect on the more polar fractions. Since the least polar fractions are the most toxic, this information is of some value. Other chromatograms that have been obtained show the effect of carbon treatment and reverse osmosis on Denver wastewater. Reverse osmosis removes ionic and highly polar impurities from water but lets some of the weakly polar fractions pass.

Fraction Examination: For further examination, fractions of the effluent from the Bondapak column were collected according to the scheme shown in Figure 7.6, and were evaporated in a Buchi rotary evaporator under low pressure at $60°$ to $70°C$ to a final volume of 2 to 3 ml. A general description of each fraction follows.

Figure 7.5: Apparatus for Pumping Sample and Gradient

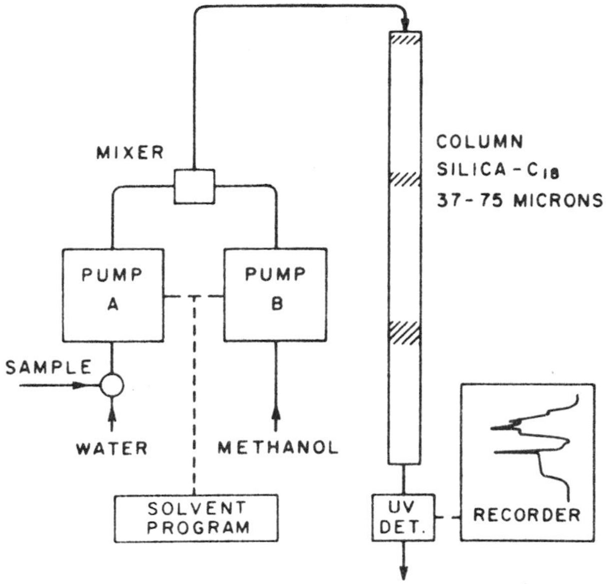

Note: Pumps are Model 6000A, controlled by Model 660 solvent programmer, all from Waters Associates; detector was either a single-wavelength model (Chromatronix Inc.) or a variable wavelength detector (Schoeffel Instrument Corp. Model SF770).

Source: EPA-600/1-79-014

The "flush peak," FP, was light brown. It appeared to contain sodium salts of aromatic acids like benzoic acid, along with neutral material. No flush peak appeared if a salt solution was used to flush the column instead of distilled water.

Fraction G1 (G = gradient) was dark brown. Fraction G2 was brilliant green; G3 was brown, and G4 light brown. G5 was light rose pink. In one experiment, each fraction was evaporated in a nitrogen stream at room temperature and the residues were weighed. The weights obtained from one liter of wastewater were: G1, 1.5 mg; G2, 0.6 mg; G3, 1.5 mg; G4, 0.7 mg; G5, 1.0 mg. Assuming that carbon accounted for one-half of the weight (a fair assumption for humic acid), the sum total of fractions G1 through G5 corresponds to 2.7 ppm dissolved organic carbon. This figure is in fair agreement with total organic carbon measurements made on the filtered wastewater before and after passing through the Bondapak column.

The brown color was due to humic substances of high molecular weight. Gel permeation chromatography of fractions G1 through G4 showed the presence of material with molecular weight 2,000 and above, and some of the material was retained on a Diaflo ultrafiltration membrane. The presence of humic material greatly complicates the detection of substances of lower molecular weight. Fraction G5 was almost free of humic material, and some success was achieved in identifying the substances that it contains.

Figure 7.6: Ultraviolet Absorbance Record (Schematic) and Scheme of Fraction Collection

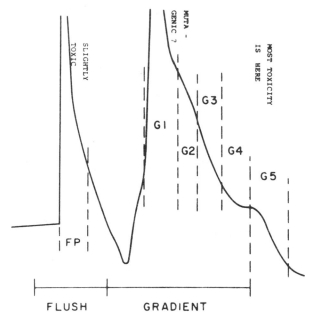

Source: EPA-600/1-79-014

Fraction G2 is distinctive for its green color. It also contains a brown component. The green and brown subfractions may be separated by treating the dry residue with pure methanol (the green dissolves, the brown does not) or by gel permeation chromatography (the brown subfraction has a high molecular weight).

[Note: The nature of tests per toxicity and mutagenicity is described in the next section.]

Secondary Liquid Chromatography: Chemical Analysis of the Fractions from the Bondapak-C_{18} Column

As has been noted, the fractions collected according to the scheme of Figure 7.6 were further resolved by chromatography on other columns. The fractions were evaporated to small volume as described above, then injected into the high-resolution columns by means of a sample loop.

The flush peak was resolved on a column of anion-exchange resin of small particle size, using ammonium acetate buffers as eluents. By changing the pH and the concentration of ammonium acetate it could be determined whether a particular peak was due to a neutral species or an anion, and if it was an anion, whether its charge was –1 or –2. At least one peak was due to a doubly charged anion, but its chemical identity has not yet been found.

Fractions G1-G4: Fractions G1-G4 were run on columns of porous polymer gels that separate compounds partly by size exclusion, partly partition. Compounds of high molecular weight (humic acids) were seen to predominate.

Fraction G5: Fraction G5 was run on a MicroBondapak-C_{18} column (Waters Associates) with 60% methanol for 10 minutes, then a 30-minute linear gradient to 100% methanol. Figure 7.7 shows a typical chromatogram. Many peaks are seen, showing the complexity of the material. A fluorescence detector, placed after the variable-wavelength UV detector, showed three strong peaks, two of them in places where no ultraviolet absorption was seen at the wavelength chosen.

Peaks "E" and "F" were collected and examined. The ultraviolet absorption spectrum of each peak was scanned and the solutions were evaporated. The weights of the residues corresponded to initial concentrations in the original wastewater of 100 $\mu g/\ell$ (100 ppb) and 150 $\mu g/\ell$, respectively. Portions of the residues, which were liquids, were introduced into a Hewlett-Packard Model 5980A mass spectrometer by means of a probe, and the mass spectra were scanned and stored as the probe was heated.

Fraction "E" was pink; the pink color appeared at the detector outlet just before the UV absorption started to rise. As the solution evaporated a bright red solid speck appeared. In the final residue the mass spectrometer showed three compounds, the first being tri(butoxyethyl) phosphate, a common plasticizer, and the second, dioctyl phthalate. The third mass spectrum, which appeared last as the probe was heated, was not identified, but seemed to be a phthalate ester. Phthalate esters show ultraviolet absorption maxima near 274 nm; fraction "E" showed a maximum at 262 nm. The UV absorption must have been due to another component, not seen in the mass spectra, and having a high absorptivity.

Fraction "E" contained at least five compounds, and fraction "F" at least two. The complexity of the analytical problem is evident. Mass spectrometry is the most powerful way of identification, but if a compound does not volatilize without decomposition it will not give a mass spectrum. Another tool of identification is infrared spectrometry. The infrared technique is to be improved to handle the very small samples that are available.

Elimination of Candidate Compounds: One route to peak identification in chromatography is to match the observed retention volumes with those of known compounds. Several known compounds were run on the MicroBondapak-

C_{18} column under the same conditions as G5 and the retention volumes were noted. The toxic pollutants benzidine, p-nitrophenol, nitrobenzene, m-chlorophenol and atrazine all came out before peak "A" of Figure 7.7, and it was concluded that these pollutants were absent from Denver secondary sewage effluent. Polychlorinated biphenyls eluted in the region of peaks B to F; however, the mass spectra of compounds containing chlorine are very characteristic, because of the chlorine isotope pair, and the mass spectra of E and F gave no sign of chlorine atoms.

Figure 7.7: Chromatogram of Fraction G5 on MicroBondapak-C_{18}

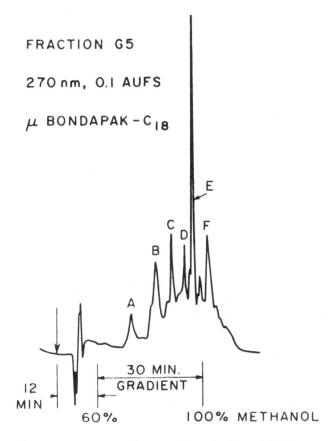

Note: In this case a 12-minute isocratic flow of 60% methanol was used, followed by a 30-minute linear gradient to 100% methanol. Later a 20-minute flow with 60% methanol was adopted.

Source: EPA-600/1-79-014

Conclusions

Most nonvolatile organic matter in secondary sewage effluent consists of highly polar, water-soluble compounds and humic material. About one-quarter of the dissolved organic carbon can be retained on an octadecyl-silica reverse-phase chromatographic adsorbent, Bondapak-C_{18}, and it can be completely removed from this adsorbent by stripping with a water-to-methanol gradient. Fractions have been collected during the stripping gradient and examined for toxicity, mutagenicity and chemical composition.

Most of the material adsorbed on the Bondapak-C consists of humic substances that are apparently nontoxic, though they may have associated with them some substances that show mutagenic activity. The toxic compounds seem to be weakly polar or nonpolar, and to amount in all to less than one milligram per liter of secondary effluent.

High-resolution liquid chromatography combined with mass spectrometry shows the presence of many compounds whose concentrations are in the low parts per billion range. Identification is difficult, but by comparing observed chromatograms with the chromatograms of known substances, it may be said that certain toxic pollutants, such as atrazine, chloro- and nitrophenols and benzidine are not present.

TOXICITY AND MUTAGENICITY TESTING SUITABLE FOR REUSED WATER

> Information in this section was based on the paper of Conference III, "The Detection of Human Cellular Toxicity Due to Environmental Substances," by C.C. Solomons, University of Colorado Medical Center.
> [Note: A discussion of the material covered in this section may also be found, in expanded form in EPA Report 600/1-79-014.]

Introduction

To determine the total health effects of a substance in the environment is a formidable task. Because of the complexity of mammalian cellular metabolism and the large variety of thousands of interacting chemical reactions in the body, it is impractical to test a suspected toxin against every known metabolic step or sequence of steps. Even if this could be done, the ability of the cell to compensate, within limits, for many types of stress would make interpretation and extrapolation extremely difficult. The situation is simplified if the compound being evaluated has a high specificity for a single enzyme system. For example, organo phosphates (parathion) specifically inhibit acetylcholinesterases and quickly disrupt the body's neuromuscular system. However, apart from acute toxicity of this type, which is relatively easy to detect, one is more concerned about the effects of chronic exposure to much less acutely toxic substances of low concentrations. Therefore, a variety of compounds, including aromatics, paraffins, and their chlorinated derivatives, were studied, as well as fractions of unknown compositions derived from treated sewage and purified water. It was also wished to measure the relative effectiveness of water purification steps such as charcoal treatment and reverse osmosis with a view to developing on-line biological testing as described in a new grant proposal.

Choice of a Metabolic Pathway

In attempting to deal with the problems of low concentration and relatively short periods of exposure, it is essential to use cells that are extremely sensitive to very small concentration changes in their immediate environment, on the order of 10^{-6} to 10^{-5} M, and which react explosively and uncontrollably once they are triggered. Two types of cells, platelets and leucocytes, which normally fulfill these requirements in the body, were studied.

Platelets: Normally, when a blood vessel is cut or damaged the platelets aggregate to each other to form a plug which stops bleeding and acts as a catalytic surface for further coagulation. In the course of aggregation the platelet becomes degranulated, releasing a number of substances, including adenosine diphosphate (ADP), serotonin and a variety of proteins. Platelet function is linked closely to adenylate metabolism and is regulated by membrane function. Consequently, lipid soluble chemicals which change membrane function can affect platelet metabolism and behavior. This concept is important not only from the viewpoint of hemostasis, but is also related to the role of platelets in interacting with bacteria and viruses.

Leucocytes: Another type of cell, which also functions explosively to a stimulus, is the white cell in the blood which forms one of the defenses against infection and malignancy. These cells can ingest or phagocytose bacteria and kill them with hydrogen-peroxide-generated metabolic action. Thus, substances which impair these functions or cause these cells to inappropriately attack the tissues of the host are of concern. The white cells, like the platelets, generate and use large quantities of high-energy-transducing purines such as adenosine triphosphate (ATP), etc., and have efficient pathways for salvaging ATP from degradation products such as hypoxanthine (HYPX).

Adenylate Control System: All choices of metabolic pathways are open to some sort of criticism. However, there is one sequence which is of central importance to both the energizing and kinetic control of all metabolic steps. This system is the adenylate control system which has come to be recognized as being of prime importance in energy transduction, storage and control of metabolic rates and directionality. The importance of the fast-acting adenylate control system cannot be exaggerated for a large number of chemical reaction sequences which typify living organisms. The adenide nucleotides interact with all sequences in a complex living cell and uncontrolled changes in the relative concentrations of ATP, ADP and adenosine monophosphate (AMP) would adversely affect the rates of all metabolic reactions and thus be highly disruptive.

It is remarkable that the role of the adenine nucleotide pool is unique in being involved in virtually every metabolic sequence in the cell. The role of the adenylates is not specific to any single pathway, but more than any other compounds, they couple and correlate all the metabolic activities of the cell, giving rise to biological homeostasis and function. The effect of stress on this pathway is to reduce ATP and increase AMP and hypoxanthine. Therefore, methods have been developed to assay adenylate pools when platelets and white cells are brought into contact with a variety of chemicals.

Methodology

Because of the nature of the experimental conditions in which radioactive adenine was used as a precursor, the only radioactive compounds formed in significant quantities were ATP, ADP and AMP, with occasional formation of inosine monophosphate (IMP) and HYPX. Dose response curves were used to express the results of known toxic compounds on adenylate metabolism as well as the effects of sewage, tap water and water effluents during treatment. In outline, the platelets were first obtained as a suspension by the standard method of differential centrifugation of anticoagulated blood. Care was taken to prevent stressing the platelets during blood drawing or subsequently in the laboratory. Thus, only a "clean" venipuncture from healthy blood donors was used and high-speed centrifugation and washing avoided. Suspensions of white cells were prepared and treated similarly.

In a typical experiment, 5 μl of U-14-C adenine (60,000 cpm) was added to a 0.5 ml suspension of platelets (5 x 10^5/mm^3, monocytes, or neutrophils, 1 x 10^4/mm^3). Ten microliters of the test fractions to be evaluated were added. After incubation at 37°C for 30 minutes the cells were cooled in ice and centrifuged at 3,000 rpm for 3 minutes. The supernatant was removed and 0.2 ml of cold 13% perchloric acid (PCA) was added to the pellet. After mixing and centrifuging, the PCA supernatant was analyzed by thin layer chromatography (TLC) and high performance liquid chromatographic systems (HPLC) described below. The TLC system allows one to measure the kinetic synthetic ability of the cells to convert U-14-C adenine to U-14-C purine nucleotides. The HPLC system measures the total pools of these substances.

Thin Layer Chromatography (TLC): Ten microliters of the PCA supernatant were applied without heat to a 2-cm strip of an Eastman Kodak Cellulose Thin Layer Chromatogram #13255 with a Mylar backing, and developed with a mixture of water:formic acid:tert-amyl alcohol 1:2:3 for 5 hours. The chromatogram was dried in air, cut into fifteen 1-cm strips, and each placed in a 5-ml counting vial with 3 ml of scintillation fluid. The vials were counted in a scintillation spectrometer and each count calculated as a percentage of the total U-14-C nucleotide pool. A typical example of the toxic effects of m-xylene shows substantial decreases in ATP and ADP and an increase in AMP. Significantly greater amounts of unmetabolized adenine are seen in the cells exposed to m-xylene. Recovery is 95 to 102%. In a large series of normal platelets carried out in connection with other projects ATP was 65 to 70%, ADP was 10 to 14% and AMP was 1 to 5%. Changes of 15% or larger in ATP levels were regarded as being above the analytical and biological noise levels for this determination.

High Performance Liquid Chromatography (HPLC): The major technical advance which makes it feasible to consider on-line capability is the use of high performance liquid chromatography (HPLC) for the rapid determination of adenine nucleotides at the rate of 15 minutes per sample. The peak heights are measured and used for calculating of pool size. Both TLC and HPLC are sensitive down to the 10^{-9} M range. With modifications the separation time can be reduced to 3 minutes.

A Waters & Associates HPLC apparatus with a U-18 MicroBondapak reversed phase column was used. Fifteen microliters extract was injected and 0.1 M KH_2PO_4 was pumped through the column at 1.5 ml/min. The nucleotides and related compounds were adequately separated in 12 to 15 minutes and were detected by UV absorption at 254 nm. Identification was obtained using retention time and the addition of known compounds to the test PCA supernatant. In the future it is planned to pump the effluent from the HPLC system into a flow-through scintillation spectrometer so that specific activity of each compound can be computed, thus obviating the need for TLC. Recovery and reproducibility of the standards was 95 to 103%. The peak height was found to be linearly proportioned to concentration, regardless of peak width, in the range 10^{-6} to 10^{-12} mol of purine compound per sample injected. The perchloric acid was neutralized by the strong buffer used and did not interfere with the results or damage the columns.

Results

The results are divided into three main sections:

> (1) Cellular effects of known toxic substances;
>
> (2) Effects of concentrated fractions of water; and
>
> (3) Study of reverse osmosis permeate.

The chemical fractionation of various waters was carried out by Dr. Walton and is fully described in the previous section.

Effects of Known Substances: Known compounds with the highest available grade of purity were added to the cell suspensions as described above. Initially, measurements were made of U-14-C adenine incorporation into ATP, ADP, and AMP, using TLC. Later on, when HPLC became available, the total adenylate pool was measured. A control with no additive was run with each batch of cells. Metabolic stress effects are indicated, either by a reduction in the 14-C or 12-C ATP pools, and similar results were obtained with each cell type.

In general, the TLC and HPLC dose response curves were in good agreement. The HPLC curves often showed a more sensitive response at the 0.1 and 1 ppm levels. The monocyte, however, was found to be most resistant to chloroform at concentrations of 0.1 and 1.0 ppm, responding at 10 ppm. Except for tetrachloroethylene the monocyte did not give a graded response for target cell release of chromium with increasing concentration. Thin layer chromatography and HPLC were more generally sensitive in detecting graded cell responses. These results were most satisfactory from a technical viewpoint and large numbers could be processed per day. In all the cells a concentration of added substance at 10 ppm was too high for the discrimination between individual compounds. The technique was more efficient at the 1 ppm level of exposure.

Effects of Concentrated Water Fractions: Concentrated fractions were produced and labeled from G1 to G9. The higher the G number the lower the polarity of the constituents of the fraction. Very significant responses were obtained, with toxicity increasing with the G number of the fraction. Thus, G2 is shown to be relatively nontoxic to neutrophils, but G4, G5 and G9 produce significant reductions in the U-14-C ATP pool.

With regard to monocytes very similar results were obtained compared to those obtained on neutrophils. These results on extracts of Pomona, California wastewater note the changes in chromium release and U-14-C ATP pools. As before, toxicity generally increases with G number. Of special interest is G4 and G4A; G4A is charcoal-treated in the plant and by comparison with the untreated G4 fraction it is seen that toxicity is reduced by charcoal treatment.

Reverse Osmosis: Concentrated samples of the permeate and reject were supplied by Dr. H. Walton and toxicity was determined as described above. The G3 fraction of the reject was more toxic than its counterpart in the permeate.

Discussion

It is difficult to decide which of these three cell models—platelets, monocytes or neutrophils—is the most useful for monitoring purposes. They all have their advantages and disadvantages. With on-line operation ultimately of prime importance, the platelet is recommended because of its stability and ease of analysis with only small amounts of blood (1 to 5 ml) needed per dose response curve. On the other hand, neutrophils and monocytes tell one more about the immune defense system. However, larger volumes of blood (on the order of 50 mℓ) are required and the behavior of the neutrophils may be subject to seasonal variations.

Distinct differences were noted in the effects of wastewater before and after charcoal treatment. Both toxic and nontoxic fractions were found in the samples. Thus, the methodology had sufficient range to distinguish biologically between fractions of different chemical polarity. The humic acid fraction was nontoxic, but less polar compounds had adverse effects on the cells.

Summary and Conclusions

(1) Several model systems for detecting cellular toxicity were developed using platelets, neutrophils, and monocytes.

(2) Testing included known substances, water fractions, and concentrates from sewage and water treatment

plants. Degrees of toxicity and the effects of purification were measured.

(3) The metabolic pathway of adenylate metabolism was found to be suitable as a rapid method of analysis and allows for a unified, theoretical approach to toxicity of a wide variety of compounds. Toxic fractions detected in this manner can be reserved for more detailed biochemical investigation.

(4) This technique is recommended for the detection of toxic compounds within hours of sampling and is thus applicable to modern water reuse technology.

Contaminants Associated
with Reuse
of Municipal Wastewater

The material in this chapter is based on EPA Report 600/1-78-019, *Contaminants Associated with Direct and Indirect Reuse of Municipal Wastewater,* prepared by SCS Engineers, Inc., Long Beach, California, for the U.S. EPA Health Effects Research Laboratory of Cincinnati, Ohio, March 1978.

The report is an overview of published data concerning the health effects associated with direct and indirect use of treated municipal wastewater for potable purposes. The chapter traces wastewater contaminants through municipal wastewater treatments, through dispersal to the environment to land or surface or groundwater, and through water treatment plants, and details the epidemiological and pathological effects on man.

The numbers in parentheses throughout the chapter refer to the references which are given in full at the end of the chapter.

INTRODUCTION

From time immemorial man has used, with varying consequences, water contaminated by other men, by animals, and by natural processes. In modern times, it has become increasingly necessary to reuse water as populations and productivity have multiplied and limited water supplies have been used up. However, this reuse has usually be done on an unplanned basis. It has been conservatively estimated that, at the present time, approximately one-third of the population in the United States derives water from sources which are degraded to some extent by wastewater discharges. Excepting the transmission of infectious diseases, little concern—until very recently—has been given to the disease-producing potential of such contamination. It is now necessary to review the health effects of this situation in a more comprehensive fashion.

Since the public health disaster of Minimata, Japan, in the late 1950s and early 1960s (caused by ingestion of shellfish contaminated with methyl mercury) there has been a great surge in research concerning environmentally induced health effects on man. It is now generally accepted that the myriad of contaminants which are continuously discharged to the environment may produce both acute and chronic repercussions on public health through daily ingestion of air, water, and food. Recently, some forms of cancer, once thought to be of genetic etiology, have been projected to be caused or stimulated by environmental contaminants.

One area of critical consideration to public health is the direct or indirect reuse of municipal wastewater for potable purposes. Municipal wastewater systems have been the repositories of virtually every chemical contaminant known to be produced by man. The very nature of municipal wastewater streams makes them of critical importance when considering the environmentally induced health effects on man. Many questions must be clearly answered before a complete understanding of the situation will occur: What are the harmful constituents of municipal wastewater? How well does the present wastewater treatment technology remove these constituents? What eventually happens to them in the environment? How well do the water treatment plants perform in providing contaminant removals and a last line of protection?

Definitions of Direct and Indirect Use

For purposes of this report, direct reuse is defined as the discharge of the treated municipal wastewater directly into a raw water supply without intervening travel, and dilution in natural surface or groundwater.

Indirect reuse is defined as the reuse of treated municipal wastewater as a raw water supply after the wastewater has entered, commingled, and essentially become a part of a natural surface or groundwater resource. A significant percentage of the nation's raw water supply is derived from surface waters such as major lakes and rivers, and consists in part of treated wastewater from other municipalities. This indirect reuse has long been accepted by the public and the waterworks industry as normal and inevitable. Indirect reuse also includes introduction of treated wastewater into groundwater aquifers through percolation or well injection. This practice is often labeled groundwater recharge and may be a formal, intentional program, or simply a result of land disposal of wastewater.

Selection of Contaminants for Consideration

The selection of wastewater contaminants for consideration in this study was difficult, because of the many public health impairing constituents found in wastewater. Several of the traditional wastewater parameters (BOD, suspended solids, etc.) pose no direct threat to public health, although some of the direct health-impairing contaminants may be associated with these traditional wastewater parameters. Therefore, some of the traditional parameters are included.

Within each section of this chapter, information is organized and presented in the following contaminant groups.

Water Quality Parameters: These are ammonia, BOD, COD, nitrates, nitrites, phosphates, SS, TDS, and TOC. Since these water quality parameters have less direct threat to public health than the other groups studied, less attention will be paid to their removal than to the removal of other contaminants, even though far more literature exists on the subject of their removal. Special attention will be paid to the nitrogenous compounds, however, since they do prove some threat to public health.

Elemental Contaminants: The elemental contaminants group consists of the ions, compounds and complexes of the following metals and metalloids: Al, Sb, As, Ba, Be, B, Cd, Cr, Co, Cu, Ge, Fe, Pb, Mn, Hg, Mo, Ni, Se, Th, Sn, U and Zn. Many of these contaminants are required in trace quantities for normal human metabolic functions, yet higher levels of these trace elements may cause significant health problems.

Biocidal Contaminants: These substances are those normally used to control insect or disease vectors. They are: DDT, DDD, DDE, aldrin, dieldrin, endrin, chlorinated hydrocarbons, arsenated hydrocarbons, organonitrogen pesticides, organophosphorus pesticides, herbicides, and soil sterilants.

Synthetic/Organic Contaminants: This group of compounds includes many synthetically produced organic chemicals that have found their way into water systems. They will be mentioned as specific compounds in various sections of this chapter.

Biological Contaminants: Traditionally, biological contaminants have received the most attention in wastewater treatment, since these contaminants may cause direct infection in the consumer. These biological contaminants will be found listed at the end of Table 8.1. Other specific organisms within this group will be considered separately at appropriate places in the chapter.

WASTEWATER INPUTS

Untreated wastewater input composition is the first point of interest in determining the pathways pollutants may follow from wastewater management systems back to man in direct and indirect reuse situations. In addition to domestic sewage, input sources may include various industrial wastes, storm water, and groundwater infiltration, in various combinations. Moreover, the input proportions of an individual system change with time; pollutant concentrations and volumes vary hourly, daily, weekly, and seasonally.

Research surveyed regarding input concentrations to municipal treatment facilities is presented in Table 8.1. Substantial literature concerning input compositions is available for water quality parameters and elemental and biological contaminants. With few exceptions, however, input concentrations of biocidal and synthetic-organic contaminants have not been investigated.

Table 8.1: Literature Reviewed and Range Pertaining to the Composition of Wastewater Inputs to Municipal Treatment Systems

Contaminant	Reference Number	Range, mg/ℓ
Water Quality Parameters		
Ammonia	22, 90, 273, 368, 390, 406, 450, 503, 516, 582, 647, 651, 700	8–50
BOD	19, 69, 171, 251, 273, 302, 345, 368, 390, 450, 503, 526, 569, 647, 651, 653, 700	30–600
COD	19, 69, 134, 171, 251, 312, 390, 391, 450, 516, 526, 582, 647, 651, 700	100–1,000
Chlorides	19, 22, 161, 450, 516	25–203
Cyanides	390	—
Fluorides	390	—
Nitrates	22, 90, 273, 368, 406, 450, 503, 510, 516, 582, 647, 651	0–3
Nitrites	90, 273, 368, 390, 406, 450, 503, 516, 582, 647, 651, 700	0–1
Oil and grease	541	1–50
Phosphates	19, 22, 69, 132, 134, 161, 273, 304, 368, 390, 406, 450, 516, 582, 647, 651, 700	5–50
Suspended solids	22, 134, 171, 312, 368, 516, 526, 582, 647, 651, 653, 700	30–350
Total dissolved solids	1, 390, 647	250–1,400
Total organic carbon	69, 134, 312, 516, 647	—
Other (general)	7, 312	—
Elemental Contaminants		
Aluminum	26, 134, 390, 538	0.3–3
Arsenic	19, 390	0.05
Barium	19, 390	0–0.02
Cadmium	19, 37, 159, 390, 391, 471, 702	0.01–0.2

(continued)

Table 8.1: (continued)

Contaminant	Reference Number	Range, mg/ℓ
Chromium	19, 134, 159, 390, 391, 462, 471, 473, 702	0.01–0.3
Cobalt	134, 273, 390, 471, 702	ND
Copper	19, 107, 134, 159, 273, 390, 471, 702	0.01–0.5
Iron	26, 134, 273, 450, 471, 538, 702	0.5–6.5
Lead	19, 107, 134, 390, 471, 493	0–1
Manganese	134, 273, 390, 450, 471, 702	0.05–0.15
Mercury	19, 392, 471	0.0002–0.003
Molybdenum	390, 702	ND
Nickel	107, 159, 273, 390, 471, 702	0.05–0.5
Selenium	19, 390, 391	0–0.11
Tin	390	ND
Zinc	19, 26, 107, 134, 159, 390, 702	0.01–2.10
Synthetic/Organic Contaminants	317, 434, 702	–
Biological Contaminants Coliforms	134, 163, 251, 368, 390, 526, 560	–
ECHO virus	560	–
Fecal streptococci	163, 236, 390, 560	–
Mycobacterium	223	–
Parasitic worms	223	–
Polio virus	560	–
Protozoa	223	–
Salmonella	223, 339	–
Shigella	223	–
Virus	198, 223	–

ND = No data available in literature.

Source: EPA-600/1-78-019

Elemental Contaminants

The type and amount of elemental contaminants contained in any treatment system input will depend primarily upon the type and amount of industrial wastes entering that system. A great deal of material is available on industrial discharges to municipal systems. A summary range of elemental influent characteristics as reported in the literature is presented in Table 8.1, above.

The literature reviewed did not provide a comprehensive survey of the sources of these metallic contaminants, but the following factors appear to be important: input water composition, input water scaling and corrosion potential, type and age of domestic water piping systems, type and amount of industrial discharges, and type of municipal system (combined or separate storm water).

Biological Contaminants

Information available in the literature concerning input concentrations of biological contaminants generally addresses primary indicator organisms rather than specific pathogens. A summary range of biological contaminants reported in this literature is presented in Table 8.2.

Table 8.2: Biological Contaminants Found in Wastewater Inputs

Contaminant	Range/100 ml
Total coliforms	$1 \times 10^6 - 4.6 \times 10^7$
Fecal coliforms	$3.4 \times 10^5 - 4.9 \times 10^7$
Fecal streptococci	$6.4 \times 10^4 - 4.5 \times 10^6$
Virus	5–100,000*

*Virus units per liter.

Source: EPA-600/1-78-019

PRIMARY TREATMENT

Primary treatment is intended to physically remove settleable solids and most of the discrete suspended and floating solids from the municipal wastewater stream preparatory to secondary treatment. In addition, primary treatment removes a limited portion of the soluble constituents.

In primary treatment, the wastewater influent is divided into three output pathways: primary effluent, primary sludge (including grit, screenings, and precipitated matter), and aerosols. Effluent from primary treatment could be directly discharged (until 1977), discharged after disinfection (again until 1977), or treated by a secondary process. Primary sludge is normally subject to additional processing. At some ocean coastal sites, however, the sludge is discharged without further treatment.

Since effluent from primary treatment may not now be discharged without further treatment, it will not be considered, due to lack of space.

SECONDARY TREATMENTS

Activated Sludge

The activated sludge process entails the growth of microorganisms in a reactor. This effects partial biological degradation of organic compounds in wastewater to simpler organic compounds, carbon dioxide, water, microorganisms, and energy (206). The basic process requires two equipment components: aeration tanks and clarifiers. Active biological sludge is separated from the effluent in a clarifier and recycled to an aeration tank.

Activated sludge, the most popular wastewater secondary treatment process, has been extensively studied. Most research has focused on water quality parameters such as BOD, COD, and suspended solids. The data are usually presented as percent removal, with removal efficiency determined by difference in influent and effluent concentrations. Removal of a specific contaminant can be accomplished by separation into the sludge or by degradation through biological activity. Aerosol generation from the aeration tank is also a possible contaminant pathway.

In view of possible health effects, the difference between separation and degradation can be significant. If the treatment process merely partitions a particular contaminant into the sludge or air, it remains available for migration back to man. In contrast, biological degradation can terminate the contaminant pathway or transform the potentially harmful substance into a nontoxic form. The separation and degradation components of the removal process are often not distinguished in the activated sludge literature.

Water Quality Parameters: Relatively high removals of most water quality contaminants can be attained by activated sludge treatment in a practical application over an extended period of time. These removal efficiencies are supported by Mitchell (453), Noland and Birkbeck (485), Huang et al (302), Rickert and Hunter (543), Lindstedt and Bennett (389), and Besik (62).

Elemental Contaminants: Although the activated sludge process efficiently removes biodegradable organic materials, only limited removal of soluble elemental contaminants from the wastewater stream can be achieved. The removal of elemental contaminants is governed by two basic mechanisms: (1) the precipitation of metal hydroxides; and (2) the adsorption of elemental contaminants by the activated sludge floc. In either case, the elemental contaminants removed will be contained in the sludge. The literature supports the thesis that the activated sludge process can reduce, but not eliminate, trace metal concentrations in the municipal wastewater stream (462)(123)(124)(453).

Synthetic/Organic Contaminants: Malaney et al (410) in a study of the removal of possible carcinogenic organic compounds by activated sludge, concluded that no significant reduction was accomplished within normal detention times at the three treatment plants studied.

Recent work by Wachinski et al (666) suggests that herbicide detoxification can be achieved with a pure oxygen-activated sludge treatment system that was determined to be both economical and ecologically safe. A proprietary strain of mutant microorganisms, Phenobac (developed by the Worne Biochemical Corp.), was utilized that was able to degrade halogenated phenols. Even with relatively high herbicide concentrations (1,380 mg/ℓ), degradation of as much as 73% was accomplished after a 16-day aeration period using optimum proportions of required nutrients, microflora, and oxygen. According to the authors, this figure represents a conservative estimate of possible reductions, since testing was conducted at 18°C, while the optimum growth temperature for Phenobac is close to 30°C.

Biological Contaminants: Activated sludge followed by secondary sedimentation can remove over 90% of coliform or pathogenic bacteria that remain after primary sedimentation; other biological pathogens are removed to varying degrees. Nonetheless, even with 90% removal, appreciable amounts of pathogens remain present in the effluent.

Pathogens can either be removed by adsorption onto the sludge flocs or destroyed by the predatory activity of the zoogleal component. A review of the literature (280)(318) reveals discussion of general wastewater removal rates with little differentiation between removals and the biocidal properties of activated sludge.

Foster and Engelbrecht (223) provided a review of pathogen removal by activated sludge processes, showing no apparent removal of amoebic cysts or helminth ova; 96 to 99% removal of salmonella; slight to 87% removal of mycobacterium; and 76 to 99% removal of virus.

Ova of intestinal parasites are apparently unaffected by the activated sludge process; in fact, the literature indicates that activated sludge-mixed liquor provides an excellent hatching medium for eggs.

The removal of viral contaminants by activated sludge has recently become the topic of considerable research. In general, viral removal of up to 90% has been observed after the activated sludge process. However, large variations in removal have been reported, probably because sampling was not temporally coordinated (242). Typical viral removals that can be expected from activated sludge treatment as reported by Bryan (88) are 0 to 90% for enteroviruses, 0 to 90% for polio viruses, 0 to 50% for coxsackie viruses, and no apparent removal of ECHO viruses.

Trickling Filter

Trickling filters have been widely used for secondary biological treatment of municipal wastewater, and substantial literature is available on this process.

The trickling filter system generally consists of a tank open on both top and bottom. The tank is filled with a rock or plastic filter media having a high surface area to allow attachment of zoogleal slimes and void fraction for movement and diffusion of oxygen. Contaminant removal is accomplished through adsorption at the surface of the biological slimes covering the filter media. Following adsorption, the organics are utilized by the slimes for growth and energy.

The trickling filter is followed by clarification to remove biological solids period-ically flushed from the filter.

Trickling filter influent is usually from a primary treatment system. System outputs include effluent, sludge, and possibly aerosols.

The literature generally refers to percent removal, with no distinction made between separation and degradation or destruction. As in the case of other secondary processes, the literature primarily addresses the general and biological contaminants and is sparse in the areas of elemental, synthetic, and biocidal contaminants.

Water Quality Parameters: The removal of BOD and suspended solids by trick-ling filters is reported to be from 65 to 95%, averaging about 85% (318)(615). The efficiency of trickling filtration decreases as temperatures fall below 20°C. Imhoff et al (318) reported that a reduction of temperature from 20° to 10°C results in an efficiency loss of about 40%. Nickerson et al (479) found that chemical addition ahead of primary clarifiers increases overall BOD and sus-pended solids removals in trickling filters. Lager and Smith (368) reported that no significant removal of total nitrogen or phosphorus occurred during the conventional trickling filter process.

Elemental Contaminants: Removal of elemental contaminants by trickling filters is not well documented. Trace metal removals by trickling filters are substantially lower than those achieved with the activated sludge process because there is less formation and sedimentation of trace metal complexes.

Biological Contaminants: Trickling filters do not effectively remove many biological pathogens. Organisms are adsorbed into the zoogleal slime but due to similar surface charges and morphology, biocidal effects are variable (318). Literature by Foster and Engelbrecht (223) revealed that trickling filters are capable of reducing paratyphoid organisms by 84 to 99%. A review by Hunter and Kotalik (311) showed 99.7% removal of *Schistosoma mansoni* ova. These authors also concluded that trickling filter effluents can contribute a major portion of the free living nematode population found in receiving waters.

Improperly operated low-rate trickling filters can provide an excellent breeding area for insects, especially filter flies (psychoda) and springtails. Trickling filters cannot be depended upon to produce significant or consistent viral reductions. Foster and Engelbrecht (223) reported removals ranging from 0 to 84%. Berg (51) speculated that even when viruses are adsorbed, they may eventually be replaced by other substances and leach out of the filter slime as a result of an equilibrium effect.

Aerated Lagoons

Aerated lagoons are aerobic or facultative ponds in which mechanical aeration is used to increase the rate at which oxygen is made available to facilitate biological stabilization. The aeration also provides mixing for suspension of micro-bial floc. The biological process does not include algae, and organic stabiliza-tion depends on the mixed liquor that develops within the pond.

Water Quality Parameters: BOD removal by aerated lagoons is a function of aeration period, temperature, and the nature of the wastewater. The aeration of a typical domestic wastewater for five days at $20^{\circ}C$ provides about 85% BOD reduction; lowering the temperature to $10^{\circ}C$ reduces the efficiency to approxi-mately 65% (280).

Biological Contaminants: A discussion of the literature by Parker (503) revealed that coliform reductions in the range of 80 to 99% can be achieved with opti-mum detention time. This is supported by the experiments of Carpenter et al (105), who reported that coliform organisms are efficiently removed by the use of aerated lagoons. Klock (357) stated that the coliform survival rate in lagoons is a function of the oxidation-reduction potential and temperature.

Berg (49) discussed the removal of viruses by stabilization ponds, concluding that virus removal can be expected to be erratic.

Ponding

An oxidation or facultative pond is generally a shallow earthen basin designed to promote a symbiotic existence between algae and bacteria (368). Algal photo-synthesis and surface reaction maintain aerobic conditions in the photic region, while anaerobic bacteria flourish in the aphotic zone. Ponds are normally oper-ated in series and are sometimes used for "polishing" effluent from conventional secondary processes.

Influent to a ponding system may be raw sanitary waste, primary effluent, or secondary effluent. Pond effluent can enter the environment by direct discharge or by seepage to the groundwater. Only a limited amount of research has ex-amined the removal of contaminants by the ponding process.

Water Quality Parameters: Oxidation pond removal efficiencies for suspended solids and BOD can vary widely and may even reach negative values (368). Removal ranges of 60 to 50% have been reported for suspended solids, and of 70 to 10% for BOD_5. This variation occurs because most influent BOD is con-verted into suspended algal mass. This mass exerts a BOD demand and provides suspended solids that may be carried out in the effluent. Bacterial decomposi-tion and algal growth are both retarded, reducing removal efficiency of the ponding process, by reduced temperatures (280).

Synthetic/Organic Contaminants: The removal of trisodium nitrilotriacetate (NTA) by ponding has been investigated by Klein (356). He found that after a two-month acclimation period, steady-state removal was in excess of 90%, with influent concentrations in the range of 30 mg/ℓ.

Biological Contaminants: Kampelmacher and Jansen (337) found that removal of salmonella by oxidation ponds was not inferior to removal achieved by conventional treatment plants. Species of the coliform group, although reduced by ponding, are not effectively eliminated according to Parhad and Rao (500). Slanetz et al (592), however, reported that if two ponds were operated in series at temperatures of 17° to 26°C, the die-off rate of coliform, fecal coliforms, and fecal streptococci ranged from 95 to 99%. During winter when temperatures were in the 1° to 10°C range, the die-off rate was 46 times lower. Berg (51) states that virus removal by ponding is erratic, ranging from 0 to 96%; virus recovery decreased as the effluent passed through a series of maturation lagoons.

TERTIARY TREATMENTS

Filtration

Inability of gravity sedimentation in secondary clarifiers to remove small particles (and associated public health impairing contaminants) is a limitation of BOD and suspended solids removal by conventional wastewater treatment. Filtration as a tertiary process upgrades treatment performance by removing a portion of the unsettled suspended solids from secondary effluents. In addition, filtration often precedes other tertiary processes such as adsorption and ion exchange since the presence of suspended solids interferes with the operation of these processes.

Filtration of wastewater to reduce the suspended solids concentration is accomplished by passage through a bed of granular particles. Single, dual, or mixed media beds may be used, composed of anthracite coal, granite, sand, and/or gravel (280). Suspended solids are removed by a variety of mechanisms: straining, impingement, settling, and adhesion. The treatment efficiency of the process is influenced by the concentration and characteristics of the wastewater solids, the characteristics of the filter media and filtering aids used, and the design and operation of the filter.

Since wastewater flow rate and solids content are variable, and processes upstream of filtration may vary in performance, the efficiency of filtration may also be expected to vary. For this reason, values presented in the following discussion should be considered as merely indicative of the range of achievable removals.

Water Quality Parameters: In general, the best effluent quality achievable by plain filtration of secondary effluent is about 5 to 10 mg/ℓ for suspended solids and BOD. The suspended solids content of secondary effluent was reduced to 5 mg with both rapid sand and mixed media filters, employed respectively at a treatment and a pilot plant. Complete removal, however, could not be effected. If further reduction is desired, chemical coagulation must precede filtration (233)(280).

Elemental Contaminants: After chemical treatment, filtration to remove residual particulate matter may provide some additional removal of elemental contaminants. Elemental contaminant removals achieved by filtration depend primarily upon the extent of suspended solids removals with which the various trace elements are associated. Argo and Culp (18) give results for sand filtration of some municipal and industrial wastes showing percent removals of elemental contaminants varying between 95 for cadmium to 2.6 for hexavalent chromium. Patterson (506) cites evidence from pilot plant studies that little or no additional removal of arsenic was afforded by filtration of chemically treated municipal wastewater.

Biological Contaminants: Several investigations have been reported concerning the removal of viruses by sand filtration. It has been shown that insignificant virus removal is achieved by rapid filtration through clean sand (14)(49). However, virus removal efficiency will be increased by impregnation of the filter medium with coagulated floc, the presence of organic matter trapped in the sand, chemical flocculation prior to filtration, or a decrease in the filtration rate. The addition of iron salts prior to filtration has resulted in significantly higher coliform reductions, as discussed by Hunter et al (313). Similarly, Robeck et al (547) noted that if a low dose of alum was fed to a rapid coal and sand filter just ahead of filtration, more than 98% of polio virus Type I could be removed. If the dosage was increased and conventional flocculators and settling were used, removal was increased to over 99%. The authors also noted a general trend toward better removal of polio virus I with slower filtration rates although their data were generally erratic.

Brown et al (81) reported 70 to 90% removals of low concentrations of either bacteriophage T2 or polio virus Type I by filtration through uncoated diatomaceous earth. However, no significant virus removals by uncoated diatomaceous earth were achieved in a laboratory study by Amirhor and Engelbrecht (14). With the polyelectrolyte-coated filter media, removals greater than 99% were consistently achieved.

In laboratory tests by Berg et al (56), from 82 to greater than 99.8% of polio virus Type I was removed from chemically treated effluent by rapid sand filtration.

Laboratory experiments on the removal of nematodes by rapid sand filtration were conducted by Wei et al (678). Removal efficiency was about 96% when all the nematodes in the influent were dead or nonmotile. However, most motile nematodes were able to penetrate the filter bed.

Sand filtration may also provide some removal of amoebic cysts and ascaris eggs, according to a literature survey by Bryan (88). He did not indicate the levels of removal afforded.

Adsorption

Adsorption refers to the removal from water or wastewater streams of dissolved contaminants by their attraction to and accumulation on the surface of an adsorbent substance. Activated carbon is the most widely used adsorbent in municipal wastewater treatment to remove trace organics. Adsorption using activated carbon is utilized as a tertiary treatment step, usually following sand or multimedia filtration.

Carbon adsorption systems generally utilized granular or powdered activated carbon packed in a column or forming a filter bed through which wastewater is passed. Three consecutive steps occur in the adsorption of wastewater contaminants by activated carbon: (1) the film diffusion phenomenon, or the transport of the adsorbate through a surface film surrounding the activated carbon; (2) the diffusion of the adsorbate within the pores of the activated carbon; and (3) adsorption on the interior surfaces of the activated carbon. Carbon adsorption of contaminants has been the topic of many research projects.

Water Quality Parameters: Adsorption is most effective for removing refractory and other organics from wastewater. This is especially important when effluents of exceptional quality are required (e.g., for groundwater recharge or other reuse applications). Adsorption can be used either as a polishing step or as the major treatment process (676). Rizzo and Schade (544) and Zanitsch and Morand (712) reported that carbon columns alone were capable of about 85% removal of BOD from wastewaters entering the columns. Bishop et al (64)(68) and Zanitsch and Morand (712) reported 75 to 80% TOC removals under the same conditions. Weber et al (676) found that a treatment system composed of primary settling, ferric chloride coagulation, and carbon adsorption could remove up to 97% of the influent BOD.

Elemental Contaminants: Not a great deal of literature is available on the removal of elemental contaminants by carbon adsorption. Such systems are not specifically designed to remove ionic elemental contaminants, but some elementals are incidentally removed. When the metallic contaminants are in an organometallic complex, carbon adsorption columns can remove specific species. Literature from several sources (315)(372) reveals that high removals (95%) of cadmium and hexavalent chromium by carbon adsorption are possible, and activated carbon treatment of a secondary-treated municipal wastewater was found to reduce selenium from 9.32 to 5.85 ppb in a study cited by Patterson (506). This represents a 37% removal efficiency. Logsden and Symons (394) found that powdered carbon, in a jar test, would adsorb both inorganic and methyl forms of mercury in excess of 70%.

Biocidal Contaminants: Carbon adsorption is widely applied to remove organic or metal-organic biocides. The removal of insecticides and pesticides has been reviewed by Hager and Flentje (278). Dieldrin, lindane, parathion, and 2,4,5-T ester were reduced below the detectable limit of 0.01 ppb with influent concentrations of 3.6 to 11.4 ppb. Influent concentrations of 3,5-dinitro-o-cresol of 30 to 180 ppb were reduced to less than 1 ppb by carbon adsorption. It was concluded that granular carbon beds will provide a margin of safety for treatment of water containing varying insecticide or pesticide residues.

Activated carbon removals of several pesticides and PCBs are well illustrated by results of laboratory studies cited by the California State Water Resources Control Board (615). A variety of pesticides were experimentally added to distilled water and passed through carbon filters to test removal efficiencies. Schwarz (570) investigated the adsorption of isopropyl N-(3-chlorophenyl)carbamate (CIPC) onto activated carbon, concluding that powdered activated carbon readily adsorbs CIPC from aqueous solution, independently of the pH range.

Grover and Smith (272) studied adsorption onto activated carbon of the acid and dimethylamine forms of 2,4-D, and dicarbamate. A strong adsorption effect was noted on both the acidic and salt forms of the compounds. This effect was expected to increase at low pH values.

On the basis of the literature which has been reviewed, it can be concluded that activated carbon adsorption is effective in the removal of some biocidal contaminants; however, further investigation of this process will be useful.

Synthetic/Organic Contaminants: Activated carbon is most effective at removing organic contaminants from aqueous solutions. It is particularly effective at removing organics of low water solubility, as are many synthetic organic compounds. In general, carbon adsorption following secondary treatment is capable of producing an effluent with from 1 to 7 mg/ℓ of organic carbon (233).

Much of the research done on the adsorption of synthetic organic compounds from wastewater has been concerned with determining mechanisms of adsorption and optimum removal conditions. The only general removal efficiency studies available report removals in terms of total organic carbon with little or no effort made to differentiate the organic compounds involved. Based on these results, adsorption can reduce the levels of synthetic organic compounds in a typical domestic wastewater by 75 to 85%. If a particular type or types of organic compounds predominate in a wastewater, these removals must be adjusted to reflect the effect of compound character on the adsorption process.

Biological Contaminants: With the exception of enteroviruses, no information was found on the adsorption of biological contaminants, although incidental removal of other organisms would be expected by filtering action. Adsorption brings about simple removal of viruses from wastewater rather than inactivation or destruction (140)(242). Consequently, viable viruses could be reintroduced to wastewater should desorption of viruses adsorbed to activated carbon occur.

Chemical Treatment

The purpose of chemical treatment is to coagulate suspended solids and cause the precipitation of phosphate and various trace metals. Chemical coagulation of secondary effluents may be accomplished by the addition of lime, alum, polymers, or iron salts, and involves three operations: (1) injection and rapid mixing of the coagulants to neutralize the predominantly negative charges on suspended matter; (2) gentle stirring to promote agglomeration of the coagulated particles into large, settleable floc; and (3) sedimentation to provide gravity separation of the flocculated material from the wastewater. The settled material is disposed to a sludge-handling system. A great deal of information is available concerning the removal of various public health impairing contaminants by chemical treatment processes.

Water Quality Parameters: Culp and Shuckrow (151) investigated chemical treatment of raw wastewater with lime and found that removals of 95 to 98% phosphorus and 99% suspended solids can be achieved with chemical clarification followed by carbon adsorption. The treatment of municipal wastewater with alum precipitation as studied by Shuckrow et al (582) resulted in removal efficiences of 85% for COD and 83% for total organic carbon.

The removal of BOD and suspended solids as reviewed by Lager and Smith (368) shows a BOD removal of 80% with lime, and 75 to 80% with ferric chloride; SS removal of 90% with lime and 95% with ferric chloride (170 mg/ℓ dose).

Phosphate removal by chemical precipitation (lime) has received considerable attention in recent years and research indicates that lime clarification usually provides removal efficiencies greater than 90% (160)(625)(59)(331).

Elemental Contaminants: The precipitation of metal hydroxides from solution is governed by the pH and the concentration of the metal ion in solution. Since many of the trace metals form insoluble hydroxides near pH 11, lime coagulation results in a reduction of these metal concentrations (615).

In a California study, arsenic, molybdenum, and selenium had relatively poor removal rates, and the potential removal of mercury was estimated to be low. Only 11% of hexavalent chromium was removed, although the trivalent form was reduced more than 99.9%. Most other metals tested were very effectively reduced at high pH. Lower removals of these same metals (usually less than 50%) can be achieved with alum coagulation at near neutral pH values (615), a fact that illustrates the dependence of precipitation on pH.

Pilot plant studies of municipal wastewater containing 5 mg/ℓ arsenic cited by Patterson (506) suggest that chemical treatment can provide efficient removal of this element. Ferric sulfate at 45 mg/ℓ Fe and pH 6.0 removed 90% of the arsenic; lime at 600 mg/ℓ and pH 11.5 removed 73%. In similar studies cited by Patterson, barium removals of 97% were obtained when municipal wastewater dosed with 5 mg/ℓ barium was treated with 45 mg/ℓ Fe at pH 6.0. Lime at 600 mg/ℓ and pH 11.5 resulted in 80% removal. The removal of cadmium from waters by sorption onto hydrous oxides of solid metals such as manganese and iron was investigated by Posselt and Weber (525). They concluded that sorptive uptake of cadmium on such materials would constitute a method easily adaptable to present treatment technology.

Biological Contaminants: Chemical treatment can be used to reduce or remove many biological pathogens present in municipal wastewater. Lindstedt and

Bennett (389) evaluated the effectiveness of lime clarification in reducing bacterial concentrations, finding that treatment effectiveness increases with increasing chemical dosage and pH. At a lime dosage of 400 mg/ℓ, fecal coliform, fecal streptococci, and total coliform concentrations could be reduced by two orders of magnitude. It was also found that about 90% removal of bacteria can be achieved through alum clarification over a broad range of alum dosage.

Jar tests employing the f2 bacteriophage virus, lake water, and a variety of chemical coagulants and polyelectrolyte coagulant aids were conducted by York and Drewry (705). Aluminum sulfate (alum), ferric chloride, ferric sulfate, ferrous sulfate, and polyelectrolyte B were found to give maximum virus removals greater than 90% at optimum dosage.

Chemical treatment (high pH) holds considerable promise as a means of effectively inactivating or destroying pathogenic organisms contained in wastewater. By itself, chemical treatment cannot be relied upon to produce a pathogen-free effluent; used in conjunction with disinfection, however, it can help ensure that such an effluent is achieved.

Ion Exchange

The process of selective ion exchange has long been utilized in the treatment of industrial process waters and in domestic water supply softening. Ion exchange resins (539) are classified by the charge of the exchangeable ion. Thus, resins may be either catonic or anionic. General purpose resins will selectively exchange both cations and anions. The operational features of the ion exchange process are well developed and reliable. Such systems offer a reliable method of removing inorganic contaminants from the wastewater stream.

Very little information is currently available on removals of contaminants from municipal wastewater by use of ion exchange techniques. The process has not been economically feasible for treatment of municipal wastewater. Several research programs focusing on the application of ion exchange to municipal wastewater treatment are presently under way. The most promising future application appears to be for ammonia or nitrate removals.

Water Quality Parameters: Eliassen and Tchobanoglous (194)(195) conducted a review of the literature. They found that removals of phosphorus and nitrogen by tertiary wastewater treatment incorporating ion exchange can reach 90%. The actual removal efficiency was seen to depend upon the type of preceding treatment. Evans (209) investigated the removal of nitrate by ion exchange, concluding that the strong acid/weak base ion exchange process is well suited for this purpose. With the exception of these few studies of phosphorus and nitrate, most research performed to date has focused on ammonium removal, since specific exchange resins are not available for either the phosphorus or nitrate ions. However, some zeolite exchange resins do have unusual selectivity for the ammonium ion. This fact has encouraged research activity.

On the basis of both pilot and laboratory scale investigations, it appears that effluent ammonia concentrations of less than 1 mg/ℓ can be expected with ion exchange (362)(438). In a pilot plant study, Mercer et al (445) used zeolite columns to test secondary effluent containing 10 to 19 mg/ℓ ammonia. Greater than 99% removal of ammonia was achieved. Similarly, 99.7% of the ammonia in activated carbon effluent was removed by a zeolite in laboratory scale experiments by McKendrick et al (438).

The Environmental Protection Agency (517) reviewed pilot plant studies involving the use of clinoptilolite—a naturally-occurring zeolite—for wastewater treatment. Ammonia removals ranged from 93 to 97%.

It should be noted that the ion exchange process using a zeolite such as clinoptilolite does not result in the production of a sludge containing the removed ammonia. Rather, the spent zeolite is regenerated with a lime slurry, which is subsequently air stripped, discharging ammonia to the atmosphere.

Elemental Contaminants: Ion exchange techniques have been principally applied for the removal of elemental contaminants from industrial waste streams (506). Few studies have dealt with the application of ion exchange techniques to municipal wastewaters for elemental contaminant removal. Lindstedt et al (391) investigated trace metal removal and concluded that a cation-anion exchange sequence was effective in reducing the concentrations of cadmium, chromium and selenium in secondary effluent.

Biocidal Contaminants: Biocidal contaminant removal through ion exchange has also received little attention in the literature. In the only study located, Grover (271) stated that trifluralin, triallate, diallate, and nonionic herbicides were readily adsorbed on both cationic and anionic exchange resins, with somewhat more adsorption occurring on the cationic than on the anionic form.

Nitrogen Removal Processes

Interim primary drinking water standards established by the EPA set a nitrate limit of 10 mg/ℓ in the nitrogen form. Nitrogen concentrations in raw municipal wastewaters generally exceed this value, ranging from 15 to 50 mg/ℓ. Unless facilities are specifically designed to remove nitrogen, much of it will remain essentially unaffected, passing through the varying stages of treatment to ultimately enter the environment. Moreover, reuse of wastewater treatment plant effluents for direct groundwater recharge, indirect groundwater recharge through land application, or indirect reuse as a potable water supply is on the increase. Such reuse policies make effective nitrogen removal an important aspect of any wastewater treatment scheme.

In raw municipal wastewater, nitrogen is primarily found in the form of both soluble and particulate organic nitrogen and as ammonium ions. Conventional primary and secondary treatment transforms some of this organic nitrogen into ammonium ions. Part of the ammonium ion is oxidized to nitrate, and about 15 to 30% of the total nitrogen is removed.

Tertiary treatment processes designed to remove wastewater constituents other than nitrogen often remove some nitrogen compounds as well. However, removal is often restricted to particulate forms, and overall efficiency is generally low. Two tertiary processes particularly designed to remove nitrogen have been developed: nitrification-denitrification and ammonia stripping. Tertiary nitrification-denitrification usually involves two stages. Nitrification occurs in an initial stage, during which ammonium ions are oxidized to nitrite and nitrate ions by nitrifying bacteria. These nitrite and nitrate ions are in turn reduced to nitrogen gas which simply escapes from the system.

Ammonia stripping is effective only in removing ammonia nitrogen from municipal wastewater and has no effect on organic nitrogen, nitrite, or nitrate. Several ammonia stripping plants are in operation in the U.S. (Lake Tahoe, California; Orange County, California), but the process has been found to be expensive. A number of technical problems remain to be solved as well (438).

Nitrification and denitrification are biological reactions which occur naturally during several conventional treatment processes such as activated sludge treatments, aerobic lagooning, and anaerobic digestion. The activated sludge process, in particular, can be closely controlled to promote nitrogen removal. Such treatment processes are not principally designed to remove nitrogen, and both nitrification and denitrification occur only as secondary reactions.

Water Quality Parameters: There is general agreement that a system incorporating secondary biological treatment and tertiary nitrification-denitrification should achieve 80 to 95% total nitrogen removal at design flows (280)(483). The nitrification process alone removes only 5 to 10% of the total nitrogen entering the process, while oxidizing up to 98% of the ammonia nitrogen present to nitrate (236).

Average nitrogen data from systems incorporating nitrification-denitrification processes recorded by an EPA Technology Transfer Publication (236) shows that the predicted effluent quality from a nitrogen-denitrification system will be 1.0 mg/ℓ organic nitrogen, 0.5 mg/ℓ ammonia nitrogen, 0.5 mg/ℓ nitrate nitrogen, and 2.0 mg/ℓ total nitrogen.

DISINFECTION

Chlorination

Until recently, chlorination was considered virtually an unmixed blessing as a cheap, effective method to destroy bacteria and viruses. It is now recognized, however, that chlorination of wastewater may create chlorinated compounds harmful to the environment and to human health. The extent of this potential hazard has not yet been determined; new and existing wastewater treatment plants continue to utilize chlorine for disinfection. The primary purpose of municipal wastewater chlorination is the destruction of pathogenic microorganisms.

Water Quality Parameters: Zaloum and Murphy (711) concluded that chlorination of treated wastewater effluents does not reduce BOD, COD, and total organic carbon. Susag (627), however, found BOD reductions by chlorination of up to 2 mg/ℓ per mg/ℓ of chlorine added. These values are somewhat misleading, in that BOD reduction was due both to oxidation of the organic material and to the formation of chlorinated organics resistant to bacterial action.

When chlorine is added to a wastewater containing ammonia nitrogen, ammonia reacts with the hypochlorous acid formed to produce chloramines. Further addition of chlorine converts the chloramines to nitrogen gas. The reaction is influenced by pH, temperature, contact time, and initial chlorine-to-ammonia ratio. If sufficient chlorine is added, 95 to 99% of the ammonia will be converted to nitrogen gas with no significant formation of nitrous oxide. The quantity of chlorine required was found to be 10 parts by weight of chlorine to 1 part of ammonia nitrogen when treating raw sewage. This ratio decreased to 9:1 for secondary effluents, and 8:1 for lime-clarified and filtered secondary effluent (627).

Elemental Contaminants: Little information is available on the minimal removal by chlorination of elemental contaminants. Andelman (16) studied the effects of chlorination on barium, copper, and nickel. The treatment effected a 34% reduction in barium, a 5% reduction in nickel, and had no effect upon copper. Kokoropoulos (360) reported hypochlorous acid reacted with soluble iron(II) and manganese(II) to form precipitates.

Synthetic/Organic Contaminants: No research was found to address removal or destruction effects of chlorination on any of the synthetic/organic contaminants. However, considerable interest has recently developed concerning the production of chlorine-containing organic compounds by chlorination. The reactions of chlorine with organic compounds in water are diverse, including oxidation, substitution, addition, and free radical reactions. Chlorination may produce several different chlorinated products from a single organic pollutant molecule. Some of these compounds have been identified as toxic to aquatic life by Snoeyink (596), Brungs (85), and others.

Jolley (334) evaluated chlorine-containing organic constituents in chlorinated effluents and found that stable chlorine-containing compounds were present after effluents had been chlorinated to a 1 to 2 mg/ℓ chlorine residual. These compounds are 2-, 3-, and 4-chlorobenzoic acid, 8-chlorocaffeine, 6-chloroguanine, 3-chloro-4-hydroxybenzoic acid, 4-chloromandelic acid, 4-chloro-3-methylphenol, 2- and 4-chlorophenol, 4-chlorophenylacetic acid, 3-chlororesorcinol, 5-chlorouracil, 5-chlorouridine, and 8-chloroxanthine.

A similar project was conducted by Glaze and Henderson (250). The chlorinated organics identified in this study may be listed as follows:

chloroform	tetrachloromethoxytoluene
dichlorobutane	dichloroaniline derivative
chlorocyclohexane	trichlorophthalate derivative

(continued)

o-dichlorobenzene	tetrachlorophthalate derivative
p-dichlorobenzene	dibromochloromethane
pentachloroacetone	3-chloro-2-methylbut-1-ene
trichlorobenzene	chloroalkyl acetate
chlorocumene	tetrachloroacetone
N-methyl-trichloroaniline	chloroethylbenzene
trichlorophenol	hexachloroacetone
chloro-α-methylbenzyl alcohol	dichloroethylbenzene
dichloromethoxytoluene	dichlorotoluene
trichloromethylstyrene	trichloroethylbenzene
dichloro-α-methylbenzyl alcohol	trichloro-N-methylanisole
dichlorobis(ethoxy)benzene	tetrachlorophenol
trichloro-α-methylbenzyl alcohol	trichlorocumene
tetrachloroethylstyrene	trichlorodimethoxybenzene
dichloroacetate derivative	

Shimizu et al (581) stated that halogenated nucleic acid bases are incorporated into the nucleic acid. Also, the incorporation of 5-deoxybromouridine in DNA and 5-fluorouracil into RNA are known to cause mutations. No work has been completed to determine how nucleic acids react with chlorine or the resulting mutations.

Biological Contaminants: The effectiveness of chlorination as a disinfection process has long been recognized. All researchers are in agreement that the effectiveness of disinfection by chlorine is influenced by time and chlorine concentration and also by whether the chlorine residual is free or combined; effectiveness of mixing; whether or not particulates are present; pH; temperature; and the concentration, condition, and nature of the organisms. Keeping these limitations in mind, an idea of the relative resistances of organisms to disinfection by chlorine can be seen in Table 8.3.

Table 8.3: Effect of Chlorination on Various Organisms (311)

Group/Organism	Chlorine Residual (mg/ℓ)	Minutes	Efficiency
Virus			
Infectious hepatitis	1	30	survived
Infectious hepatitis	15	30	inactivated
Coxsackie	5	2.5	survived
Coxsackie	1.0	3	99.6% inactivated
ECHO	1.95	6.5	survived
Polio virus I	0.53	14	survived
Coliphage B	0.03	10	20% survival
Theiler phage	0.03	10	inactivated
Bacteria			
M. tuberculosis	1-5	120	99% kill
M. tuberculosis	2	30	99% kill
M. tuberculosis	1	30	destroyed
E. coli	0.14	3	99.9% kill
Coliforms	0.03	10	52% kill
Coliforms	1-1.2	15	99% kill
Total count	trace	15	98-99% kill

(continued)

Table 8.3: (continued)

Group/Organism	Chlorine Residual (mg/ℓ)	Minutes	Efficiency
Nematodes			
Diplogaster	2.5–3	120	survived and mobile
Cheilobus	15–45	1	survived and mobile
Others			
S. mansoni*	0.2–0.6	30	killed
S. japonicum*	0.2–0.6	30	killed

*Ova and miracidia.

Source: EPA-600/1-78-019

Many other studies of chlorine disinfection have been made. Examples of such studies are references (195)(621)(562)(158)(311)(585)(659) and (71).

Ozonation

Ozone, an allotropic form of oxygen, is a powerful oxidizing agent for the disinfection of wastewater. Ozone is used in over 100 municipalities in Europe for disinfection of drinking water. Certain chemical features make ozone treatment a particularly attractive method of water purification: It is a powerful oxidant which reacts rapidly with most organic compounds and microorganisms in wastewater. It does not impart taste and odor to potable water. It is produced from oxygen in air by means of electric energy.

On the negative side, the cost of ozonation is not presently competitive with chlorine disinfection. Moreover, long-term residual disinfection capabilities are lacking, and the instability of ozone generally necessitates its generation on-site (660).

The principal ozone decomposition products in aqueous solution are molecular oxygen and the highly reactive free radicals HO_2^-, OH^-, and H^+. Very little is known about the significance of the free radical intermediates on the germicidal properties of ozone solutions. The same free radicals are produced by irradiation of water, and it has been reported that HO_2^- and OH^- radicals contribute significantly to the killing of bacteria by this process.

A considerable amount of information is available on the destruction of various pathogens by ozonation; however, little information was found on the effect of ozone upon other contaminants.

Water Quality Parameters: Because of its strong oxidizing character, ozone is very reactive toward the organic compounds which make up the BOD, COD, and the total organic carbon. Under ideal conditions the reactions would result in almost complete oxidation and only carbon dioxide as a reaction product. In practice, ozonation results in only partial oxidation and produces simpler organic molecules. Both Ghan (244) and Nebel (474) reported COD removals of less than 40%. Morris (463) found that the apparent BOD of a wastewater can increase after ozonation as a result of refractory organic molecules being oxidized to simpler, biodegradable compounds. If the ozone is applied after other treatment processes (as is normal), the increase in organic nutrient molecules can lead to the growth in the distribution system of algae, slime bacteria, and the possible regrowth of any pathogens not destroyed during treatment.

Ozone is effective at decreasing concentrations of organic suspended solids and organic nitrogen through oxidation. Ozonation can assist in suspended solids removal through froth flotation mechanisms induced through the process. Ozone will also oxidize nitrites to nitrates, but will not react with ammonia (332). There is little evidence to date that ozonation will produce any toxic or carcinogenic oxidation by-products as will chlorination.

Biological Contaminants: The use of ozone as a wastewater disinfectant was reviewed by Venosa (660). It was concluded that with 0.1 mg/ℓ of active chlorine, 4 hours would be required to kill 6×10^4 E. coli cells in water, whereas with 0.1 mg/ℓ of ozone only 5 seconds would be necessary. When the temperature was raised from 22° to 37°C, the ozone inactivation time decreased from 5 to 0.5 second. These investigations revealed that the contact time with ozone necessary for 99% destruction of E. coli was only one-seventh that observed with the same concentration of hypochlorous acid. The death rate for spores of Bacillus species was about 300 times greater with ozone than with chlorine.

In the same study, Venosa also described bacteriological studies performed on secondary effluent from an extended aeration pilot plant in the Metropolitan Sewer District of Louisville, Kentucky. Using an average applied ozone dosage of 15.2 mg/ℓ for an average contact time of 22 minutes, fecal coliform reductions of greater than 99% were achieved, resulting in a mean fecal coliform concentration of 103 cells per 100 ml, a mean total coliform concentration of 500 cells per 100 ml, and a mean fecal streptococci concentration of 8 cells per 100 ml in the final effluent. Laboratory results with raw sewage indicated that ozone could be successfully used to sterilize sewage containing Bacillus anthracis, influenza virus, and B. subtilis morph. globibii, and to inactivate toxins of Clostridium botulinum. Ozone consumption was 100 to 200 mg/ℓ for 30 minutes. Finally, Venosa found ozone to be many times more effective than chlorine in inactivating poliomyelitis virus. Identical dilutions of the same strain and pool of virus, when exposed to 0.5 to 1.0 mg/ℓ of chlorine and 0.05 to 0.45 mg/ℓ of ozone, were devitalized within 1.5 to 2 hours by chlorine, while only 2 minutes of exposure were required with ozone.

WASTEWATER DISPOSAL

By Land to Groundwater

Hundreds of municipal and industrial wastewater treatment plants dispose of their effluents to the land. Thousands of wastewater lagoons percolate effluents into the ground. Millions of septic tank systems leach their wastewater into the ground. Most of these wastewaters travel through the soil and eventually reach groundwater aquifers. Unplanned groundwater recharge with wastewaters, therefore, must be recognized as occurring on a large scale.

The present interest in planned regulated wastewater reuse projects is bringing into focus an informal practice which has existed "in the closet" for a long time. The question is not whether wastewater reuse is acceptable, but rather how best to control what is an existing practice.

Groundwater recharge with treated municipal wastewater is accomplished by either planned or unplanned processes. Planned processes consist of two basic methods: (1) conveying the treated effluent to shallow spreading basins and allowing the water to percolate through the soil to the groundwater or (2) conveying the effluent to a well field and injecting the water directly into the aquifer. The major intent of these formal processes is to replenish groundwater basins, to establish saltwater intrusion barriers in threatened coastal aquifers, or to provide further treatment for ultimate extraction and reuse.

A number of factors determine the degree to which groundwater may be contaminated by wastewater that is applied to land. Depth to the groundwater table and distance to an extraction point affect residual levels of phosphorus, bacteria, and other constituents for which removal appears to be a function of travel distance. Soil characteristics, native groundwater quality, assimilation capacity of the aquifer, and method of waste application also determine groundwater degradation and consequent health problems (568). Cation exchange and adsorptive capacities important in the removal of metal ions and viruses and of trace organics and solids are determined by soil composition. Porosity regulates infiltration rates to some extent, affecting contaminant residence time in surface layers. Residence time may, in turn, determine aerobic or anaerobic conditions.

Total groundwater volume cannot necessarily be considered an effective diluting agent. Uniform diffusion of recharged water cannot be guaranteed, and water quality may vary considerably both in area and in depth.

Nitrogen Removal: In an acidic environment, nitrite has been found to react with secondary amines to produce nitrosamines. These compounds have recently been labeled carcinogenic, teratogenic, and mutagenic. The health hazards associated with nitrite and other forms of nitrogen in drinking water and crops have been delineated by the U.S. Department of Agriculture (663).

The most definitive study of nitrogen removal by land application of wastewater effluent was conducted by H. Bouwer at Flushing Meadows, Arizona (73). He found that short flooding periods (two days flooding followed by five days drying) did not provide sufficient time to develop the anaerobic conditions for nitrate denitrification. A longer flooding period of ten days followed by two weeks of drying proved to be more favorable.

A study by Preul (532) in 1966 provided the following observations of the movement and conversion of nitrogen in soil and the potential dangers of nitrate contamination:

- Biological oxidation is the dominant mechanism affecting ammonia nitrogen as it passes through the soil. This action initially occurs at a high rate, and to a large extent, within several feet of the point of release of the septic tank effluent, if soil conditions are well aerated.

- Nitrate contamination of groundwaters is a serious threat from shallow soil adsorption systems. High concentrations of ammonia nitrogen in septic tank effluents are quickly nitrified to high concentrations of nitrate, which pollute the groundwater. Dilution from groundwater or soil moisture and possibly denitrification aid in the deterrence of nitrate.

- The effectiveness of adsorption in deterring the travel of nitrogen is limited, because of the rapid conversion of ammonia to nitrate. Laboratory experiments have shown that ammonium can be readily removed in soil by adsorption; but, under aerated soil circumstances, nitrification of these ions occurs before the flow can contact a sufficiently effective volume of soil.

Similarly, results of a study by Chapman et al (115) have shown that, in Texas, irrigation with a sewage effluent was a potential source of nitrate pollution of the local groundwater. Other studies on nitrogen removal are found in the following references: (441)(572)(72).

In summary, data indicate that, under proper management conditions, land application of wastewater effluent offers the potential to efficiently remove nitrogen from wastewater and protect groundwater from nitrate contamination. The most successful programs stressed an appropriate flooding/drying schedule to promote both aerobic nitrification and anaerobic denitrification processes, in order to ultimately convert ammonia nitrogen in the wastewater to nitrogen gas. However, if not properly managed, a definite danger exists of polluting groundwater resources with excess nitrates.

Phosphate Removal: Recent studies of land application of wastewater effluent indicate that the soil system is highly efficient in removing phosphates from wastewater (299)(22)(185)(73)(45). Phosphate removal is both a function of soil composition and travel distance. In most soils, phosphorus not taken up by plants is immobilized due to the adsorption of phosphate onto the soil. Adsorption is followed by precipitation into various forms of calcium phosphate if the soil is basic (72). These reaction products are sufficiently insoluble, so that phosphorus is held in the upper few centimeters of most soils, and very little phosphorus moves into the groundwater (388). However, in the case of acidic, sandy soils with no iron or aluminum oxides, little phosphate is fixed. Thus, it may be necessary to remove phosphorus from wastewater before its application to such soils (72).

Elemental Contaminants: Municipal wastewater contains small amounts of nearly all metals. The degree to which a particular soil will protect underlying groundwater through removal of contaminants is primarily determined by the chemical and physical composition of the soil. Removal can occur through such processes as precipitation of solid phases, ion exchange, and adsorption. These processes are in turn controlled by soil pH, the oxidation/reduction potential, clay content, the presence and type of organic material, and the extent of soil saturation. The following references discuss removal of various metal contaminants by land spreading: (79)(388)(615)(72)(533)(374)(552)(73)(15)(685) and (535).

Biocidal Contaminants: A California State Water Resources Control Board report (615) mentioned that pesticides are adsorbed by soil clays, iron aluminum oxides, and especially by organic colloids, and that they are susceptible to microbial decomposition. However, the amount of biocides in average municipal wastewater was found to be so minimal that the spreading of municipal waste on land offers extremely low potential for groundwater biocide contamination.

Synthetic/Organic Contaminants: One of the most intensely debated questions regarding land application for treatment and/or disposal of municipal wastewater concerns the problem of residual organic contaminants. Refractory organic compounds may survive conventional treatment processes and penetrate through the soil to contaminate groundwater supplies. The controversy centers around the fate of residual organics within the soil systems, including such issues as the synergistic effects between organics and inorganics or other groundwater and soil constituents, or conversion of safe organics to hazardous compounds in the soil. Despite this controversy, no literature was found concerning groundwater pollution by the synthetic/organic contaminants in municipal wastewater as a result of land application.

Biological Contaminants: Most available data suggest that virus, bacteria, and other biological pathogens present in wastewater are removed or inactivated by percolation through soil.

The California State Water Resources Control Board study (615) states that most of these pathogens prefer warm-blooded animals as their habitat and do not flourish in the soil environment. When introduced into soils, the pathogens do not compete well with the vast number and variety of normal soil inhabitants and are subject to attack by antagonistic soil species. The time necessary for their ultimate destruction varies, according to species and environmental conditions. A compilation of pathogen survival data in the literature is shown in Table 8.4.

Table 8.4: Survival of Pathogens in Soils (615)

Ascaris lumbricoides ova	2.5–7 years
Entamoeba histolytica cysts	8 days
Salmonella species	6 hours
Coliform group organisms	133–147 days
Q-fever organisms	148 days
Brucella abortus	30–100 days
Tuberculosis bacteria	6 months
Enteroviruses	12 days

Source: EPA-600/1-78-019

Various studies (553)(441)(73)(569)(685) showed that fecal coliforms were removed effectively by soil percolation. However, full-scale, long-term waste-water reclamation studies by CSWRCB (615) concluded that, although soil is an excellent media for removing bacteria, a small fraction of the fecal coliform bacteria therein may reach groundwater reservoirs at high percolation rates.

Definitive work on virus interaction with soil was conducted at Santee, California, where extensive studies showed that percolation through several hundred feet of soil consistently removed all virus from secondary effluent (569). Other studies also supported the conclusion that soil effectively removes viruses (185) (441)(73)(247).

To Fresh Surface Water

Approximately two-thirds of the water supplies in the U.S. are drawn from surface waters. Direct discharge of treated wastewater to these fresh surface waters is the most popular method of wastewater disposal and the most significant pathway for wastewater contaminants to reach potable water supply systems. In addition, relatively minor quantities of wastewater contaminants may indirectly reach fresh surface waters through runoff or percolation from land disposal of wastewater effluents. This section of the chapter discusses current knowledge about the fate of various effluent contaminants in freshwater systems.

Most major river systems in the United States contain wastewater effluent from upstream municipalities and industries, the percentage of effluent wastewater volume varying from negligible to over 10%. Potable water systems utilizing these rivers as a source supply are, of course, reusing wastewater. Therefore, there is intense interest in the subject of contaminant changes which may occur in the freshwater system between waste discharge points and water intake locations.

Much of the material relative to this section is discussed in the following references: (162)(211)(239)(326)(534)(591) and (624).

Elemental Contaminants: The behavior of elemental contaminants in freshwater systems is very complex. Elemental contaminant transport mechanisms can generally be divided into either elements in solution or elements associated with inorganic or biological particulates. Each of these mechanisms can be broken down still further. Dissolved elements may occur as unassociated ions or as inorganic or organic complexes. Elementals/inorganic particulate associations include coulombic attraction, as in conventional adsorption; ionic bonding, as in ion exchange; precipitated or coprecipitated metal coating; or incorporation into particulate crystalline lattices. Elementals/biological particulate associations include surface adsorption, ingested particulation, and biochemical incorporation into the organism. The particular transport mechanism that will predominate in a given water system depends, in part, on the geohydrologic environment, mineralogy/petrology of the river or lake bed, pH, temperature, dissolved organic or oxygen content, biological activity, elemental type and source, and nonelemental chemical composition of the water.

This variety of factors does much to explain the seeming discrepancies in the work of different researchers attempting to establish element distributions in freshwater systems. The complexity of the chemistry, biology, and physics involved in water behavior of elements precludes a detailed discussion. Instead, a brief discussion is presented of a few sample elements (mercury, arsenic, lead, cadmium, copper) to demonstrate the principles involved.

Mercury — Mercury from wastewater enters a water system primarily as the metal or divalent cation. Although of limited solubility, it can reach concentrations of 100 ppb in aerated water (234). Metallic mercury alone is soluble up to 25 ppb and will hydrolize to soluble $Hg(OH)_2$ in oxygenated systems, increasing the overall solubility and water content. Despite these solubility figures, mercury concentrations seldom exceed 5 ppb except in polluted water.

Inorganic and biological adsorption, absorption, and precipitation serve to keep the concentrations of dissolved mercury much lower than the theoretical maximum. In general, the bulk of the mercury in a given water system is in the sediments. In reducing sediments, mercury is tied up as the sulfide, although if the system becomes sufficiently alkaline, $HgS_2^=$ may be released into solution. Should the sediments become aerobic, the sulfide will be oxidized to sulfate, and the mercury will be released.

All soluble mercury species except mercuric sulfide can be absorbed by bacteria. Once the mercury is in the bacteria, a series of transformations—possibly via a detoxification mechanism—convert the incorporated mercury into mono- and dimethyl mercury, both soluble at low concentrations and readily released into solution. The methyl mercury compounds are much more lipid-preferring than the inorganic forms and are quickly absorbed by living tissues. As a rule, mercury concentrations tend to increase in organisms up the food chain, so that the highest concentrations are found in fish. This is partly due to absorption of methyl mercury from the water and partly from ingestion of plants or smaller organisms containing methyl mercury. When the organisms die, the mercury returns to the sediments, where most of the bacterial methylation occurs.

Arsenic — Arsenic, selenium, and antimony are chemically similar and exhibit analogous environmental behavior. Arsenic has been studied far more than either selenium or antimony. The following discussion of arsenic is largely applicable to selenium and antimony as well.

Arsenic has an unusually complex chemistry in aquatic systems: oxidation-reduction, ligand exchange, precipitation, adsorption, and biomethylation reactions all take place. Arsenic species can be removed from water via surface adsorption and coprecipitation with metal ions; both arsenate (AsO_4^{-3}) and arsenite (AsO_3^{-3}) have a high affinity for hydrous iron oxides and readily coprecipitate with or adsorb onto them. Significantly, iron ores are always enriched with arsenic (214). Aluminum hydroxide and clays adsorb arsenate species, although to a lesser degree.

Microbial transformations of arsenic, while demonstrable in the laboratory, have not been positively identified in natural water systems. The two most commonly postulated transformations are oxidation of arsenite and methylation. Methylation is important because it could be a means by which sediment arsenic is recycled back into the water system; natural aquatic methylation has not been demonstrated.

Cadmium — Cadmium readily precipitates as the hydroxide or carbonate and consequently is not normally found in high concentrations in surface waters. In fact, several researchers (188)(461) have noted that high soluble cadmium concentrations are invariably associated with polluted water that receives a steady cadmium source, such as industrial wastewater.

Cadmium(II) readily hydrolyzes and forms transitory inorganic complexes, such as chloride complexes that have a limited affinity for hydrous iron and manganese oxides, and organic particulates. The organic affinity probably indicates a reaction between the cadmium and sulfur-containing compounds.

Cadmium forms the insoluble hydroxide at pH levels of 7 and above; it forms the insoluble carbonate under oxidizing conditions, particularly in soft waters where cadmium does not have to compete with calcium and magnesium for the carbonate anion. Once cadmium has precipitated and settled into the sediments, it is not readily removed. Consequently, if cadmium additions are reduced, a water body will tend to purify itself of soluble cadmium.

Copper — Copper, and to a lesser extent nickel, occupy an unusual position in water chemistry and biology because they are both nutrients and toxins. This has a pronounced effect on their water chemistry. Copper contained in wastewater may be either soluble or particulate; neither form predominates as a rule. Copper adsorbs readily onto clay and organic particulates. Copper also forms several very stable complexes. In pure water, while the aquo complex may predominate, the carbonate, chloride, and amine inorganic complexes are much more stable.

Ultimately, the soluble stability of copper can be attributed to organic complexes, since copper forms coordination complexes with virtually every conceivable organic ligand. These complexes are very stable thermodynamically and are also resistant to microbial attack, a mechanism responsible for the destruction of most organic complexes. Copper is a bacterial toxin and, if released from its complex by microbial attack, simply kills the offending bacteria and forms a new complex (461).

Copper is removed from solution via precipitation or biological incorporation. Since the most common precipitate is the carbonate, most sediment copper is in the carbonate form (140)(461). An essential trace nutrient, copper is readily incorporated into aquatic plants and animals.

Lead — The main soluble species of lead in wastewater are the lead(II) cation and the hydrolyzed complex $Pb(OH)_3^-$. Lead forms a variety of stable complexes as well; researchers (381) have identified both $PbOH^+$ and $Pb(CO_3)_2^{-2}$ in natural water systems. Lead complexes easily with a variety of organic chelates, forming very stable complexes. Some of these complexes are more stable than the sediment lead precipitates; therefore, they will actually dissolve otherwise insoluble lead. A case in point is nitrilotriacetate, which can solubilize lead from lead carbonate precipitates (268).

Low water organic content generally prevents solution lead concentrations from exceeding a few parts per billion. In most water systems, lead introduced with wastewater readily forms insoluble $Pb(OH)_2$ and $PbCO_3$, which will precipitate and adsorb onto suspended particulates. Ionic lead is not so strongly adsorbed, although it does have some affinity for clays.

Hydrous iron oxides strongly sorb ionic lead at neutral to slightly acidic pH levels. Some ionic or complexed lead adsorbs onto or is chelated with the surface mucilage of algae, and microorganisms immobilize substantial quantities of inorganic lead, presumably on or in all membranes (648). As a result of all of these mechanisms, most of the water lead burden is associated with particulate matter, and most of the lead entering a normal water system ultimately finds its way into the sediment.

Summary — Natural water bodies normally contain very low dissolved concentrations of the more harmful elemental contaminants. Unless wastewater additions are voluminous and repeated, natural water chemistry can purify the water of soluble species fairly well. However, there is a buildup of these elements in the sediments. This means that if the local water chemistry should change significantly, the elements can still be released to solution. Natural water purification mechanisms can only change the wastewater element problem from a real to a potential hazard; they cannot solve the problem of element contamination.

Biocidal Contaminants: In general, municipal wastewater will have detectable quantities of biocides only if it contains biocide manufacturing wastes. The single most important source of biocidal contaminants in freshwater bodies is surface runoff, followed by aerial fallout and industrial waste discharge from plants manufacturing biocides. Cleanup and disposal by households, farmers, gardeners, etc., contribute minimally to the overall wastewater burden.

Biocides are classed here as chlorinated hydrocarbons, organophosphates, carbamates, and ionic biocides. Biocides can be transported or removed from the system by microbial or chemical degradation, photodegradation, adsorption to sediment or humic matter, adsorption, volatilization, and biological uptake. All of these mechanisms are in turn affected by pH, temperature, salt or organic content, and bioproductivity.

Various transport mechanisms affect the biocide classes differently. This is demonstrated in Table 8.5, which compares the persistence of selected chlorinated hydrocarbons, organophosphates, and carbamates in river water. Because of these differences, the biocide classes will be discussed separately.

Table 8.5: Persistence of Compounds in River Water (415)

Compound	Original Compound Found, percent				
	0 Time	1 Week	2 Weeks	4 Weeks	8 Weeks
Organochlorine					
BHC	100	100	100	100	100
Heptachlor	100	25	0	0	0
Aldrin	100	100	80	40	20
Heptachlor epoxide	100	100	100	100	100
Telodrin	100	25	10	0	0
Endosulfan	100	30	5	0	0
Dieldrin	100	100	100	100	100
DDE	100	100	100	100	100
DDT	100	100	100	100	100
DDD	100	100	100	100	100
Chlordane (technical)	100	90	85	85	85
Endrin	100	100	100	100	100
Organophosphorus					
Parathion	100	50	30	<5	0
Methyl parathion	80	25	10	0	0
Malathion	100	25	10	0	0
Ethion	100	90	75	50	50
Trithion	90	25	10	0	0
Fenthion	100	50	10	0	0
Dimethoate	100	100	85	75	50
Merphos	0	0	0	0	0
Merphos recovered as DEF	100	50	30	10	<5
Azodrin	100	100	100	100	100
Carbamate					
Sevin	90	5	0	0	0
Zectran	100	25	0	0	0
Matacil	100	60	10	0	0
Mesurol	90	0	0	0	0
Baygon	100	50	30	10	5
Monuron	80	40	30	20	0
Fenuron	80	60	20	0	0

Source: EPA-600/1-78-019

Chlorinated Hydrocarbons — The chlorinated hydrocarbon pesticides are all insoluble in water, with the exception of lindane, which is sparingly soluble to 10 ppm (211). They are generally resistant to microbial and chemical degradation. These pesticides are somewhat more susceptible to photodegradation, although the degradation products are often as toxic as the parent compound, regardless of the type of degradation. DDT is decomposed chemically to DDD and DDE and photochemically to PCBs (162)(550); aldrin is photooxidized to the more toxic dieldrin (162); and methoxychlor is degraded to methoxychlor DDE (501). Surface oil slicks tend to concentrate chlorinated hydrocarbons and thus make them more available for photochemical degradation (162). Chlorinated hydrocarbons in general readily adsorb onto fungi, algae, and floc-forming bacteria (385)(501), and thus tend to concentrate in biological communities. When ingested by higher organisms, they accumulate in lipid tissues; consequently, chlorinated hydrocarbons tend to concentrate up the food chain.

Chlorinated hydrocarbon insecticides differ in chemical structure, but they all exhibit affinity for organic sediments and resistance to microbial attack. As a result they accumulate in bottom sediment. The highest reported concentrations of several pesticides in major U.S. river basins from 1958 to 1965 were as follows: dieldrin, 0.100 $\mu g/\ell$; endrin 0.116 $\mu g/\ell$; and DDT, 0.148 $\mu g/\ell$. Dieldrin was the most widely found pesticide (679).

Organophosphorus Biocides — The organophosphorus biocides are more soluble than the chlorinated hydrocarbons. These solubilities range from 1 ppm for ethion to 20,000 ppm for dimethoate; most fall in the 25 to 150 ppm range (211). The organophosphorus biocides are also more amenable to both microbial and chemical degradation. Even parathion, the most chemically resistant of the organophosphates, will degrade via ester linkage hydrolysis in a few months under normal conditions. The degradation takes place in just a few weeks in polluted water with a high bacteria count (264).

Interestingly, the degradation of organophosphates can be inhibited by the presence of other synthetic organic chemicals. Experiments were conducted with two detergent surfactants, alkyl benzene sulfonate (ABS) and linear alkyl benzene sulfonate (LAS). These experiments demonstrated increased persistence for several organophosphate insecticides, especially parathion and diazinon (162). As a result, highly polluted water may exhibit accumulations or half-lives far beyond the normal for organophosphates, which, as a rule, neither persist nor accumulate in the environment, but are removed entirely within a few months.

Carbamate Biocides — Carbamate biocides are moderately soluble, ranging from 7 ppm for Terbutol to 250 ppm for Prophem and averaging around 100 ppm (211). In general, they decompose easily and show little tendency toward adsorption on suspended material, but hydrolyze readily. The hydrolysis is particularly pH dependent, virtually ceasing entirely below pH 5 (211) and increasing as the pH and temperature rise. High salt content affects the hydrolysis rate inversely, slowing the rate as the salt concentration increases (211). Carbamates photodecompose readily, increasingly so as the pH rises, and can be rapidly biodegraded under normal circumstances (550). Carbamates are not, then, persistent in normal water systems, lasting only a few days to a few weeks, but remain as a stable compound in acidic waters (211).

Ionic Biocides — Ionic biocides are a broad class embracing a variety of chemical types and uses. They are all considered soluble in water, with solubilities ranging from 100 to more than 1,000,000 ppm. Ionic biocides that are marginally soluble in pure water have increased solubilities in natural waters high in humic acid salts (211). With few exceptions, these biocides do not accumulate or persist and, consequently, are seldom found in high concentrations.

Ionic biocides are, however, strongly adsorbed onto soil particles, all types of clay, humic matter, and organisms—in short, onto anything with a partial charge or an ion exchange capability (211). They are generally resistant to chemical attack but photodegrade readily, except when adsorbed onto particulate matter (211). Ionic biocides respond differently to microbial attack, but are absorbed by many organisms. As a result, they tend to concentrate in organisms and up the food chain. Research on TCDD, an ionic herbicide residue, demonstrated that accumulation was directly related to water concentrations (0.05 to 1,330 ppb) and averaged between 400,000 and 2,000,000 times the water concentration (321).

Synthetic/Organic Contaminants: Recently, there has been a great interest in identifying synthetic/organic trace compounds in water supplies drawn from rivers and in other water bodies receiving treated wastewater. Although studies have been made of the concentrations found in various water systems, neither the environmental pathways nor the potential health effects to man of these substances have been studied to any great extent.

Over 100 synthetic/organic compounds have been identified in various drinking water sources. Table 8.6 lists the results of organic analyses of several domestic water supply sources.

Table 8.6: Molecular Constituents Identified in Natural Water Samples (615)

Constituent	Sample Source*	Concentration (mg/ℓ)
p-Cresol	3	7
Diethylene glycol	5	1
Ethylene glycol	5	20
Glycerine	1, 2, 3, 4, 5	1–20
Glycine	1	2
Mannitol	5	2
Methyl-α-D-glucopyranoside	4	30
Methyl-β-D-glucopyranoside	4	3
Sucrose	1, 5	2
Xylitol	5	1
Urea	1, 2	4

(continued)

Table 8.6: (continued)

Constituent	Sample Source*	Concentration (mg/ℓ)
Inositol	1, 2, 3, 4, 5	0.5–1
O-methylinositol	1, 2, 3, 4, 5	0.3–10
Linoleic acid	1, 5	1
Oleic acid	1, 5	1
Palmitic acid	1, 5	0.4
Stearic acid	1	0.5
2,2'-Bipyridine	4	4

*1 = Lake Marion; 2 = Fort Loudon Lake; 3 = Holston River;
4 = Mississippi River; 5 = Watts Bar Lake.

Source: EPA-600/1-78-019

The differences in manmade synthetic/organic compounds exceed the similarities, but in general, these compounds are persistent and resist microbial degradation. Beyond that generalization, research has been too limited to discuss specific compounds in detail.

Polychlorinated biphenyls (PCBs) are the only class of synthetic/organic contaminants that have been studied in detail. They are virtually insoluble in water, which, combined with a high specific gravity and volatility, serves to keep solution PCB concentrations low. However, they are strongly adsorbed onto suspended particulate matter and transported through the water system. Because of their heavy, insoluble character and sediment affinity, they tend to accumulate in bottom sediments. PCBs are fairly stable in freshwater systems, resisting hydrolysis and chemical degradation, and are not amenable to photodegradation (481). Theoretically, they should readily vaporize from solution, but this is prevented by their tendency to sink or strongly adsorb onto suspended matter. Only PCBs that are associated with floatables or oil slicks appear to vaporize to any great degree. The lower isomers (four or fewer chlorine atoms) are somewhat responsive to biodegradation, but the degradation products are frequently more toxic than the PCB itself (481). The higher isomers resist microbial attack. PCBs are thus quite persistent in water/sediment systems, and lifetimes of years or even decades have been postulated (481).

The continued presence of PCBs makes it inevitable that they will enter the food chain. As they tend to accumulate in lipid tissues in higher plants and animals, it has been estimated that PCBs will concentrate up the food chain to as much as 10^7 times the water concentration (482).

Biological Contaminants: An important pathway for certain communicable disease transmission to man is the consumption of contaminated water. Direct disposal of wastewater is the principal contamination route. Land disposal of wastewater is not an important pathway, as pathogenic organisms have limited mobility in soil and seldom migrate far enough to contaminate water supplies (296). However, in contrast to their restricted mobility in soils, biological contaminants are readily dispersed and transported by receiving waters. Consequently, there is a high potential for direct public contact through drinking or recreational use. Wastewater treatment has diminished this threat by reducing the number of organisms in the wastewater. This, combined with natural pathogen mortalities, has greatly lessened the outbreak of water-borne disease attributable to public water supplies.

Pathogenic bacteria are best adapted to survival in the human body or to conditions resembling those found in the body. Consequently, natural water systems are a hostile environment. However, cool water is generally more hospitable than warm water because of the depressed metabolism of both the bacteria and their predators. Predatory organisms, especially in slightly polluted waters, are a major contributor to bacteria die-off. For instance, Barua (35) noted that *Vibrio cholerae* survived one to two weeks in clean water as opposed to one to two days in water with a large bacterial population.

Pathogenic bacteria also suffer from a lack of proper nutrition in clean waters; low nutrient levels prevent reproduction. Since die-off rates exceed growth rates, the overall population will decline. Other factors affecting die-off are ultraviolet radiation in sunlight, pH extremes, natural antibiotics, and chemical toxins.

In contrast to bacteria, viruses do not multiply in water and, therefore, their number in a water body can never exceed the number introduced into that body by waste disposal. Typically, viruses are much more resistant to external environmental factors (chemical content, pH, temperature, time, etc.) and survive longer than bacteria (136)(198). It was long suspected that algae could inactivate viruses through some process because of low virus concentrations in algae-rich waters. It is now believed that the high pH and dissolved oxygen in the vicinity of algal blooms are responsible for the inactivation. Virus inactivation in lake water is further enhanced by the presence of proteolytic bacteria which degrade the viral coat (292). Coxsackie is particularly susceptible to proteolytic bacteria, while polio virus is generally resistant except to *Pseudomonas aeruginosa* (292). Otherwise, the mechanisms of virus removal are obscure.

Transport mechanisms for pathogens include physical current motion, organism motility, adsorption, ingestion, and aerosolization. As most pathogens readily adsorb onto suspended matter, sediment pathogen concentrations may greatly exceed water concentrations. Filter feeding organisms, such as freshwater shellfish, tend to concentrate pathogenic organisms. Consequently, shellfish can be a major factor in the spreading of certain communicable diseases.

CONVENTIONAL WATER TREATMENTS

Chemical Coagulation and Flocculation plus Solids Separation

Chemical coagulation and flocculation, followed by clarification or filtration, is common water treatment practice for the treatment of surface waters. The primary purpose is to remove suspended and colloidal solids. The overall process takes place in three distinct phases. Coagulation involves destabilization of the colloids by rapid mixing of the chemical coagulant with the water in some type of agitated rapid mix tank. Retention time in rapid mixing is very brief, on the order of a few minutes. Flocculation follows in which the wastewater is gently stirred with paddles, allowing the particles to collide and aggregate into larger flocs. Depending on temperature, concentration of the solids, and the type and dosage of coagulant, flocculation requires from 15 minutes to 1 hour. Clarification and/or filtration usually follows, to provide solids separation.

The most commonly used coagulant is $Al_2(SO_4)_3 \cdot 18H_2O$, which is known as filter alum. The amount of hydrolysis which occurs when filter alum is introduced to the water is a function of the pH of the water, with optimum efficiency achieved at a pH of 7 to 8 (506).

Because chemical coagulation and clarification is probably the most popular water treatment technique, there exists a substantial volume of information on this technology. Most research work has been performed on the elemental group of contaminants as many of the metals are most efficiently removed by chemical precipitation. Substantial study of turbidity removal and virus inactivation/removal has also been conducted with the current focus on the synthetic/ organic and biocidal contaminants in water supplies and their potential carcinogenic effects with long-term ingestion, a surge in research in these areas is anticipated.

Asbestos Removal: Asbestos has recently been implicated as a carcinogen of potential danger to workers breathing the fiber in asbestos manufacturing plants. Thus, it is feared that the incidence of asbestos in drinking water supplies may also be a health hazard.

Several studies have investigated the ability of chemical coagulation followed by clarification and/or filtration to remove asbestos from water intended for potable purposes. Lawrence et al (375) examined the effectiveness of various methods and found that the most effective method involved chemical coagulation with iron salts and polyelectrolytes followed by filtration, which resulted in better than 99.8% removal from water containing 12×10^6 fibers per liter. The optimum ferric chloride dosage was found to range from 6 to 8 mg/ℓ; satisfactory flocs were formed at all test temperatures.

Elemental Contaminants: Many elemental contaminants are readily removed by chemical coagulation and subsequent solids separation steps (settling or filtration). As some of the elemental contaminants are being more closely reviewed for possible long-term health effects, the importance of chemical coagulation as a removal process becomes more pronounced.

Arsenic is one element being closely watched in water supplies as it has a relatively high toxicity, accumulates in the body, and has been associated with the occurrence of cancer (39). Several studies on arsenic removal are available. Some 1,056 cases of black-foot disease and skin cancer have been reported in the southwest part of Taiwan. According to statistical data, there is a close relationship between these diseases and the high arsenic content (0.6 to 2.0 mg/ℓ) in deep-well water used for drinking (577). Since there is no other available water source in the area, some practical and economical method to remove the arsenic compounds was urgently needed. To satisfy this need, Shen (576) performed a lengthy analysis of treatability tests to evaluate the arsenic removal capability of coagulation/settling/filtration processes. Initial coagulant tests showed ferric chloride to be the best chemical, achieving 92% As removal at a 30 mg/ℓ dosage. Subsequent testing, however, showed that these removals could be improved by preoxidation before coagulation. Adding 20 mg/ℓ of chlorine and then coagulating with 50 mg/ℓ of ferric chloride provided the best results, achieving 97.7% As removal. Further studies on As removal are found in references (275) (396)(280).

Removals of antimony, barium, cadmium, cobalt, chromium, iron and manganese have been studied primarily in wastewater treatments. The following references relate to the removal of these contaminants: (537)(588)(396)(157) (480)(470) and (130).

Recent attention has been focused on the contamination of water supplies by organic and inorganic mercury by industrial discharges. Fortunately, recent tests by the EPA of 273 water supplies across the country showed very low mercury levels in nearly all of them. Even so, the performance of conventional water treatment technologies and new techniques for removing mercury from water is of interest. Logsdon and Symons (394) investigated the efficiency of conventional water treatment processes in removing mercury and concluded that as long as environmental levels of mercury in raw water remain low (near drinking water standards), extremely high removals will not be required, and conventional technology should be sufficient.

Biocidal Contaminants: Recently, there has been increased awareness of the potential health hazards of biocidals. Limited data, however, are available in the literature regarding the removal of these constituents from water supplies by chemical coagulation. Robeck et al (546) studied the effects of various water treatment processes on pesticides. Their results, in regard to pesticide removal via chemical coagulation (alum) and filtration, are shown in Table 8.7.

As can be seen in the table, DDT was readily removed, whereas lindane, parathion, and endrin were not. Dieldrin and 2,4,5-T ester are removed at slightly better than 50%. Softening with lime and soda ash and with an iron salt as a coagulant did not improve on the removals obtained with alum coagulation alone.

Another study (380) evaluated the effect of $KMnO_4$ as an oxidant and precipitating agent. It was found that $KMnO_4$ was not significantly effective in removing lindane, but was capable of removing over 80% of the heptachlor present in under 5 hours. Removals of DDT were less than 20% in 48 hours, and endrin was totally unaffected by the process.

Table 8.7: Percentage of Pesticide Removed by Conventional Water Treatment

Pesticide	1	5	10	25
	. . . . (%)			
Lindane	<10	<10	<10	–
Dieldrin	55	55	55	–
DDT	–	–	98	97
Parathion	–	–	20	–
2,4,5-T ester	–	–	63	–
Endrin	35	–	35	–

Note: Total hardness as $CaCO_3$ reduced from 260 to 33 ppm and pH increased from 7.6 to 10.4.

Source: EPA-600/1-78-019

Synthetic/Organic Contaminants: In recent years, concern has been expressed over the possible occurrence of certain carcinogenic compounds in drinking water (World Health Organization, 1964). A group of compounds which has received particular attention is the polynuclear (polycyclic) aromatic hydrocarbons (PAH), some of which are potent carcinogens under certain conditions. It is, however, far from certain that these compounds are significant when present in the trace amounts found in drinking water. Clearly, further research is needed into both the levels and health effects of PAH in the environment (284).

Symons et al (632) found that precipitative softening at water treatment plants increased the concentration of trihalomethane in the product water from an average of 0.49 $\mu m/\ell$ (80 locations) to 0.84 $\mu m/\ell$ (17 plants with softening). This indicates that chlorination at a higher pH will produce higher concentrations of trihalomethanes.

Kinoshita and Sunada (352) performed an experiment on the removal of PCB by chemical coagulation. Bentonite, sodium carbonate, and aluminum sulfate were added to a solution of 100 ppb PCB. After settling, the PCB concentration has been reduced 90%, suggesting that conventional water treatment by coagulation and settling or filtration provides a margin of safety against the ingestion of PCBs in raw water supplies.

Biological Contaminants: The use of diatomite filtration with and without chemical addition is capable of removing bacteria from water supplies (435).

Amirhor and Englebrecht (14) analyzed the potential use of uncoated polyelectrolyte-aided diatomaceous earth filtration for bacterial virus removal. They concluded that uncoated DE filtration was not effective for virus removal, but that precoating of cationic polyelectrolyte greatly improved removals. Certain variables such as pH level and concentration of polyelectrolyte coating, and virus concentration affected removals.

Wolfe et al (700) conducted a large-scale pilot study of virus removal by both lime and alum. They demonstrated that virus removals from secondary effluents by alum coagulation-sedimentation and coagulation-sedimentation-filtration processes are essentially the same as described in the literature using smaller scale processes. Removals of bacterial virus as high as 99.845% for coagulation-sedimentation and 99.985% for coagulation-sedimentation-filtration processes were observed at an Al:P ratio of 7:1.

At a lower alum dose there was a marked decrease in virus removals. At an Al:P ratio of 0.44:1, removals of only 46% of f_2 coliphage and 63% of polio virus by the coagulation-sedimentation process per se were observed. High lime treatment of secondary effluents has achieved high degrees of virus removal, but the percentage has not been quantified (116).

The current state of knowledge indicates that chemical flocculation, settling, and filtration are effective in removing virus from water. Removals of 99+% have been reported under proper operating conditions. However, more research is still needed in the area to fully determine the most effective doses of coagulants and coagulant aids, the physiochemical effects of turbidity, pH, temperature, and colloidal charge, and to develop optimal operating parameters (56) (198)(547).

Chang et al (113) performed comprehensive studies of the dynamics of removal of bacterial virus by aluminum sulfate flocculation. From their observations they concluded that flocculation by aluminum sulfate can remove high percentages of virus, and within the zone of flocculation, higher doses produced greater efficiency. They also found that the virus is concentrated in the floc sediment and is not destroyed, but only temporarily inactivated. It will become active again, if dissociated from the aluminum.

Disinfection

Disinfection refers to the inactivation or destruction of pathogenic microorganisms. Disinfectants (chlorine, ozone, ultraviolet and ionizing radiation) also have secondary applications, particularly as oxidants for the removal of organic contaminants. The types of disinfectants have been discussed under tertiary wastewater treatments, earlier in this chapter. All of the disinfectants have disadvantages that prevent any of them from being universally applicable. For a given situation the choice depends largely on the water quality, types of microorganisms in the water, desirability of nondisinfection applications, and cost.

Water Quality Parameters: The organics, as represented by BOD, COD, and total organic carbon, in drinking water are susceptible to oxidation by disinfectants. However, reactions other than oxidation may produce potentially hazardous compounds. For instance, Rook (555) and McClanahan (332) reported that chlorine reacted with humic and fulvic substances, forming chlorinated organic compounds. These chlorinated compounds are much more resistant than the precursor compounds to both biodegradation and chemical oxidation. Consequently they persist in a water supply that is not treated any further than chlorination. Some of the chlorinated compounds formed are suspected to have carcinogenic properties.

Ozone is even more reactive toward organic compounds than is chlorine. With ozone, though, the reactions are almost exclusively oxidation, with few if any hazardous compounds formed in side reactions.

It should be noted that nonbiological contaminants interfere with the primary disinfection role of these chemicals by consuming the disinfectants. Achieving proper disinfection in highly organic waters, for instance, requires large increases in applied dosages. Some water-borne disease outbreaks are attributed to improper disinfection of highly organic water supplies.

Elemental Contaminants: In general, the disinfectants have no effect on elemental concentrations. Elements would have to be in a reduced state before oxidizing disinfectants could have an impact. This is not likely in most drinking water supplies. Exceptions are iron and manganese, which are readily oxidized by ozone to their insoluble oxides which can then be removed by filtration (465).

Biocidal Contaminants: Chlorinated hydrocarbon biocides are generally resistant to chemical oxidations. Stone et al (537) reported that chlorine was not a particularly effective oxidant for such biocides. Ozone was more effective, but removal efficiencies varied widely from 16 to 93%, depending on the type of biocide, ozone concentration, and contact time. Stone et al reported other ozone studies that yielded 50% removal of endrin, 75% removal of lindane, and approximately 100% removal of dieldrin and aldrin. They also stated that ultraviolet radiation could completely eliminate carbamate biocides, reduce aldrin by 45%, and reduce endrin and dieldrin by 18%.

Synthetic/Organic Contaminants: As previously mentioned, both chlorine and ozone readily react with dissolved organics. However, synthetic organics are often more resistant to oxidation than the natural organics. Rosenblatt (332) indicated that chlorine reacted with many organics to give both chlorinated and oxidation products, but that there was no reaction with any others. Ozone is an effective oxidant against the phenolics and organic nitrogen compounds, but not against many of the simpler organic molecules, such as ethanol. It was reported by Harrison et al (284) that chlorine was more effective than ozone against benzo[a]pyrene.

Many of these synthetic organics, such as nitrobenzene, benzo[a]pyrene, aniline, and ethylbenzene are reportedly carcinogenic. While these chemicals are seldom found in drinking water supplies at concentrations exceeding a few parts per million, the postulated no-threshold-dose character of many carcinogens makes even one molecule a potential hazard. Note also that chlorine is suspected of producing chlorinated organic compounds which may themselves be carcinogenic.

Kinoshita and Sunada (352) investigated the effects of irradiation on PCB in water. They concluded that PCB in aqueous microparticulate colloidal solution is destroyed by ionizing irradiation (up to 95%), but that its resistance to radiation is far greater than other chlorinated hydrocarbons used such as pentachlorophenol or DDT, and other pesticides such as parathion. They also found that the acute toxicity of the irradiated PCB solution was far less than the nonirradiated solution for striped shrimps.

Biological Contaminants: The major application of disinfectants is against biological contaminants. In this light, the disinfectants have been evaluated primarily on their effectiveness in controlling biologicals (e.g., bacteria, viruses, protozoa, parasitic worms).

Chlorine is the traditional disinfectant in the United States. It is effective to some extent against all types of pathogenic organisms found in water. Bacterial kills of at least 99% are considered normal (537), and 4 to 5 log reductions are not unusual. Both Sobsey (600) and Long (399) reported virus reductions of up to 99.99%. Reference (136) summarized research on virus destruction by chlorine. Chlorine can be effective when used with filtration against free-swimming protozoa and parasitic worms. However, chlorine is relatively ineffectual against their ova and cysts that are resistant to oxidation. Chlorine has the further advantage of persistence given a sufficiently large dose; a low residual chlorine concentration will remain in the water after treatment, providing continued disinfectant action. This prevents regrowth and protects against accidental contamination during distribution.

Despite chlorine's widespread use and some reports of effective virus kill, other reports are less optimistic about its performance against virus. Clarke et al (129) and Sobsey (600) reported the isolation of viruses in chlorinated drinking water in Paris (1 pfu/300 ℓ) and South Africa (1 pfu/10 ℓ). In view of the fact that only one or two viruses of some types are sufficient to cause infection, anything less than 100% inactivation may be unacceptable. But with chlorine, even the absence of any "living" viruses still may not be acceptable. McClanahan (429) reported that chlorine removes the protein coat of a virus—thus rendering the virus technically nonviable—but may leave the infectious nucleic acid core intact. Consequently, a water supply free of any living viruses may still be infectious.

Ozone is equally as effective as chlorine against bacteria and viruses and has a much faster reaction rate. Once the proper "threshold" ozone dose is applied (usually less than 5 mg/ℓ), the bactericidal action is almost instantaneous. Tests have shown ozone to be between 600 and 3,000 times more rapid than chlorine in its destruction of bacteria (429). McClanahan (429) was unable to recover viable nucleic acids from ozonated water, suggesting that virus destruction was complete, as opposed to the action of chlorine. Venosa (660) reported that protozoal cysts resistant to chlorine were easily inactivated by ozone. Furthermore, the biocidal character of ozone is not affected by pH, as is the biocidal character of chlorine.

Ozone is not without problems, however; ozone leaves no residual. It has a fairly short half-life in water and rapidly loses all disinfectant ability. Experience in Europe has revealed few problems along these lines, but the added margin of safety with chlorine has worked against the adoption of ozone in the United States. The versatility of ozone and its relatively greater disinfecting ability has led to the suggestion that initial ozonation could be followed by low-level chlorination to provide a residual. However, little research has been conducted along these lines.

Murphy (469) and Vajdic (656) both reported that gamma radiation was as good a disinfectant as chlorine against bacteria and was somewhat better against the more chlorine-resistant biologicals. Ultraviolet is a proven bactericide, but research on other biocidal characteristics has been limited. Nevertheless, any radiation treatment suffers from operational difficulties, and, like ozone, provides no residuals.

ADVANCED WATER TREATMENT

Adsorption onto Activated Carbon and Other Materials

Activated carbon adsorption (or simply carbon adsorption) is employed to remove color, odor, taste, and refractory organic compounds from water. Many water treatment plants presently pass their effluent through a carbon column or fine-grain carbon bed to polish the final product. Available data indicate that carbon adsorption is an effective method for removing synthetic and natural organic contaminants, particularly chlorinated hydrocarbons and organophosphorus pesticides, from water. Carbon adsorption may also be used to remove some metals. There is some adsorption of the free metal, but metal removal can be greatly enhanced by the addition of an organic chelating agent prior to passage through the carbon. The carbon will readily adsorb the chelating agent, thereby also removing the complexed metal.

The major portion of the research to date on the effectiveness of the adsorption process in potable water treatment has involved tertiary wastewater treatment application, and has been discussed earlier in this chapter.

In addition to activated carbon, synthetic polymeric adsorbents have been extensively tested and show promise for potable water treatment. They are not widely used in water treatment plants but have been tested in pilot-scale installations. Some tests have indicated higher removal efficiencies for synthetic adsorbents than for activated carbon for some contaminants. Inorganic adsorbents, such as clays and magnetite, are also capable of contaminant removal.

Water Quality Parameters: Activated carbon is commonly used for removing tastes and odors from water. Undesirable odors in water are caused by the vapors from many chemicals, including halogens, sulfides, ammonia, turpentine, phenols and cresols, picrates, and various hydrocarbons and unsaturated organic compounds, some of which have not been identified. Tastes and odors are also caused by substances produced by living microorganisms or decaying organic matter. Some inorganic substances, such as metal ions in high concentrations (especially iron), also impart taste and odor to water. Removal of many tastes and odors with activated carbon approaches 100% (276)(524)(282)(316).

Elemental Contaminants: Although little data from municipal water purification applications are available, it appears that activated carbon can provide some removal of heavy metals (506)(467)(394). Direct adsorption provides some removal, but efficiencies can be increased to nearly 100% by adding an organic chelating agent (537). The carbon removes the complex by adsorbing the organic agent, removing the metal along with it.

Biocidal Contaminants: As with other synthetic/organic compounds, some of the organic pesticides and herbicides that are resistant to removal by conventional treatment techniques are effectively removed by adsorption. David Volkert and Associates (157) cited evidence that over 99% of the following chlorinated hydrocarbons can be adsorbed by activated carbon: DDT, aldrin, dieldrin, endrin, chlordane, heptachlor epoxide, lindane, methoxychlor, and toxaphene.

Laboratory studies cited by Stone (537) have shown that reductions from 50 to 99% in chlorinated hydrocarbon concentrations can be achieved by contacting with appropriate doses of activated carbon. Activated carbon removals of several pesticides are well illustrated by results of laboratory studies cited by the California State Water Resources Control Board (615).

According to reference (570), the available data on organophosphorus pesticide removal indicate that the efficiency of activated carbon ranges from 50 to over 99%.

Synthetic/Organic Contaminants: Adsorption is commonly cited as a presently available technology for removing particulate, colloidal, and soluble organic contaminants from water. Many of the organics present in water supplies—particularly the soluble and colloidal organics—are of a refractory nature, i.e., they resist removal by conventional methods. A number of these are potentially toxic or carcinogenic and, as a result, their detection, identification, and treatment in water is receiving increasing attention. These substances, even in small amounts, contribute to taste and odor conditions and may pose a chronic health hazard. As has been discussed, activated carbon is widely applied for taste and odor removal; however, its effectiveness for removing residual organics has just come under study in recent years. The more common parameters used as a measure of organics include carbon chloroform extract (CCE), liquid extraction, paper and gas chromatography, fluorescent spectroscopy, and radiation.

Traditionally, carbon life expectancy has been based on the capability of the carbon to adsorb tastes and odors. But research has shown that the life expectancy of carbon to reduce carbon chloroform extract or organic compounds is somewhat less than that to remove tastes and odors (442). Medlar (442) suggested that monitoring carbon chloroform extract concentration in carbon filtered water would provide a conservative estimate of filter performance, but noted that the CCE test may not encompass all the compounds that should be considered.

The adsorption of polycyclic (polynuclear) aromatic hydrocarbons (PAH) from water by activated carbon was discussed by Harrison et al (284). These compounds are potential carcinogens under certain conditions. Carbon adsorption has been shown to give 99% removal of PAH from water filtered by prior seepage through river bank soil.

Bis-ethers are synthetic organic compounds that may occur in water associated with industrial discharges. Stone and Company (537) cited laboratory tests of activated carbon treatment in which isopropyl ether concentrations were reduced from 1,023 to 20 mg/ℓ, butyl ether concentrations from 197 mg/ℓ to nil, and dichloroisopropyl ether concentrations from 1,008 mg/ℓ to nil.

Patterson (506) has used adsorption onto activated carbon to remove over 99% of the phenol present in process waters with initial concentrations ranging from 5,325 to 0.12 mg/ℓ.

Foaming agents such as linear alkylbenzene sulfonate in concentrations up to 5 mg/ℓ can be removed by activated carbon with 90 to 100% efficiency according to evidence cited by David Volkert and Associates (157). Phillips and Shell (515) present data on activated carbon filtration at the Colorado Springs pilot plant showing 97% removal of alkylbenzene sulfonate (ABS). Stander and Funke (610) reported reduction of ABS from 4 to 0.7 mg/ℓ at the Windhoek pilot plant. Organic acids are also reported to have been reduced from 1 to 0.4 mg/ℓ.

Morton and Sawyer (467) studied the adsorption of two organic compounds—diethylstilbestrol (DES), which is a hormone and aflatoxin, which is a natural toxin produced by fungi—onto attapulgite clay. Attapulgite is a magnesium aluminum silicate clay that exhibits a high degree of adsorption for low-weight organic molecules. In laboratory experiments, DES at a concentration of 5 ppb was decreased 68 and 76% by contacting with 1.1 and 10% (by weight) clay suspensions, while in a 50 ppb solution the removals were 68 and 89%, respectively. More than 98% of the aflatoxin at concentrations of 0.5 and 5.0 ppb was removed by both 1.1 and 10% clay suspensions.

The Amberlite adsorbents represent a new technology for adsorbing organic molecules from water. They are used specifically for adsorbing aromatic and aliphatic compounds. Simpson (589) cited a laboratory study in which the removal efficiency of Amberlite XAD-2 for a list of organics at flow rates of 1.25 gpm/ft^3 was determined. Nonionic compounds were removed with 100% efficiency while ionized compounds were less effectively removed.

In the nationwide study of water supplies and water treatment facilities by

Symons et al (632), it was concluded that both powdered and granular activated carbon treatment significantly reduced the trace concentrations of total trihalomethane in the product water.

Biological Contaminants: The limited efficiency of activated carbon in removing viruses from wastewater has been discussed in the advanced wastewater treatment section of this report. Results show that activated carbon is inefficient in removing viruses from drinking water.

Ion Exchange

Ion exchange has its greatest current application in industrial and small-scale potable water supply operations. The most common use of ion exchange is for removal of hardness (calcium and magnesium cations) from municipal, industrial, household, and laboratory water supplies. It is particularly suited for desalting brackish water, pretreating water that must be almost completely demineralized for industrial use, and removing metals from industrial metal plating rinse wastewaters.

No one ion exchange resin is capable of removing all ionic contaminants. Various resins, depending upon their chemical nature, show preferential selectivity for specific ions.

The more strongly a resin adsorbs a particular ion, the more complete the ion removal. However, a high affinity between a particular resin and a specific ion also means greater difficulty in regenerating the resin; that is, it is more difficult to release the adsorbed ions to make the resin reuseable. As a result, regeneration of an effective resin is seldom carried to completion, and the operational capacity of an ion exchange resin may be reduced to 50 to 60% of theoretical capacity.

In the past, application of ion exchange processes was confined to the removal of ionic contaminants. Recently, however, some ion exchangers have been developed that can remove nonionic species. Resinous adsorbents are also available that are particularly suited for removing organic compounds, including biocidal and synthetic/organic contaminants, from water. While often used in conjunction with true ion exchange processes, the mechanism of organic removal is actually adsorption; therefore, the resinous or polymeric adsorbents (as they are called) have been discussed in the previous section of this chapter.

Reverse Osmosis

Initial investigators thought that osmotic membranes acted as strainer-type materials with such small pore sizes that most ionic and biological molecules were too large to pass through. Recent studies with electron microscopes have shown that removals are controlled by molecular diffusion through the membrane and that salts and other impurities diffuse much more slowly than water (652). The differential pressure to provide a driving force through the membrane is supplied by pumps. The discarded flow of concentrated contaminants is continuous, and its volume normally equals from 5 to 30% of the volume of the process influent volume. Membrane fouling by suspended solids, organic slimes, and precipitates is a problem unless substantial pretreatment of the influent water is provided. Therefore, reverse osmosis (RO) is normally located as the last unit process in the water treatment chain.

Reverse osmosis may become more important in the future as both a tertiary wastewater and raw water supply treatment process, because of its capability to remove a high percentage of all types of general, elemental, and biological contaminants as well as many synthetic/organic biocidal constituents. With the recent concern over even very small concentrations of heavy metals, residual organics, and toxic compounds in water supplies, RO with its $>99\%$ removal efficiency may see increased usage, albeit at a high cost.

Various types of membrane systems have been tested on a variety of wastewater effluents from primary to highly treated tertiary. Laboratory tests have also been conducted on the removal of many synthetic/organic chemicals and biocidal compounds. The RO process does not destroy any of the input contaminants, but only separates them into two streams, with the waste stream containing the rejected materials. Depending upon the feed conditions and the desired objectives, the product water volume can range up to 95% of the total influent, with the remainder representing the discarded flow. The characteristics of RO membranes can be controlled within a wide range by controlling the manufacturing variables. In general, as one improves the contaminant removal efficiencies, the flux per unit area decreased. This type of trade-off implies that the systems can be optimally designed to achieve the desired objectives.

Water Quality Parameters: RO systems are not commonly used specifically for general contaminant removal from water supplies (with the exception of TDS), as these constituents can be sufficiently removed by other less expensive treatment units. However, the performance of RO systems in terms of percent removal is excellent (90 to 99+%) for all general contaminants except for low molecular components of BOD, or COD, and nitrate.

ABS — Several references discussed the removal of ABS from solution. The presence of highly nonbiodegradable alkylbenzene sulfonate (ABS) even in concentrations of only 1 mg/ℓ can produce undesirable frothing and foams although health implications do not appear significant. Removals of 90 to 99+% were reported (286)(46)(449).

Elemental Contaminants: A good deal of available literature on RO membranes deals with the removal of elemental contaminants. RO systems can be designed to remove almost any elemental contaminant existing in either an ionic form or colloidal form in water. Generally, multivalent ions (Fe^{+3}, Cu^{++}, Zn^{++}, $SO_4^{=}$) are rejected more effectively than monovalent ions (NO_3^{-}). As previously mentioned, the percentage removal will depend upon specific membrane and manufacturing procedures. References (154)(294) and (615) provide typical summaries of the performance of reverse osmosis units in removing elemental contaminants. Results are shown in Table 8.8. As shown, RO is generally very effective.

Table 8.8: Reverse Osmosis Removal of Elemental Contaminants

Contaminant	. . . . Percent Removal (Single Pass)		
	Reference (154)	Reference (294)	Reference (615)
Aluminum	—	97	—
Arsenic	90–95	—	—
Barium	90–95	—	—
Boron	—	50	—
Cadmium	90–98	68–70	66–98
Chromium	90–97	93–98	82–98
Fluorides	90–97	88–98	—
Copper	90–97	82–96	99
Lead	90–99	—	99
Iron	90–99	95–98	94–99
Manganese	90–99	—	—
Mercury	90–97	—	—
Nickel	—	—	98–99
Selenium	90–97	—	—
Silver	90–97	—	96
Zinc	90–99	—	97

Source: EPA-600/1-78-019

Biocidal Contaminants: A few studies have been conducted on the removal of biocidals by osmotic membranes (46)(126)(191). Excellent removals were reported for a wide variety of pesticides, insecticides, and herbicides including chlorinated hydrocarbons, organophosphorus compounds, and halogenous cyclodienes. However, a considerable amount of this removal can be attributed to adsorption or absorption on the membrane itself. Since these tests were for short time periods relative to commercial application, the long-term rejection may be more complex and may depend upon whether the contaminant is adsorbed or absorbed and upon the diffusion rates through the membrane.

The literature data indicate that removal of biocidals is highly variable, depending not only on contaminant concentrations and membrane characteristics, but on synergistic effects of other components in the water. In any case, RO provides a high level of treatment for many common pesticides and insecticides.

Synthetic/Organic Contaminants: The performance of RO membranes with respect to removal of synthetic/organic contaminants is similar to that of many of the biocides. In general, these contaminants can be adsorbed, absorbed, rejected or transmitted by the membrane, with removals depending on chemical species and membrane type. In general, larger molecular weight compounds are readily rejected or sorbed by the membrane, whereas low molecular weight compounds are more likely to pass through (189)(281)(46).

The classes of compounds that do not appear to be well rejected and are present in wastewater effluents include compounds such as methanol, ethanol, and phenol. No data were found on the low-molecular weight halogenated hydrocarbons such as chloroform, bromoform, halogenated ethane, or ethylene compounds; but, based on the present theoretical knowledge, removals would be expected to be poor.

Biological Contaminants: Due to the large size of biological contaminants, including virus, relative to the effective pore size of RO membranes, high reductions of these contaminants can be expected.

Hindin and Bennet (294) conducted microbiological studies to determine the permeation through a porous cellulose acetate membrane of microorganisms found in sewage effluent. Their results showed that *Escherichia coli, Aerobacter aerogenes,* coliphage T-7 and X-175, and *Streptococcus narcesence* were all removed 100% by the RO unit, with the exception of one test in which a leak in the membrane may have permitted permeation.

Cruver (148) reports that several studies have shown that 99.9% removals of bacteria and virus can be attained. However, even with these excellent removals, RO processes are not used alone for disinfection because of the presence of imperfections in the membranes. These systems are primarily designed for TDS removal in which small leaks through the membrane and at seal joints are generally inconsequential. Nevertheless, these leaks could be significant when they reduce the removal of virus and bacteria from 99.9999 to 98%. To depend upon these systems for 100% biological contaminant removal would require continuous monitoring for biologicals and a degree of quality control that would be considered beyond the state of the art for field systems.

The literature indicates that whereas removals of biological contaminants with RO are very good, they are not as high or as fail-safe as other disinfection practices (chlorination, ozonation). It should also be remembered that RO is only a separation process, not a destruction unit, and that the biological contaminants, once removed, will remain in the waste solution.

REFERENCES

(1) Adams, A.P. and Spendlove, J.C., "Coliform Aerosols Emitted by Sewage Treatment Plants," *Science*, 169(3951):1218-1220 (September 18, 1970).

(2) Adams, B.J. and Grimmell, R.S., "Performance of Regionally Related Wastewater Treatment Plants," *JWPCF*, 45(10):2088-2163 (October 1973).

(3) Adams, C.E., "Removing Nitrogen from Wastewater," *Environmental Science and Technology*, 7(8):696-701 (August 1973).

(4) Adams, C.E., Krenkel, P.A., and Bingham, E.C., "Investigation into the Reduction of High Nitrogen Concentrations," *Advances in Water Pollution Research*, 1970(1): 13/1-13.

(5) Adams, V.D., Middlebrooks, E.J., and Nance, P.D., "Organic Residue in a Recycled Effluent, Part I," *Water and Sewage Works*, 122(6):82-84 (September 1975).

(6) *Advances in Wastewater Treatment*, Advanced Wastewater Treatment Research Facility, Pomona, CA.

(7) Agnew, R.W., et al, "A Biological Adsorption System for the Treatment of Combined Sewer Overflow," presented at the 46th Water Pollution Control Federation Annual Conference, Cleveland, Ohio (October 2, 1973).

(8) Akin, E.W., Benton, W.H., and Hill, W.F., Jr., "Enteric Viruses in Ground and Surface Waters: A Review of Their Occurrence and Survival," *Proceedings, Thirteenth Water Quality Conference at University of Illinois*, pp 59-74 (February 1971).

(9) Al-Layla, M.A. and Middlebrooks, E.J., "Optimum Values for Operational Variables in Turbidity Removal," *Water and Sewage Works*, 121(8):66-69 (August 1974).

(10) Albertson, O.E. and Sherwood, R.J., "Phosphate Extraction Process," *JWPCF*, 41(8): 1467-1490 (August 1969).

(11) Albone, E.S., et al, "Fate of DDT in Severn Estuary Sediments," *Environmental Science and Technology*, 6(10):914-919 (October 1979).

(12) Alsentzer, H.A., "Ion Exchange in Water Treatment," *JAWWA*, 55(6):742-748 (June 1963).

(13) Ames, L.L., Jr. and Dean, R.B., "Phosphorus Removal from Effluents in Alumina Columns," *JWPCF*, 42(5):R161-R172 (May 1970).

(14) Amirhor, P. and Engelbrecht, R.S., "Virus Removal by Polyelectrolyte-Aided Filtration," *JAWWA*, 67(4):187-192 (April 1975).

(15) Amramy, A., "Waste Treatment for Ground Water Recharge," *Advances in Water Pollution Research*, 1964(2):147-168.

(16) Andelman, J.B., "The Effect of Water Treatment and Distribution on Trace Element Concentrations," in *Chemistry of Water Supply Treatment and Distribution*, A.J. Rubin, ed., Ann Arbor Science Publishers, Ann Arbor, Michigan, pp 423-440 (1975).

(17) Andelman, J.B. and Suess, M.J., "Polynuclear Aromatic Hydrocarbons in the Water Environment," *Bulletin of the World Health Organization*, 43:479-508 (1970).

(18) Argo, D.G. and Culp, G.L., "Heavy Metals Removal in Wastewater Treatment Processes, Part 1," *Water and Sewage Works*, 119(8):62-65 (August 1972).

(19) Argo, D.G. and Culp, G.L., "Heavy Metals Removal in Wastewater Treatment Processes, Part 2. Pilot Plant Operation," *Water and Sewage Works*, 119(9):128-133 (September 1972).

(20) Arpa, S.S., *Nitrogen Removal Obtained Through Heterotrophic Growth in Trickling Filters*, NTIS/PB-239-925 (August 1974).

(21) Atkins, P.D., Jr., et al, "Ammonia Removal by Physical-Chemical Treatment," *JWPCF*, 45(11):2372-2388 (November 1973).

(22) Aulenback, D.B., et al, "Water Renovation Using Deep Natural Sand Beds," *JAWWA*, 67(9):510-515 (September 1975).

(23) Axelson, O., et al, "Herbicide Exposure—Mortality and Tumor Incidence: An Epidemiological Survey of Swedish Railway Workers," *Pesticide Abstracts*, 75:1886 (1975).

(24) Balakrishnan, S. and Eckenfelder, W.W., "Nitrogen Removal by Modified Activated Sludge Process," *Journal of the Environmental Engineering Division*, ASCE, 96(SA3):501-512 (April 1970).

(25) Balakrishnan, S., Eckenfelder, W.W., and Brown, C., "Organics Removed by a Selected Trickling Filter Media," *Water and Wastes Engineering*, 6(1):A22-A25 (January 1969).

(26) Bargman, R.B., Betz, J.M., and Garber, W.F., "Nitrogen-Phosphate Relationships and Removals Obtained by Treatment Processes at the Hyperion Treatment Plant," *Advances in Water Pollution Research*, 1970(1):14/1-17.

(27) Barnard, J.L., "Cut P and N Without Chemicals," *Water and Wastes Engineering*, 11:33-36 (July 1974).

(28) Barnes, G.E., "Disposal and Recovery of Electroplating Wastes," *JWPCF*, 40(8):1459-1470 (August 1968).

(29) Baroni, C., Van Esch, G.J., and Saffiotti, V., "Carcinogenesis Tests of Two Inorganic Arsenicals," *Archives of Environmental Health*, 7:668-674 (1963).

(30) Barrow, N.J., "Effect of Previous Additions of Phosphate on Phosphate Adsorption by Soils," *Soil Science*, 118:82-89 (August 1974).

(31) Barth, E.F., et al, "Field Survey of Four Municipal Wastewater Treatment Plants Receiving Metallic Wastes," *JWPCF*, 37(8):1101-1117 (August 1965).

(32) Barth, E.F., et al, "Phosphorus Removal from Wastewater by Direct Dosing of Aluminate to a Trickling Filter," *JWPCF*, 41(11):1932-1942 (November 1969).

(33) Barth, E.F., et al, "Summary Report on the Effects of Heavy Metals on the Biological Treatment Processes," *JWPCF*, 37(1):86-96 (January 1965).

(34) Barton, R.R., et al, *UV-Ozone Water-Oxidation/Sterilization Process*, NTIS/AD/A-004 205/1WP (September 1974).

(35) Barua, D., "Survival of Cholera Vibrios in Food, Water, and Fomites," *Principals and Practice of Cholera Control*, pp 29-31 (1970).

(36) Bauer, R.C. and Snoeyink, V.L., "Reactions of Chloramines with Active Carbon," *JWPCF*, 45(11):2290-2301 (November 1973).

(37) Baughman, G.L., et al, *Chemistry of Organo-Mercurials in Aquatic Systems*, EPA-660/3-73-012 (September 1973).

(38) Bausum, H.T., et al, *Bacterial Aerosols Resulting from Spray Irrigation with Wastewater*, U.S. Army Medical Research and Development Laboratory, Fort Detrick, MD (June 1976).

(39) Bean, E.L., "Potable Water—Quality Goals," *JAWWA*, 66(4):221-230 (April 1974).

(40) Beckman, W.J., et al, "Combined Carbon Oxidation-Nitrification," *JWPCF*, 44(10):1916-1930 (October 1972).

(41) Bellar, T.A., Lichtenberg, J.J., and Kroner, R.C., *The Occurrence of Organohalides in Chlorinated Drinking Waters*, NTIS/PB-238 589 (November 1974).

(42) Bellar, T.A., Lichtenberg, J.J., and Kroner, R.C., "The Occurrence of Organohalides in Chlorinated Drinking Waters," *JAWWA*, 166:703-706 (December 1974).

(43) Bellin, J.S. and Chow, I., "Biochemical Effects of Chronic Low-Level Exposure to Pesticides," *Research Communications in Clinical Pathology and Pharmacology*, 9(2):325-337 (October 1974).

(44) Benarde, M.A., "Land Disposal and Sewage Effluent: Appraisal of Health Effects of Pathogenic Organisms," *JAWWA*, 65(6):432-440 (June 1973).

(45) Bendixen, T.W., et al, "Cannery Waste Treatment by Spray Irrigation-Runoff," *JWPCF*, 41(3):385-391 (March 1969).

(46) Bennett, P.J., Narayarian, S., and Hindin, E., "Removal of Organic Refractories by Reverse Osmosis," *Proceedings, 23rd Purdue Industrial Waste Conference*, pp 1000-1017 (May 1968).

(47) Berg, E.L., Brunner, C.A., and Williams, R.T., "Single Stage Lime Clarification of Secondary Effluent," *Water and Wastes Engineering*, 7(3):42-46 (March 1970).

(48) Berg, G., "Integrated Approach to Problem of Viruses in Water," *Journal of the Sanitary Engineering Division, ASCE*, 97(SA6):867-882 (December 1971).

(49) Berg, G., "Removal of Viruses from Sewage, Effluents, and Waters. 1: A Review," *World Health Organization Bulletin*, 49:451-460 (May 1973).

(50) Berg, G., "Removal of Viruses from Sewage, Effluents and Waters. 2: Present and Future Trends," *World Health Organization Bulletin*, 49:461-469 (May 1973).

(51) Berg, G., "Removal of Viruses from Water and Wastewater," *Proceedings, Thirteenth Water Quality Conference at University of Illinois*, pp 126-136 (February 1971).

(52) Berg, G., *Transmission of Viruses by the Water Route*, Interscience Publishers, New York (December 1965).

(53) Berg, G., "Virus Transmission by the Water Vehicle. I: Viruses," *Health Laboratory Science*, 3(2):86-88 (April 1966).

(54) Berg, G., "Virus Transmission by the Water Vehicle. II: Virus Removal by Sewage Treatment Procedures," *Health Laboratory Science*, 3(2):90-100 (April 1966).

(55) Berg, G., "Virus Transmission by the Water Vehicle. III: Removal of Viruses by Water Treatment Procedures," *Health Laboratory Science*, 3(3):170-181 (July 1966).

(56) Berg, G., Dean, R.B., and Dahling, D.R., "Removal of Poliovirus 1 from Secondary Effluents by Lime Flocculation and Rapid Sand Filtration," *JAWWA*, 60(2):193-198 (February 1968).

(57) Berg, J.W. and Burbank, F., "Correlations Between Carcinogenic Trace Metals in Water Supplies and Cancer Mortality," *Annals of the New York Academy of Sciences*, 199:249-261 (June 28, 1972).

(58) Bernardin, F.E., "Cyanide Detoxification Using Adsorption and Catalytic Oxidation on Granular Activated Carbon," *JWPCF*, 45(2):221-231 (February 1973).

(59) Bernhardt, H., et al, "Phosphate and Turbidity Control by Flocculation and Filtration," *JAWWA*, 63(6):355-368 (June 1971).

(60) Bertucci, J., Zenz, D., and Lue-Hing, C., *Report on the Virological Studies of Big Creek and Evelyn Reservoir in Fulton County, Illinois, February, 1973*, Metropolitan Sanitary District of Greater Chicago (September 6, 1973).

(61) Besik, F.K., "Renovating Domestic Sewage to Drinking Water Quality," *Water and Pollution Control*, 111(4):58-63, 97 (April 1973).

(62) Besik, F.K., "Wastewater Reclamation in a Closed System," *Water and Sewage Works*, 118(7):213-219 (July 1971).

(63) Betz Laboratories, *Betz Handbook of Industrial Water Conditioning* (1962).

(64) Bishop, D.F., et al, "Physical-Chemical Treatment of Municipal Wastewater," *JWPCF*, 44(3):361-371 (March 1972).

(65) Bishop, D.F., et al, *Physical-Chemical Treatment of Raw Municipal Wastewater*, EPA-670/2-73-070 (September 1973).

(66) Bishop, D.F., Heidman, J.A., and Stamberg, J.B., *Single-Stage Nitrification-Denitrification*, EPA-670/2-75-051 (June 1975).

(67) Bishop, D.F., Heidman, J.A., and Stamberg, J.B., "Single-Stage Nitrification-Denitrification," *JWPCF*, 48(3):520-532 (March 1976).

(68) Bishop, D.F., et al, "Studies on Activated Carbon Treatment," *JWPCF*, 39(2):188-203 (February 1967).

(69) Black, A.P., DuBose, A.T., and Vogh, R.P., *Physical-Chemical Treatment of Municipal Wastes by Recycled Magnesium Carbonate*, EPA/660/2-74-055 (June 1974).

(70) Blanck, C.A. and Sulick, D.J., "Activated Carbon Fights Bad Taste," *Water and Wastes Engineering*, 12(9):71-74 (September 1975).

(71) Boardman, G. and Sproul, O.J., "Protection of Viruses During Disinfection by Adsorption to Particulate Matter," presented at the 48th Annual Conference, Water Pollution Control Federation, Miami, Florida (October 1975).

(72) Bouwer, H., "Use of the Earth's Crust for Treatment or Storage of Sewage Effluent and Other Waste Fluids," *CRC Critical Reviews in Environmental Control*, pp 111-130 (March 1976).

(73) Bouwer, H., Lance, J.C., and Riggs, M.S., "High-Rate Land Treatment II: Water Quality and Economic Aspects of the Flushing Meadows Project," *JWPCF*, 46(5): 844-859 (May 1974).

(74) Boyden, C.R., "Trace Element Content and Body Size in Mollusks," *Nature*, 51:311-314 (September 1974).

(75) Braswell, J.R. and Hoadley, A.W., "Recovery of *Escherichia coli* from Chlorinated Secondary Sewage," *Applied Microbiology*, 28:328-329 (August 1974).

(76) Brewer, R.F., "Fluorine," in *Diagnostic Criteria for Plants and Soils*, H.D. Chapman, ed., Quality Printing Company, Abilene, Texas, pp 180-196 (1973).

(77) Brinska, G.A., "Sludge Disposal by Incineration at Alcosan," *Proceedings of the National Conference on Municipal Sludge Management*, pp 157-161 (June 11-13, 1974).

(78) Brown, J.R. and Chow, L.Y., "Comparative Study of DDT and Its Derivatives in Human Blood Samples in Norfolk County and Holland Marsh, Ontario," *Bulletin of Environmental Contamination and Toxicology*, 13(4):483-488.

(79) Brown, R.E., "Significance of Trace Metals and Nitrates in Sludge Soils," *JWPCF*, 47(12):2863-2875 (December 1975).

(80) Brown, T.S., et al, "Virus Removal by Diatomaceous Earth Filtration—Part I," *JAWWA*, 66(2):98-102.

(81) Brown, T.S., Malina, J.F., Jr., and Moore, B.D., "Virus Removal by Diatomaceous Earth Filtration—Part 2," *JAWWA*, 66:735-738 (December 1974).

(82) Brown, T.S., et al, "Virus Removal by Diatomaceous Earth Filtration," in *Virus Survival in Water and Wastewater Systems*, Malina and Sagik, ed., Water Resources Symposium No. 7, pp 129-144 (1974).

(83) Browning, G.E. and Mankin, J.O., "Gastroenteritis Epidemic Owing to Sewage Contamination of Public Water Supply," *JAWWA*, 81(11):1465-1470 (November 1966).

(84) Browning, J.E., "New Water Cleanup Roles for Powdered Activated Carbon," *Chemical Engineering*, 79:36-48 (February 21, 1972).

(85) Brungs, W.A., "Effects of Residual Chlorine on Aquatic Life," *JWPCF*, 45(10):2180-2193 (October 1973).

(86) Brunner, D.R. and Sproul, O.J., "Virus Inactivation During Phosphate Precipitation," *Journal of the Sanitary Engineering Division, ASCE*, 96(SA2):365-379 (April 1970).

(87) Bryan, E.H., "Concentrations of Lead in Urban Storm Water," *JWPCF*, 46(10):2419-2421.

(88) Bryan, F.L., "Diseases Transmitted by Foods Contaminated by Wastewater," in *Wastewater Use in the Production of Food and Fiber—Proceedings*, EPA-660/2-74-041, pp 16-45 (June 1974).

(89) Buelow, R.W. and Walton, G., "Bacteriological Quality vs Residual Chlorine," *JAWWA*, 63(1):28-35 (January 1971).

(90) Buelow, R.W., et al, "Nitrate Removal by Anion-Exchange Resins," *JAWWA*, 67(9):528-534 (September 1975).

(91) Buescher, C.A., Dougherty, J.H., and Skrinde, R.T., "Chemical Oxidation of Selected Organic Pesticides," *JWPCF*, 36(8):1005-1014 (August 1964).

(92) Burns, D.E. and Shell, G.L., "Carbon Treatment of a Municipal Wastewater," *JWPCF*, 46(1):148-164 (January 1974).

(93) Burns, D.E., Baumann, E.R., and Oulman, C.S., "Particulate Removal on Coated Filter Media," *JAWWA*, 62(2):121-126 (February 1970).

(94) Cabelli, V.J. and Heffernan, W.P., "Elimination of Bacteria by the Soft Shell Clam, *Mya arenaria*," *Journal of the Fisheries Research Board of Canada*, 27:1579-1586 (1970).

(95) Cabelli, V.J., et al, "The Impact of Pollution on Marine Bathing Beaches: An Epidemiological Study," personal communication (1975).

(96) Caldwell, G.G., et al, "Epidemic of Adenovirus Type 7 Acute Conjunctivitis in Swimmers," *American Journal of Epidemiology*, 99(3):230-234 (March 1974).

(97) *California Morbidity, Weekly Report from the Infectious Disease Section*, California State Dept. of Health (June 11, 1976).

(98) *California Morbidity, Weekly Report from the Infectious Disease Section*, California State Dept. of Health (October 8, 1976).

(99) Calmon, C., notes and comments relative to an article, "Arsenic Removal from Potable Water," by Ervin Bellack which appeared in the July 1971 Journal, *JAWWA*, 65(8):568-569 (August 1973).

(100) Calmon, C., "Trace Heavy Metal Removal by Ion Exchange," personal communication.

(101) Calmon, C. and Gold, H., "Treatment of Industrial Waste by Ion Exchange," *Proceedings of the Second National Conference on Complete Water Reuse*, American Institute of Chemical Engineers, New York, pp 820-842 (1975).

(102) Carlson, R.M., et al, "Facile Incorporation of Chlorine into Aromatic Systems During Aqueous Chlorination Process," *Environmental Science and Technology*, 9:674-675 (August 1975).

(103) Carnes, B.A., Eller, J.M., and Martin, J.C., *Integrated Reuse-Recycle Treatment Processes Applicable to Refinery and Petrochemical Wastewaters*, American Society of Mechanical Engineers, New York (1971).

(104) Carney, J.F., Carty, C.E., and Colwell, R.R., "Seasonal Occurrence and Distribution of Microbial Indicators and Pathogens in the Rhode River of Chesapeake Bay," *Applied Microbiology*, 30(5):771-780 (November 1975).

(105) Carpenter, R.L., et al, "The Evaluation of Microbial Pathogens in Sewage and Sewage-Grown Fish," *Wastewater Use in the Production of Food and Fiber—Proceedings*, EPA-660/2-74-041, pp 46-55 (June 1974).

(106) Case, O.P., *Metallic Recovery from Wastewaters Utilizing Cementation*, EPA-670/2-74-008 (January 1974).

(107) Cassel, A.F. and Mohr, R.T., "Sludge Handling and Disposal at Blue Plains, *Proceedings of the National Conference on Municipal Sludge Management*, pp 171-176 (June 11-13, 1974).

(108) Chahal, K.S., *Microbial Activities During Sewage Treatment in Lagoons*, NTIS/PB-237 501/2WP (1974).

(109) Chambers, D.W., "Chlorination for Control of Bacteria and Viruses in Treatment Plant Effluents," *JWPCF*, 43(2):228-241 (February 1971).

(110) Chang, P.W., *Effect of Ozonation on Human Enteric Viruses in Water from Rhode Island Rivers*, NTIS/PB-236 421/4WP (July 1974).

(111) Chang, S.L., "Modern Concept of Disinfection," *Journal of the Sanitary Engineering Division, ASCE*, 97(SA5):689-707 (October 1971).

(112) Chang, S.L., et al, "Removal of Coxsackie and Bacterial Viruses in Water by Flocculation," *American Journal of Public Health*, 48:51-61 (January 1958).

(113) Chang, S.L., Isaacs, P.C.G., and Baine, N., "Studies on Destruction of Bacterial Virus," *American Journal of Hygiene*, 57(3):253-266 (May 1953).

(114) Chapman, B., "Sponsors of Science Inc. on Safety of 2,4,5-T and Dioxin," *Clinical Toxicology*, 7(4):413-421 (1974).

(115) Chapman, S.W., Jr., Sweazy, R.M., and Wells, D.M., *Nitrogen Mass Balance Determination for Simulated Wastewater Land Spreading Operations*, NTIS/PB-239-406 (December 1974).

(116) Chaudhuri, M. and Engelbrecht, R.S., "Removal of Viruses from Water by Chemical Coagulation and Flocculation," *JAWWA*, 62(9):563-567 (September 1970).

(117) Chaudhuri, M. and Engelbrecht, R.S., "Virus Removal in Wastewater Renovation by Chemical Coagulation and Flocculation," *Advances in Water Pollution Research*, 1970(1):II/201-22.

(118) Chen, C.L., "Virus Removal," personal communication (September 1975).

(119) Chen, C.L. and Miele, R.P., *Wastewater Demineralization by Continuous Counter-Current Ion Exchange Process*, Contract No. 14-12-150, National Environmental Research Center, Cincinnati, Ohio (1972).

(120) Chen, C.L. and Miele, R.P., *Wastewater Demineralization by Tubular Reverse Osmosis Process*, Contract No. 14-12-150, National Environmental Research Center, EPA, Cincinnati, Ohio.

(121) Chen, C.L. and Miele, R.P., *Wastewater Demineralization by Two-Stage Fixed-Bed Ion Exchange Process*, Advanced Treatment Research Center, EPA.

(122) Chen, C.W. and Orlob, G.T., "The Accumulation and Significance of Sludge Near San Diego Outfall," *JWPCF*, 44(7):1362-1371 (July 1972).

(123) Chen, K. and Hendricks, T., *Trace Metals on Suspended Particulates*, Southern California Coastal Water Research Project annual report, El Segundo, CA, pp 147-152 (June 30, 1974).

(124) Chen, K.Y. and Lockwood, R.A., "Evaluation Strategies of Metal Pollution in Oceans," *Journal of the Environmental Engineering Division, ASCE*, 102(EE 2): 347-359 (April 1976).

(125) Chen, M.H., et al, "Heavy Metals Uptake by Activated Sludge," *JWPCF*, 47(2):362-376 (February 1975).

(126) Chian, E.S.K., Bruce, W.N., and Fang, H.H.P., "Removal of Pesticides by Reverse Osmosis," *Environmental Science and Technology*, 9(1):52-59 (January 1975).

(127) Christensen, G.L., "Use of Ozone and Oxygen in Advanced Wastewater Treatment," *JWPCF*, 46(8):2054-2055 (August 1974).

(128) Ciaccio, L., *Water and Water Pollution Handbook*, Vol. 4, Marcel Dekker, New York (1971).

(129) Clarke, N.A., et al, "Virus Study for Drinking Water Supplies," *JAWWA*, 68(4):192-197 (April 1976).

(130) Cleasby, J.L., "Iron and Manganese Removal—A Case Study," *JAWWA*, 67(3):147-149 (March 1975).

(131) Cleasby, J.L., et al, "Trickling Filtration of a Waste Containing NTA," *JWPCF*, 46(8):1872-1887 (August 1974).

(132) Cliver, D.O. and Herrmann, J.F., "Proteolytic and Microbial Inactivation of Enteroviruses," *Water Research*, 6(7):797-805 (July 1972).

(133) Cliver, D.O., Green, K.M., and Bouma, J., *Viruses and Septic Tank Effluent*, Small Scale Waste Management Project, University of Wisconsin, Madison, Wisconsin (1975).

(134) Colston, N.V., Jr., *Characterization and Treatment of Urban Land Runoff*, EPA-670/2-714-096 (December 1974).

(135) Comer, S.W., et al, "Exposure of Workers to Carbaryl," *Bulletin of Environmental Contamination and Toxicology*, 13(4):385-391 (1975).

(136) Committee on Public Health Activities, "Coliform Organisms as an Index of Water Safety," *Journal of the Sanitary Engineering Division, ASCE*, 87(SA6):41-58 (November 1961).

(137) Conley, W.R., "High-Rate Filtration," *JAWWA*, 64(3):203-206 (March 1972).

(138) Cookson, J.T., "The Chemistry of Virus Concentration by Chemical Methods," *Developments in Industrial Microbiology*, 15:160-173 (1973).

(139) Cookson, J.T., "Removal of Submicron Particles in Packed Beds," *Environmental Science and Technology*, 4:128-134 (February 1970).

(140) Cooper, B.S. and Harris, R.C., "Heavy Metals in Organic Phases of River and Estuarine Sediment," *Marine Pollution Bulletin*, 5(2):24-26 (February 1974).

(141) Cooper, R.C., "Health Considerations in Use of Tertiary Effluents," *Journal of the Environmental Engineering Division, ASCE*, 103(EE1):37-47 (February 1977).

(142) Cooper, R.C., *Wastewater Contaminants and their Effects on Public Health*, California State Water Resources Control Board (1975).

(143) Cortinovis, D., "Activated Biofilter: A Modesto Invention Gains Acceptance Throughout North America," *The Bulletin (California Water Pollution Control Association)*, 12(2):38-41 (October 1975).

(144) Craun, G.F., "Microbiology—Waterborne Outbreaks," *JWPCF*, 47(6):1566-1581 (June 1975).

(145) Craun, G.F. and McCabe, L.J., "Review of the Causes of Waterborne-Disease Outbreaks," *JAWWA*, 65(1):74-84 (January 1973).

(146) Crump-Weisner, H.J., Feltz, H.R., and Yates, M.L., "A Study of the Distribution of Polychlorinated Biphenyls in the Aquatic Environment," *U.S. Geological Survey Journal of Research*, 1:603-607 (September 1973).

(147) Cruver, J.E. and Nusbaum, I., "Application of Reverse Osmosis to Wastewater Treatment," *JWPCF*, 46(2):301-311 (February 1974).

(148) Cruver, J.E., "Reverse Osmosis—Where it Stands Today," *Water and Sewage Works*, 120(10):74-78 (October 1973).

(149) Cruver, J.E. and Nusbaum, I., "Application of Reverse Osmosis to Wastewater Treatment," *JWPCF*, 46(2):301-311 (February 1974).

(150) Culbertson, C.G., "The Pathogenicity of Soil Amebas," *Annual Review of Microbiology*, 25:231 (1971).

(151) Culp, G.L. and Shuckrow, A.J., "Physical-Chemical Techniques for Treatment of Raw Wastewaters," *Public Works*, 103(7):56-60 (July 1972).

(152) Culp, R.L., "Breakpoint Chlorination for Virus Inactivation," *JAWWA*, 66:699-703 (December 1974).

(153) Culp, R.L., "Breakpoint Chlorination for Virus Inactivation," *Virus Survival in Water and Wastewater Systems*, Malina and Sagik, eds., Water Resources Symposium No. 7, pp 158-165 (1974).

(154) Culp, R.L., "Virus and Bacteria Removal in Advanced Wastewater Treatment," *Public Works*, 102:84-88 (June 1971).

(155) Culp, R.L., "Wastewater Reclamation at South Tahoe Public Utilities District," *JAWWA*, 60(1):84-94 (January 1968).

(156) Daniels, S.L. and Parker, D.G., "Removing Phosphorus from Wastewater," *Environmental Science and Technology*, 7(8):690-694 (August 1973).

(157) David Volkert and Associates, *Monograph on the Effectiveness and Cost of Water Treatment Processes for the Removal of Specific Contaminants*, Contract No. 68-01-1833, EPA, Office of Air and Water (August 1974).

(158) Davis, E.M. and Keen, S.R., "Municipal Wastewater Bacteria Capable of Surviving Chlorination," *Health Laboratory Science*, 11:268-274 (October 1974).

(159) Davis, J.A., III and Jacknow, J., "Heavy Metals in Wastewater in Three Urban Areas," *JWPCF*, 47(9):2292-2297 (September 1975).

(160) Davis, W.K., "Land Disposal III: Land Use Planning," *JWPCF*, 45(7):1485-1488 (July 1973).

(161) DeBoise, J.N. and Thomas, J.F., "Chemical Treatment for Phosphate Control," *JWPCF*, 47(9):2246-2255 (September 1975).

(162) *Degradation of Synthetic Organic Molecules in the Biosphere: Natural, Pesticidal, and Various Other Man-Made Compounds*, National Academy of Sciences, Washington, DC (1972).

(163) DeMichele, E., "Pathogenic Organisms in the Murderkill River Estuary," *JWPCF*, 46(4):772-776 (April 1974).

(164) DeMichele, E., "Water Reuse, Virus Removal and Public Health," in *Virus Survival in Water and Wastewater Systems*, Malina and Sagik, eds., Water Resources Symposium No. 7, pp 45-56 (1974).

(165) Dennis, J.M., "1955-1956 Infectious Hepatitis Epidemic in Delhi, India," *JAWWA*, 51:1288-1296 (October 1959).

(166) de Vries, J., "Soil Filtration of Wastewater Effluent and the Mechanism of Pore Clogging," *JWPCF*, 44(4):565-573 (April 1972).

(167) DeWalle, F.B. and Chian, E.S.K., "Removal of Organic Matter by Activated Carbon Columns," *Journal of the Environmental Engineering Division, ASCE*, 100(EE5):1089-1104 (October 1974).

(168) Diaper, E.W.J., "Disinfection of Water and Wastewater Using Ozone," in Johnson, J.D. *Disinfection—Water and Wastewater*, Ann Arbor Science Publishers, Ann Arbor, MI, pp 211-231 (1975).

(169) Diaper, E.W.J., "Microstraining and Ozonation of Water and Wastewater," *Water and Wastes Engineering*, 5(2):56-58 (February 1968).

(170) Diaper, E.W.J., "Practical Aspects of Water and Wastewater Treatment by Ozone," in *Ozone in Water and Wastewater Treatment*, Ann Arbor Science Publishers, Ann Arbor, MI, pp 145-179 (1972).

(171) Diaper, E.W.J. and Glover, G.E., "Microstraining of Combined Sewer Overflows," *JWPCF*, 43(10):2101-2113 (October 1971).

(172) Directo, L.S. and Chen, C., "Pilot Plant Study of Physical-Chemical Treatment," 47th Annual Water Pollution Control Federation Conference, Denver, Colorado, October 1974.

(173) Directo, L.S., Miele, R.P., and Masse, A.N., "Phosphate Removal by Mineral Addition to Secondary and Tertiary Treatment Systems," presented at the 27th Purdue Industrial Waste Conference, May 1972.

(174) Directo, L.S., Chen, C., and Miele, R.P., *Physical Chemical Treatment of Raw Sewage*, Advanced Waste Treatment Research Laboratory, EPA.

(175) Directo, L.S., Chen, C., and Miele, R.P., *Two-Stage Granular Activated Carbon Treatment*, Advanced Waste Treatment Research Center, EPA.

(176) *Disinfection of Wastewater, Task Force Report*, EPA Office of Research and Development (July 1975).

(177) Dismukes, W.E., et al, "An Outbreak of Gastroenteritis and Infectious Hepatitis Attributed to Raw Clams," *American Journal of Epidemiology*, 89(5):555-561 (1969).

(178) "Disposal of Wastes from Water Treatment Plants—Part I," *JAWWA*, 61(10):541-566 (October 1967).

(179) Dixon, J.K. and Zielyk, M.W., "Control of the Bacterial Content of Water with Synthetic Polymeric Flocculants," *Environmental Science and Technology*, 3:551-558 (June 1969).

(180) Dowty, B., et al, "Halogenated Hydrocarbons in New Orleans Drinking Water and Blood Plasma," *Science*, 187(4171):75-77 (January 10, 1975).

(181) Dreisbach, R.H., *Handbook of Poisoning: Diagnosis and Treatment*, Lange Medical Publications, Los Altos, CA (1971).

(182) Dryden, F.D., "Mineral Removal by Ion Exchange, Reverse Osmosis and Electrodialysis," presented at the Workshop on Wastewater and Reuse, South Lake Tahoe, CA, June 25-26, 1970.

(183) Duddles, G.A., Richardson, S.F., and Barth, E.F., "Plastic-Medium Trickling Filters for Biological Nitrogen Control," *JWPCF*, 46(5):937-947 (May 1974).

(184) Dugan, G.L., et al, "Land Disposal of Sewage in Hawaii a Reality?" *Water and Sewage Works*, 121(11):64-65 (November 1974).

(185) Dugan, G.L., et al, "Land Disposal of Wastewater in Hawaii," *JWPCF*, 47(8):2067-2087 (August 1975).

(186) Dugan, P.R., *Bioflocculation and the Accumulation of Chemicals by Floc-Forming Organisms*, EPA-600/2-75-032 (September 1975).

(187) Dunham, J., O'Gara, R.W., and Taylor, F.B., "Studies on Pollutants from Processed Water: Collection from Three Stations and Biologic Testing for Toxicity and Carcinogenesis," *American Journal of Public Health*, 57(12):2178-2185 (December 1967).

(188) Durum, W.H. and Hem, J.D., "An Overview of Trace Element Distribution Patterns in Water," *Annals, New York Academy of Science*, 199:26-36 (June 28, 1972).

(189) Duvel, W.A., Jr. and Helfgott, T., "Removal of Wastewater Organics by Reverse Osmosis," *JWPCF*, 47(1):57-65 (January 1975).

(190) Eckenfelder, W.W., Jr., "Wastewater Treatment Design: Economics and Techniques, Part I," *Water and Sewage Works*, 122(6):62-65 (September 1975).

(191) Edwards, V.H. and Schubert, P.C., "Removal of 2,4-D and Other Persistent Organic Molecules from Water Supplies by Reverse Osmosis," *JAWWA*, 66(10):610-616 (October 1974).

(192) Eichelberger, J.W. and Lichtenberg, J.J., "Carbon Adsorption for Recovery of Organic Pesticides," *JAWWA*, 63(1):25-27 (January 1971).

(193) El-Dib, M.A., Ramadan, F.M., and Ismail, M., "Adsorption of Sevin and Baygon on Granular Activated Carbon," *Water Research*, 9:795-798 (1975).

(194) Eliassen, R. and Tchobanoglous, G., "Chemical Processing of Wastewater for Nutrient Removal," *JWPCF*, 40(5):R171-R180 (May 1968).

(195) Eliassen, R. and Tchobanoglous, G., "Removal of Nitrogen and Phosphorus from Wastewater," *Environmental Science and Technology*, 3:536-541 (June 1969).

(196) Eliassen, R., Wyckoff, B.M., and Tonkin, C.D., "Ion Exchange for Reclamation of Reusable Supplies," *JAWWA*, 57(9):1113-1122 (September 1965).

(197) Ember, L., "The Specter of Cancer," *Environmental Science and Technology*, 9(13):1116-1121 (December 1975).

(198) Engineering Evaluation of Virus Hazard in Water, *Journal of the Sanitary Engineering Division, ASCE*, 96(SA1):111-160 (February 1970).

(199) England, B., "Recovery of Viruses from Waste and Other Waters by Chemical Methods," *Developments in Industrial Microbiology*, 15:174-183 (1973).

(200) England, B., et al, "Virologic Assessment of Sewage Treatment at Santee, California," in *Transmission of Viruses by the Water Route*, G. Berg, ed., John Wiley, New York, pp 401-417 (1965).

(201) Englebrecht, R.S., et al, *New Microbial Indicators of Wastewater Chlorination Efficiency*, EPA-670/2-73-082 (February 1974).

(202) English, J.N., et al, "Denitrification in Granular Carbon and Sand Columns," *JWPCF*, 46(1):28-42 (January 1974).

(203) English, J.N., Linstedt, K.D., and Bennett, E.R., *Research Required to Establish Confidence in the Potable Reuse of Wastewater*, U.S. Environmental Protection Agency, Cincinnati, Ohio (1975).

(204) Ericsson, B., "Nitrogen Removal in a Pilot Plant," *JWPCF*, 47(4):727-740 (April 1975).

(205) Esvelt, L.A., Kaufman, W.J., and Selleck, R.E., "Toxicity Assessment of Treated Municipal Wastewaters," *JWPCF*, 45(7):1558-1572 (July 1973).

(206) *Evaluation of Municipal Sewage Treatment Alternatives*, NTIS/PB-233 489 (February 1974).

(207) Evans, F.L., III, "Ozone Technology: Current Status," in *Ozone in Water and Wastewater Treatment*, Ann Arbor Science Publishers, Ann Arbor, Michigan, pp 1-13 (1972).

(208) Evans, F.L., III, et al, "Treatment of Urban Stormwater Runoff," *JWPCF*, 40(5): R162-R170 (May 1968).

(209) Evans, S., "Nitrate Removal by Ion Exchange," *JWPCF*, 45(1):632-636 (April 1973).

(210) Fannin, K.F., et al, *Field Studies on Coliphages and Coliforms as Indicators of Airborne Animal Viral Contamination from Wastewater Treatment Facilities*, Water Research, Dept. of Environmental Health and Epidemiology, School of Public Health, University of Michigan, Ann Arbor.

(211) *Fate of Organic Pesticides in the Aquatic Environment*, Advances in Chemistry Series No. 111, American Chemical Society, Washington, DC (1972).

(212) Feinstone, S.M., Kapikian, A.Z., and Purcell, R.H., "Hepatitis A: Detection by Immune Electron Microscopy of a Viruslike Antigen Associated with Acute Illness," *Science*, 182:1026-1028 (December 7, 1973).

(213) Ferens, M.C., *A Review of the Physiological Impact of Mercurials*, EPA-660/3-73-022 (February 1974).

(214) Ferguson, J.F. and J. Gavis, "A Review of the Arsenic Cycle in Natural Waters," *Water Research*, 6:1259-1274 (1972).

(215) Ferguson, J.F., Jenkins, D., and Eastman, J., "Calcium Phosphate Precipitation at Slight Alkaline pH Values," *JWPCF*, 45(4):620-631 (April 1973).

(216) Finberg, L., "Interaction of the Chemical Environment with the Infant and Young Child," *Pediatrics*, 53:831-837 (1974).

(217) Focht, D.D., "Microbial Degradation of DDT Metabolites to Carbon Dioxide, Water, and Chloride," *Bulletin of Environmental Contamination and Toxicology*, 7(1):52-56 (January 1972).

(218) Folk, G., "Phosphorus Removal with Liquid Alum," *WPCF Highlights*, pp 8-9 (February 1976).

(219) Folkman, Y. and Wachs, A.M., "Filtration of Chlorella through Dune-Sand," *Journal of the Sanitary Engineering Division, ASCE*, 96(SA3):675-689 (June 1970).

(220) *Foodborne and Waterborne Disease Outbreaks Annual Summary 1973*, U.S. Center for Disease Control, HEW (1974).

(221) *Foodborne and Waterborne Disease Outbreaks Annual Summary 1975*, U.S. Center for Disease Control, HEW (September 1976).

(222) Fossum, G.O., *Water Balance in Sewage Stabilization Lagoons*, NTIS/PB-233-482 (August 1971).

(223) Foster, D.H. and Engelbrecht, R.S., "Microbial Hazards in Disposing of Wastewater on Soil," in *Conference on Recycling Treated Municipal Wastewater Through Forest and Cropland*, W.E. Sopper and L.T. Kardos, eds., EPA-660/2-74-003, pp 217-241 (March 1974).

(224) Frank, R., et al, "Organochlorine Insecticide Residues in Sediment and Fish Tissues," Ontario, Canada, *Pesticides Monitoring Journal*, 7:165-180 (March 1974).

(225) Frissora, F.V., "An Advanced Water Filtration Plant," *Water and Sewage Works*, 118(11):365-369 (November 1971).

(226) Fulton, G.P. and Bryant, E.A., "Pilot Plant Program—Treatment of NYC Water Supply," *Civil Engineering—ASCE*, 46(6):52-55.

(227) Furgason, R.R. and Day, R.O., "Iron and Manganese Removal with Ozone, Part I," *Water and Sewage Works*, 122(6):42, 45-47 (June 1975).

(228) Furgason, R.R. and Day, R.O., "Iron and Manganese Removal with Ozone, Part II," *Water and Sewage Works*, 122(7):61-63 (July 1975).

(229) Gaitan, E., "Waterborne Goitrogens and Their Role in the Etiology of Endemic Goiter," *World Review of Nutrition and Dietetics*, 17:53-90 (1973).

(230) Gambrell, R.P. and Weed, S.B., "The Fate of Fertilizer Nutrients as Related to Water Quality in the North Carolina Coastal Plain," NTIS/PB-238 001/2WP (August 1974).

(231) Ganczarczyk, J., "Nitrogen Transformation in Activated Sludge Treatment," *Journal of the Sanitary Engineering Division, ASCE*, 98(SA5):783 (October 1972).

(232) Gangoli, N. and Thodos, G., "Phosphate Adsorption Studies," *JWPCF*, 45(5):842-849 (May 1973).

(233) Gavis, J., *Wastewater Reuse*, National Technical Information Service, Springfield, VA (1971).

(234) Gavis, J. and Ferguson, J.F., "The Cycling of Mercury Through the Environment," *Water Research*, 6:989-1008 (1972).

(235) Geldreich, E.E. and Clarke, N.A., "The Coliform Test: A Criterion for Viral Safety of Water," in *Proceedings, 13th Water Quality Conference*, Urbana, Illinois, pp 103-113 (1971).

(236) Geldreich, E.E. and Kenner, A., "Concepts of Fecal Streptococci in Stream Pollution," *JWPCF*, 41(8):R336-R352 (August 1969).

(237) Geldreich, E.E. and Bordner, R.H., "Fecal Contamination of Fruits and Vegetables During Cultivation and Processing for Market; a Review," *Journal of Milk and Food Technology*, 34(4):184-195 (April 1971).

(238) George, A. and Zajicek, O.T., "Ion Exchange Equilibria. Chloride-Phosphate Exchange with a Strong Base Anion Exchanger," *Environmental Science and Technology*, 2(7):540-542 (July 1968).

(239) Gerakis, P.A. and Sficas, A.G., "The Presence and Cycling of Pesticides in the Ecosphere," *Residue Reviews*, 52:69-87 (1974).

(240) Gerba, C.P., et al, "Adsorption of Poliovirus onto Activated Carbon in Wastewater," *Environmental Science and Technology*, 9:727-731 (August 1975).

(241) Gerba, C.P., et al, "Enhancement of Poliovirus Adsorption in Wastewater on Activated Carbon," in *Virus Survival in Water and Wastewater Systems*, Malina and Sagik, eds., Water Resources Symposium No. 7, pp 115-126 (1974).

(242) Gerba, C.P., Wallis, C., and Melnick, J.L., "Viruses in Water: The Problem, Some Solutions," *Environmental Science and Technology*, 9(13):1122-1126 (December 1975).

(243) Ghan, H.B., Chen, C., and Miele, R.P., "Disinfection and Color Removal with Ozone (Draft Report)," EPA Advanced Waste Treatment Research Laboratory, Cincinnati, Ohio.

(244) Ghan, H.B., et al, "Wastewater Disinfection with Ozone Works Best with a Clean Effluent and Multiple, Low-Dosage Injection Points," *Bulletin (California Water Pollution Control Association)*, 12(2):47-53 (October 1975).

(245) Ghosh, M.M. and Zugger, P.D., "Toxic Effects of Mercury on the Activated Sludge Process," *JWPCF*, 45(3):424-433 (March 1973).

(246) Gibbs, R.J., "Mechanisms of Trace Metal Transport in Rivers," *Science*, 180:71-73 (April 1973).

(247) Gilbert, R.G., et al, "Wastewater Renovation and Reuse: Virus Removal by Soil Filtration," *Science*, 192:1004-1005 (June 4, 1976).

(248) Gilliam, J.W., Daniels, R.B., and Lutz, J.F., "Nitrogen Content of Shallow Groundwater in the North Carolina Coastal Plain," *Journal of Environmental Quality*, 3: 147-151 (April 1974).

(249) Giusti, D.M., Conway, R.A., and Lawson, C.T., "Activated Carbon Adsorption of Petrochemicals," *JWPCF*, 46(5):947-965 (May 1974).

(250) Glaze, W.H. and Henderson, J.E., IV, "Formation of Organochlorine Compounds from the Chlorination of a Municipal Secondary Effluent," *JWPCF*, 47(10):2510-2515 (October 1975).

(251) Glover, G.E. and Hubert, G.R., *Microstraining and Disinfection of Combined Sewer Overflows—Phase II*, EPA-R2-73-124 (January 1973).

(252) Gloyna, E.F., Brady, S.O., and Lyles, H., "Use of Aerated Lagoons and Ponds in Refinery and Chemical Waste Treatment," *JWPCF*, 41(3):429-439 (March 1969).

(253) Godfrey, K.A., Jr., "Land Treatment of Municipal Sewage," *Civil Engineering*, 43(9): 103-109 (September 1973).

(254) Goff, G.D., et al, "Emission of Microbial Aerosols from Sewage Treatment Plants that Use Trickling Filters," *Health Service Reports*, 88(7):640-651 (August-September 1973).

(255) Gold, H. and Todisco, A., "Wastewater Reuse by Continuous Ion Exchange," in *Complete Water Reuse*, L.K. Cecil, ed., American Institute of Chemical Engineers, New York, pp 96-103 (1973).

(256) Goldman, J.C., et al, "Inorganic Nitrogen Removal in a Combined Tertiary Treatment Marine Aquaculture System—I: Removal Efficiencies," *Water Research*, 8:45-54 (1974).

(257) Goldman, J.C., et al, "Inorganic Nitrogen Removal in a Combined Tertiary Treatment Marine Aquaculture System—II: Algal Biomass," *Water Research*, 8:55-59 (1974).

(258) Gossling, J. and Slack, J.M., "Predominant Gram-Positive Bacteria in Human Feces: Numbers, Variety, and Persistence," *Infection and Immunity*, 9:719-729 (April 1974).

(259) Grabow, W.O.K., "The Virology of Wastewater Treatment," *Water Research*, 2(10): 675-701 (November 1968).

(260) Grabow, W.O.K. and Nupen, E.M., "The Load of Infectious Microorganisms in the Wastewater of Two South African Hospitals," *Water Research*, 6:1557-1563 (1972).

(261) Graeser, H.J., "Dallas' Wastewater-Reclamation Studies," *JAWWA*, 63(10):634-640 (October 1971).

(262) Graeser, H.J., "Water Reuse: Resource of the Future," *JAWWA*, 66(10):575-578 (October 1974).

(263) Graetz, D.A., Hammond, L.C., and Davidson, J.M., "Nitrate Movement in a Eustis Fine Sand Planted to Millet," *Soil and Crop Science Society of Florida Proceedings*, 33:157-160 (November 27-29, 1973).

(264) Graetz, D.A., et al, "Parathion Degradation in Lake Sediments," *JWPCF*, 42(2): R76-R94 (February 1970).

(265) Granata, A., et al, "Relationship Between Cancer Mortality and Urban Drinking Water Metal Ion Content," *Minerva Medica*, 61:1941 (May 1970).

(266) Greenberg, A.E. and Kupka, E., "Tuberculosis Transmission by Wastewaters—A Review," *Sewage and Industrial Wastes*, 29(5):524-537 (May 1957).

(267) Gregg, J.C., "Nitrate Removed at Water Treatment Plant," *Civil Engineering, ASCE*, 43(4):45-47 (April 1973).

(268) Gregor, C.D., "Solubilization of Lead in Lakes and Reservoir Sediments by NTA," *Environmental Science and Technology*, 6(3):278-279 (March 1972).

(269) Grigoropoulos, S.G., Vidder, R.C., and Max, D.W., "Fate of Aluminum-Precipitated Phosphorus in Activated Sludge and Anaerobic Digestion," *JWPCF*, 43(12):2366-2382 (December 1971).

(270) Grinstein, S., Melnick, J.L., and Wallis, C., "Virus Isolations from Sewage and from a Stream Receiving Effluents of Sewage Treatment Plants," *Bulletin of the World Health Organization*, 42:291-296 (1970).

(271) Grover, R., "Adsorption and Desorption of Trifluralin, Triallate, and Diallate by Various Adsorbents," *Weed Science*, 22:405-408 (July 1974).

(272) Grover, R. and Smith, A.E., "Adsorption Studies with the Acid and Dimethylamine Forms of 2,4-D and Dicambra," *Canadian Journal of Soil Science*, 54:179-186 (May 1974).

(273) Gruenwald, A., "Drinking Water from Sewage?" *The American City*, 82(3):92-93 (March 1967).

(274) Gruninger, R.M., "Chemical Treatment for Surface Water," *Water and Sewage Works*, 121(6):110-114 (June 1974).

(275) Gulledge, J.H. and O'Connor, J.T., "Removal of Arsenic(V) from Water by Adsorption on Aluminum and Ferric Hydroxides," *JAWWA*, 65(8):548-552.

(276) Hager, D.G., "Adsorption and Filtration with Granular Activated Carbon," *Water and Wastes Engineering*, 6(8):39-43 (August 1969).

(277) Hager, D.G. and Reilly, P.B., "Clarification-Adsorption in the Treatment of Municipal and Industrial Wastewater," *JWPCF*, 42(5):794-800 (May 1970).

(278) Hager, D.G. and Flentje, M.E., "Removal of Organic Contaminants by Granular-Carbon Filtration," *JAWWA*, 57(11):1440-1450 (November 1965).

(279) Hall, H.E. and Hauser, G.H., "Examination of Feces from Food Handlers for Salmonellae, Enteropathogenic *Escherichia coli*, and *Clostridium perfringens. Applied Microbiology*, 14(6):928-932 (November 1966).

(280) Hammer, N.J., *Water and Wastewater Technology*, Wiley, New York (1975).

(281) Hamoda, M.F., et al, "Organics Removal by Low-Pressure Osmosis," *JWPCF*, 45(10): 2146-2154 (October 1973).

(282) Hansen, R.E., "Granular Carbon Filters for Taste and Odor Removal," *JAWWA*, 64(3):176-181 (March 1972).

(283) Harris, W.C., "Ozone Disinfection," *JAWWA*, 64(3):182-183 (March 1972).

(284) Harrison, R.M., Perry, R., and Wellings, R.A., "Polynuclear Aromatic Hydrocarbons in Raw, Potable and Wastewaters," *Water Research*, 9:331-346 (1975).

(285) Hatch, M.J. and Wolochow, H., "Bacterial Survival: Consequence of the Airborne State," in *An Introduction to Experimental Aerobiology*, R.L. Dimmick and A.B. Akers, eds., Wiley, New York, pp 267-295 (1969).

(286) Hauck, A.R. and Sourirajan, S., "Performance of Porous Cellulose Acetate Membranes for the Reverse Osmosis Treatment of Hard and Wastewaters," *Environmental Science and Technology*, 3(12):1269-1275.

(287) Haug, R.T. and McCarty, P.L., "Nitrification with Submerged Filters," *JWPCF*, 44(11):2086-2102 (November 1972).

(288) *Heavy Metals in the Environment*, Water Resources Research Institute, Oregon State University, Corvallis (January 1973).

(289) Hentschel, M.L. and Cox, T.L., "Effluent Water Treating at Charter International Oil Company's Houston Refinery," *AIChE Symposium Series*, 69(135):151-153 (1973).

(290) *Hepatitis Surveillance*, Center for Disease Control Report 37, U.S. Public Health Service, HEW (June 1975).

(291) *Hepatitis Surveillance*, Center for Disease Control Report 38, U.S. Public Health Service, HEW (September 1976).

(292) Herrmann, J.E., Kostenbader, K.D., and Cliver, D.O., "Persistence of Enteroviruses in Lake Water," *Applied Microbiology*, 28:895-896 (November 1974).

(293) Hickey, J.L.S. and Reist, P.C., "Health Significance of Airborne Microorganisms from Wastewater Treatment Processes," *JWPCF*, 47(12):2741-2757 (December 1975).

(294) Hindin, E. and Bennett, P.J., "Water Reclamation by Reverse Osmosis," *Water and Sewage Works*, 116(2):66-73 (February 1969).

(295) Hinesly, T.D., Braids, O.D., and Molina, J.E., *Agricultural Benefits and Environmental Changes Resulting from the Use of Digested Sewage Sludge on Field Crops*, Environmental Protection Agency (1971).

(296) Hoadley, A.W. and Goyal, S.M., *Public Health Implications of the Application of Wastewaters to the Land*, School of Civil Engineering, Georgia Institute of Technology, Atlanta, Georgia.

(297) Holzmacher, R.G., "Nitrate Removal from a Groundwater Supply," *Water and Sewage Works*, 118(7):210-213 (July 1971).

(298) Hom, L.W., "Kinetics of Chlorine Disinfection in an Ecosystem," *Journal of the Sanitary Engineering Division, ASCE*, 98(SA1):183-193 (February 1972).

(299) Hook, J.E., Kardos, L.T., and Sopper, W.E., "Effects of Land Disposal of Wastewaters on Soil Phosphorus Relations," in *Conference on Recycling Treated Municipal Wastewater through Forest and Cropland*, W.E. Sopper and L.T. Kardos, EPA-660/2-74-003, pp 179-195 (March 1974).

(300) Hornick, R.B., et al, "Typhoid Fever: Pathogenesis and Immunologic Control," *New England Journal of Medicine*, 283:739-746 (October 1, 1970).

(301) Hsu, D.Y. and Pipes, W.O., "Aluminum Hydroxide Effects on Wastewater Treatment Processes," *JWPCF*, 45(4):681-697 (April 1973).

(302) Huang, C.H., Feuerstein, D.L., and Miller, E.L., *Demonstration of a High-Rate Activated Sludge System*, EPA-670/2-75-037 (March 1975).

(303) Huang, C.P. and Wu, M.H., "Chromium Removal by Carbon Adsorption," *JWPCF*, 47(10):2437-2446 (October 1975).

(304) Huang, P.M. and Hwang, C.P., "Inorganic and Organic Phosphorus Distribution in Domestic and Municipal Sewage," *Water and Sewage Works*, 120(6):82-83 (June 1973).

(305) Hudson, H.E., "High-Quality Water Production and Viral Disease," *JAWWA*, 54(10): 1265-1274 (October 1962).

(306) Heuper, W.C. and Payne, W.W., "Carcinogenic Effects of Adsorbates of Raw and Finished Water Supplies," *American Journal of Clinical Pathology*, 39(5):475-481 (May 1963).

(307) Hulka, S.C., et al, "Sediment Coliform Populations and Post Chlorination Behavior of Wastewater Bacteria," *Water and Sewage Works*, 120(10):79-81 (October 1973).

(308) Hume, N.B. and Garber, W.F., "Marine Disposal of Digested Screened Wastewater Solids," *Advances in Water Pollution Research*, 1966(3):243-262.

(309) Humenick, M.J., Jr. and Schnoor, J.L., "Improving Mercury(II) Removal by Activated Carbon," *Journal of the Environmental Engineering Division, ASCE*, 100 (EE6):1249-1262 (December 1974).

(310) Humenick, M.J. and Kaufman, W.J., "An Integrated Biological-Chemical Process for Municipal Wastewater Treatment," *Advances in Water Pollution Research*, 1970(1): I-19/1-18.

(311) Hunter, J.V. and Kotalik, T.A., "Chemical and Biological Quality of Sewage Effluents," in *Conference on Recycling Treated Municipal Wastewater Through Forest and Cropland*, W.E. Sopper and L. Kardos, eds., EPA-660/2-74-003, pp 6-27 (March 1974).

(312) Hunter, J.V. and Heukelekian, H., "The Composition of Domestic Sewage Fractions," *JWPCF*, 37(8):1142-1163 (August 1965).

(313) Hunter, J.V., Bell, G.R., and Henderson, C.N., "Coliform Organism Removals by Diatomite Filtration," *JAWWA*, 58(9):1160-1169 (September 1966).

(314) Hutton, W.D. and LaRocca, S.A., "Biological Treatment of Concentrated Ammonia Wastewaters," *JWPCF*, 47(5):989-997 (May 1975).

(315) Hyde, H.C., "Sewage Sludge Utilization for Agricultural Soil Enrichment," presented at 7th Annual Western Regional Solid Waste Symposium (April 7-8, 1975).

(316) Hyndshaw, A.Y., "Activated Carbon to Remove Organic Contaminants from Water," *JAWWA*, 64(5):309-311 (May 1972).

(317) *Identification of Organic Compounds in Effluents from Industrial Sources*, EPA-68-01-2926 (April 1975).

(318) Imhoff, K., Muller, W.J., and Thistlethwayte, D.K.B., *Disposal of Sewage and Other Waterborne Wastes*, Ann Arbor Science Publishers, Ann Arbor, Michigan (1974).

(319) Ingols, R.S., "Chlorination of Water—Potable, Possibly: Wastewater, No!" *Water and Sewage Works*, 122(2):82-83 (February 1975).

(320) *Interaction of Heavy Metals and Biological Sewage Treatment Processes*, U.S. Public Health Service, Cincinnati, Ohio (May 1965).

(321) Isensee, A.R. and Jones, G.E., "Distribution of 2,3,7,8-Tetrachlorodibenzo-p-dioxin (TCDD) in Aquatic Model Ecosystem," *Environmental Science and Technology*, 9:688-672 (July 1975).

(322) Ishizaki, C. and Cookson, J.J., Jr., "Influence of Surface Oxides on Adsorption and Catalysis with Activated Carbon," in *Chemistry of Water Supply, Treatment, and Distribution*, J. Rubin, ed., Ann Arbor Science Publishers, Ann Arbor, Michigan, pp 201-231 (1975).

(323) Jamieson, W., "*Candida albicans* as an Indicator of Pollution in Estuarine Water," PhD Thesis, New York University (1974).

(324) Jebens, H.J. and Boyle, W.C., "Enhanced Phosphorus Removal in Trickling Filters," *Journal of the Sanitary Engineering Division, ASCE*, 98(SA3):547-660 (June 1972).

(325) Jenkins, S.R., Engeset, J., and Hasfurther, V.R., "Model Sand Filters for the Removal of Colloidal Manganese Oxides Using Selected Cations as Filter Aids," in *Chemistry of Water Supply, Treatment, and Distribution*, A.J. Rubin, ed., Ann Arbor Science Publishers, Ann Arbor, Michigan, pp 181-199 (1975).

(326) Jenne, E.A. and Luoma, S.N., *Forms of Trace Elements in Soils, Sediments, and Associated Waters: An Overview of Their Determination and Biological Availability*, U.S. Geological Survey, Menlo Park, CA (1975).

(327) Jeris, J.S. and Owens, R.W., "Pilot-Scale High-Rate Biological Denitrification," *JWPCF*, 47(8):2043-2057 (August 1975).

(328) Jeris, J.S., Beer, C., and Mueller, J.A., "High-Rate Biological Denitrification Using a Granular Fluidized Bed," *JWPCF*, 46(9):2118-2128 (September 1974).

(329) Jernelov, A. and Jensen, S., "Biological Methylation of Mercury in Aquatic Organisms," *Nature*, 223:753-754 (August 1969).

(330) Jewell, W.J. and Cummings, R.J., "Denitrification of Concentrated Nitrate Wastewaters," *JWPCF*, 45(9):2281-2291 (September 1975).

(331) Johnson, E.L., Beeghly, J.H., and Wukasch, R.F., "Phosphorus Removal with Iron and Polyelectrolytes," *Public Works*, 100:66-68, 142 (November 1969).

(332) Johnson, J.D., *Disinfection: Water and Wastewater*, Ann Arbor Science Publishers, Ann Arbor, Michigan (1975).

(333) Johnson, J.E., "The Public Health Implications of Widespread Use of the Phenoxy Herbicides and Picloram," *Bio-Science*, 21(17):899-905 (September 1971).

(334) Jolley, R.L., "Chlorine-Containing Organic Constituents in Chlorinated Effluents," *JWPCF*, 47(3):601-618 (March 1975).

(335) Jordan, T.A., Ghosh, M.M., and Boyd, R.H., Jr., "Physico-Chemical Aspects of Deep-Bed Filtration," *JWPCF*, 46(12):2745-2754 (December 1974).

(336) Kalinske, A.A., "Enhancement of Biological Oxidation of Organic Wastes Using Activated Carbon in Microbial Suspensions," *Water and Sewage Works*, 119(6):62-64 (June 1972).

(337) Kampelmacher, E.H. and van Noorle Jansen, L.M., "Occurrence of Salmonella in Oxidation Ditches," *JWPCF*, 45(2):348-352 (February 1973).

(338) Kampelmacher, E.H. and van Noorle Jansen, L.M., "Reduction of Bacteria in Sludge Treatment," *JWPCF*, 44(2):309-313 (February 1972).

(339) Kampelmacher, E.H. and van Noorle Jansen, L.M., "Salmonella—Its Presence in and Removal from a Wastewater System," *JWPCF*, 42(12):2069-2073 (December 1970).

(340) Kanisawa, M. and Schroeder, H.A., "Life Term Studies on the Effects of Arsenic, Germanium, Tin, and Vanadium on Spontaneous Tumors in Mice," *Cancer Research*, 27:1192-1195 (July 1967).

(341) Kapikian, A.Z., et al, "Visualization by Immune Electron Microscopy of a 27-nm Particle Associated with Acute Infectious Nonbacterial Gastroenteritis," *Journal of Virology*, 10:1075-1081 (1972).

(342) Kardos, L.T., et al, *Renovation of Secondary Effluent for Reuse as a Water Resource*, EPA-660/2-74-016 (February 1974).

(343) Katzenelson, E., Kletter, B., and Shuval, H.I., "Inactivation Kinetics of Viruses and Bacteria in Water by Use of Ozone," *JAWWA*, 66:725-729 (December 1974).

(344) Katzenelson, E., et al, "Inactivation of Viruses and Bacteria by Ozone," in *Chemistry of Water Supply, Treatment, and Distribution*, A.J. Rubin, ed., Ann Arbor Science Publishers, Ann Arbor, Michigan, pp 409-421 (1975).

(345) Keeney, D.R., Lee, K.W., and Walsh, L.M., "Guidelines for the Application of Wastewater Sludge to Agricultural Land in Wisconsin," Technical Bulletin No. 88, Dept. of Natural Resources, Madison, Wisconsin (1975).

(346) Kenard, R.P. and Valentine, R.S., "Rapid Determination of the Presence of Enteric Bacteria in Water," *Applied Microbiology*, 27(3):484-487 (1974).

(347) Kenline, P.A. and Scarpino, P.V., "Bacterial Air Pollution from Sewage Treatment Plants," *American Industrial Hygiene Association Journals*, 33:346-352 (May 1972).

(348) Kerfoot, W.B. and Ketchum, B.T., *Cape Cod Wastewater Renovation and Retrieval System, a Study of Water Treatment and Conservation*, Woods Hole Oceanographic Institute (February 1974).

(349) Ketchum, L.H., Jr. and Weber, W.J., Jr., "Coagulation of Stormwaters and Low Alkalinity Wastewaters," *JWPCF*, 46(1):53-62 (January 1974).

(350) King, P.H., et al, "Distribution of Pesticides in Surface Waters," *JAWWA*, 61(9):483-486 (September 1969).

(351) Kinman, R.N., "Ozone in Water Disinfection," in *Ozone in Water and Wastewater Treatment*, Ann Arbor Science Publishers, Ann Arbor, Michigan, pp 123-143 (1973).

(352) Kinoshita, S. and Sunada, T., "On the Treatment of Polychlorinated Biphenyl in Water by Ionizing Radiation," in *Advances in Wastewater Research*, Pergamon Press, New York, C/12/26/1-6 (1972).

(353) Kirk, B.S., McNabney, R., and Wynn, C.S., "Pilot Plant Studies of Tertiary Wastewater Treatment with Ozone," in *Ozone in Water and Wastewater Treatment*, Ann Arbor Science Publishers, Ann Arbor, Michigan, pp 61-82 (1972).

(354) Kirkham, M.B. and Dotson, G.K., "Growth of Barley Irrigated with Wastewater Sludge Containing Phosphate Precipitants," *Proceedings of the National Conference on Municipal Sludge Management*, pp 97-106 (June 11-13, 1974).

(355) Klein, L.A., et al, "Sources of Metal in New York City Wastewater," *Metal Finishing*, 72:34-35 (July 1974).

(356) Klein, S.A., "NTA Removal in Septic Tank and Oxidation Pond Systems," *JWPCF*, 46(1):78-88 (January 1974).

(357) Klock, J.W., "Survival of Coliform Bacteria in Wastewater Treatment Lagoons," *JWPCF*, 43(10):2071-2083 (October 1971).

(358) Knittel, M.D., "Occurrence of *Klebsiella pneumoniae* in Surface Waters," *Applied Microbiology*, 29(5):595-597 (May 1975).

(359) Koerts, K. "Selective Removal of Mercury, Lead, Zinc, Copper, and Silver," in *Proceedings of the Second National Conference on Complete Water Reuse*, American Institute of Chemical Engineers, New York, pp 260-262 (1975).

(360) Kokoropoulos, P., "Designing Post-Chlorination by Chemical Reactor Approach," *JWPCF*, 45(10):2155-2165 (October 1973).

(361) Kokoropoulos, P. and Manos, G.P., "Kinetics as Design Criteria for Post-Chlorination," *Journal of the Environmental Engineering Division, ASCE*, 99(EE1):73-88 (February 1973).

(362) Koon, J.H. and Kaufman, W.J., "Ammonia Removal from Municipal Wastewaters by Ion Exchange," *JWPCF*, 47(3):448-465 (March 1975).

(363) Kopp, J.F., "The Occurrence of Trace Elements in Water," *Proceedings of the Third Annual Conference on Trace Substances in Environmental Health*, University of Missouri, Columbia, D.D. Hemphill, ed., pp 59-73 (1969).

(364) Kott, Y., et al, "Bacteriophages as Viral Pollution Indicators," *Water Research*, 8(3): 165-171 (1974).

(365) Kruse, C.W., Oliveri, V.P., and Kawata, K., "The Enhancement of Viral Inactivation of Halogens," *Proceedings Thirteenth Quality Conference; Virus and Water Quality: Occurrence and Control, University of Illinois*, pp 197-209 (February 1971).

(366) Kuiper, D. and Wechsler, R., "Domestic Wastewater Reuse Aspects of the Treatment System," *Water Research*, 9:655-657 (1975).

(367) Labadie, J.W., *Optimization Technique for Minimization of Combined Sewer Overflow*, NTIS/PB-234 331/7WP (June 1973).

(368) Lager, J.A. and Smith, W.G., *Urban Stormwater Management and Technology: An Assessment*, EPA-670/2-74-040 (December 1974).

(369) Lance, J.C., Gerba, C.P., and Melnick, J.L., "Virus Movement in Soil Columns Flooded with Secondary Sewage Effluent," *Applied and Environmental Microbiology*, 32(4):520-526 (October 1976).

(370) Lanouette, K.H., "Removing Heavy Metals from Wastewater," *Environmental Science and Technology*, 6(6):518-522 (June 1972).

(371) Larson, T.J. and Argo, D.G., "Large-Scale Water Reclamation by Reverse Osmosis," presented at the First Desalination Conference of the American Continent, Mexico City (October 24-29, 1976).

(372) Lawrence, A.W., *Kinetics of Microbiologically Mediated Transformations of Heavy Metals in Aquatic Environments*, NTIS/PB-239 148 (June 1974).

(373) Lawrence, J. and Tosine, H.M., "Adsorption of Polychlorinated Biphenyls from Aqueous Solutions and Sewage," *Environmental Science and Technology*, 10(4): 381-383 (April 1976).

(374) Lawrence, J. and Zimmerman, H.W., "Potable Water Treatment for Some Asbestiform Minerals: Optimization and Turbidity Data," *Water Research*, 10:195-198 (1976).

(375) Lawrence, J., et al, "Removal of Asbestos Fibers from Potable Water by Coagulation and Filtration," *Water Research*, 9:397-400 (1975).

(376) Leary, R.D., *Two-Hundred MGD Activated Sludge Plant Removes Phosphorus by Pickle Liquor*, EPA-670/2-73-050 (September 1973).

(377) Lee, J.A., et al, "Filtering Combined Sewer Overflows," *JWPCF*, 44(7):1317-1333 (July 1972).

(378) Lee, P.E., "Activated Carbon Removes Sulfide Odor," *Water and Sewage Works*, 121(9):116-117 (September 1974).

(379) LeGendre, G.R. and Runnels, D.D., "Removal of Dissolved Molybdenum from Wastewaters by Precipitates of Iron," *Environmental Science and Technology*, 9:744-749 (August 1975).

(380) Leigh, G.M., "Degradation of Selected Chlorinated Hydrocarbon Insecticides," *JWPCF*, 41(11):R450-R460 (November 1969).

(381) Leland, H.V., Bruce, W.N., and Shimp, N.F., "Chlorinated Hydrocarbon Insecticides in Sediments of Southern Lake Michigan," *Environmental Science and Technology*, 7(9):833-838 (September 1973).

(382) Leland, H.V., Shukla, S.S., and Shimp, N.F., "Factors Affecting Distribution of Lead and Other Trace Elements in Sediments of Southern Lake Michigan," in *Trace Metals and Metal-Organic Interactions in Natural Waters*, P.C. Singer, ed., Ann Arbor Science Publishers, Ann Arbor, Michigan, pp 89-129 (1974).

(383) Lennette, E.H., Spaulding, E.H., and Truant, J.P., *Manual of Clinical Microbiology*, 2nd Edition, American Society for Microbiology, Washington, DC (1974).

(384) Lerman, A. and Childs, C.W., "Metal-Organic Complexes in Natural Waters: Control of Distribution by Thermodynamic, Kinetic and Physical Factors," in *Trace Metals and Metal-Organic Interactions in Natural Waters*, Ann Arbor Science Publishers, Ann Arbor, Michigan, pp 201-235 (1974).

(385) Leshniowsky, W.O., et al, "Aldrin: Removal from Lake Water by Flocculent Bacteria," *Science*, 169(3949):993-995 (September 4, 1970).

(386) Levin, G.V. and Shapiro, J., "Metabolic Uptake of Phosphorus by Wastewater Organisms," *JWPCF*, 37(6):800-818 (June 1965).

(387) Lin, S.S. and Carlson, D.A., "Phosphorus Removal by the Addition of Aluminum(III) to the Activated Sludge Process," *JWPCF*, 47(7):1978-1986 (July 1975).

(388) Lindsay, W.L., "Inorganic Reactions of Sewage Wastes with Soils," in *Recycling Municipal Sludges and Effluents on Land; Proceedings of the Joint Conference, July 9-13, 1973*, pp 91-96.

(389) Lindstedt, K.D. and Bennett, E.R., *Evaluation of Treatment for Urban Wastewater Reuse*, EPA-R2-73-122 (July 1973).

(390) Lindstedt, K.D., Bennett, E.R., and Work, S.W., "Quality Considerations in Successive Water Use," *JWPCF*, 43(8):1681-1694 (August 1971).

(391) Lindstedt, K.D., Houck, C.P., and O'Connor, J.T., "Trace Element Removals in Advanced Wastewater Treatment Processes," *JWPCF*, 43(7):1507-1513 (July 1971).

(392) Lingle, J.W. and Hermann, E.R., "Mercury in Anaerobic Sludge Digestion," *JWPCF*, 47(3):466-471 (March 1975).

(393) Loehr, R.C. and deNavarra, C.T., Jr., "Grease Removal at a Municipal Treatment Facility," *JWPCF*, 41(5):R142-R154 (May 1969).

(394) Logsdon, G.S. and Symons, J.M., "Mercury Removal by Conventional Water-Treatment Techniques," *JAWWA*, 65(8):554-562 (August 1973).

(395) Logsdon, G.S. and Edgerley, E., Jr., "Sludge Dewatering by Freezing," *JAWWA*, 63(11):734-740 (November 1971).

(396) Logsdon, G.S., Sarg, T.S., and Symons, J.M., "Removal of Heavy Metals by Conventional Treatment," in *Proceedings, 16th Water Quality Conference, University of Illinois at Urbana-Champaign*, pp 111-133 (1974).

(397) Long, D.A. and Nesbitt, J.B., "Removal of Soluble Phosphorus in an Activated Sludge Plant," *JWPCF*, 47(1):170-184 (January 1975).

(398) Long, D.A., Nesbitt, J.R., and Kountz, R.R., *Soluble Phosphorus Removal in the Activated Sludge Process, Part I*, Water Quality Office, U.S. Environmental Protection Agency (August 1971).

(399) Long, W.N. and Bell, F.A., Jr., "Health Factors and Reused Waters," *JAWWA*, 64(4):220-225 (April 1972).

(400) Longley, E., et al, "Enhancement of Terminal Disinfection of a Wastewater Treatment System," in *Virus Survival by Water and Wastewater Systems*, Malina and Sagik, eds., Water Resources Symposium No. 7, pp 166-179 (1974).

(401) Lothrop, T.L. and Sproul, O.J., "High-Level Inactivation of Viruses in Wastewater by Chlorination," *JWPCF*, 41(4):567-575 (April 1969).

(402) Lowndes, M.R., "Ozone for Water and Effluent Treatment," *Chemistry and Industry*, 34:951-956 (August 21, 1971).

(403) Ludzack, F.J. and Noran, D.K., "Tolerance of High Salinities by Conventional Wastewater Treatment Processes," *JWPCF*, 37(10):1404-1416 (October 1965).

(404) Lund, E., "Inactivation of Viruses," *Progress in Water Technology*, 3:95-97 (1973).

(405) Lutin, P.A. "Removal of Organic Nitrites from Wastewater Systems," *JWPCF*, 42(9): 1632-1642 (September 1970).

(406) Mackenthern, K.M., *Nitrogen and Phosphorus in Water: An Annotated Selected Bibliography of Their Biological Effects*, U.S. Public Health Service, Division of Water Supply and Pollution Control (1965).

(407) Mackenthern, K.M. and Keup, L.E., "Biological Problems Encountered in Water Supplies," *JAWWA*, 62(8):520-526 (August 1970).

(408) MacKenzie, R.D., et al, "Chronic Toxicity Studies. II: Hexavalent and Trivalent Chromium Administered in Drinking Water to Rats," *AMA Archives of Industrial Health*, 18:232-234 (1958).

(409) Majumdar, S.B., et al, "Inactivation of Poliovirus in Water by Ozonation," *JWPCF*, 45(12):2433-2443 (December 1973).

(410) Malaney, G.W., et al, "Resistance of Carcinogenic Organic Compounds to Oxidation by Activated Sludge," *JWPCF*, 39(12):2020-2029 (December 1967).

(411) Malina, J.F., et al, "Poliovirus Inactivation by Activated Sludge," in *Virus Survival in Water and Wastewater Systems*, Malina and Sagik, eds., Water Resources Symposium No. 7, pp 95-106 (1974).

(412) Malina, J.F., et al, "Poliovirus Inactivation by Activated Sludge," *JWPCF*, 47(8): 2178-2183 (August 1975).

(413) Malone, J.R. and Bailey, T.L., "Oxidation Ponds Remove Bacteria," *Water and Sewage Works*, 116(4):136-140 (April 1969).

(414) Mangravite, F.J., Jr., et al, "Removal of Humic Acid by Coagulation and Microflotation," *JAWWA*, 67(2):88-94 (February 1975).

(415) Manske, D.D. and Corneliussen, P.E., "Pesticide Residues in Total Diet Samples (VII)," *Pesticides Monitoring Journal*, 8(2):110-124 (September 1974).

(416) Manwaring, J.F., "Removal of Viruses by Coagulation and Flocculation," *JAWWA*, 63(5):298-300 (May 1971).

(417) Mara, D.D., "Fecal Bacterial Kinetics in Stabilization Ponds," *Journal of the Environmental Engineering Division, ASCE*, 100(EE5):1191-1192 (October 1974).

(418) Marais, G.V.R., "Faecal Bacterial Kinetics in Stabilization Ponds," *Journal of the Environmental Engineering Division, ASCE*, 100(EE1):119-139 (February 1974).

(419) Maruyama, T., Hannah, S.A., and Cohen, J.M., "Metal Removal by Physical and Chemical Treatment Processes," *JWPCF*, 47:962-975 (May 1973).

(420) Marx, J.L., "Drinking Water: Another Source of Carcinogens," *Science*, 86:809-811 (November 1974).

(421) Matsumura, F., Gotoh, Y., and Boush, G.M., "Factors Influencing Translocation and Transformation of Mercury in River Sediment," *Bulletin of Environmental Contamination and Toxicology*, 8(5):267-272 (November 1972).

(422) Mattson, J.S. and Kennedy, F.W., "Evaluation Criteria for Granular Activated Carbons," *JWPCF*, 43(11):2210-2217 (November 1971).

(423) Maxwell, K.E., *Environment of Life*, Dickenson Publishing Company, Encino, CA (1976).

(424) Mayer, B.W. and Schlackman, N., "Organo-Phosphates—A Pediatric Hazard," *American Family Physician*, 11(5):121-124 (May 1975).

(425) Mayrose, D.F., "Heat Treatment and Incineration," *Proceedings of the National Conference on Municipal Sludge Management*, pp 87-91 (June 11-13, 1974).

(426) McAchran, G.E. and Hogue, R.D., "Phosphate Removal from Municipal Sewage," *Water and Sewage Works*, 118(2):36-39 (February 1971).

(427) McCarthy, J.J. and Smith, C.H., "A Review of Ozone and Its Application to Domestic Wastewater Treatment," *JAWWA*, 66:718-725 (December 1974).

(428) McCarty, P.L., "Biological Processes for Nitrogen Removal—Theory and Application," *Proceedings, Twelfth Sanitary Engineering Conference; Nitrate and Water Supply: Source and Control, University of Illinois*, pp 136-152 (February 1970).

(429) McClanahan, M.A., "Recycle—What Disinfectant for Safe Water Then?" in Johnson, J.D., *Disinfection—Water and Wastewater*, Ann Arbor Science Publishers, Ann Arbor, Michigan, pp 49-66 (1975).

(430) McDermott, G.N., et al, "Effects of Copper on Aerobic Biological Sewage Treatment," *JWPCF*, 35(2):227-241 (February 1963).

(431) McDermott, G.N., et al, "Nickel in Relation to Activated Sludge and Anaerobic Digestion Process," *JWPCF*, 37(2):163-177 (February 1965).

(432) McGarry, M.G., "Algal Flocculation with Aluminum Sulfate and Polyelectrolytes," *JWPCF*, 42(5):R191-R201 (May 1970).

(433) McGregor, W.C. and Finn, R.K., "Factors Affecting the Flocculation of Bacteria by Chemical Additives," *Biotechnology and Bioengineering*, 11(2):127-138 (March 1969).

(434) McGuire, J.H., Alford, A.L., and Carter, M.H., *Organic Pollutant Identification Utilizing Mass Spectrometry*, EPA-R2-73-234 (July 1973).

(435) McIndoe, R.W., "Diatomaceous Earth Filtration for Water Supplies/2," *Water and Wastes Engineering*, 6(11):48-52 (November 1969).

(436) McKee, J.E. and Wolf, H.W., *Water Quality Criteria*, 2nd Edition, California State Water Quality Board (1963).

(437) McKee, J.E., Brokaw, C.H., and McLaughlin, R.T., "Chemical and Colicidal Effects of Halogens in Sewage," *JWPCF*, 32(8):795-819 (August 1960).

(438) McKendrick, J., Bates, G.R., and Swart, E.R., "The Physico-Chemical Treatment of Crude Sewage," *Water Pollution Control*, 74(2):155-159 (1975).

(439) McLean, D.M, Brown, J.R., and Laak, R., "Virus Dispersal by Water," *JAWWA*, 58(7):920-928 (July 1966).

(440) McLellon, M., Kunath, T.M., and Chao, C., "Coagulation of Colloidal- and Solution-Phase Impurities in Trickling Filter Effluents," *JWPCF*, 44(1):77-91 (January 1972)

(441) McMichael, F.C. and McKee, J.E., *Wastewater Reclamation at Whittier Narrows, California*, California Institute of Technology (September 30, 1965).

(442) Medlar, S., "Operating Experiences with Activated Granular Carbon," *Water and Sewage Works*, 122(2):70-73 (February 1975).

(443) Mennell, M., et al, "Treatment of Primary Effluent by Lime Precipitation and Dissolved Air Flotation," *JWPCF*, 46(11):2472-2485 (November 1974).

(444) Mercado-Burgos, N., Hoehn, R.C., and Holliman, R.B., "Effect of Halogens and Ozone on Schistosoma Ova," *JWPCF*, 47(10):2411-2419 (October 1974).

(445) Mercer, B.W., et al, "Ammonia Removal from Secondary Effluents by Selective Ion Exchange," *JWPCF*, 42(2):R95-R107 (February 1970).

(446) Merrell, J.C. and Katko, A., "Reclaimed Wastewater for Santee Recreational Lakes," *JWPCF*, 38(8):1310-1318 (August 1966).

(447) Merrell, J.C. and Ward, P.C., "Virus Control at the Santee, California Project," *JAWWA*, 61(2):145-153 (February 1968).

(448) Merson, M.H. and Barker, W.H., Jr., "Outbreaks of Waterborne Disease in the United States, 1971-1972," *Journal of Infectious Diseases*, 129(5):614-616 (May 1974).

(449) Merten, U. and Bray, D.T., "Reverse Osmosis for Water Reclamation," *Advances in Water Pollution Research*, 1966(3):315-331.

(450) Metzler, D.F., et al, "Emergency Use of Reclaimed Water for Potable Supply at Chanute, Kansas," *JAWWA*, 50(8):1021-1057 (August 1958).

(451) Meyer, W.T., "Epidemic Giardiasis: A Continued Elusive Entity," *Rocky Mountain Medical Journal*, 70:48-49 (October 1973).

(452) Michelsen, D.L., "The Removal of Soluble Mercury from Wastewater by Complexing Techniques," NTIS/PB-232 256/8WP (1973).

(453) Mitchell, F.K., "Comparison of Primary and Secondary Treatment," *Southern California Coastal Water Research Project Annual Report*, El Segundo, CA, pp 163-165 (June 30, 1974).

(454) Monroe, D.W. and Phillips, D.C., "Chlorine Disinfection in Final Settling Basins," *Journal of the Sanitary Engineering Division, ASCE*, 98(SA2):287-297 (April 1972).

(455) Montalvo, J.G., Jr. and Lee, C.G., "Analytical Notes—Removal of Organics from Water: Evaluating Activated Carbon," *JAWWA*, 68(4):211-215 (April 1976).

(456) Moore, W.A., et al, "Effects of Chromium on the Activated Sludge Process," *JWPCF*, 33(1):54-72 (January 1961).

(457) *Morbidity and Mortality Weekly Report*, U.S. Center for Disease Control, HEW, 23(34) (August 24, 1974).

(458) *Morbidity and Mortality Weekly Report*, U.S. Center for Disease Control, HEW, 24(28) (July 12,1975).

(459) *Morbidity and Mortality Weekly Report*, U.S. Center for Disease Control, HEW, 24(29) (July 19, 1975).

(460) *Morbidity and Mortality Weekly Report*, U.S. Center for Disease Control, HEW, 24(43) (October 1975).

(461) Morel, F., McDuff, R.E., and Morgan, J.J., "Interactions and Chemostasis in Aquatic Chemical Systems: Role of pH, pE, Solubility, and Complexation," in *Trace Metals and Metal-Organic Interactions in Natural Waters*, P.C. Singer, ed., Ann Arbor Science Publishers, Ann Arbor, Michigan, pp 157-200 (1974).

(462) Morgan, J.J., "Physical-Chemical Forms of Chromium in Sewers, Treatment Works, and Coastal Water Environments," (personal communication) (1975).

(463) Morris, J.C., "Chlorination and Disinfection—State of the Art," *JAWWA*, 63(12): 769-774 (December 1971).

(464) Morris, J.C., *Formation of Halogenated Organics by Chlorination of Water Supplies (A Review)*, EPA-600/1-75-002 (March 1975).

(465) Morris, J.C., "The Role of Ozone in Water Treatment," in *Proceedings, 96th Annual Conference American Water Works Association*, 29-6 (June 20-25, 1976).

(466) Morris, R.L., Johnson, L.G., and Ebert, D.W., "Pesticides and Heavy Metals in the Aquatic Environment," *Health Laboratory Science*, 9:145-151 (April 1972).

(467) Morton, S.D. and Sawyer, E.W., "Clay Minerals Remove Organics, Viruses and Heavy Metals from Water," *Water and Sewage Works*, Reference Issue 116-120 (April 30, 1976).

(468) Mosley, J.W., "Transmission of Viral Diseases by Drinking Water," in *Transmission of Viruses by the Water Route*, G. Berg, ed., Wiley, New York, pp 5-23 (1965).

(469) Murphy, K.L., "Gamma Radiation as an Effective Disinfectant," *Water and Pollution Control*, 112(4):24-28 (April 1974).

(470) Muzzarelli, R.A., "Selective Collection of Trace Metal Ions by Precipitation of Chitosan, and New Derivatives of Chitosan," *Analytica Chimica Acta*, 54:133-142 (1971).

(471) Mytelka, A.I., et al, "Heavy Metals in Wastewater and Treatment Plant Effluents," *JWPCF*, 45(9):1859-1864 (September 1973).

(472) Napolitano, P.J. and Rowe, D.R., "Microbial Content of Air Near Sewage Treatment Plants," *Water and Sewage Works*, 113(12):480-483 (December 1966).

(473) *National Emissions Inventory of Sources and Emissions of Chromium*, EPA-450/3-74-012 (May 1973).

(474) Nebel, C., et al, "Ozone Disinfection of Industrial-Municipal Secondary Effluents," *JWPCF*, 45(12):2493-2507 (December 1973).

(475) Nelson, D.W., Owens, L.B., and Terry, R.E., *Denitrification as a Pathway for Nitrate Removal in Aquatic Systems*, NTIS/PB-231 305/4WP (December 1973).

(476) Neufeld, R.D. and Hermann, E.R., "Heavy Metal Removal by Acclimated Activated Sludge," *JWPCF*, 47(2):310-329 (February 1975).

(477) "New Process Detoxifies Cyanide Wastes," *Environmental Science and Technology*, 5(6):496-497 (June 1971).

(478) Newton, C.D., Shephard, W.W., and Coleman, M.S., "Street Runoff as a Source of Lead Pollution," *JWPCF*, 46(5):999-1000 (May 1974).

(479) Nickerson, G.L., et al, "Chemical Addition to Trickling Filter Plants," *JWPCF*, 46(1):133-147 (January 1974).

(480) Nilsson, R., "Removal of Metals by Chemical Treatment of Municipal Wastewater," *Water Research*, 5:51-60 (1971).

(481) Nisbet, I.C.T., *Criteria Document for PCB's*, EPA-440/9-76-021 (July 1976).

(482) Nisbet, I.C.T. and Sarofim, A.F., "Rates and Routes of Transport of PCB's in the Environment," *Environmental Health Perspectives*, 1:21-38 (April 1972).

(483) *Nitrification and Denitrification Facilities: Wastewater Treatment*, EPA Technology Transfer (August 1973).

(484) *Nitrogenous Compounds in the Environment*, EPA-5AB-73-001 (December 1973).

(485) Noland, R.F. and Birkbeck, R., "Two-Stage Biological Process Provides High Degree of Treatment," 1973 Water Pollution Control Conference, Cleveland, Ohio (October 2, 1973).

(486) Nomura, M.M. and Young, R.H.F., *Fate of Heavy Metals in the Sewage Treatment Process*, Water Resources Research Center Technical Report No. 82, University of Hawaii, Honolulu (September 1974).

(487) Nupen, E.M., "Virus Studies on the Windhoek Wastewater Reclamation Plant (South-West Africa)," *Water Research*, 4:661-672 (1970).

(488) Nupen, E.M., Bateman, B.W., and McKenny, N.C., "The Reduction of Virus by the Various Unit Processes Used in the Reclamation of Sewage to Potable Waters," in *Virus Survival in Water and Wastewater Systems*, Malina and Sagik, eds., Water Resources Symposium No. 7, pp 107-114 (1974).

(489) Ockershausen, R.W., " Alum vs Phosphates: It's No Contest," *Water and Wastes Engineering*, 11:54-61 (November 1974).

(490) Ockershausen, R.W., "In-Plant Usage Works and Works," *Environmental Science and Technology*, 865:420-423 (May 1974).

(491) O'Connor, J.T., "Removal of Trace Inorganic Constituents by Conventional Water Treatment Processes," in *Proceedings, 16th Water Quality Conference, University of Illinois at Urbana-Champaign*, pp 99-110 (1974).

(492) O'Farrell, T.P., et al, "Nitrogen Removal by Ammonia Stripping," *JWPCF*, 44(8): 1527-1535 (August 1972).

(493) Oliver, B.G., et al, "Chloride and Lead in Urban Snow," *JWPCF*, 46(4):766-771 (April 1974).

(494) Olson, L.L. and Binning, C.D., "Interactions of Aqueous Chlorine with Activated Carbon," in *Chemistry of Water Supply, Treatment, and Distribution*, A.J. Rubin, ed., Ann Arbor Science Publishers, Ann Arbor, Michigan pp 253-295 (1975).

(495) O'Shaughnessy, J.C., et al, *Soluble Phosphorus Removal in the Activated Sludge Process. Part II: Sludge Digestion Study*, Water Quality Office, EPA (October 1971).

(496) Ottoboni, A. and Greenberg, A.E., "Toxicological Aspects of Wastewater Reclamation—A Preliminary Report," *JWPCF*, 42(4):493-499 (April 1970).

(497) Owens, L.B. and Nelson, D.W., *Relationship of Various Indices of Water Quality to Denitrification in Surface Waters*, NTIS/PB-237 702/6WP (1972).

(498) Oza, P.P. and Chaudhuri, M., "Removal of Viruses from Water by Sorption on Coal," *Water Research*, 9:707-712 (1975).

(499) Palin, A.T., "Chemistry of Modern Chlorination," *Water Services*, 78:7-12, 53-55 (January 1974).

(500) Parhad, N.M. and Rao, N.U., "Effect of pH on Survival of *Escherichia coli*," *JWPCF*, 46(5):980-986 (May 1974).

(501) Paris, D.F., et al, *Microbial Degradation and Accumulation of Pesticides in Aquatic Systems*, EPA-660/3-75-007 (March 1975).

(502) Park, J.W., *An Evaluation of Three Combined Sewer Overflow Treatment Alternatives*, EPA-670/2-74-079 (December 1974).

(503) Parker, C.D., "Microbiological Aspects of Lagoon Treatment," *JWPCF*, 34(2):149-161 (February 1962).

(504) Parkhurst, J.D., *Virus Study: Supplement to the Project Report for Facilities Planning Study*, Los Angeles County Sanitation District (November 1974).

(505) Parkhurst, J.D., et al, "Demineralization of Wastewater by Ion Exchange," *Advances in Water Pollution Research*, 1972(1):I-20/1-15.

(506) Patterson, J.W., *Wastewater Treatment Technology*, Ann Arbor Science Publishers, Ann Arbor, Michigan (1975).

(507) Patterson, J.W., Shimada, P., and Haas, C.N., "Heavy Metals Transport Through Municipal Sewage Treatment Plants," Second National Conference on Complete Water Reuse, Chicago (1975).

(508) Pavoni, J.L. and Tittlebaum, M.E., "Virus Inactivation in Secondary Wastewater Treatment Plant Effluent Using Ozone," in *Virus Survival in Water and Wastewater Systems*, Malina & Sagik, eds., Water Resources Symposium No. 7, pp 180-198 (1974).

(509) Pavoni, J.L., et al, "Virus Removal from Wastewater Using Ozone," *Water and Sewage Works*, 119(12):59-67 (December 1972).

(510) Pearson, F. and Metcalf, T.G., *The Use of Magnetic Iron Oxide for Recovery of Virus from Water*, NTIS/PB-234 626/OWP (1974).

(511) Pennypacker, S.P., Sopper, W.E., and Kardos, L.F., "Renovation of Wastewater Effluent by Irrigation of Forest Land," *JWPCF*, 39(2):285-296 (February 1967).

(512) Perhac, R.M., "Distribution of Cd, Co, Cu, Fe, Mn, Ni, Pb and Zn in Dissolved and Particulate Solids from Two Streams in Tennessee," *Journal of Hydrology*, 15:177-186 (1972).

(513) Perry, R., *Mercury Recovery from Contaminated Wastewater and Sludges*, EPA-660/2-74-086 (December 1974).

(514) Pfeiffer, K.R., "The Homestead Typhoid Outbreak," *JAWWA*, 65(12):803-805 (December 1973).

(515) Phillips, J.D. and Shell, G.L., Pilot Plant Studies of Effluent Reclamation," *Water and Wastes Engineering*, 6(11):38-41 (November 1969).

(516) Phillips, W.J., II, "The Direct Reuse of Reclaimed Wastewater: Pros, Cons, and Alternatives," *JAWWA*, 66(4):231-237 (April 1974).

(517) *Physical-Chemical Nitrogen Removal: Wastewater Treatment*, EPA Technology Transfer (July 1974).

(518) *Physical-Chemical Wastewater Treatment Plant Design*, EPA Technology Transfer (August 1973).

(519) Pillay, K.K.S., et al, "Mercury Pollution of Lake Erie Ecosphere," *Environmental Research*, 5:172-181 (May 1972).

(520) Pitt, W.W., Jolley, R.L., and Katz, S., *Automated Analysis of Individual Refractory Organics in Polluted Water*, EPA/660-2-74-076 (August 1974).

(521) Pittwell, L.R., "Metals Coordinated by Ligands Normally Found in Natural Waters," *Journal of Hydrology*, 21:301-304 (1974).

(522) Pokornts, Y. and Kulikova, K., "Effects of Pesticides on Reservoir Water," *Pesticide Abstracts*, 74-1874 (1974).

(523) Poon, C.P.C., "Studies on the Instantaneous Death of Airborne *Escherichia coli*," *American Journal of Epidemiology*, 84(1):1-19 (July 1966).

(524) Popalisky, J.R. and Pogge, F.W., "Detecting and Treating Organic Taste & Order (!) Compounds in the Missouri River," *JAWWA*, 64(8):505-511 (August 1972).

(525) Posselt, H.S. and Weber, W.J., Jr., "Removal of Cadmium from Waters and Wastes by Sorption on Hydrous Metal Oxides for Water Treatment," in *Chemistry of Water Supply, Treatment, and Distribution*, A.J. Rubin, ed., Ann Arbor Science Publishers, Ann Arbor, Michigan, pp 89-108 (1975).

(526) Pound, C.E. and Crites, R.W., "Characteristics of Municipal Effluents," in *Recycling Municipal Sludges and Effluents on Land; Proceedings of the Joint Conference, July 9-13, 1973*, pp 49-61.

(527) Prakasam, T.B.S. and Loehr, R.C., "Microbial Nitrification and Denitrification in Concentrated Wastes," *Water Research*, 6:859-869 (July 1972).

(528) Prasad, D. and Jones, P.H., "Degradation or Organic Nitrogenous Compounds by Psychrophilic Bacteria," *JWPCF*, 46(7):1686-1691 (July 1974).

(529) *Preliminary Investigation of Effects on the Environment of Boron, Indium, Nickel, Selenium, Tin, Vanadium, and Their Compounds. Vol. IV: Selenium*, EPA-560/2-75-005D (August 1975).

(530) Premi, P.R. and Cornfield, A.H., "Incubation Study of Nitrogen Mineralization of Soil Treated with Dried Sewage Sludge," *Environmental Pollution*, 2(1):1-5 (July 1971).

(531) Pressley, T.A., Bishop, D.F., and Roan, S.G., "Ammonia-Nitrogen Removal by Breakpoint Chlorination," *Environmental Science and Technology*, 6(7):622-626 (July 1972).

(532) Preul, H.C., "Underground Movement of Nitrogen," *Advances in Water Pollution Research*, 1966(1):309-328.

(533) *Process Design Manual for Nitrogen Control*, EPA Technology Transfer (October 1975).

(534) Radding, S.B., et al, *Review of the Environmental Fate of Selected Chemicals*, EPA-560/5-75-001 (January 1975).

(535) Ragone, S.E., Vecchioli, J., and Ku, H.F.H., "Short-Term Effect of Injection of Tertiary Treated Sewage on Iron Concentration of Water in Magothy Aquifer, Bay Park, New York," in *Reprints of Paper Presented at the International Symposium on Underground Waste Management and Artificial Recharge*, J. Braustein, ed., G. Banta, Menasha, WI, 1:273-290 (1973).

(536) Rains, B.A., DePrimo, M.J., and Groseclose, T.L., *Odors Emitted from Raw and Digested Sewage Sludge*, EPA-670/2-73-098 (December 1973).

(537) Ralph Stone and Company, *Treatment Effectiveness for the Removal of Selected Contaminants from Drinking Water; Final Report*, Water Supply Division, EPA (March 1975).

(538) "Recycling Sludge and Sewage Effluent by Land Disposal," *Environmental Science and Technology*, 6(10):871-873 (October 1972).

(539) Reeves, T.G., "Nitrogen Removal: A Literature Review," *JWPCF*, 44(10):1895-1908 (October 1972).

(540) Reid, G.W., et al, "Effects of Metallic Ions on Biological Waste Treatment Processes," *Water and Sewage Works*, 115(7):320-325 (July 1968).

(541) "Research Foundation to Undertake Study on Organics Removal," *Watercare*, San Jose, CA (September 1975).

(542) Richardson, E.W., Stobbe, E.D., and Bernstein, B., "Ion Exchange Traps Chromates for Reuse," *Environmental Science and Technology*, 2(11):1006-1016.

(543) Rickert, D.A. and Hunter, J.V., "Effects of Aeration Time on Soluble Organics During Activated Sludge Treatment," *JWPCF*, 43(9):134-138 (January 1971).

(544) Rizzo, J.L. and Schade, R.E., "Secondary Treatment with Granular Activated Carbon," *Water and Sewage Works*, 116(8):307-312 (August 1969).

(545) Roan, S.G., Bishop, D.F., and Pressley, T.A., *Laboratory Ozonation of Municipal Wastewaters*, EPA-670/2-73-075 (September 1973).

(546) Robeck, G.G., et al, "Effectiveness of Water Treatment Processes in Pesticide Removal," *JAWWA*, 57(2):181-199 (February 1965).

(547) Robeck, G.G., Clarke, N.H., and Dostal, K.A., "Effectiveness of Water Treatment Processes in Virus Removal," *JAWWA*, 54(10):1275-1292 (October 1962).

(548) Robinson, C.N., Jr., "Polyelectrolytes as Primary Coagulants for Potable-Water Systems," *JAWWA*, 66(4):252-257 (April 1974).

(549) Roersma, R.E., Alsema, G.J., and Anthonissen, I.H., "Removal of Hexavalent Chromium by Activated Carbon," *Chemical Abstracts*, 83:65112w (1975).

(550) Rogers, C.J. and Landreth, R.L., *Degradation Mechanisms: Controlling the Bioaccumulation of Hazardous Materials*, EPA-670/2-75-005 (January 1975).

(551) Rohm and Haas, "Summary Bulletin: Amberlite Polymeric Adsorbents," Philadelphia, PA (February 1975).

(552) "The Role of Soils and Sediments in Reducing the Concentration of Heavy Metals, Fluorides, and Pesticides in Percolating Waste Discharges (Memorandum Report)," State of California Resources Agency, Department of Water Resources (June 1972).

(553) Romero, J.C., "The Movement of Bacteria and Viruses through Porous Media," *Groundwater*, 8(2):34-48 (March-April 1970).

(554) Rook, J.J., "Formation of Haloforms During Chlorination of Natural Waters," *Water Treatment and Examination*, 23:234 (1974).

(555) Rook, J.J., "Haloforms in Drinking Water," *JAWWA*, 68(3):168-172 (March 1976).

(556) Rosen, H.M., "Use of Ozone and Oxygen in Advanced Wastewater Treatment," *JWPCF*, 45(12):2521-2536 (December 1973).

(557) Rosen, H.M., Lowther, F.E., and Clark, R.G., "Economical Wastewater Disinfection with Ozone," in Johnson, J.D., *Disinfection—Water and Wastewater*, Ann Arbor Science Publishers, Ann Arbor, Michigan, pp 233-248 (1975).

(558) Routh, J.D., "DDT Residues in Salinas River Sediments," *Bulletin of Environmental Contamination and Toxicology*, 7(2/3):168-176 (February/March 1972).

(559) Rozell, R.B. and Swain, H.A., Jr., *Removal of Manganese from Mine Drainage by Ozone and Chlorine*, EPA-670/2-75-006 (March 1975).

(560) Rubenstein, S.H., et al, "Viruses in Metropolitan Waters: Concentration by Polyelectrolytes, Freeze Concentration, and Ultrafiltration," *JAWWA*, 65(3):200-202 (March 1973).

(561) Rubin, A.J. and Hanna, G.P., "Coagulation of Bacterium *Escherichia coli* by Aluminum Nitrate," *Environmental Science and Technology*, 2(5):358-362 (May 1968).

(562) Rudolfs, W., Folk, L.L., and Rogotzkie, R.A., "Contamination of Vegetables Grown in Polluted Soil. Part V: Helminthic Decontamination," *Sewage and Industrial Wastes*, 23:853-860 (1951).

(563) *Salmonella Surveillance*, U.S. Center for Disease Control, HEW, Report No. 122 (February 1975).

(564) Scarpino, P.V., et al, "Effectiveness of Hypochlorous Acid and Hypochlorite Ion in Destruction of Viruses and Bacteria," in *Chemistry of Water Supply, Treatment and Distribution*, A.J. Rubin, ed., Ann Arbor Science Publishers, Ann Arbor, Michigan, pp 359-368 (1975).

(565) Schaub, S.A., et al, *Land Application of Wastewater: The Fate of Viruses, Bacteria, and Heavy Metals at a Rapid Infiltration Site*, NTIS/AD-A011263 (May 1975).

(566) *Schistosomiasis Control: Report of a WHO Expert Committee*, Geneva (July 3-7, 1972).

(567) Schmid, L.A. and McKinney, R.E., "Phosphate Removal by a Lime-Biological Treatment Scheme," *JWPCF*, 41(7):1259-1276 (July 1969).

(568) Schmidt, C.J. and Clements, E.V., III, *Reuse of Municipal Wastewater for Groundwater Recharge*, EPA-68-03-2140 (1975).

(569) Schmidt, C.J., Kugelman, I., and Clements, E.V., III, "Municipal Wastewater Reuse in the U.S.," *JWPCF*, 47(9):2229-2245 (September 1975).

(570) Schwartz, H.G., Jr., "Adsorption of Selected Pesticides on Activated Carbon and Mineral Surfaces," *Environmental Science and Technology*, 1(4):332-337 (April 1967).

(571) Selleck, R.E., Bracewell, L.W., and Carter, R., *The Significance and Control of Wastewater Floatables in Coastal Waters*, EPA/660-3-74-016 (January 1974).

(572) Sepp, E., *Nitrogen Cycle in Groundwater*, Bureau of Sanitary Engineering, State of California (1970).

(573) Seppäläinen, A.M. and Häkkinen, "Electrophysiological Findings in Diphenyl Poisoning," *Journal of Neurology, Neurosurgery, and Psychiatry*, 38(3):248-252 (1975).

(574) Shane, M.S., Wilson, S.B., and Fries, C.R., "Virus-Host System for Use in the Study of Virus Removal," *JAWWA*, 75(9):1184-1186 (September 1967).

(575) Shelton, S.P. and Drewry, W.A., "Tests of Coagulants for the Reduction of Viruses, Turbidity, and Chemical Oxygen Demand," *JAWWA*, 65(10):627-635 (October 1973).

(576) Shen, Y.S., "Study of Arsenic Removal from Drinking Water," *JAWWA*, 65(8):543-548 (August 1973).

(577) Shen, Y.S. and Shen, C.S., "Relation Between Blackfoot Disease and the Pollution of Drinking Water by Arsenic in Taiwan," *JWPCF*, 36(3):281 (March 1964).

(578) Shields, C.P., "Reverse Osmosis for Municipal Water Supply," *Water and Sewage Works*, 119(1):61-70 (January 1972).

(579) *Shigella Surveillance*, U.S. Center for Disease Control, HEW (1974).

(580) *Shigella Surveillance Annual Summary*, U.S. Center for Disease Control, HEW, Report No. 38 (September 1976).

(581) Shimizu, Y., et al, *Further Studies of the Interaction of Chlorine and Organic Molecules in Water*, OWRR: B-057-RI, Office of Water Research and Technology, U.S. Department of the Interior.

(582) Shuckrow, A.J., et al, "Treatment of Raw and Combined Sewage," *Water and Sewage Works*, 118(4):104-111 (April 1971).

(583) Shuval, H.I., "Health Factors in the Reuse of Wastewater for Agricultural, Industrial, and Municipal Purposes," in *Problems in Community Wastes Management*, World Health Organization, pp 76-89 (1969).

(584) Shuval, H.I., et al, "Chlorination of Wastewater for Virus Control," *Munich Abstracts—Section II*, 38(3):343.

(585) Shuval, H.I., et al, "The Inactivation of Enteroviruses in Sewage by Chlorination," *Advances in Water Pollution Research*, 1966(2):37-51.

(586) Shuval, H.I., Katzenelson, E., and Butum, I., "Risk of Communicable Disease Infection Associated with Wastewater Irrigation in Agricultural Settlements," *Science*, 194:944-946 (November 26, 1976).

(587) Sierka, R.A., *Activated Carbon Treatment and Ozonation of MUST Hospital Composite and Individual Component Wastewaters and MUST Laundry Composite Wastewaters*, NTIS/AS-A008 347/7WR (May 1975).

(588) Sigworth, E.A. and Smith, S.B., "Adsorption of Inorganic Compounds by Activated Carbon," *JAWWA*, 64(6):386-391 (June 1972).

(589) Simpson, R.M., "The Separation of Organic Chemicals from Water," presented at the 3rd Symposium of the Institute of Advanced Sanitation Research, International (April 13, 1972).

(590) Singer, P.C., "Anaerobic Control of Phosphate by Ferrous Iron," *JWPCF*, 44(4): 663-669 (April 1972).

(591) Singer, P.C., *Trace Metals and Metal-Organic Interactions in Natural Waters*, Ann Arbor Science Publishers, Ann Arbor, Michigan (1974).

(592) Slanetz, L.W., et al, *Survival of Enteric Bacteria and Viruses in Oxidation Pond Systems*, University of New Hampshire (1972).

(593) Smith, J.M., Masse, A.N., and Miele, R.P., *Renovation of Municipal Wastewater by Reverse Osmosis. Water Pollution Control Research Series*, 17040-05/70 (May 1970).

(594) Smith, J.M. et al, "Nitrogen Removal from Municipal Wastewater by Columnar Denitrification," *Environmental Science and Technology*, 6(3):260-267 (March 1972).

(595) Smith, R.J., et al, "Relationships of Indicator and Pathogenic Bacteria in Stream Waters," *JWPCF*, 45(8):1736-1745 (August 1973).

(596) Snoeyink, V.L. and Markus, F.I., *Chlorine Residuals in Treated Effluents*, NTIS/PB-227-268 (August 1975).

(597) Snoeyink, V.L. and Markus, F.I., "Chlorine Residuals in Treated Effluents," *Water and Sewage Works*, 121(4):35-38 (April 1974).

(598) Snoeyink, V.L., et al, "Active Carbon: Dechlorination and the Adsorption of Organic Compounds," in *Chemistry of Water Supply, Treatment, and Distribution*, A.J. Rubin, ed., Ann Arbor Science Publishers, Ann Arbor, Michigan, pp 233-252 (1975).

(599) Snoeyink, V.L., Weber, W.J., and Mark, H.B., "Sorption of Phenol and Nitrophenol by Activated Carbon," *Environmental Science and Technology*, 8:918-926 (October 1969).

(600) Sobsey, M.D., "Enteric Viruses and Drinking-Water Supplies," *JAWWA*, 67(8):414-418 (August 1975).

(601) Sobsey, M.D., et al, "Virus Removal and Inactivation by Physical-Chemical Waste Treatment," *Journal of the Environmental Engineering Division, ASCE*, 99(EE3): 245-252 (June 1973).

(602) Sorber, C.A., Schaub, S.A., and Bausum, H.T., "An Assessment of a Potential Virus Hazard Associated with Spray Irrigation of Domestic Wastewaters," in *Virus Survival in Water and Wastewater Systems*, Malina and Sagik, eds., Water Resources Symposium No. 7, pp 241-352 (1974).

(603) Sorber, C.A., Bausum, H.T., and Schaub, S.A., "Bacterial Aerosols Created by Spray Irrigation of Wastewater," presented at the 1975 Sprinkler Irrigation Association Technical Conference, Atlanta, Georgia (February 1975).

(604) Sorber, C.A., Schaub, S.A., and Guter, K.M., *Problem Definition Study: Evaluation of Health and Hygiene Aspects of Land Disposal of Wastewater at Military Installations*, Army Medical Environmental Engineering Research Unit (August 1972).

(605) Spear, R.C., Jenkins, D.L., and Milby, T.H., "Pesticide Residues and Field Workers," *Environmental Science and Technology*, 9(4):308-313 (April 1975).

(606) Spody, B. and Adams, S.D., *Improved Activated Sludge Treatment with Carbon*, Deeds and Data (January 1976).

(607) Spohr, G. and Talts, A., "Phosphate Removal by pH Controlled Lime Dosage," *Public Works*, 101:63-66 (July 1966).

(608) Sproul, O.J., "Virus Inactivation by Water Treatment," *JAWWA*, 64(1):31-35 (January 1972).

(609) Sproul, O.J., et al, "Virus Removal by Adsorption in Wastewater Treatment Process," *Advances in Water Pollution Research*, 1969:541-554.

(610) Stander, G.J. and Funke, J.W., "Direct Cycle Water Reuse Provides Drinking Water Supply in South Africa," *Water and Wastes Engineering*, 6(5):66-67 (May 1969).

(611) Stander, G.J. and Van Vuuren, L.R.J., "The Reclamation of Potable Water from Wastewater," *JWPCF*, 41(3):355-365 (March 1969).

(612) Stanford, G.B. and Tuburan, R., "Morbidity Risk Factors from Spray Irrigation with Treated Wastewaters," in *Wastewater Use in the Production of Food and Fiber—Proceedings*, EPA-660/2-74-041, pp 56-64 (June 1974).

(613) Starkey, R.J., Jr., et al, *An Investigation of Ion Removal from Water and Wastewater*, EPA/660/3-74-022 (August 1973).

(614) Stasiuk, W.N., Jr., Hitling, L.J., and Shuster, W.W., "Nitrogen Removal by Catalyst-Aided Breakpoint Chlorination," *JWPCF*, 46(8):1974-1983 (August 1974).

(615) *"State of the Art" Review of Health Aspects of Wastewater Reclamation for Groundwater Recharge*, State of California Water Resources Control Board (November 1975).

(616) Stevens, A.A., et al, "Chlorination of Organics in Drinking Water," *JAWWA*, 68(11): 615-619 (November 1976).

(617) Stobbe, H., et al, "Fundamental Remarks on the Problem of Occupationally Caused Leukemias," *Pesticide Abstracts*, 75-0812 (1975).

(618) Stone, R. and Smallwood, H., *Intermedia Aspects of Air and Water Pollution Control*, EPA-660/5-73-003 (1973).

(619) Stoveken, J. and Sproston, T., *Ozone and Chlorine Degradation of Wastewater Pollutants*, NTIS/PB-238 365/1WP (June 1974).

(620) Stover, E.L. and Kincannon, D.F., "One- Versus Two-Stage Nitrification in the Activated Sludge Process," *JWPCF*, 48(4):645-651 (April 1976).

(621) Stringer, R. and Krusé, C.W., "Amoebic Cysticidal Properties of Halogens in Water," *Journal of the Sanitary Engineering Division, ASCE*, 97(SA6):801-811 (December 1971).

(622) Stukenberg, J.R., "Biological-Chemical Wastewater Treatment," *JWPCF*, 43(9):1791-1806 (September 1971).

(623) Stukenberg, J.R., "Physical-Chemical Wastewater Treatment Using a Coagulation-Adsorption Process," *JWPCF*, 47(2):338-353 (February 1975).

(624) Stumm, W. and Morgan, J.J., *Aquatic Chemistry: An Introduction Emphasizing Chemical Equilibria in Natural Waters*, Wiley-Interscience, New York (1970).

(625) Sturm, M. and Hatch, N.N., "The Sarasota Phosphate Removal Project," *Water and Sewage Works*, 121(3):39-40, 42-43, 59 (March 1974).

(626) Sunshine, I., *Handbook of Analytical Toxicology*, Chemical Rubber Company, Cleveland, Ohio (1969).

(627) Susag, R.H., "BOD Reduction by Chlorination," *JWPCF*, 40(11):R434-R444 (November 1968).

(628) Sutton, P.M., et al, "Efficacy of Biological Nitrification," Water Pollution Control Federation," 47th Annual Conference, Denver, Colorado (October 1974).

(629) Sutton, P.M., et al, "Low-Temperature Biological Denitrification of Wastewater," *JWPCF*, 47(1):122-134 (January 1975).

(630) Sutton, P.M., Murphy, K.L., and Jank, B.E., "Nitrogen Control: A Basis for Design with Activated Sludge Systems," Conference on Nitrogen as a Water Pollutant, Copenhagen, Denmark (August 1975).

(631) Swanson, C.L., et al, "Mercury Removal from Wastewater with Starch Xanthate-Cationic Polymer Complex," *Environmental Science and Technology*, 7:614-619 (July 1973).

(632) Symons, J.M., et al, "National Organics Reconnaissance Survey for Halogenated Organics," *JAWWA*, 47(11):634-648 (November 1975).

(633) Talbot, P. and Harris, R.H., *The Implications of Cancer-Causing Substances in Mississippi River Water*, Environmental Defense Fund, Washington, DC (November 1974).

(634) Tamura, O., et al, "Relationship Between Consumption of Pesticides and Chronological Changes in Myopia in School Children in Tokushima Prefecture," *Pesticides Abstracts*, 75-1893 (1975).

(635) Tank, N.H., *Relationship Between BOD Removal and LAS Detergent Removal*, NTIS/PB-232 997/7WP (May 1974).

(636) Tardiff, R.G. and Deinzer, M., "Toxicity of Organic Compounds in Drinking Water," *Proceedings of 15th Water Quality Conference, Champaign, Illinois*, pp 23-32 (February 1973).

(637) Taylor, F.B., "Viruses—What is Their Significance in Water Supplies?" *JAWWA*, 66(5):306-311 (May 1974).

(638) Tchobanoglous, G., "Filtration Techniques in Tertiary Treatment," *JWPCF*, 42(4): 604-623 (April 1970).

(639) Thayer, S.E. and Sproul, O.J., "Virus Inactivation in Water-Softening Precipitation Processes," *JAWWA*, 58(8):1063-1074 (August 1966).

(640) Thiem, L.T., "Removal of Mercury from Drinking Water Using Powdered Activated Carbon," in *Proceedings, 96th Annual American Water Works Conference*, pp 17-33 (June 20-25, 1976).

(641) Thiem, L.T., "Removal of Mercury from Drinking Water Using Powdered Activated Carbon," *Water and Sewage Works*, 123(8):71 (August 1976).

(642) Thimann, K.V., "Herbicides in Vietnam," *Science*, 185(4147):207 (July 19, 1974).

(643) Thorup, R.T., et al, "Virus Removal by Coagulation with Polyelectrolytes," *JAWWA*, 62(2):97-101 (February 1970).

(644) "Three Summary Tables Relating to Metals Removal," Dallas Water Utilities Water Reclamation Research Center, Dallas, Texas (September 1975).

(645) Tinsley, T. and Melnick, J.L., "Potential Ecological Hazards of Pesticide Viruses," *Intervirology*, 2(3):206-208 (1973/74).

(646) Tofflemire, T.J. and Brizner, G.P., "Deep-Well Injection of Wastewater," *JWPCF*, 43(7):1468-1479 (July 1971).

(647) Tofflemire, T.J., et al, "Activated Carbon Adsorption and Polishing of Strong Wastewater," *JWPCF*, 45(10):2166-2179 (October 1973).

(648) Tornabene, T.G. and Edwards, H.W., "Microbial Uptake of Lead," *Science*, 176: 1334-1335 (June 1972).

(649) Tossey, D., et al, "Tertiary Treatment by Flocculation and Filtration," *Journal of the Sanitary Engineering Division, ASCE*, 96(SA1):75-90 (February 1970).

(650) Tromp, S.W., "Possible Effects of Geophysical and Geochemical Factors on Development and Geographic Distribution of Cancer," *Schweizerische Zeitschrift fur Allgemeine Pathologie und Bakteriologie*, 18(5):929-939 (1955).

(651) Ulmgren, L., "Swedish Experiences in Chemical Treatment of Wastewater," *JWPCF*, 47(4):696-703 (April 1975).

(652) UOP Fluid Systems Division, *Reverse Osmosis*, San Diego, California (1977).

(653) *Upgrading Existing Wastewater Treatment Plants: Case Histories*, EPA Technology Transfer (August 1973).

(654) *Upgrading Lagoons*, EPA Technology Transfer (August 1973).

(655) Vacker, R., Connell, C.H., and Walls, W.N., "Phosphate Removal through Municipal Wastewater Treatment at San Antonio, Texas," *JWPCF*, 39(5):750-771 (May 1967).

(656) Vajdick, A.H., "Gamma Rays vs the *E. coli* Monster," *Water and Wastes Engineering*, 12:29-32 (July 1975).

(657) Vale, J.A. and Scott, G.W., "Organophosphorus Poisoning," *Guy's Hospital Reports*, 123(13):13-25 (1974).

(658) Van Bladel, R. and Moreale, A., "Adsorption of Fenuron and Monuron (Substantial Ureas) by Two Montmorillonite Clays," *Soil Science Proceedings*, 38:244-249 (March 1974).

(659) Varma, M.W., Christian, B.A., and McKinstry, D.W., "Inactivation of Sabin Oral Poliomyelitis Type I Virus," *JWPCF*, 46(5):987-992 (May 1974).

(660) Venosa, A.D., "Ozone as a Water and Wastewater Disinfectant: A Literature Review," in *Ozone in Water and Wastewater Treatment*, Ann Arbor Science Publishers, Ann Arbor, Michigan, pp 83-100 (1972).

(661) Venosa, A.D. and Chambers, C.W., "Bactericidal Effect of Various Combinations of Gamma Radiation and Chloramine on Aqueous Suspensions of *Escherichia coli*," *Applied Microbiology*, 25:735-744 (May 1973).

(662) Versteeg, J.P.J. and Jager, K.W., "Long-Term Occupational Exposure to the Insecticides Aldrin, Dieldrin, Endrin, and Telodrin," *British Journal of Industrial Medicine*, 30(2):201-202 (1973).

(663) Viets, F.G., Jr. and Hageman, R.H., *Factors Affecting the Accumulation of Nitrate in Soil, Water, and Plants. Agricultural Handbook No. 413*, U.S. Department of Agriculture, Washington, D.C. (November 1971).

(664) "Viruses in Water," *JAWWA*, 61(10):491-494 (October 1969).

(665) Voelkel, K.G., Martin, D.W., and Deering, R.W., "Joint Treatment of Municipal and Pulp Mill Effluents," *JWPCF*, 46(4):634-656 (April 1974).

(666) Wachinski, A.M., Adams, V.D., and Reynolds, J.H., *Biological Treatment of the Phenoxy Herbicides 2,4-D and 2,4,5-T in a Closed System*, Utah Water Research Laboratory, Utah State University (March 1974).

(667) Wallace, R.N. and Burns, D.E., "Factors Affecting Powdered Carbon Treatment of a Municipal Wastewater," *JWPCF*, 48(3):511-519 (March 1976).

(668) Waller, D.H., "Pollution from Combined Sewer Overflows," *Proceedings of the Conference on Pollution. St. Mary's University, Halifax*, pp 67-80 (August 1969).

(669) Ward, P.S., "Carcinogens Complicate Chlorine Question," *JWPCF*, 46(12):2638-2640 (December 1974).

(670) *Wastewater Filtration: Design Considerations*, EPA Technology Transfer (July 1974).

(671) Water Purification Associates, *Innovative Technology Study Prepared for the National Commission on Water Quality* (August 1975).

(672) *Water Quality Criteria 1972*, U.S. Environmental Protection Agency (1972).

(673) Watkins, S.H., *Coliform Bacteria Growth and Control in Aerated Stabilization Basins*, EPA-660/2-73-028 (December 1973).

(674) Weber, W.J. and Morris, J.C., "Equilibria and Capacities for Adsorption on Carbon," *Journal of the Sanitary Engineering Division, ASCE*, 90(SA3):79-107 (June 1964).

(675) Weber, W.J., Jr. and Ketchum, L.H., Jr., *Activated Silica in Wastewater Coagulation*, EPA-670/2-74-047 (June 1974).

(676) Weber, W.J., Jr., Hopkins, C.B., and Bloom, R., Jr., "Physicochemical Treatment of Wastewater," *JWPCF*, 42(1):83-99 (January 1970).

(677) Wei, I.W. and Morris, C., "Dynamics of Breakout Chlorination," in *Chemistry of Water Supply, Treatment, and Distribution*, A.J. Rubin, ed., Ann Arbor Science Publishers, Ann Arbor, Michigan, pp 297-332 (1975).

(678) Wei, I.W., Engelbrecht, R.S., and Austin, J.H., "Removal of Nematodes by Rapid Sand Filtration," *Journal of the Sanitary Engineering Division, ASCE*, 95(SA1):1-16 (February 1969).

(679) Weibel, S.R., et al, "Characterization, Treatment, and Disposal of Urban Stormwater," *Advances in Water Pollution Research*, 1966(1):329-352.

(680) Weibel, S.R., et al, "Pesticides and Other Contaminants in Rainfall and Runoff," *JAWWA*, 58(8):1075-1084 (August 1966).

(681) Wellings, F.M., Lewis, A.L., and Mountain, C.W., *The Demonstration of Solids-Associated Virus in Wastewater and Sludge*, Epidemiology Research Center, State of Florida Division of Public Health.

(682) Wellings, F.M., et al, "Demonstration of Virus in Groundwater after Effluent Discharge onto Soil," *Applied Microbiology,* 49(6):751-757 (June 1975).

(683) Wellings, F.M., Lewis, A.L., and Mountain, C.W., "Pathogen Viruses May Thwart Land Disposal," *Water and Wastes Engineering*, 12:70-74 (March 1975).

(684) Weng, C. and Molof, A.H., "Nitrification in the Biological Fixed-Film Rotating Disk System," *JWPCF*, 46(7):1674-1685 (July 1974).

(685) Wesner, G.M. and Baier, D.C., "Injection of Reclaimed Wastewater into Confined Aquifers," *JAWWA*, 62(3):203-210 (March 1970).

(686) Westing, A.H., "Ecocide: Our Last Gift to Indochina," *Environmental Quality*, 36-42, 62-65 (May 1973).

(687) White, G.C., "Disinfecting Wastewater with Chlorination/Dechlorination. Part I," *Water and Sewage Works*, 121(8):70-71 (August 1974).

(688) White, G.C., "Disinfection: The Last Line of Defense for Potable Water," *JAWWA*, 67(8):410-413 (August 1975).

(689) White, G.C., "Disinfection Practices in the San Francisco Bay Area," *JWPCF*, 46(1):87-101 (January 1974).

(690) Wilhelmi, A.R. and Ely, R.B., "A Two-Step Process for Toxic Wastewaters," *Chemical Engineering*, 83(4):105-109 (February 16, 1976).

(691) Willenbrink, R., *Wastewater Reuse and In-Plant Treatment. AIChe Symposium Series*, 69(135):153-154 (1973).

(692) Williams, L.G., Joyce, J.C., and Monk, J.T., Jr., "Stream-Velocity Effects on the Heavy Metal Concentrations," *JAWWA*, 64(4):275-279 (April 1973).

(693) Williams, T.C. and Malhotra, S.K., "Phosphorus Removal for Aerated Lagoon Effluent," *JWPCF*, 46(12):2696-2703 (December 1974).

(694) Wilson, T.E. and Riddell, M.D.R., "Nitrogen Removal: Where Do We Stand?" *Water and Wastes Engineering*, 11:56-61 (October 1974).

(695) Windom, H.L., "Mercury Distribution in Estuarine-Nearshore Environment," *Journal of the Waterways, Harbors, and Coastal Engineering Division, ASCE*, 99:257-265 (May 1973).

(696) Wing, R.E., "Cornstarch Compound Recovers Metals from Water," *Industrial Wastes*, 21(1):26-27 (January/February 1975).

(697) Wing, R.E., et al, "Heavy Metal Removal with Starch Xanthate-Cationic Polymer Complex," *JWPCF*, 46(8):2043-2047 (August 1974).

(698) Wing, R.E., Doane, W.M., and Russell, C.R., "Insoluble Starch Xanthate: Use in Heavy Metal Removal," *Journal of Applied Polymer Science*, 19:847-854 (1975).

(699) Wolf, H.W., "Biological Aspects of Water," *JAWWA*, 63(3):181-188 (March 1971).

(700) Wolf, H.W., et al, "Virus Inactivation During Tertiary Treatment," *JAWWA*, 66(9): 526-553 (September 1974).

(701) Wolf, H.W., et al, "Virus Inactivation During Tertiary Treatment," in *Virus Survival in Water and Wastewater Systems*, Malina and Sagik, eds., Water Resources Symposium No. 7, pp 145-157 (1974).

(702) Wood, D.K. and Tchobanoglous, G., "Trace Elements in Biological Waste Treatment," *JWPCF*, 47(7):1933-1945 (July 1975).

(703) Woodward, W.W., et al, "Acute Diarrhea on an Apache Indian Reservation," *American Journal of Epidemiology*, 99(4):281-190 (1974).

(704) Worrell, C.L., "Management of Organophosphate Intoxication," *Southern Medical Journal*, 68(3):335-339 (March 1975).

(705) York, D.W. and Drewry, W.A., "Virus Removal by Chemical Coagulation," *JAWWA*, 66:711-716 (December 1974).

(706) Young, J.C., et al, "Packed-Bed Reactors for Secondary Effluent BOD and Ammonia Removal," *JWPCF*, 47(1):46-56 (January 1975).

(707) Young, R.A., Cheremisinoff, P.N., and Feller, S.M., "Tertiary Treatment: Advanced Wastewater Techniques," *Pollution Engineering*, 7(4):26-33 (April 1975).

(708) Young, R.H.F. and Burbank, N.C., Jr., "Virus Removal in Hawaiian Soils," *JAWWA*, 65:598-604 (September 1973).

(709) Yu, C.C. and Sanborn, J.R., "The Fate of Parathion in a Model Ecosystem," *Bulletin of Environmental Contamination and Toxicology*, 13:543-550 (May 1975).

(710) Yu, W.C., "Selective Removal of Mixed Phosphates by Activated Alumina," *JAWWA*, 58(2):239-247 (February 1966).

(711) Zaloum, R. and Murphy, K.L., "Reduction of Oxygen Demand of Treated Wastewater by Chlorination," *JWPCF*, 46(12):2770-2777 (December 1974).

(712) Zanitsch, R.H. and Morand, J.M., "Tertiary Treatment of Combined Wastewater with Granular Activated Carbon," *Water and Wastes Engineering*, 7:58-60 (September 1970).

(713) Zellich, J.A., "Toxicity of Combined Chlorine Residuals to Freshwater Fish," *JWPCF*, 44(2):212-220 (February 1972).

(714) Zimansky, G.M., "Removal of Trace Metals During Conventional Water Treatment," *JAWWA*, 66(10):606-609 (October 1974).

(715) Zitko, V. and Carson, W.V., "Release of Heavy Metals from Sediments by Nitrilotriacetic Acid (NTA)," *Chemosphere*, 1(3):113-118 (May 1972).

(716) ZoBell, C.E., "Carcinogenic Hydrocarbons as Marine Environmental Pollutants: A Preliminary Report," in *Sources and Biodegradation of Carcinogenic Hydrocarbons*, API/EPA/USCG Conference on the Prevention and Control of Oil Spills, pp 441-451 (1971).

Health Effects of Wastewater Reuse

EPIDEMIOLOGICAL AND PATHOLOGICAL EVALUATION OF WASTE-
WATER CONTAMINANTS

The material in this section is based on Section II of
EPA Report 600/1-78-019, *Contaminants Associated
with Reuse of Municipal Wastewater,* prepared by SCS
Engineers, Inc. for the U.S. EPA Health Effects Research
Laboratory of Cincinnati, Ohio, March 1978. The num-
bers in parentheses throughout the section refer to the
references given at the end of the previous chapter
(Chapter 8).

Introduction

Many contaminants contained in municipal wastewater are known to produce adverse human health effects. A number of elemental, biocidal, and syn-
thetic/organic constituents have been clearly identified as potential carcinogens;
some have even been identified as being mutagenic or teratogenic. Although
the epidemiological effects of various viruses and bacteria are known and pre-
dictable, knowledge of the health risks of certain other contaminants is incomplete or lacking. Moreover, some chemical substances work not only in
isolation within the human body, but may react synergistically (two or more
chemicals combining to produce a net effect that is greater or lesser than that
produced if the chemicals act independently). A multiplicity of factors is involved in such reactions, and knowledge of potential health risks is scant.

Present standards controlling wastewater discharges and drinking water supplies have been assumed by many to guarantee adequate protection of public
health. However, recent investigation has shown that some residual organics,
carcinogenic chlorinated hydrocarbons, synthetic compounds, trace elements,

and biocides are harmful even in extremely small concentrations. Existing standards are called into question by this increasing knowledge; there may be no "safe" threshold for some of these chemicals. Growing epidemiological and pathological evidence must be taken into account if discharge and drinking water standards are to safely ensure public well-being.

Water Quality Parameters

Suspended solids, BOD, TOC, and most other constituents of general water quality have no direct effect on public health. However, nitrogen species present in wastewater can directly affect human health.

Nitrogen: Nitrogen in wastewater effluent is usually found in one of the stable forms (ammonia, nitrate, or organic nitrogen) rather than the more hazardous nitrite form. Nitrates and nitrites occur in drugs, food, and water. Man is continually exposed to small amounts of these substances, which usually cause no harm. In high concentrations and under special circumstances, however, they may cause illness and even death. Sepp (572) and the Hazardous Waste Advisory Committee of the EPA (484) consider nitrite, in particular, a significant health problem.

Nitrite toxicity is the major health problem associated with these nitrogen species since nitrate easily reduces to the toxic nitrite form. Such a conversion may occur outside the human body in food or water containing nitrates or inside the body through the action of intestinal bacteria on ingested nitrates.

Nitrate/nitrite conversion that occurs during digestion requires special conditions likely to be present only in infants. The foremost prerequisite is the presence of nitrate-reducing bacteria in the upper gastrointestinal tract. They are not normally present so high up in the intestinal tract but may be in infants, particularly those with gastrointestinal infections and a gastric pH insufficiently acidic to kill the bacteria. Acute nitrite toxicity (methemoglobinemia) occurs when hemoglobin is oxidized into methemoglobin (a brown pigment incapable of carrying oxygen). Cyanosis results when roughly 15% of the hemoglobin is converted into methemoglobin; when methemoglobin constitutes 70% or more of the total hemoglobin, oxygen transport is severely impeded, and death may occur (484).

Consumption of water with high levels of nitrates has accounted for many more cases of methemoglobinemia than all other causes combined. Methemoglobinemia of such etiology has been reported only in infants, but one study documents one occurrence due to the use of nitrate-contaminated well water for peritoneal dialysis in an adult. In the United States only one case has been associated with water from a public water supply, the rest, about 300, were due to well water (484).

Reliable data are lacking on physiologic effects of chronic nitrate/nitrite toxicity or of mild, noncyanotic methemoglobinemia. Chronically elevated methemoglobin levels may affect the brain; abnormal changes on electroencephalograms have been seen in rats fed 100 to 2,000 mg/ℓ of sodium nitrite daily for two weeks. A Russian study indicates decreased response to visual and auditory stimuli in school children with a mean methemoglobin level of 5.3% of total hemoglobin, but the study was poorly controlled, and results, inconclusive. Nitrosamines formed by reacting nitrites and amines have been proved hazardous to human health. Nitrosamines have potent biological effects, including acute cellular injury (primarily involving the liver), carcinogenesis, mutagenesis, and teratogenesis. To date, about 100 nitrosamines have been tested in animals and found carcinogenic. Diverse animals are susceptible to the cancer-producing effects, which can be elicited experimentally by various routes of administration (oral, intravenous, inhalation) at extremely low doses. Cancer can develop after a single exposure (484).

Concerns about potential nitrosamine hazards to human health arise from the possibility for (1) contact with preformed carcinogenic nitrosamines and (2) the formation of carcinogenic nitrosamines within the human body after exposure to precursor nitrites and amines.

Elemental Contaminants

It is often difficult to assess the health effects of metals and their compounds: many metals are essential to life at low concentrations but toxic when concentrations exceed tolerance in man. The situation is further complicated because the various chemical states of metals (pure metal, inorganic or organic-metallic compounds) react differently within the body.

However, five heavy metals—cadmium, lead, mercury, nickel as nickel carbonyl, and beryllium—represent known hazards to human health. Lead, mercury, and cadmium are particularly insidious, because they can be retained in the body for a relatively long time and can accumulate as poisons. Antimony, arsenic, cadmium, lead, and mercuric salts are the most toxic.

Lead: Lead is a cumulative poison. However, except in cases of prolonged exposure at high concentrations, most of it is absorbed into the blood and is later excreted in the urine. The blood lead does not rise to acute levels; however, a small portion of the daily lead intake gradually accumulates in bones, where it is normally insoluble and harmless. Under certain conditions, such as periods of high calcium metabolism in feverish illness, cortisone therapy, or old age, this accumulated lead can be released suddenly into the blood at toxic levels. A fatal dose of absorbed lead has been estimated to be 0.5 g; ingestion of more than 0.5 mg/ℓ/day may, because of the abovementioned accumulation, cause toxicity and death.

There are up to 100 cases of lead poisoning reported in the U.S. annually; an average of 10 are fatal. Most of the fatalities are related to children who ingested lead-based paint from homes built before 1940; however, 7 cases of lead poisoning were reported from drinking well water in Australia in 1973 (57) (144). The well water contained a soluble lead content of about 14 mg/ℓ.

Mercury: Neither methyl nor elemental mercury is normally found in dangerous concentrations in air, water, or most common foodstuffs. There are three principal ways in which man can be poisoned by methyl mercury: (1) when food is consumed that has been contaminated with methyl mercury, e.g., seed containing mercury fungicides ($HgCl_2$); (2) when methyl mercury used or formed in industrial processes is intentionally or unintentionally dumped into natural waters, reaching man directly through the water and indirectly through the food chain; and (3) when nontoxic inorganic or organic phenyl mercury is converted into toxic alkyl mercury compounds by microorganisms in the environment and is passed on to man through the food chain (329).

Cadmium: Cadmium has become the most recent and perhaps the most acute menace among the widely used heavy metals. A great amount of current research is being conducted regarding the fate and distribution of cadmium to the environment.

Nearly all the literature concerns the quantification of cadmium in wastewater and sludges, and the effects of disposal to land and water systems. However, there is little information available concerning the direct health hazards of cadmium present in wastewater and water supplies. The average American citizen's daily intake of cadmium from foods and water supplies is estimated to be between 0.02 and 0.1 mg/d. The oral dose of cadmium producing toxicity is about 3 mg, but its fatal dose is not known.

Cadmium has reportedly caused a number of deaths from oral ingestion of the metal in food or water. For example, Japanese people living along the Jintsu River suffered for years from an unknown malady characterized by kidney malfunction, a drop in the phosphate level of the blood serum, loss of minerals from the bones, and osteomalacia resulting in bone fractures causing intense pain. One of several causes of the malady implicated was a cadmium, zinc, and lead mine that was discharging wastewater into the river. The disease, known as *itai itai,* was contracted either by drinking water from the river or by eating rice that had accumulated the metal from irrigation water (123).

Chromium: Experiments on rats showed no toxic response from drinking water containing 0.45 to 25 mg/ℓ in chromate and chromium ion form (408).

Although a potential health hazard exists, evidence of health problems resulting from chromium present in wastewaters is lacking in the literature.

Arsenic: Arsenic is widely distributed in nature. It is present in toxic concentrations in many water supplies; cattle in New Zealand have died from drinking water containing natural arsenic, and there are several areas of the world where there is a high incidence of skin cancer among people drinking well water that contains natural arsenic (423). In 1971 the U.S. Geological Survey found that 2% of the samples drawn from 720 waterways were above their standard of 0.05 ppm for arsenic.

Arsenic is suspected to be carcinogenic but not tumorigenic (29)(340)(363). Chronic exposure to arsenic-contaminated water of 0.3 mg/ℓ is also suspected to be related to the increased incidence of hyperkeratosis (hypertrophy of the horny layer of the epidermis) and skin cancer; chronic exposure at levels of 0.8 mg/ℓ may be related to gangrene of the lower limbs (265).

Biocidal Contaminants

There is significant information in the literature concerning biocidal contaminants, their chemcial and physical characteristics, toxicology, analytical chemistry, and impacts on health and the environment. In both chemical and medical literature, hundreds of cases of acute poisoning resulting directly or indirectly from such pesticides have been reported. Table 9.1 summarizes the various levels at which LD_{50}, fatal dose, chronic poisoning, and acute poisoning occur.

Table 9.1: Biocides in the Environment and Their Toxicity*

Biocide	LD_{50} (oral) (mg/kg)	Fatal Doses (g/kg)	Chronic Poisoning	Acute Poisoning
DDT	Rat 285 Rabbit 325	0.4	Not substantiated. Having 648 ppm in their body remained well.	Severe vomiting within 30 min to 1 hr of 5 g. Weakness and numbness of the extremities. Apprehension and excitement are marked.
Dieldrin	Rat 60 Dog 68 Rabbit 45	0.07	Not been established in man. Impair liver function in animals, occasional epileptiform convulsions.	Hyperexcitability, tremors, ataxia, convulsions.
Lindane (benzene hexachloride)	Rat 135 Dog 120 Rabbit 130	0.6	In animals, liver necrosis.	Vomiting and diarrhea, convulsions, circulatory failure.
Malathion	Rat 2500	0.86	In animals, cholinesterase levels of red blood cells and plasma are reduced markedly.	Headache, tremors, nausea, abdominal cramps, diarrhea, coma, heart block.
Parathion	Rat 4	0.0014	Not established in man.	Similar to those of malathion, but more severe and fatal.
2,4-D	Mouse 375	0.7	Weakness, fall of blood pressure, muscle damage.	Burning pain, painful and tender muscle, fever, paralysis, irreversible fall of blood pressure.
2,4,5-T	Rat 300 Dog 100	0.6	Similar to 2,4-D	Similar to 2,4-D.

*Data primarily from Sunshine (626), Dreisbach (181), and McKee and Wolfe (436).

Source: EPA-600/1-78-019

PCBs: To date limited study in this area indicates that uncontaminated PCBs have a very low toxicity to man. According to the Food and Drug Administration, the average PCB concentration in a normal American diet is only about 10% of the strict safety levels set in 1971 for food, food packaging materials, and animal feeds.

Synthetic/Organic Contaminants

Recently diverse compounds identified in water supplies drawn from the Mississippi River have been discovered in the blood serum of local residents using the water supply. This has created great concern over chemicals found in drinking water. The presence of small amounts of synthetic/organic chemicals in treated reclaimed water has been recognized as a potential health hazard.

The list of compounds identified in drinking waters is rapidly growing larger. This is due primarily to the continual introduction of new chemicals but also to the development of sensitive analytical techniques that measure trace quantities of the chemicals. There is very little evidence available concerning the relation between the presence of these compounds in water and human disease. Information on classical acute health effects of relatively toxic chemicals can be obtained from physicians' manuals. However, knowledge of the chronic health effects associated with long-term exposure to low-level concentrations of chemical substances is not well documented. The possibility that cancer may result from long-term exposure to low concentrations of carcinogens is of utmost concern.

Carbon-Chloroform Extractables (CCE) and Carbon Alcohol Extractables (CAE): The Committee on Water Quality Criteria (672) suggested that absorbable organic carbon in public water supply sources should not exceed the carbon chloroform extractables (CCE) level of 0.7 mg/ℓ. [No level has been established for carbon alcohol extractables (CAE)]. The establishment of this level was based upon the adverse physiological effects of CCE as well as aesthetic considerations. To date, laboratory testing of the epidemiological and pathological effects of trace organics has been restricted to mice and fish and results are not clear-cut.

Organohalides: Occurrence and formation of organohalides such as $CHCl_3$, $CHCl_2Br$, $CHClBr_2$, and $CHBr_3$ were reported when water containing organic substances was chlorinated (41)(554). Of the haloforms, chloroform ($CHCl_3$) was reported as the predominant organohalide, with concentrations ranging from 54 to 150 $\mu g/\ell$. The level of risk for chloroform, estimated from consideration of the worst case and for the expected cancer site, such as the liver, might be extrapolated to account for up to 40% of the observed liver cancer. The toxicity of chloroform has been well demonstrated in lethal-dose studies.

An LD_{50} (lethal dose, 50%) value ranging from 89 to 35 mg/kg was observed by Tardiff and Deinzer (636) when CCE obtained from the Kanawha River in West Virginia was introduced into mice via an intraperitoneal route. The differences among these LD_{50} values were shown to be due to the amount of chloroform present in the extract, indicating the toxicity of chloroform. The CAE obtained from the same river showed an LD_{50} of 84 mg/kg. The LD_{50} for the concentrated organics from Cincinnati tap water was shown to be 65 to 290 mg/kg.

The same authors also reported the identification of 60 compounds from drinking water. Of the compounds, 1 was classified as nontoxic; 14 moderately toxic; 16, very toxic; 2, extremely toxic; and 27, unknown.

However, it is difficult at this time to determine the relationships of the toxicities of these compounds in humans to the level of the compounds present in water and wastewater. Careful interpretation of the toxicity data, such as the LD_{50} value obtained from concentrated extracts, is necessary when these values are to be used to set toxicity levels in drinking water.

Polynuclear Aromatic Hydrocarbons (PAH): Occurrence, formation, concentration, activity, carcinogenicity, and degradation of polynuclear aromatic hydrocarbons (PAH) in water are well documented (17).

Of the PAH, 3,4-benzpyrene has been generally recognized as the most potent carcinogen. Minimal carcinogenic doses of three of the most potent hydrocarbons in susceptible experimental animals are shown in Table 9.2.

Table 9.2: The Minimal Carcinogenic Dose for Three of the Most Potent Carcinogenic Hydrocarbons in Susceptible Experimental Animals (716)

Carcinogen	Animal	Least Amount Which Caused Cancer* (μg)
3,4-Benzpyrene	Mouse	4.0
3,4-Benzpyrene	Rat	50.0
1,2,5,6-Dibenzanthracene	Mouse	2.5
20-Methylcholanthrene	Mouse	4.5
	Rat	20.0

*Only one dose was administered subcutaneously.

Source: EPA-600/1-78-019

Miscellaneous Organic Compounds: A preliminary experiment was designed to study the toxicity of organic compounds present in a secondary treatment plant effluent. Rats were supplied with filter-sterilized effluent from an activated sludge plant as the sole source of drinking water. Two of the 10 rats developed massive tumors. Also, the exposed female rats developed significantly smaller adrenal glands than the control rats that were provided with the local water supply (496).

An epidemiologic study on the toxicity of compounds present in drinking water was cited by Andelman and Suess (17). This study indicated fewer cancer mortalities in a London borough that was supplied with well water than in boroughs supplied with river water. This could mean that the river water receives more carcinogenic waste material.

Similar findings reported by Tromp (650) showed that areas using municipal water systems had lower cancer death rates than those using other systems. However, the cancer death rate was higher among areas that received municipal water from a river than among those that received municipal water from wells.

When other factors such as food, air quality, and individual habits (i.e., cigarette smoking) are considered, the importance of trace carcinogens in water supplies may not be significant. However, several observations have been made correlating water supply quality and cancer incidence. For example, Talbot and Harris (633) established a correlation between cancer mortality in white males and water supply source, between mortality and urbanization, and between mortality and income. When occupational variables are not considered, lung cancer mortality rates were found to be correlated with surface water sources, but there were no correlations found in other cancers.

Low Molecular Sulfurated Hydrocarbons: A case history study of the waterborne goitrogens and their role in the etiology of endemic goiter was recently reported from Colombia, South America (229). The potential presence of low molecular weight compounds (less than 220), such as sulfurated hydrocarbons in water and wastewater, received careful evaluation. The compounds (sulfurated hydrocarbons) were known to be related to the high incidence of goiter among children and were regarded as waterborne goitrogens. The study also reported a 10-fold increase in cancer of the thyroid where endemic goiter was observed (229).

Biological Contaminants

Epidemics of waterborne diseases have largely been eliminated, due mainly to the advancement of sanitary engineering, enforcement of public health regulations, and preventive medical practices; however, waterborne disease data from the last three decades indicate that outbreaks are no longer on the decline in the United States. During the 25-year period from 1946 to 1970, there were 358 recognized outbreaks (72,358 individuals involved) of disease or chemical poisoning attributed to contaminated drinking water (145)(220).

According to the reports of the Center for Disease Control (221), during the four years from 1972 to 1975, 105 waterborne disease outbreaks were reported, involving 22,650 cases.

Table 9.3 shows the number of outbreaks and cases by etiology and type of water system. The category with the most outbreaks is acute gastrointestinal illness. This category includes outbreaks characterized by upper and/or lower gastrointestinal symptomatology for which no specific etiologic agent was identified. In previous years, these outbreaks were considered sewage poisoning. One outbreak each was caused by giardiasis, shigellosis, enterotoxigenic *E. coli*, and hepatitis A. There were no reported deaths associated with waterborne disease outbreaks in 1975 (221).

Table 9.3: Waterborne Disease Outbreaks, 1975 (221)

	. .Municipal . .		. . Semipublic . .		. .Individual . .		. . . .Total. . . .	
	Outbreaks	Cases	Outbreaks	Cases	Outbreaks	Cases	Outbreaks	Cases
Acute gastro-intestinal illness	4	7,300	13	2,460	–	–	17	9,760
Chemical poisoning	2	11	1	26	–	–	3	37
Giardiasis	–	–	–	–	1	9	1	9
Shigellosis	–	–	1	56	–	–	1	56
Enterotoxigenic E. coli	–	–	1	1,000	–	–	1	1,000
Hepatitis	–	–	–	–	1	17	1	17
Total	6	7,311	16	3,542	2	26	24	10,879

Source: EPA-600/1-78-019

Protozoan and Other Parasites: A number of intestinal parasite infections can be introduced into man directly from water supplies and indirectly through waste-water discharges. Under normal conditions, the potable-water route of infection is quite unimportant. However, the reuse of treated waste effluents for potable purposes requires that this problem be reexamined.

Amoebic dysentery (or amebiasis) appears to be the most important parasitic disease associated with wastewater in the United States. It is caused by *Entamoeba histolytica,* a protozoan. Today, the prevalence rate of *E. histolytica* in the general population of the United States is considered to be around 3 to 5% (383). The prevalence of the intestinal protozoa varies considerably in different population groups and is generally correlated with socioeconomic conditions.

In an experiment with volunteers, it has been demonstrated that up to 25% could be infected by a dose containing less than 10 organisms of entamoeba; the remainder required a minimal dose of 10,000 organisms to become infected. However, the infected volunteers did not manifest any signs of illness.

Giardia lamblia, a flagellated protozoan of the small intestine, often implicated epidemiologically with drinking water, is the etiological agent for giardiasis. An outbreak has been reported (460) in Rome, New York, where the water supply could have been contaminated by untreated human waste. Another outbreak of giardiasis by *G. lamblia* was reported in September 1976 in Idaho. The source was purported to be from untreated surface water of an individual water system (290).

In moderate climates, the human contribution of ova to wastewater would appear to be no greater than 10%, but may reach 30% in subtropical regions such as the southern extremities of the United States. The remainder of the ova is of animal origin. Various authors have reported 59 to 80 worm eggs/ℓ sewage (223). The eggs are generally resistant to environmental conditions, having a thick outer covering to protect them against desiccation. In one study, 90% of ascaris ova was destroyed after 15 days at 29°C; the ova may survive for up to 60 days at 40°C (223).

Ova from the giant roundworm *Ascaris lumbricoides*, the pinworm *Oxyuris vermicularis*, the whipworm *Trichuris trichuria*, the tapeworm *Taenia saginata*, and possibly the hookworm are reported to be present in wastewater (223).

Free-living nematodes are widely found in municipal water supplies. Their potential as carriers of *Enterococci, Salmonella,* and *Shigella* has been demonstrated (699). Although free-living nematodes are not important as health threats in conventional waterworks practice, their significance in a reclaimed water situation needs evaluation.

Dracontiasis, or guinea worm infection, is a disease primarily associated with poverty (especially inadequate water supplies and wastewater treatment), and is common in India and West Africa. Vector species of Cyclops persisting in ponds used for drinking water must be controlled (usually by the use of Abate at a concentration of 1 mg/ℓ).

In summary, it may be stated that a large quantity of a variety of ova from parasitic worms may be present in wastewater, and that the ova possess a high degree of resistance to many environmental stresses.

Fungi: *C. albicans* may cause oral thrush, corneal ulcers, and other ocular infections. One survey analyzed 20 weekly samples collected at three stations on the North Shore of Great South Bay, Long Island. It was reported that the estuarine water samples contained between 1,000 to 11,000 or more cells/ℓ (323).

This fungus retained an infectivity and pathogenicity to mice after it was exposed to seawater for eight weeks (323). In the open ocean, there is a concentration of 200 to 300 fungal cells/ℓ; in moderately contaminated beach areas, there are levels of 10,000 to 20,000 cells/ℓ; and in heavily contaminated estuaries, up to 100,000 cells/ℓ (323). The overall trend was a gradual increase in concentrations during summer months, from June to September, after which the concentration declined (323).

Bacteria: *Salmonellosis* — A wide variety of species that are pathogenic to man and animals belongs to the genus *Salmonella*. Water and food, as well as personal contact, are the main routes for transmission of the species from man to man.

Relatively few outbreaks of typhoid fever and salmonellosis associated with drinking water were reported in the United States during 1971 to 1973 (220) (448). The reported isolation rates for humans in the United States in 1972 was 12.5/100,000; the fatality rate between 1962 and 1972 was 0.43%, mostly among the very young and very old.

In 1974, *S. typhimurium* (30.8%), *S. newport* (6.9%), and *S. enteritides* (6.0%) were the first, second, and third most commonly isolated serotypes, (563). The annual incidence of reported human isolations of salmonella has remained relatively constant since 1963 (563).

Shigellosis — *Shigellae* cause bacillary dysentery in man and in higher apes. Although person-to-person transmission is the predominant mode of spreading shigellosis, waterborne outbreaks have played a significant role in the overall epidemiology of the disease in the United States (579)(612). In 1975, 14,757 *Shigella* isolations from humans were reported to the Center of Disease Control (CDC). This was a decrease of 24.0% from the 19,420 isolations reported in 1974 (580). Utilizing population estimates for July 1, 1975, approximately 69.2 isolations were reported for each million population of the United States in 1975. *Shigella sonnei* (60.3%) was the most common etiological agent in all these cases, followed by *S. flexneri* (38.2%). Between January 17 and March 15, 1974, approximately 1,200 cases of acute gastrointestinal illness occurred in Richmond Heights, Florida. The outbreak was caused by a failure in the chlorination process of well water, which allowed insufficiently chlorinated water from a contaminated well (located near a church's septic tank) to be distributed to the community (144).

Most instances of *Shigellae*-induced illnesses reported in the past several years have involved small wells, temporary breakdowns of chlorinated systems in water supply, and swimming in waters contaminated with sewage. The isolation rate in the United States is approximately 15/1,000,000 population.

Gastroenteritis — There are many reports of waterborne gastroenteritis of unknown etiology in which bacterial infections are suspected. These include outbreaks characterized by nausea, vomiting, diarrhea, and fever, for which no specific etiologic agent could be identified.

In 1971, a waterborne gastroenteritis outbreak was reported in Pico Rivera, California, in which 11,000 residents became ill with diarrhea and abdominal cramps. No pathogens were isolated from any cases. The source of water was responsible for the outbreak; chlorination at the reservoir had been interrupted when the chlorine supply was exhausted. One of the major outbreaks involving over 1,000 persons occurred at Crater Lake National Park, Oregon, in July 1975. The illness was reported to be associated with sewage-contaminated water (459). Enterotoxigenic *E. coli*, Serotype 06:H16, was isolated from ill park residents and from the park's water supply (221).

Viruses: In the past, transmission of waterborne viral diseases was rarely recognized, due largely to lack of sensitive virus-detection methods and precise quantification. With improved techniques for concentrating viruses from large water samples, increasing occurrences of viruses in water and wastewaters have been reported. Viral transmission through water may take place in various ways: bathing in contaminated water, eating contaminated seafood, drinking from untreated or improperly treated water sources, or contacting contaminated waters. Enteric viruses have been investigated with greater emphasis than any other group of viruses, mainly because any virus excreted in the feces and capable of producing infection when ingested is theoretically transmissible by water. The human enteric viruses and the diseases associated with them are listed in Table 9.4.

Table 9.4: The Human Enteric Viruses and Diseases Associated with Them (142)

Virus Subgroup	Number of Types	Disease
Polio virus	3	Paralytic poliomyelitis, aseptic meningitis
Coxsackie virus		
Group A	26	Herpangina, aseptic meningitis,
Group B	6	paralysis pleurodynia, aseptic meningitis, acute infantile myocarditis
ECHO virus	34	Aseptic meningitis, rash and fever, diarrheal disease, respiratory illnesses
Infectious hepatitis	1 (?)	Infectious hepatitis
Reovirus	3	Fever, respiratory infections, diarrhea
Adenovirus	32	Respiratory and eye infections

Source: EPA-600/1-78-019

Infectious Hepatitis — Apart from theoretical considerations, there are very few viruses for which epidemiological evidence suggests transmission by water. Infectious hepatitis (hepatitis A) is the only disease caused by an agent having the characteristics of a virus for which evidence of waterborne transmission has been accepted by all workers in the field (468). Therefore, it is regarded as the viral disease of greatest importance in wastewater.

In 1973 alone, a total of 59,200 cases of viral hepatitis A, B, and a type unspecified were reported (221). In 1974, a total of 59,340 cases of viral hepatitis, hepatitis A, B, and type unspecified, were reported to CDC. This represents a rate of 28.1 cases/100,000 population, approximately the same rate as for 1973. Since 1971, 1974 is the first year to have shown rate increases for two quarters; the increase in cases began in the fourth quarter of 1973. The seasonal variation noted in the 1950s and early 1960s was not seen in 1974. The 48,709 cases of acute hepatitis A and hepatitis, type unspecified, constituted 82.1% of the total cases of viral hepatitis reported in 1974 (291). Waterborne outbreaks of hepatitis A continue to occur in the United States. From 1971 to 1973, these documented outbreaks were associated with contaminated drinking water from either municipal, semipublic, or individual water systems (144) (448). Use of contaminated spring or groundwater without proper treatment or disinfection, and back-siphonage of contaminated water into the distribution system were reported to be causes of the outbreaks. The majority of documented hepatitis A outbreaks in municipal water systems in the United States between 1946 and 1971 occurred as a result of distribution system contamination, primarily through cross-connections and back-siphonage.

As far as the magnitude of waterborne infectious hepatitis is concerned, the water route still only accounts for up to 1% of reported cases at any time for which information is available (468).

Despite the increased interest and concern in infectious hepatitis, its infectious agent has not yet been isolated and cultured. One recent report (212) using microscopic techniques was able to show the presence of viruslike particles, immunologically distinct from hepatitis B, in infected stools.

Poliomyelitis — The infectivity of feces from persons with poliomyelitis and the characteristic fecal excretion of the diseased persons have been documented for years. The polio virus has been sought and detected in sewage. Accordingly, the water route of transmission has been implicated in several outbreaks of poliomyelitis. Many cases of epidemics of poliomyelitis were attributed to waterborne transmission through contaminated or untreated water, but the evidence is not sufficient. It appears that water transmission of the polio virus may be a rare occurrence in the United States, but common in parts of the world lacking adequate sanitary facilities. Six of the outbreaks attributed to drinking water occurred in Sweden during the 1930s and 1940s (468) and led to the early recognition of the importance of the fecal-oral route in poliomyelitis.

Viral Gastroenteritis — When a recognized pathogen cannot be isolated in cases of gastroenteritis and diarrhea, the term viral is often used to describe the symptoms. It is quite possible that forms of gastroenteritis and diarrhea transmissible from person to person are due to viruses.

Gastroenteritis and diarrheal disease are believed to have accounted for approximately 60% of all epidemics of waterborne diseases throughout history. The number of these cases that was due to viral agents is not known; if, however, only a small portion of the cases was due to viral agents, this number would still be quite substantial.

A viruslike particle, similar in appearance but immunologically distinct from the hepatitis A, has been reported to be associated with an acute infectious nonbacterial gastroenteritis (341). Shellfish-associated gastroenteritis has also been reported (177).

Infective Dose of Viruses — Virologists feel that one plaque-forming unit (pfu), one viral particle that grows in the laboratory media, constitutes an infectious viral dose. However, there is a difference between infection and disease (637); the diseased person manifests a variety of symptoms and readily recognizes that he is sick; an infected person has the material in his system, but does not necessarily show symptoms of the disease. It has been estimated that of every 100 to 1,000 people who are infected, only one will manifest the clinical symptoms of disease. However, it is not quite as simple as these statistics suggest, for an infected individual can serve as a carrier or source within the community and transmit this disease to other people (637).

It has been mentioned that infection with small amounts of virus in water would probably immunize individuals rather than produce disease. This may be substantiated by the fact that sewage workers continually exposed to small amounts of infected material had the lowest rate of absenteeism among all the occupation groups studied (52).

An adequate biological indicator for viruses in various waters is not currently available; however, efforts are being made to find better indicators. For example, ratios of coliphages to human enteric viruses and the coliform-virus ratio have been investigated (235)(364). Also, a high degree of coliforms and coliphages occurring in water samples (346) as well as a yeast and two acid-fast bacilli recovered from wastewater, resist chlorination at a level sufficient to inactivate viruses. This suggests that they may be useful indicators of wastewater chlorination efficiency (201).

EVALUATION OF TOXIC EFFECTS OF ORGANIC CONTAMINANTS IN RECYCLED WATER

The material in this section is based on EPA Report 600/1-78-068 of the above title, by Dr. N. Gruener, then of the Gulf South Research Institute, for the U.S. EPA Health Effects Research Laboratory of Cincinnati. An abstract of this volume, also written by Dr. Gruener, in 1979 at Tulane University's School of Public Health, appears in Conference III.

Introduction

Water used to be one of our cheapest natural resources. In recent years, we have discovered that water is no longer an abundant commodity in many places in the United States and other countries of the world. Reasons for this include population growth, increases in the average water consumption for domestic and industrial purposes, pollution, and climatic changes. Although there are annual changes in our water reservoirs, the long-term trends show that shortage of water is going to be a problem in many places that have not experienced this phenomenon before.

One of the approaches to remedy this situation is conservation. Natural reuse of water or unintentional reuse by humans has been known for many years. But the presence of thousands of compounds in our wastewater, among them known toxins and carcinogens, should alarm us to take a more cautious approach when we consider wide-scale usage of treated wastewater. Treated wastewater can be used for a variety of purposes, agriculture, industry, recreation, drinking and other nonpotable applications. Treated wastewater may be used for drinking water in several ways, such as recharge of groundwater or direct supply with or without other sources of water. None of these strategic approaches have been dealt with in a practical way. Obviously, water should get special toxicological consideration since it is a general daily commodity used throughout our life and by everyone in population.

Evaluation Method

For the purpose of the evaluation of the health effects of long-term consumption of reused water, an extensive toxicological study was planned. A preliminary problem was sample preparation. Because of the inherent weakness of a toxicological experiment with regard to extrapolation to humans, levels at least 100 times the human daily consumption had to be evaluated. The water, therefore, had to be concentrated.

Water Concentration: Many concentration systems are inappropriate because the end product is selective both in relation to removal of original compounds or addition of contaminants. Preliminary laboratory studies showed that the best way to concentrate the water was through reverse osmosis technology. Since the study was intended to test only the organic soluble fraction, we decided to use charged membranes to remove much of the inorganic fraction. This was necessary for toxicological and nutritional reasons. Some 400,000 liters of advanced treated wastewater was concentrated down to 200 liters through several steps. The first step was done in the treatment plant and took almost 2 months. The first concentrate (757 liters) was then taken to the laboratory where the additional steps were carried out.

Diet Preparation: Table 9.5 shows the various stages of sample preparation with the total organic carbon recovery values. The concentrated water was incorporated into a gel-type diet which was balanced with regard to the inorganic ions based on the concentrations found in the concentrated sample. Chemical analysis of the concentrate is shown in Table 9.6.

As can be seen, all of the toxic heavy metals were present at low concentrations or could not be detected. The project included 900 mice of the strain CFI, males and females. There were five groups in each study: controls and four others exposed to 45, 90, 180 and 360 milligrams TOC per kilogram of food. The intake of the TOC in the different groups was in the range of 5-150 mg TOC/kg BW/day, according to the exposure level, age and sex. These levels are 25-2,500 times the levels to which humans are normally exposed.

Table 9.5: Organic Levels at Various Stages of Sample Preparation

Process Step	Sample Volume (ℓ)	Sample TOC (mg/ℓ)	Mass of Organics (g)	Total Organic Mass Retention (%)	Step-Wise Organic Mass Retention (%)
Initial reverse osmosis concentration	757	530	402.1	53.0	53.0
Alkaline precipitation/filtration	757	384	290.7	38.3	72.5
Closed-loop dialysis	757	260	196.8	26.0	67.7
Final reverse osmosis concentration	204	907	185.5	24.5	94.3
$SO_4^=$ precipitation filtration	204	704	144	19.0	77.6

Source: EPA-600/1-78-068

Table 9.6: Chemical Analysis of the Concentrate

Parameter	Milligrams per Liter	Parameter	
As	<0.01	Total hardness (as $CaCO_3$), mg/ℓ	1,640
Ba	<0.5	Mg hardness (as $CaCO_3$), mg/ℓ	60
Cu	<0.10	Total alkalinity, mg/ℓ	270
Al	0.40	Total dissolved solids, mg/ℓ	132,000
Cr	<0.01	pH	5.5
Zn	2.00	Stability index	7.3
Pb	<0.01	Saturating index	0.9
Ag	<0.01	Odor threshold	4
Hg	<0.01	Turbidity	3.2
Se	<0.01	Color PCU	260
Mn	0.17	Total organic carbon, mg/ℓ	704
Fe	1.70		
Co	<0.20		
B	<15		
Si	1.3		
NH_3-N	<0.1		
NO_3-N	<0.01		
F	2.6		
Na	1,300		
K	4,300		
Ca	632		
Mg	15		
Cl	4,400		
SO_4	2,650		
PO_4	1,500		
I	2.9		

Testing: The toxicological tests that were carried out are exhibited in Table 9.7.

Table 9.7: Toxicological Tests (in vivo)

General physiology
Food consumption
Body weight
Hematology
  Hemoglobin
  Red blood cell count
  White blood cell count
Mixed function oxidase activity
Motor activity
Reproduction
Dominant lethal mutation
Pathology
  Heart
  Lungs
  Spleen
  Liver
  Kidney
  Adrenals
  Brain
  Testes
  Ovaries
  Microscopy and tissue weights

Blood chemistry
  Glucose
  Chloresterol
  Triglyceride
  Total protein
  Albumin
  Calcium
  Phosphorus
  Sodium
  Potassium
  Chloride
  Carbon dioxide
  Urea nitrogen
  Uric acid
  Total bilirubin
  Creatinine
  Alkaline phosphatase
  LDH
  GOT
  GPT
  CPK

Source: EPA-600/1-78-068

The mice in the preliminary 14-day experiment were checked for body weight, food consumption and general physiology. They also were tested for mutagenicity by the dominant lethal mutation test. In Study I, the mice were tested by all the above tests and also for hematology, blood chemistry, mixed function oxidase activity, and motor activity. Similar tests were performed in Studies II, III, and IV.

Results

Toxicity: The results of the different tests which were run during the various studies showed that there were no significant differences in the hematological determinations, motor activity measurements, mixed function oxidase activities or body weight values. The reproduction tests did not show any physiological deviations. In the blood chemistry determinations, which include 20 tests per group, there were small numbers of parameters which were found to be significant (P is lower than 0.05).

When dealing with a large number of variables and a rather large number of animals, one can expect that there will be significant differences between experimental and control values for some of the parameters. It was therefore decided that experimentally significant results would be only those which were found in more than one experimental group.

Males in Study I showed higher levels of sodium, chloride and CO_2 in the serum of experimental groups. Males in Study II had lower urea values in the experimental groups and higher levels of serum proteins. Males in Study III had lower glucose values, lower alkaline phosphatase activity and lower triglycerides. In the females of this study, cholesterol showed lower values in the experimental groups. As a whole, the blood chemistry did not indicate a specific or general pathological situation in these animals. Among the tissues, the spleen mean weight was higher in males of Studies II and III, and in females of Study III. The adrenals were bigger in males and females of Study III.

Mutagenicity: The evaluation of the mutagenic potential of this water was done in in vivo and in vitro experiments.

The mean of the dead fetuses was found to be significantly higher than the control. In a second experiment, in spite of the fact that the mean of the dead fetuses was even higher, the difference between the experimental and the control group was found to be insignificant.

To try to resolve this discrepancy, other mutagenicity tests were tried: a microbiological test using the *Salmonella* strains, and the mammalian mutagenicity assay. The microbiological tests did not show any mutagenicity. The experiment with mammalian cultures was done with V79 hamster cells. In this test, the cells were checked for the presence of forwarded mutation, in this case, ouabain-resistant cells. The results presented in Table 9.8 show that, at the dose of 200 μg of TOC (0.3 ml of water), the mutagenicity rate is 20 times the control.

Table 9.8: Mutagenicity of Concentrated Recycled Water (First Run)*

Sample	Toxicity (% Plating Efficiency)	Colonies per 16 Plates	Ouabain-Resistant Mutants per 10^6 Survivors
Control	88	1	0.5
Control + S9	78	0	0.0
0.1 ml H_2O + S9	44	1	1.0
0.2 ml H_2O + S9	46	4	3.8
0.3 ml H_2O + S9	24	6	10.9
0.5 μg BP + S9	55	54	43.8
1.0 μg BP + S9	38	104	142.2

*H_2O mixed 1:1 with 2 x MEM and added to each sample with 1 ml S9 mix plus PBS to give 2 ml final volume. TOC level in water was 700 μg/ml. Cells incubated with S9 alone have a plating efficiency of 70%. S9 is the rat liver homogenate supernate after centrifugation at 9,000 grams BP-benzo(a)pyrene.

Source: EPA-600/1-78-086

In vitro toxicity tests were run with human lung fibroblasts (W138). Toxicity was shown to increase with time. The presence of the liver activation system significantly increased the toxicity. Both experiments were done in the presence of 150 μg TOC.

Summary

In summary, concentrated recycled water with TOC levels up to about one thousand times the expected human exposure did not cause pathological changes in the various toxicological tests done in mice after exposure for up to five months. On the other hand, the concentrated water was found to be mutagenic. More studies on the mutagenicity and carcinogenicity of renovated water are necessary before conclusions can be made.

REMOVAL OF MUTAGENS AND CARCINOGENS DURING AWT

The information in this section was abstracted from a paper of Conference III, "Occurrence of Mutagens/Carcinogens in Municipal Wastewaters and Their Removal During Advanced Wastewater Treatment," by J Saxena, D.J. Schwartz and M.W. Neal, all of the Center for Chemical Hazard Assessment, Syracuse Research Corp.

Introduction

As clean water resources become scarce and the need to protect our environment becomes urgent, wastewater reclamation will be increasingly practiced. Advanced Wastewater Treatment (AWT) processes are used following conventional treatment, not only to protect certain lakes and rivers but also to produce high quality water for reuse. Prior to considering reuse of renovated wastewaters for potable purposes, the potential hazards from the consumption of renovated wastewaters must be assessed. Wastewaters contain many hazardous chemicals for which currently no criteria exist. The AWT technology available today leaves many potentially hazardous chemicals unchanged and in some instances introduces new and potentially toxic chemicals. Further complications arise from the fact that residual or introduced trace pollutants vary from one situation to the next depending upon the nature of the industrial waste which enters the sewage system.

In view of the growing recognition that the majority of human cancers are due to the presence of chemicals in the environment, the possible occurrence of carcinogenic chemicals in renovated wastewater is of particular concern. In the described investigation the physical-chemical treatment process used at the Piscataway, MD pilot wastewater treatment plant was examined for its ability to remove (or introduce) mutagenic/carcinogenic substances from wastewaters. Further, the distribution of the detected activity among various classes of chemical compounds was studied in an attempt to identify the active fraction(s).

Experimental

Piscataway, MD Model AWT Plant (High Lime Process): This is a 5 million gallon per day plant. The treatment consists of lime addition, recarbonation, dual media filtration, breakpoint chlorination and activated carbon filtration.

Samples and Sampling Procedure: Three sampling points were selected for these studies. These included influent for AWT, which is the secondary effluent from conventional treatment process, effluent after liming and recarbonation step (henceforth referred to as intermediate effluent), and tertiary effluent.

Mutagenicity studies on the unconcentrated wastewaters were performed on twenty-four-hour composite samples collected in glass container with the help of an ISCO automatic composite sampler. The rate of sample collection was maintained at approximately 250 ml every 30 minutes. All samples were kept in wet ice during the compositing period and transporting. In view of the generally recognized quality fluctuations of the influent wastewaters, two samples, which were collected several weeks apart were tested. Samples were sterilized by serial filtration with 1,200 nm, 450 nm and finally 200 nm membrane filters (Millipore Corp.).

The concentration of trace organics from wastewaters by XAD and polyurethane foam was performed at the treatment site using a portable apparatus which allowed maintenance of optimum conditions for recovery. Following exposure to an adequate volume of wastewater, the sorbent material was brought to the laboratory for further processing. This helped overcome the difficulties associated with shipping large volumes of samples for concentration, and possible deterioration of samples during transportation and storage. For recovery of organics by liquid-liquid extraction, wastewater samples were brought to the laboratory. These samples were preserved in transit by saturating with 2% methylene chloride and kept cold.

Recovery of Trace Organics from Wastewater: In order to recover a wide variety of organic contaminants from wastewaters, three concentration methods were employed: Polyurethane foam plugs, macroreticular resin (XAD), and liquid-liquid extraction employing 15% methylene chloride in hexane. The wastewaters were filtered through glass wool prior to subjecting them to any concentration procedure. Liquid extractions were performed by mixing wastewater overnight with methylene chloride-hexane (70 ml solvent/ℓ wastewater).

Fractionation of Recovered Organics into Major Chemical Classes: The crude organic concentrates were separated into major classes of organic compounds according to their solubility under acidic, basic and neutral conditions. The major classes of compounds isolated were: ether insolubles, water soluble, bases, amphoterics, strong acids, weak acids, and neutrals. The neutral fraction was subfractionated into aliphatic aromatic and oxygenated fractions by chromatography or silica gel.

Mutagenicity Assay: Ames *Salmonella typhimurium* assay employing strain TA 100 and TA 1535 as base pair substitution mutants and strain TA 98 and TA 1538 as frameshift mutants was used in these studies. To facilitate detection of low concentrations of mutagens suspected in unconcentrated wastewaters, the bioassays were performed by preparing the assay media (base agar layer) with the filter sterilized wastewaters under investigation. Thus, suspected mutagens would be present in the bottom agar, whereas bacteria and mammalian activation systems (where added) would be in the agar overlay. This modification of the assay permitted incorporation of up to 20 ml wastewater/assay (70% v/v). Metabolic activation of mutagens was achieved by incorporating rat liver homogenate plus necessary cofactors in the assay. The procedure used for preparation of the liver homogenate and liver homogenate-cofactor mix was the same as described by Ames [*Mutation Research* 31:347 (1975)]. Mutagenicity assays on various unconcentrated wastewaters collected at a particular date were carried out at the same time together with distilled demineralized water controls for spontaneous reversion rate and positive mutagenesis controls. The results for unconcentrated wastewaters are expressed as averages of triplicate determination.

For mutagenicity assays on crude wastewater concentrates and separated fractions, samples were evaporated to dryness and reconstituted with dimethyl sulfoxide. Preliminary experiments showed that liquid suspension assay, which involved exposing the organism to the test mixture in a liquid suspension prior to plating in agar medium, detected mutagens more effectively than the conventional plate incorporation assay or spot test. Therefore, liquid suspension assays were routinely used in these studies. The incubation medium contained 1 ml minimal medium, 0.5 ml S-9 mix where added, 0.1 ml of appropriate tester strain (5×10^8 cells), 4 μg histidine and 6 μg biotin, and appropriate amounts of the test organic mixture. Identical control tubes were set up without the test organic mixture. Following a 60 min incubation at 37°C, 3 ml soft agar containing 8 μg histidine and 12 μg biotin/ml was added and the contents were overlaid on minimal glucose agar. Mutagenicity was shown by an increase in the number of revertants over spontaneous (control). Assays were carried out in duplicate.

Results and Discussion

Identification of every compound of concern in complex uncharacterized medium such as municipal wastewater is an extremely difficult task. Even if identification could be accomplished, nothing would be revealed from the data with respect to any health effects linked to their presence in wastewaters except in a few cases where information is available in the literature. An alternate strategy is to use rapid in vitro bioassays for detecting presumptive biological activity in wastewater samples and locating active fractions, and then subjecting the active fraction to physiochemical analysis to fix molecular composition. This strategy would eliminate the need for laborious analysis of samples that do not, in fact, contain hazardous compounds. In addition, this will enable detection of unknown biologically active compounds. In this investigation this approach was utilized to identify mutagenic/carcinogenic components of municipal wastewater and to examine their fate during AWT treatment.

Mutagenic Activity of Unconcentrated Wastewaters: Secondary as well as AWT effluent showed significant mutagenesis in the base pair substitution mutants TA 100 and TA 1538 of *S. typhimurium*. The mutagens responsible for the effect were inactivated to a large extent by the presence of mammalian liver enzymes in the assay. The wastewaters failed to revert the frameshift mutant TA 98 but exhibited strong toxicity towards this strain, decreasing the spontaneous reversion rate as much as three-fold in some samples. The inability to detect frameshift mutagens may be linked to the high sensitivity of this strain towards toxicants in wastewaters. Decreasing the volume of wastewaters in the assay relieved the inhibition without inducing mutagenic response.

In view of the low levels of mutagenic activity observed, it became important to determine if histidine was present in these wastewaters and if so whether histidine was artifactually responsible for the increased number of revertant. Assay of the wastewaters for histidine by a specific enzymatic method having a detection limit of 1 μg/ml revealed that histidine was not present in measurable amounts. Furthermore, wastewaters spiked with <1 μg/ml histidine failed to exhibit any significant influence on the spontaneous reversion rate. Thus wastewater-induced increase in the reversion rate was true mutagenesis and not due to histidine.

Chemical mutagens that enter the human body through the diet or in other ways are often excreted unchanged as conjugates. Thus the possibility exists for the presence of some mutagens in municipal wastewaters as conjugates such as glucuronides. The incorporation of β-glucuronidase in the assay did not result in increased mutagenicity with any of the wastewater samples studied, demonstrating that any mutagens present were not conjugated as glucuronides.

Comparison of the mutagenic response of AWT influent and AWT midpoint effluent showed that lime addition and/or recarbonation were capable of promoting synthesis of mutagens. Some of these compounds were direct acting, whereas others required metabolic activation. The mutagens formed in these treatment processes were partially removed during breakpoint chlorination and/or carbon filtration. However, the overall concentration of mutagens present in the final effluent was no less than that present in the influent wastewaters.

Recovery of Organics from Wastewaters and Mutagenicity Assay of the Concentrates: The total organic carbon content of the wastewaters and the proportion recovered by various concentration methods are shown in Table 9.9. Although polyurethane foam collected the least amount of organic carbon, the recovered carbon possessed mutagenic activity roughly equivalent to that recovered with XAD and solvent suggesting some specificity of foam plugs for recovering mutagens. The organic mixture recovered from AWT influent was mutagenic for *Salmonella* strain TA 100 but not to a significant extent in TA 1538. Following liming and/or recarbonation of the influent the mutagenic response shown by TA 100 remained unaffected but there was a significant increase in mutagenicity with TA 1538. The findings show that liming and/or recarbonation processes have the potential of introducing compounds capable of causing frameshift mutation.

The final AWT effluent did not exhibit significant mutagenic activity in any of the *Salmonella* strains tested. This does not show that the mutagens present in influent wastewaters and those introduced during liming and/or recarbonation were effectively removed during the final stage of treatment, since mutagens were detected in unconcentrated samples of AWT effluents. The inability of the concentration methods to recover these mutagenic substances from AWT effluent appears to be responsible for their absence.

Table 9.9: Recovery of Organic Compounds from Wastewaters by Different Collection Methods

| | | ... Percent Carbon Recovered by ... | | |
| | Total Organic Carbon | | | Extraction by Methylene Chloride- |
Sample	(ppm)	Foam	XAD	Hexane
Secondary effluent	12.2	2	9.8	24.6
Intermediate effluent	2.8	8.9	13.6	7.8
Tertiary effluent	1.4	6.8	46.0	10.0

Source: NSA/RA-790224

Mutagenicity Assay of the Major Fractions of Wastewater Concentrates: The solubility separation of the crude mixtures into chemical classes and measurement of mutagenic activity of these classes were undertaken in order to identify the active fraction(s). It was noted that the combined activity of all the fractions was generally greater than that of the crude concentrate. The increase may be linked to the enrichment of mutagenic substances in selected fractions separated from toxicants or due to the dilution of toxic material present in the crude mixture. In terms of the quantities and classes of mutagenic substances recovered by the concentration procedures employed, the performance of polyurethane foam plugs was best, solvent extraction being the next, and XAD being the poorest.

XAD, however, appeared extremely efficient in recovering toxic components of wastewater. The mutagenic activity recovered by polyurethane foam from AWT influent was distributed largely in basic, strong acid and neutral fraction. The response was noted in strain TA 100 and TA 98 without the presence of the mammalian activation system. Breakpoint chlorination/recarbonation resulted in an increase in the number of fractions which were mutagenic. For example, ether-insoluble, amphoteric, and weak acid fractions of polyurethane foam concentrate of AWT influent were nonmutagenic, whereas similar fractions representing intermediate-stage effluent were weakly to moderately mutagenic. This provides further support to the earlier observation that liming and/or recarbonation processes introduce mutagens. Similar increase in the number of mutagenic classes was not noted with the activity recovered by solvent extraction or XAD adsorption. The final AWT effluent generally appeared to contain a high concentration of toxicants. These toxicants were not present in the intermediate level effluent and therefore their synthesis probably occurred during breakpoint chlorination or carbon filtration. Significant levels of mutagenic activity were not detected in any of the fractions of AWT effluent. This was in agreement with the earlier findings with crude concentrates.

Neutral fractions recovered by polyurethane foam, XAD or solvent extraction were generally toxic to the *Salmonella* tester strains and therefore were subfractionated into aliphatic, aromatic and oxygenated fractions prior to bioassay. Nearly all the mutagenic activity for the neutral fraction of AWT influent was located in the oxygenated fraction. Efficient recovery of these compounds was achieved by solvent extraction. XAD adsorption partially recovered these compounds but polyurethane foam failed to recover them. Oxygenated mutagenic compounds were also detected in the intermediate effluent; however, these appeared to be of a different chemical nature, as they could be recovered by polyurethane foam. Furthermore, XAD adsorption and solvent extraction proved ineffective in recovering these mutagens.

The final AWT effluent, while it was free of any oxygenated mutagens, contained activity in the aromatic fraction. Since no activity in this fraction was detected in the intermediate effluents, these mutagens appeared to have been synthesized during treatment. The aliphatic and the oxygenated neutrals of the AWT effluent at the concentration used were toxic to the bacteria and therefore it cannot be said with certainty that mutagenic compounds were present in these fractions.

The results showed that the physiochemical AWT method studied was able to adequately remove mutagenic compounds which were susceptible to recovery by adsorption on solid sorbent such as XAD and polyurethane foam, and by liquid-liquid extraction. Mutagens of a highly polar nature which were difficult to concentrate from water were also the ones which were difficult to treat. Indeed, some treatment steps showed a potential for introducing mutagenic substances. Further studies are required to determine the nature of the introduced compounds and to examine their presence in final effluents. The reuse of renovated wastewaters for potable purposes at the present time may present a hazard to health.

Sources Utilized

EPA-600/2-77-210

Wastewater Characterization and Process Reliability for Potable Wastewater Reclamation, prepared by A.C. Petrasek, Jr., of Dallas Water Utilities for Municipal Environmental Research Laboratory, U.S. EPA, Cincinnati, Ohio, November 1977.

EPA-600/1-78-019

Contaminants Associated with Direct and Indirect Reuse of Municipal Wastewater, prepared by SCS Engineers, Inc., Long Beach, CA for HERL, U.S. EPA, Cincinnati, Ohio, March 1978.

EPA-600/1-78-068

Evaluation of Toxic Effects of Organic Contaminants in Recycled Water, prepared by Dr. N. Gruener of Gulf South Research Institute for U.S. EPA Health Effects Research Laboratory, Cincinnati, Ohio, December 1978.

EPA-600/1-79-014

Health Effects of Consumption of Renovated Water: Chemistry and Cytotoxicity, prepared by W.R. Chappell, C.C. Solomons, Harold F. Walton, and W.L. Weston, all of Environmental Trace Substances Research Program, University of Colorado, for Field Studies Division, Health Effects Research Laboratory, U.S. EPA, Cincinnati, Ohio, March 1979.

NSF/RA-790224
NSF/RA-790225
NSF/RA-790226

Water Reuse—From Research to Application. Proceedings of Water Reuse Symposium Held at Washington, D.C. on March 25-30, 1979, prepared

by the American Water Works Association Research Foundation for the
National Science Foundation, March 1979. [Volume 1 (NSF/RA-790224)
is referred to in the text as "Conference I," Volume 2 (NSF/RA-790225)
as "Conference II," and Volume 3 (NSF/RA-790226) as "Conference
III."]

NTIS PB-289 386

*Water Reuse Highlights, A Summary Volume of Wastewater Reclamation
and Reuse Information*, prepared by the American Water Works Association Research Foundation for the OWRT of the U.S. Department of the
Interior, January 1978.

List of Abbreviations

AWT	advanced water treatment
AWWA	American Water Works Association
BOD_5	5-day biological oxygen demand
CCE	carbon-chloroform extract
COD	chemical oxygen demand
DO	dissolved oxygen
FTU	formazin turbidity unit
GAC	granulated activated carbon
GC	gas chromatography
gpcpd	gallons per capita per day
HERL	Health Effects Research Laboratory
JAWWA	Journal of the American Water Works Association
JTU	Jackson turbidity unit
JWPCF	Journal of the Water Pollution Control Federation
MCL	maximum contaminant level
MLSS	maximum level suspended solids
MS	mass spectroscopy
NAS	National Academy of Science
(N)IPDWR	National Interim Primary Drinking Water Regulations
NTU	nephelometric turbidity unit
OWRT	Office of Water Research and Technology (U.S. Dept. of the Interior)
PACT	powdered activated carbon
PAH	polynuclear aromatic hydrocarbons
RO	reverse osmosis
SRT	sludge retention time
SS	suspended solids
TDS	total dissolved solids
THM	trihalomethanes
TKN	total Kjeldahl nitrogen
TOC	total organic carbon
TPC	total purgeable carbon
TU	turbidity units
UF	ultrafiltration
U.S. EPA	United States Environmental Protection Agency
USPHS	United States Public Health Service
VOA	volatile organic analysis
VSS	volatile suspended solids

Other Noyes Publications

WASTEWATER REUSE AND RECYCLING TECHNOLOGY 1980

by Gordon Culp, George Wesner, Robert Williams and Mark V. Hughes, Jr.

Pollution Technology Review No. 72

This volume describes and evaluates the technology for water reuse and recycling; as well as describing the magnitude of the potential for reusing and recycling industrial, agricultural, and municipal wastewaters.

Wastewaters available for reuse and recycling include discharges from municipalities, industries, steam electric plants and agricultural irrigation return water. The potential uses for reclaimed water are agricultural irrigation, landscape irrigation, cooling in steam electric plants, and other industrial uses.

The beneficial uses for water considered for reuse or recycling are those projected to require either the greatest quantities of water or those that are impacted because of projected water shortages. This book identifies the areas requiring large quantities of water, water-short areas, and areas having potential conflicts among the uses of available water.

The major portion of this volume contains an extensive evaluation of current wastewater treatment technology including water quality criteria, primary treatment and many secondary treatment methods such as trickling filters, extended aeration, rotating biological contactors, coagulation-sedimentation, etc. Listed below is a summarized table of contents illustrating the **chapter headings and some important subtitles.**

I. EVALUATION OF NEEDS AND POTENTIAL

1. **EXISTING AND PROPOSED WATER REUSE PROJECTS**

2. **WATER QUALITY REQUIREMENTS**

II. EVALUATION OF TREATMENT TECHNOLOGY

1. **INTRODUCTION**

2. **BENEFICIAL USES OF RECLAIMED WASTEWATER**

3. **WATER QUALITY CRITERIA FOR BENEFICIAL USES**

4. **WASTEWATER TREATMENT PROCESS EVALUATION**
Statistical Analyses
Wastewater Characterization
Primary Treatment
Activated Sludge
Extended Aeration
Nitrification
Denitrification
Trickling Filters
Rotating Biological Contactors
Coagulation-Sedimentation
Filtration
Recarbonation
Activated Carbon Adsorption
Ammonia Stripping
Selective Ion Exchange
Breakpoint Chlorination
Reverse Osmosis
Chlorination
Ozonation
Irrigation
Infiltration-Percolation
Overland Flow
Sludge Processing and Disposal

5. **SPECIAL TREATMENT CONSIDERATIONS**
Pathogens, Organics, and Heavy Metals

6. **WASTEWATER TREATMENT SYSTEMS**
Sludge Processing and Disposal
Treatment Energy and Cost Summary

7. **TREATMENT SYSTEM COMPATIBILITY WITH REUSE APPLICATIONS**
Treatment Level Compatibility
with Beneficial Uses
Economics of Wastewater Reuse
Feasibility of Wastewater Reuse

8. **THRUST OF CURRENT RESEARCH**
Future Research Needs

Appendix A: Unit Treatment Processes
Appendix B: Treatment System Reliability
Appendix C: Cost Information
Appendix D: Chlorination Systems
Appendix E: Analytical Methods

ISBN 0-8155-0829-8

838 pages

Other Noyes Publications

DESALINATION OF SEAWATER BY REVERSE OSMOSIS

Edited by Jeanette Scott

Pollution Technology Review No. 75

A study of reverse osmosis technology involved with desalting of seawater is offered in this volume. The current technology is covered with 150 processes described in detail. Emphasis is placed on the composition of the membranes from natural and synthetic materials, membrane configurations including the tubular and hollow fiber units, supports, membrane maintenance to ensure trouble-free production and modified reverse osmosis techniques with other energy sources.

In addition, an introductory overview discusses the reverse osmosis process with varied membrane designs and recent cost estimates and analyses for construction and operation of 0.01 to 5 MGD capacity desalting plants.

A summarized table of contents with **selected chapters and subtitles** is given below; in parentheses is the number of processes per topic.

INTRODUCTION
The Reverse Osmosis Process
 Process Description
 Membrane Designs
Cost Analysis
 Basis for Cost Estimates
 Costs

1. NATURAL MEMBRANE MATERIALS (19)
Cellulosic
 Crosslinked with Methacrylate
 Polyaminoethylene Grafts
Discrete Particles
 Bentonite Clay
 Dual-Layer Membranes

2. SYNTHETIC MEMBRANE MATERIALS (32)
Polyamides
 N-3-Hydroxyalkyl Acrylamide
 Polypiperazide Amides
Polybenzimidazoles and
 Polyoxadiazoles
Other Nitrogen-Containing Polymers
 Polymeric Epoxides
 Cyclic Polyureas
Polyethers

3. MEMBRANE SUPPORTS AND CASTING (22)
Membrane Supports
 Permeable Ceramic Supports
 Glass Fiber Mat

 Porous Rigid PVC
Casting Tubular Membranes
Casting Ultrathin Membranes
Casting Asymmetric Membranes

4. MEMBRANE TREATMENT AND CLEANING (17)
Tannin Treatment
Acid Treatments
Cleaning and Scale Prevention
 Cleaning with Oxalic Acid
 Tubular Membrane with Cleaning
 Ball Delivery System
 Backflushing with Hot Acid/Surfactant
 Cleaning Solution
 Controlling Concentration of Dissolved
 Solids on Membrane Surfaces

5. MEMBRANE CONFIGURATIONS (19)
Tubular Units
 Module Design
 Two Stream Process
 Porous Glass Membranes
Hollow Fibers
 Acid-Grafted Nylon Membranes
 Hollow Fibers in U-Shaped Loop
Spirally Wound Modules
 Three-Ply Layup Leaves
Stacked Assemblies

6. EQUIPMENT AND PROCESS DESIGN (10)
Multistage Units
Minimizing Deposits and Polarization
 Layers

7. MODIFIED REVERSE OSMOSIS TECHNIQUES (21)
Vapor Permeation
 Stacked Membrane Distillation System
Other Energy Sources
 Cavitational Unit
 Infrasonic Activation
 Thermo-Osmosis
 Magnetic Field
Solution Modifications

8. SPECIAL UNITS (9)
Submerged Units
 Emergency Seawater Purification
 Submerged Installations
Portable Units
 Hand-Operated Pump
 Use of Osmotic Pressure to Drive
 Reverse Osmosis

ISBN 0-8155-0837-9 (1981)

431 pages